Luminos is the Open Access monograph publishing program from UC Press. Luminos provides a framework for preserving and reinvigorating monograph publishing for the future and increases the reach and visibility of important scholarly work. Titles published in the UC Press Luminos model are published with the same high standards for selection, peer review, production, and marketing as those in our traditional program. www.luminosoa.org

The publisher and the University of California Press Foundation gratefully acknowledge the generous support of the Ahmanson Foundation Endowment Fund in Humanities.

Impersonations

Impersonations

The Artifice of Brahmin Masculinity in South Indian Dance

Harshita Mruthinti Kamath

UNIVERSITY OF CALIFORNIA PRESS

University of California Press, one of the most distinguished university presses in the United States, enriches lives around the world by advancing scholarship in the humanities, social sciences, and natural sciences. Its activities are supported by the UC Press Foundation and by philanthropic contributions from individuals and institutions. For more information, visit www.ucpress.edu.

University of California Press
Oakland, California

Suggested citation: Kamath, H. M. *Impersonations: The Artifice of Brahmin Masculinity in South Indian Dance.* Oakland: University of California Press, 2019. DOI: https://doi.org/10.1525/luminos.72

Library of Congress Cataloging-in-Publication Data

Names: Kamath, Harshita Mruthinti, 1982- author.
Title: Impersonations : the artifice of Brahmin masculinity in South Indian dance / Harshita Mruthinti Kamath.
Description: Oakland, California : University of California Press, [2019] | Includes bibliographical references and index. |
Identifiers: LCCN 2018061418 (print) | LCCN 2019003975 (ebook) | ISBN 9780520972230 (Epub) | ISBN 9780520301665 (pbk. : alk. paper)
Subjects: LCSH: Brahmans—India, South--Social life and customs. | Gender identity in dance—India, South. | Female impersonators—India, South—Social life and customs. | Kuchipudi (Dance)—Social aspects—India, South.
Classification: LCC DS432.B73 (ebook) | LCC DS432.B73 K36 2019 (print) | DDC 306.4/846081109548—dc23
LC record available at https://lccn.loc.gov/2018061418

28 27 26 25 24 23 22 21 20 19
10 9 8 7 6 5 4 3 2 1

for Baliakka

CONTENTS

List of Illustrations ix
Acknowledgments xi
Note on Transliteration xv

Introduction 1

1. Taking Center Stage: The Poet-Saint and the Impersonator of Kuchipudi Dance History 33
2. "I am Satyabhama": Constructing Hegemonic Brahmin Masculinity in the Kuchipudi Village 55
3. Constructing Artifice, Interrogating Impersonation: Madhavi as *Vidūṣaka* in Village *Bhāmākalāpam* Performance 80
4. *Bhāmākalāpam* beyond the Village: Transgressing Norms of Gender and Sexuality in Urban and Transnational Kuchipudi Dance 104
5. Longing to Dance: Stories of Kuchipudi Brahmin Women 134

Conclusion: Rewriting the Script for Kuchipudi Dance 159

Notes 169
Bibliography 193
Index 219

ILLUSTRATIONS

FIGURES

1–2. Vedantam Satyanarayana Sarma in the village of Kuchipudi *3*
3. Ramalingeshvara and Balatripurasundari temple in the center of the Kuchipudi village *15*
4. Siddhendra's *mūrti* (image) in a temple in the Kuchipudi village *45*
5–11. Vedantam Venkata Naga Chalapathi Rao donning Satyabhama's *strī-vēṣam* *60–61*
12. Chinta Ravi Balakrishna as the *sūtradhāra* *83*
13. Satyabhama addressing Madhavi *84*
14. Madhavi and Satyabhama offer flowers to Krishna (performed by Yeleswarapu Srinivas) *90*
15. Sasikala Penumarthi enacts Satyabhama *110*
16. Vedantam Raghava as the *sūtradhāra* *112*
17. Madhavi and Satyabhama *113*
18. Madhavi wears Satyabhama's nose ring *115*
19. Satyabhama combs Madhavi's hair *126*
20. Author impersonates Krishna *129*
21. Vedantam Rajyalakshmi in her home in the Kuchipudi village *139*
22. Chavali Balatripurasundari in her home in Hyderabad *151*

MAPS

1. India (2018) *16*
2. The Kuchipudi village *17*

TABLE

1. *Sūtradhāra*/Madhavi/Madhava across *Bhāmākalāpam* performance contexts *117*

ACKNOWLEDGMENTS

Writing is a performative act that demands collective labor in the guise, or *vēṣam*, of a singular voice. Although a monograph, this book would not be possible without the collective efforts of teachers, mentors, colleagues, and friends. My Kuchipudi guru, Sasikala Penumarthi, first introduced me to Kuchipudi through her exquisite skills in performance. Chavali Balatripurasundari, the daughter of guru Vempati Chinna Satyam, deepened my knowledge of Kuchipudi through her persistent dedication to her father's legacy. Inspired by Baliakka's story, I dedicate this book to her.

I am deeply indebted to Joyce Burkhalter Flueckiger, my incredibly generous advisor who has supported me throughout, from the start of this project to its finish. Joyce's intellectual insights, deep love of India, and commitment to her students are truly remarkable, and she has been the single force that has shaped my academic training over the years. Velcheru Narayana Rao has sparked my interest in all things Telugu since the day I met him. I am grateful not only for Narayana Rao's unbridled enthusiasm for reading Telugu texts, but also for his insightful observations and inspirational claims. My mentor at the University of Hyderabad, Anuradha Jonnalagadda, has been a guiding force through this project. Anuradha's expansive knowledge of Kuchipudi dance history is an inspiration, and she is the single most influential scholar of Kuchipudi dance to date. I also thank the other scholars who influenced the shape of this book, including Laurie Louise Patton, an intellectual tour de force who prompted me on the path of scholarly work in South Asian studies. Vasudha Narayanan, the authority on South India, has shaped the arc of my scholarship from dissertation to book. I am extremely grateful to Anne Monius for her ongoing support of my research and scholarly career, as well as her insightful feedback on drafts of the book. I also thank Sara McClintock for her careful eye when reading early versions of the book in its dissertation stage.

I extend my gratitude to the many members of the Kuchipudi dance community who supported my fieldwork in India. In particular, I am indebted to the late Vempati Ravi Shankar for the countless hours spent discussing dance, Vedantam Venkata Naga Chalapathi Rao for his enthusiasm, Vedantam Raghava for his insights, and my dear friend Pasumarti Mrutyumjaya for his continuing encouragement. I thank the women of Kuchipudi village families who I interviewed in 2014, particularly Vedantam Rajyalakshmi, Vedantam Lakshminarasamma, Vempati Swarajyalakshmi, and Chavali Balatripurasundari, for their insights. Baliakka's daughter, Sarvani, brought joy to my fieldwork. In addition, I am incredibly grateful to the following members of the Siddhendra Kalakshetra who took time to answer my questions, teach me dance, and support my project: Pasumarti Rattayya Sarma, Vedantam Radheshyam, Vedantam Ramalingasastry, Chinta Ravi Balakrishna, Yeleswarapu Srinivas, and Pasumarti Haranadh. I am also grateful to Vedantam Satyanarayana Sarma, P.V.G. Krishna, Pasumarti Keshav Prasad, Nataraja Ramakrishna, Kalakrishna, Uma Rama Rao, Ajay Kumar, and Haleem Khan, as well as my remaining interlocutors for their willingness to speak with me. I thank Madhavi Puranam, Aruna Bhikshu, and the late G.M. Sarma for their support of this research. Finally, I am deeply grateful to the late Modali Nagabhushana Sarma for his willingness to meet with me in Hyderabad for hours upon end to discuss Kuchipudi dance history.

The research for this book was supported by grants from the United States Department of Education's Fulbright-Hays Doctoral Dissertation Research Abroad program and Emory University's Graduate Division of Religion's Initiative in Religious Practices & Practical Theology. I also received support from the American Association of University Women (AAUW) American Fellowships Research Publication Grant and Emory University's Center for Faculty Development and Excellence Scholarly Writing and Publishing Fund to complete the manuscript.

I thank Reed Malcolm, Archna Patel, Emilia Thiuri, Paul Tyler, Tom Sullivan, and the editorial board at the University of California Press for their support. I also thank the anonymous reviewers for their feedback to the manuscript. I am indebted to my outstanding editor, Petra Shenk, for her keen eye and insightful comments on many drafts. I am grateful to the staff at the Sangeet Natak Akademi Archives in New Delhi and the Tirupati Oriental Research Library in Tirupati, Andhra Pradesh. In addition, I thank Velcheru Narayana Rao, P. Venugopala Rao, Bethavolu Ramabrahmam, and Durga Yerramalli for their assistance in translating my primary source materials from Telugu into English. I am grateful to Carla Freeman at Emory College of Arts and Sciences and Sarah McKee at Emory University's Fox Center for Humanistic Inquiry for their support in publishing this book as an open access monograph. Thanks also to Ben Pease for his detailed maps, Uzma Ansari for her beautiful photographs, and Chris Dodge for indexing.

I am indebted to my colleagues at Emory University for supporting my scholarship, particularly Devin Stewart, Scott Kugle, Ruby Lal, Vincent Cornell, Rkia Cornell, Roxani Margarati, Ofra Yeglin, Brajesh Samarth, Juana McGhee, Paul Courtright, Arun Jones, Ellen Gough, Bobbi Patterson and Jim Hoesterey. I also thank my colleagues at my previous institutions, UNC–Chapel Hill and Middlebury College, particularly Pamela Lothspeich, Juliane Hammer, Jessica Boon, Brandon Bayne, Lauren Leve, Barbara Ambros, Carl Ernst, Randall Styers, Townsend Middleton, Elizabeth Morrison, and Sujata Moorti. I am grateful for the feedback from colleagues at Syracuse University, University of California–Santa Barbara, and Case Western University, including Ann Gold, Susan Wadley, Carol Babiracki, Chandra Talpade Mohanty, Emera Bridger, Romita Kapoor, Barbara Holdrege, and Deepak Sarma. Barbara, in particular, has been a wonderful conversation partner throughout the years, particularly about themes of embodiment.

I am particularly indebted to Stanley I. Thangaraj for his generosity and enormously helpful comments on my manuscript. I thank Amy-Ruth Holt and Karen Pechilis for their insightful comments on my analysis of *bhakti* poets in the Krishna district. I also thank John Stratton Hawley for his ongoing discussions of *bhakti,* which have shaped the trajectory of this book and my future research. My fellow Telugu scholars, including David Shulman, R.V.S. Sundaram, Bethavolu Ramabrahmam, Karri Ramachandra Reddy, Ilanit Loewy Shacham, Jamal Jones, Gautham Reddy, Vimala Katikaneni, Afsar Mohammad, Srinivas Reddy, and, of course, Velcheru Narayana Rao, shape the field of Telugu studies. I am particularly indebted to Narayana Rao, David, Sundaram, Ramabrahmam, and Vimala for their efforts in reading Telugu texts with me in early stages of my research. I am also grateful to Indira Gummuluri and Lavanya Vankayala for organizing my first trip to Kuchipudi village in 2006 through the AIIS Summer Language Program in Telugu. Davesh Soneji's groundbreaking research in South Asian dance and performance and Rumya Putcha's work on Kuchipudi historiography contributed to my understanding of Kuchipudi dance.

I thank Arthi Devarajan, my colleague and friend, particularly for her encouragement and willingness to read through last minute drafts. I thank Pamela Lothspeich, Christian Novetzke, Claire Pamment, Kellen Hoxworth, Aftab Jassal, Sumathi Ramaswamy, Rich Freeman, and the other attendees at the Impersonation in South Asia Symposium at the Annual Conference on South Asia in October 2018 for their input on this project and the forthcoming edited volume, *Mimetic Desires: Impersonation and Guising Across South Asia*. I am grateful for friends and colleagues from my graduate programs: Katherine Zubko, Steven Vose, Gil Ben-Herut, Michael Allen, Manuela Ceballos, Gloria Hernandez, Jenn Ortegren, and Amy Allocco. I could not have made it through these years without the support of my writing group: Jeremy Posadas, Nikki Young, Susannah Laramee-Kidd, Letitia Campbell, and Cayenne Claassen-Luttner. My fellow members of the Intersectional Hindu Studies Collective—Sailaja Krishnamurti, Shana Sippy,

Tanisha Ramachandran, and Shreena Gandhi—have inspired me in countless ways. Also, many thanks to the attendees at the Wabash Workshop for Early Career Religion Faculty of Asian Descent, particularly Samira Mehta, David Kamitsuka, Zayn Kassam, and Roshan Iqbal for helping me locate my voice in my work.

I thank my parents, Shyamala and Swamy Mruthinti, for encouraging me in every step of my academic career. They are my academic role models. My two amazing sisters, Navyata and Namrata, have always been willing to stand by my side whenever I needed their support. I thank the extended members of the Mruthinti and Kamath families, particularly my paternal great-aunt, V. Vijaya, for housing me during my time in Hyderabad. I wish my maternal grandmother, Sarvepalli Indira, could have been alive to read this book, which is inspired by her in so many ways. Finally, I am deeply indebted to my partner, Vasant, for his unwavering love and support. Vasant has been by my side through every step of the research and writing process and I could not have done any of it without him. And last, but not least, I thank the two people I cherish most in this whole wide world, my Gopal and Indira.

NOTE ON TRANSLITERATION

All italicized technical words in Sanskrit and Telugu and the titles of literary works have been transliterated according to the system followed by the Library of Congress (e.g., *Nāṭyaśāstra, Bhāmākalāpam*). Proper names, such as Satyabhama and Krishna, appear without diacritic marks or italicization according to common Anglicized-Indian usage.

Sanskrit words ending in long vowels are kept long if the reference primarily draws from a well-known Sanskrit source, concept, or term (e.g., *māyā*). By comparison, words drawing from a Telugu literary source or contemporary Telugu discourse do not include elongated vowel endings. However, in the case of Telugu sources, if the word is found in a compound, then the lengthening of the vowel is maintained in the middle of the word (e.g., *Bhāmākalāpam* or *strī-vēṣam).* In Telugu sources and/or discourses, the -ē- is lengthened (e.g., *vēṣam*) to reflect the Library of Congress transliteration system. Plurals of Sanskrit or Telugu words include the affix "-s" for ease of English reading comprehension.

All cited material in quotes is given with the spelling and style with which it appears in the original publication. For example, Satyabhama will also appear as Satyabhāmā and Krishna will also appear as Kṛṣṇa in direct quotations. Titles of contemporary performances are spelled as they appear in program notes, written publications, or performance scripts (e.g., Vempati Chinna Satyam's *Sri Krishna Parijatam* would appear as *Śrī Kṛṣṇa Pārijātam* in diacritics).

Finally, the term "brahmin" appears without diacritic marks or italicization according to common Anglicized-Indian usage. However, unlike other proper names in this book, I have chosen not to capitalize this term in order to signal a decentering of power commonly attributed to upper-caste, brahminical identity. When quoted, the term also appears as "Brahmin."

Introduction

A balding elderly man sits in front of a mirror applying dark kohl around the edges of his large eyes and across the arches of his brow. Dabbing the tip of a thin brush into a tube of red lipstick, he carefully traces the curves of his mouth and draws a teardrop shape in the space between his eyebrows. After that, he reaches over to a wig of thick black hair lying next to him and places it on his head. Then, firmly holding down the center parting, he secures it in position and nimbly weaves the hair into a long braid, adorns the parting of the wig with a glistening ornament, and fastens hanging earrings onto his ears. Pausing to assess his progress, the man looks into the mirror to see his altered reflection. The image of Satyabhama, the wife of the Hindu deity Krishna and the lead character of the Kuchipudi dance drama *Bhāmākalāpam,* looks back. In front of the mirror sits Vedantam Satyanarayana Sarma, a male Kuchipudi dancer skilled at donning the *strī-vēṣam,* translated here as "woman's guise." As Satyanarayana Sarma looks into his reflection to see Satyabhama, he begins to hum the lyrics to her *pravēśa daruvu,* or introductory song:

> I am Bhama, I am Satyabhama.
> I am the most beautiful Satyabhama.
> Among all 16,000 women,
> I alone stole Krishna's heart.
> I am Bhama, I am Satyabhama.[1]

. . .

I first met Vedantam Satyanarayana Sarma, one of the most famous dancers from the Kuchipudi village in Telugu-speaking South India, in the summer of

2006.[2] As a dancer trained in Kuchipudi, the eponymous dance form originating from the village, I was well aware of Satyanarayana Sarma's reputation as a male Kuchipudi dancer skilled in donning the *strī-vēṣam*, particularly during the height of his career in the 1960s and 1970s. While I sat on Satyanarayana Sarma's veranda and listened to him talk on that hot summer afternoon, I was struck by the incongruity between the elderly bald man clad in a freshly pressed button-down shirt and his reputation as the living embodiment of Satyabhama, the heroine of the *Bhāmākalāpam* dance drama. All that was soon forgotten as he began to sing the lyrics to Satyabhama's *pravēśa daruvu*, accompanied by mimetic hand gestures and facial expressions (see Figures 1 and 2). As I watched Satyanarayana Sarma transform into Satyabhama, exemplifying what Dell Hymes (2015, 31) refers to as a "breakthrough" into full performance, I realized that I was witnessing a man who could impersonate Satyabhama better than me or any other woman.

In the years following my initial encounter with Satyanarayana Sarma, I came to understand that his enactment of Satyabhama was more than an impromptu performance on the veranda of his house; it was also a paradigmatic example of the gender and caste norms of the Kuchipudi village. Kuchipudi men from a select group of hereditary brahmin families are expected to don the *strī-vēṣam* and impersonate female characters onstage, particularly the character of Satyabhama in the dance drama *Bhāmākalāpam*. According to the hagiography of Siddhendra, the founding saint of Kuchipudi dance and the purported author of *Bhāmākalāpam*, every brahmin man from a hereditary Kuchipudi family must don Satyabhama's *vēṣam* at least once in his life, a prescription that still resonates in the village today. Impersonation, the term I use to indicate the donning of a gender guise (*vēṣam*), is not simply a performative mandate for Kuchipudi brahmin men but also a practice of power that creates normative ideals of brahmin masculinity in village performance and everyday life.

This book analyzes the practice of impersonation across a series of boundaries—village to urban to transnational, brahmin to nonbrahmin, hegemonic to nonnormative—to explore the artifice of brahmin masculinity in contemporary South Indian dance. Drawing on multisited ethnographic fieldwork and performance analysis, *Impersonations* begins with a hereditary community of brahmin men from the village of Kuchipudi in Telugu-speaking South India. Contrary to Euro-American assumptions about hypermasculinity, the Kuchipudi village presents us with a distinct understanding of normative masculinity, particularly as it relates to caste. In the Kuchipudi village, donning a woman's guise (*strī-vēṣam*) is not considered to be a subversive or unusual act; rather, impersonation enables village brahmin men to achieve normative and even hegemonic forms of masculinity in their everyday lives (Connell 1987). However, the construction of brahmin masculinity against the backdrop of impersonation is highly contingent, particularly due to the expansion of Kuchipudi in the latter half of the twentieth century from

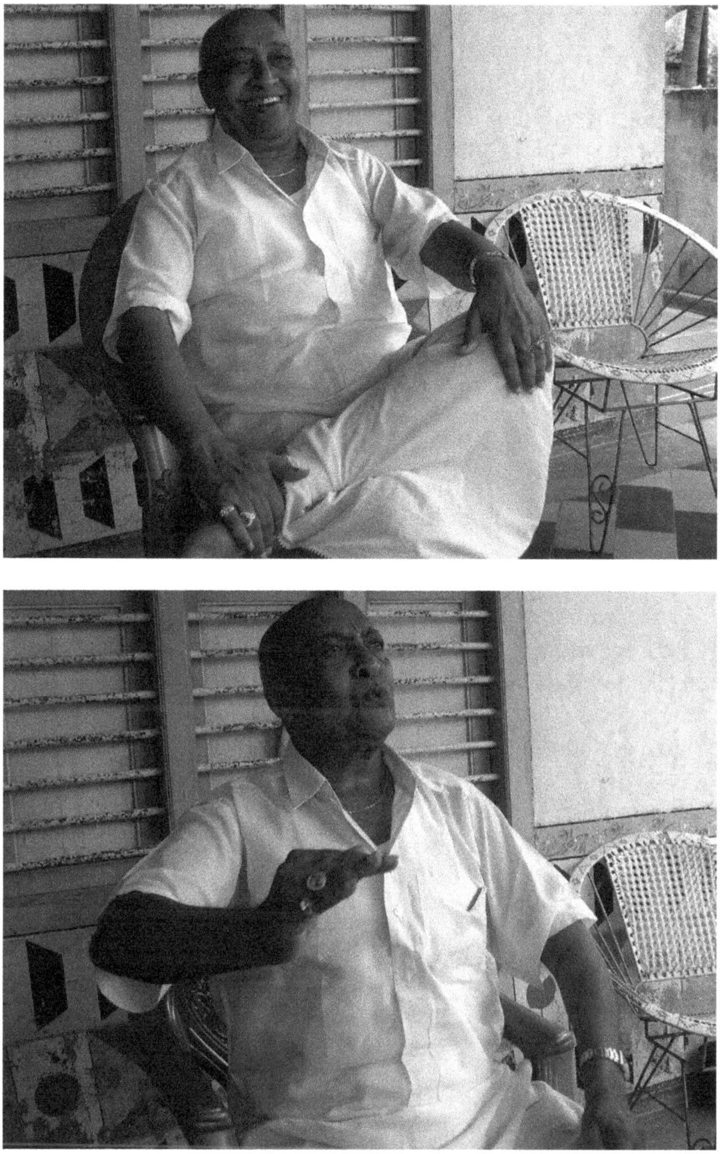

FIGURES 1 AND 2. Vedantam Satyanarayana Sarma in the village of Kuchipudi in July 2006. Photo by author.

a localized village performance to a transnationally recognized "classical" Indian dance style. While impersonation in the village is read as a powerful expression of brahmin masculinity, the very same practice is reinterpreted in urban contexts as obsolete, especially given the growing numbers of women who have begun to learn and perform Kuchipudi dance from the mid-twentieth century onwards. In the words of my interlocutors, "There is no need for men to dance as women when women are dancing themselves." The authority of hegemonic brahmin masculinity in the village is displaced in urban and transnational forms of Kuchipudi dance, in which the brahmin man in *strī-vēṣam* comes to symbolize an outdated mode of tradition.

Impersonations examines the simultaneous construction and displacement of hegemonic brahmin masculinity in the wake of transnational change. The Kuchipudi brahmin man, much like his white heterosexual male counterpart in the West, ostensibly occupies a seat of power at the center of his societal and cultural contexts (Marcus 2005, 213).[3] As Charu Gupta (2016, 111) observes, "In India the propertied, high-caste, heterosexual Hindu male is at the top of religious and caste hierarchies, and this is taken as normal, natural, and beyond reproach."[4] Yet, this power itself is transient as broader configurations of gender and sexuality call into question the authority of the brahmin male body in *strī-vēṣam*. By shifting from village to urban and transnational forms of Kuchipudi dance, I trace the technologies of normativity that create, sustain, and undermine normative ideals of gender, caste, and sexuality through the embodied practice of impersonation in contemporary South India.

In framing my study of brahmin masculinity, I engage Mrinalini Sinha's (2012) call for a global perspective on gender that is radically contextualized. Sinha challenges long-standing Euro-American approaches to gender that link the category with the binary relationship of man/woman. Sinha (2012, 357) writes:

> While we certainly have a great deal of scholarship on women's and gender history *in* global contexts, we have not learned sufficiently from these contexts to begin to open up the concept of gender itself to different meanings. We must distinguish between merely exporting gender as an analytical category to different parts of the world and rethinking the category itself in the light of those different locations. In other words, what do these different global locations contribute to the meaning of gender *theoretically?* [Emphasis in original]

The larger point, Sinha argues, is not simply to enumerate gender in multiple contexts, but rather to analyze the theoretical implications of these contextual interpretations of gender for both feminist scholarship and feminist practice.[5]

This study extends Sinha's analysis by utilizing impersonation as an avenue for theorizing gender within a highly localized South Asian context, while also considering the transnational implications of vernacular gender performance. In my analysis of Kuchipudi brahmin masculinity, I read gender as forged at the intersection of other salient categories, namely caste and sexuality (Crenshaw 1989; Mohanty 1991; Sinha 2012). In focusing on both gender *and* caste, I am aware of the shifting axes of domination that exist across intersectional frameworks. In the words of Sonja Thomas (2018, 8), who cites the foundational work of Kimberlé Crenshaw (1989): "the point of intersectionality is not to diagnose where the intersections of race, class, caste, gender, and religion are at work in India but to go back to Kimberlé Crenshaw's important critique of how certain experiences of oppression can be privileged over others in attempts at redress." Thomas calls upon a dynamic analysis of power and subordination that does not view caste, gender, and religion through a single-axis frame (9).[6] The shifting negotiations across caste and gender are apparent in chapter 5, in which I examine the experiences of brahmin women in the Kuchipudi village community.

As the primary theoretical contribution of the book, I interpret brahmin masculinity through the lens of *māyā*, a term that I translate as "constructed artifice."[7] In my conversations with performers from the Kuchipudi village, I was struck by their repeated invocation of the Sanskrit term *māyā*. Familiar with *māyā* as an Indian philosophical concept that connotes a range of meanings including illusion or artifice, I was surprised to hear Kuchipudi performers invoke the term to describe what appeared to me to be an instance of gender role-play onstage. For my interlocutors, *māyā* explains how a single performer can enact three characters through the course of the *Bhāmākalāpam* dance drama: the *sūtradhāra* (the director-cum-narrator of the dance drama), Madhavi (the female confidante of Satyabhama), and Madhava (the male confidant of Krishna). In the words of senior Kuchipudi guru Pasumarti Rattayya Sarma (translated here from Telugu to English):

> Do you know this character of Madhavi? She's a kind of *māyā*. What is *māyā?* This *māyā* is what Krishna has sent. When she comes near Satyabhama, she actually appears like a woman. But when she goes to Krishna, she becomes Madhava [a man]. The difference is clear. This is unique to Kuchipudi and is not found elsewhere.

The invocation of *māyā* was not limited to Rattayya Sarma but appeared repeatedly in my discussions with other Kuchipudi brahmin performers (see chapter 3). While I am fully aware of the problematic attempts to Sanskritize Indian dance through the invocation of Sanskrit categories and texts (Coorlawala 2004), I believe these performers were on to something by suggesting that impersonation can be envisioned as *māyā*, a term that both means illusion and eludes any single definition.

The theoretical approach to *māyā* that I put forth in chapter 3 expresses an awareness of the multiple resonances and contested history of the term in Indian textual and philosophical traditions, while also expanding its connotative possibilities beyond magic, illusion, deception, or creative power, to interrogate brahmin masculinity in its many guises. By privileging the specific context in which *māyā* is invoked, rather than its Sanskrit textual history, I reposition *māyā* as a vernacular category and address Sinha's (2012, 357) call to reframe gender by giving "theoretical weight to the particular contexts in which it is articulated." *Māyā*, or constructed artifice, is one such example of gender theory arising from a highly localized vernacular context. Although Kuchipudi dancers may invoke *māyā* for its theological import, I reframe the term as a theoretical category to analyze the contingency of brahmin masculinity in Kuchipudi dance. The hermeneutics of constructed artifice (*māyā*) proposed here is also shaped by feminist theorizations that envision gender as a "changeable and revisable reality" (Butler [1990] 2008, xxiv). As such, the practice of impersonation paradoxically enables the construction of hegemonic brahmin masculinity, while simultaneously exposing it as artifice. A hermeneutics of constructed artifice, forged at the juncture of vernacular Kuchipudi discourse and feminist thought, prompts a critical inquiry into brahmin masculinity and its constraints.

DEFINING THE TERMS: IMPERSONATION AND *VĒṢAM*

In the South Indian language of Telugu, the primary language of many Kuchipudi dancers, the term *vēṣam* (guising) is used to indicate the practice of impersonation. *Vēṣam* (Telugu) or *veṣa* (Sanskrit) is derived from the Sanskrit root √*viṣ*. In Sanskrit, *veṣa* can mean "dress, apparel, ornament, artificial exterior, assumed appearance (often also = look, exterior, appearance in general)" (Monier-Williams [1899] 1960, 1019).[8] In the Sanskrit-Telugu dictionary *Sarva Śabda Saṃbōdhinyākhyōyam* ([1875] 2004, 877), the Telugu term *vēṣam* is translated as "dress that is unlike your real appearance." During my fieldwork, scholars and practitioners of Kuchipudi dance used the English term "female impersonation" as a translation of the Telugu idiom for taking on the *strī-vēṣam* within performance.[9] When speaking in Telugu, my interlocutors usually employed the Sanskritized Telugu term *strī-vēṣam*, as opposed to the Telugu alternative of *āḍa-vēṣam*.[10] Given the prominence of these two terms in the lexicon of my interlocutors, I will outline my usage of impersonation and *vēṣam* in the context of this study.

Drawing directly on vernacular and scholarly usages, I employ the term "impersonation" as a broad analytic category that connotes the practice of donning a gender *vēṣam* (guise) either onstage or in everyday life. Impersonation can also be expanded to indicate the temporary assumption of an identity or guise of a group which is not inherently one's own, regardless of whether this assumption is an intentional or deliberate act.[11] While impersonation may contain a negative connotation in popular English idiom (e.g., impersonating a police officer), the term lacks such semantic resonances in South Asia, particularly among my interlocutors who used it freely whenever speaking in English about guising practices. Published works on Kuchipudi and other Indian dance and theatrical forms also employ the term "impersonation" and/or "impersonator" to refer to the practice of gender guising.[12] I use the term "impersonation" to translate to a broader English readership and also to appeal to wider scholarly discourses on gender and performance beyond South Asia or the South Asian diaspora.

Notably, impersonation is a practice that appears across transnational contexts, spanning from Japanese kabuki theatre (Mezur 2005) to Javanese dance performance (Sunardi 2015) to the Shakespearean stage (Orgel 1996). Within South Asia, impersonation is ubiquitous: it is attested in a range of literary sources including Sanskrit epic texts (Goldman 1993; Doniger 2000, 2004; Vanita and Kidwai 2001), *bhakti* devotional literature (Ramanujan 1989; Hawley 2000; Pechilis 2012), and Sufi and Urdu poetry (Petievich 2008; Kugle 2013). Scholars of South Asia have noted the significance of impersonation in staged performance, particularly the practice of "female impersonation" (a male-identified performer donning a woman's guise) in Indian theatre (Hansen 1999, 2002) and dance (Pitkow 2011).[13] Also significant are the myriad forms of gender ambiguity across the South Asian landscape; spanning from premodern literary sources to contemporary performances, it is often the case that men become women, women become men, humans become gods, and ambiguous gender identities are openly described and, in some cases, valorized.[14]

Like "impersonation," *vēṣam* is also a capacious term that has theoretical significance in South Asian theatre and performance.[15] Joyce Flueckiger (2013) underscores the broad analytic potential of *vēṣam,* which she translates as "guising," as a means for recognizing everyday expressions of gender and divinity. In her study of the Gangamma *jātara* festival in the South Indian temple town of Tirupati, Andhra Pradesh, the repertoire of *vēṣam*s spans from the ritual guises of the goddess Gangamma by male participants to women's application of auspicious golden turmeric (*pasupu*) on their faces (54). Flueckiger's interpretation of *vēṣam* as an analytic category extends its scope beyond men's dramatic ritual enactments of guising to include women's everyday practices. *Impersonations* focuses on *vēṣam* in a highly stylized performance or presentational context (Sunardi 2015, 13), as opposed to everyday sartorial practices, such as those found among *hijṛā* communities in urban Telugu South India (Reddy 2005).[16] Notably, the practice of donning the *strī-vēṣam* in the Kuchipudi village does not take on the same ritual significance of guising in the Gangamma *jātara,* in which male ritual participants not only take on the guises of the goddess, but also *become* ritual manifestations of her (Handelman 1994, 333). However, like the everyday guising practices of female participants of the Gangamma *jātara* (Flueckiger 2013), sartorial guising by Kuchipudi brahmin men is not simply a dramatic act onstage. Instead, the donning of Satyabhama's *strī-vēṣam* by village brahmin men engenders expressions of power, both in staged performance and in everyday village life.

In forging a connection between the terms *vēṣam* and impersonation, my objective is to ground this study in the South Asian vernacular, while also engaging broader theoretical discourses on gender and sexuality in which impersonation is a salient analytic category. Feminist theorists have expanded the scope of impersonation beyond staged performance to reimagine the theoretical possibilities of gender more broadly.[17] Esther Newton's (1979) study of drag performers, whom she refers to as "female impersonators," is foundational to later feminist theorizations of gender, most notably the work of Judith Butler ([1990] 2008, [1993] 2011). Drawing on Newton's ethnographic work, Butler ([1990] 2008, 137) argues that drag not only parodies a particular gender identity, but also reveals the imitative structure of gender itself, as well as its inherent potential for disruption.[18] Donning the *strī-vēṣam* in Kuchipudi dance is, at the very least, functionally distinct from American drag, which can be envisioned as a parodic performance that "self-referentially draws attention to its not-quite-rightness" (Drouin 2008, 25). By contrast, guising in the Kuchipudi village is a dramatic performance that produces a stylized gender enactment onstage. That said, both practices use gender performance through sartorial guising to entertain audiences. *Vēṣam* and drag can thereby be envisioned as two culturally specific examples of the broader analytic category of impersonation. In line with the lexicon of my interlocutors and broader scholarship on Kuchipudi dance, I use the terms "impersonation" and "*vēṣam*" interchangeably in this study.

Given recent feminist scholarship, I have opted *not* to describe the practice of impersonation in gender binaries, i.e., female impersonation or male impersonation. I also do not characterize impersonation as cross-dressing or cross-gender guising because such terms presuppose that binary gender identities are being crossed through sartorial transformations.[19] I avoid the terms "transvestism" and "theatrical transvestism," which are often used interchangeably with cross-dressing in scholarship across American and South Asian performance.[20] Instead, I envision impersonation as a broad analytic category that includes not only instances of what is commonly referred to as cross-dressing or transvestism—i.e., men impersonating women and women impersonating men—but also other possibilities of guising, such as men impersonating men, women impersonating women, deities impersonating humans, and the presentation of ambiguous gender identities within narrative or performance. Nevertheless, this book is a contemporary ethnographic study circumscribed by everyday verbal discourse in which gender binaries are often directly employed or subtly invoked. Given the situatedness of this study in contemporary South India, I use gendered language—man/woman, male/female, male-identified/female-identified, and masculine/feminine—to describe the staged practice of Kuchipudi impersonation and its implications in both shaping and destabilizing constructions of hegemonic brahmin masculinity.

SOUTH ASIAN MASCULINITIES

In positing masculinity as the central focus of this study, I follow Raewyn Connell's (1995) emphasis on masculinity as an inherently relational, social practice of the body, particularly in an effort to avoid reifying Euro-American gender binaries that do not translate across global contexts (Sinha 2012). Masculinity, as Connell (2000, 10) reminds us, is a term that should be used in the plural: "We need to speak of 'masculinities', not masculinity. Different cultures, and different periods of history, construct gender differently."[21] Connell's well-known discussion of hegemonic masculinity (1987) is equally relevant to this study. Drawing on Gramsci's (1971) analysis of hegemony, Connell defines the term "hegemonic masculinity" as the practice that enables men's dominance over women and other subordinated masculinities (183–90).[22]

In a later essay outlining the state of the field of scholarship on hegemonic masculinity, Connell and James W. Messerschmidt (2005, 832) put forth the following definition:

> Hegemonic masculinity was distinguished from other masculinities, especially subordinated masculinities. Hegemonic masculinity was not assumed to be normal in the statistical sense; only a minority of men might enact it. But it was certainly normative. It embodied the currently most honored way of being a man, it required all other men to position themselves in relation to it, and it ideologically legitimated the global subordination of women to men.

Given this definition, I use the term "hegemonic masculinity" to signify the ideal form of masculinity attainable for Kuchipudi brahmin men through the practice of impersonation. The ability to excel in donning the *strī-vēṣam* is the primary marker for achieving hegemonic masculinity for Kuchipudi brahmin men, particularly as they exert authority over brahmin women and nonbrahmin men. Yet, as I will discuss in chapter 2, only one brahmin dancer—Vedantam Satyanarayana Sarma—fully embodies hegemonic masculinity in village performance and everyday life. Other brahmins in the Kuchipudi village adhere to standards of normative masculinity—the processual or emergent form of hegemonic masculinity—even if they fail to achieve the ideal of hegemonic masculinity itself.[23] For Kuchipudi brahmins, hegemonic masculinity is challenged by the presence of nonbrahmin men and brahmin women who desire to participate in performance (see chapter 5).

It is also worth noting that the category of masculinity is not a gender characteristic limited to the world of men (Connell 1995, 69; Chopra et al. 2004, 8–9). As Jack Halberstam (1998, 2) argues, there are many expressions of masculinity that exceed the male body, especially the white male middle-class body.[24] In other words, Halberstam seeks to theorize masculinity *without* men. Halberstam's decoupling of masculinity from the purview of men extends post-structuralist theorizations, which critique the presumed relationship between a prediscursive biological "sex" and a culturally constructed "gender" (Connell 1995; Butler [1990] 2008). In contemporary feminist discourse, gender is a stylized repetition of acts that conceal the processes of its very formation and, as a result, is vulnerable to disruption (Butler [1990] 2008, 190–92). In other words, masculinity, in this case brahmin masculinity, is dramatically contingent.

In focusing on brahmin masculinity, this book contributes to the burgeoning study of South Asian and South Asian American masculinities (Sinha 1995; Osella and Osella 2006; Alter 2011; Whitaker 2011; Gupta 2016, among others).[25] Throughout this expanding body of scholarship, brahmin masculinity as a distinct gender and caste category is rarely mentioned and quite often undertheorized.[26] Considering that the brahmin male body constitutes the central focus of Hindu religious texts and practices from the Vedic period onwards, the lack of scholarship on the construction of brahmin masculinity as a performative gender and caste category is remarkable.[27] While there is a vast array of scholarship on brahminical caste status (Dumont 1980; Kinsley 1993; Chakravarti 2003; Knipe 2015; Pandian 2016), as well as analysis of the masculinity of upper-caste Hindus in the colonial period (Nandy [1983] 2009; Sinha 1995; Krishnaswamy 2011), there is a considerable lacuna of scholarship on the figure of the brahmin man in relation to his gender identity, particularly in the contemporary context.[28] Questions about brahmin masculinity, particularly as it operates in regional *jāti* groups in contemporary South Asia, remain largely unanswered. In what ways does the brahmin man attain authoritative brahminhood? How does he achieve and perform societal markers of masculinity? How does brahmin masculinity emerge in both village and cosmopolitan spaces in contemporary South Asia?

Caroline Osella and Filippo Osella (2006) address some of these questions in their ethnographic study of masculinity and manhood in a rural paddy-growing village in central Kerala. As part of their broader exploration of South Asian masculinity in relation to kinship, Osella and Osella discuss rites of passage for the brahmins of the village, including the *upanayanam,* or investiture of the sacred thread, which signifies a brahmin's twice-born (*dvija*) status (32–39).[29] For Osella and Osella's interlocutors, the *upanayanam* is followed by a three-year *brahmacārya* phase in which the initiate (*brahmacārin*) masters ritual knowledge, after which a new three-stranded sacred thread is given in the *samāvartanam* (lit., "bringing to life") ceremony.[30] Upon completion of these rites of initiation, the boy achieves the symbolic capital (Bourdieu 1977) of brahminhood:

> There is a sense here of status achieved: in discourse, the boy becomes unequivocally Brahmin and masculine, utterly different from non-Brahmin men and women, including Brahmins. He is putatively the most perfect form of human being. Taking the thread is second birth, and it is what differentiates adult Brahmin males—the twice-born, the most perfect form of human beings—from the rest of society (Osella and Osella 2006, 34).

For Osella and Osella's interlocutors, mastery of ritual knowledge, particularly memorizing Sanskrit *mantra*s and performing rituals, functions as significant means for achieving the status of brahminhood.[31] The ethnographic detail provided in their account aligns, in varying degree, with other examples across India and the United States in which an expedited version of the *upanayanam* ceremony, often performed just prior to marriage, is an important marker for the achievement and construction of brahminhood (Fuller and Narasimhan 2014, 191; Flueckiger 2015, 172–73; Knipe 2015, 142–44).

In examining brahmin communities of South India, it is also necessary to point to the scholarship of Mary Hancock (1999), Indira Viswanathan Peterson and Davesh Soneji (2008), and Kristen Rudisill (2007, 2012). Hancock's (1999) book, *Womanhood in the Making*, is a comprehensive study of Smartas, a prominent South Indian group of brahmins, which includes Kuchipudi brahmins.[32] Focusing on Tamil-speaking Smarta brahmins, Hancock (1999) argues that Smartas function as "cultural brokers" who shape discourses on national culture by occupying the dialectical position between modernity and tradition (64–67).[33] Peterson and Soneji (2008, 19) build on Hancock's (1999) work to suggest that the brahmin elites of Madras (present-day Chennai) have dominated the South Indian music and dance scene.[34] Beginning with the establishment of the Music Academy in Madras in 1928, Tamil brahmins, including E. Krishna Iyer and Rukmini Arundale, underwrote the construction of "classical" arts for middle-class consumption in urban South India (Peterson and Soneji 2008, 19–20).[35] Similarly, Rudisill (2007) posits the notion of "Brahmin taste" in relation to the field of artistic production in contemporary Chennai: "[Tamil brahmins] are truly the taste-makers of the city and both construct and embody Tamil notions of good taste" (93). Through the *sabha*, which are the voluntary cultural organizations that stage performances across the city of Chennai, Tamil brahmins use humor as the vehicle for expressing brahminical taste and cultural ideals (62).[36]

Impersonations contributes to this growing field of scholarship on South Asian masculinities and contemporary brahmin communities by focusing on the brahmins of the Kuchipudi village who use performance to craft their gender and caste identities. Kuchipudi brahmins self-identify as Vaidiki (alt., Vaidika), a sect of Telugu-speaking Smarta brahmins whose occupational practices traditionally focus on conducting priestly rituals.[37] Kuchipudi Vaidiki brahmins, like their Smarta counterparts in Tamil South India, promulgate their own vision of brahminical taste through performance. As bearers of tradition, or what is known in Telugu as *sāmpradāyam*, Kuchipudi brahmins dance to exemplify and preserve their brahminical identity. However, the shift from open-air village performance to urban theatre, particularly with the migration of Kuchipudi *gurus* to the city of Madras in the mid-twentieth century, threatens the utility of the brahmin male dancer as women take over the cosmopolitan Kuchipudi stage (see chapter 4). Building on the aforementioned studies, *Impersonations* engages scholarship on South Asian masculinities, South Indian performance, and brahmin communities to examine the simultaneous authority and fragility of brahmin masculinity in the ever-changing landscape of South Indian dance.

While this study focuses on a relatively obscure community of Vaidiki Smarta brahmin men in a South Indian village, it has bearing on broader scholarship on caste, gender, and power. Indebted to Michel Foucault's ([1976] 1990) theorizations on power and discourse, I also take a cue from Christian Novetzke's discussions of brahmin identity in the context of precolonial Marathi literature. For Novetzke (2011, 236), the term "brahmin" is imbued with discursive power enacted in the public sphere: "the power to mediate, and to some degree control, the production of knowledge in various contexts . . . Thus, the symbolic capital of Brahminism is discursive power, whether it is literary or performative, it is the power to use language to shape society, politics and culture." The theme of brahminical authority, I argue, must be coupled with explorations of masculinity and sexuality in public performance; brahminical power, at least in the context of the Kuchipudi village, is primarily circumscribed to the purview of hereditary male dancers.

Although the brahmins of the Kuchipudi village share power and privilege like their South Indian brahmin counterparts, there are certain ways that their community is idiosyncratic, particularly when viewed against other ethnographic accounts and archival research, such as those provided by Osella and Osella (2006) and C.J. Fuller and Haripriya Narasimhan (2014) in their respective studies.[38] Countering the trend of Tamil brahmin migration from village to urban settings, the brahmins of the Kuchipudi village have a vibrant *agrahāram* (brahmin quarters) occupied by many members of the hereditary families listed on the 1763 property document described in the next section.[39] Although younger Kuchipudi brahmins are moving from the village to nearby urban settings, including Vijayawada and Hyderabad, as well as abroad, their rootedness in the village has not been lost. During my fieldwork in the village, it was not uncommon to see Vedantam Venkata Naga Chalapathi Rao, a younger brahmin male performer and Vijayawada resident (at the time), traversing the streets on his motorcycle, which he frequently rode into the village to visit his family.[40] Pasumarti Haranadh, another younger brahmin man from Kuchipudi who resides in Vijayawada, commutes daily to play *mṛdaṅgam* (a barrel-shaped, double-headed South Indian drum) at the village's dance institute. Kuchipudi brahmins living abroad maintain ties to the village, often visiting on their return trips to India. By contrast, members of the older generation of the Kuchipudi brahmin community continue to live in the village, maintaining the boundaries of the brahmin *agrahāram.*

The second noted difference relates to occupation. Although Kuchipudi brahmin men undergo an *upanayanam* (thread ceremony), they do not actively engage in rituals within a temple or domestic context; these ritual obligations are set aside for Vaidiki brahmins trained in priestly duties who have migrated into the village from neighboring areas. Unlike the trends observed by Fuller and Narasimhan (2014) regarding occupational shifts of Tamil brahmins into fields such as engineering, medicine, and IT, the brahmin men of the Kuchipudi village are predominantly associated with performance.[41] I would even argue that, for the brahmin men of Kuchipudi, the *upanayanam* does not function as the critical rite of passage for marking the status of authoritative brahminhood. Instead, the significant rite of passage for Kuchipudi brahmin men is to impersonate by donning the *strī-vēṣam* of Satyabhama, the wife of the Hindu deity Krishna and the heroine of the dance drama *Bhāmākalāpam*. The brahmins of the Kuchipudi village aspire to attain hegemonic brahmin masculinity by virtue of their ascribed brahminhood, yet the ways in which they achieve their gender and caste norms are idiosyncratic in comparison to those adopted in many brahmin communities across other parts of India.

Residents of the Kuchipudi village also vocalize distinct views on gender and sexuality. Living within the confines of a selective brahmin enclave, the brahmins of the Kuchipudi village reside, relatively, outside the boundaries of transnational discourses, debates, and practices of nonnormative sexualities (Reddy 2005).[42] Village brahmins are certainly aware of such discourses, especially given how often they engage with urban communities, particularly in the regionally proximate cities of Vijayawada, Hyderabad, and Chennai. While I can never be certain of the sexual practices of Kuchipudi brahmin men in their private lives, it is clear that these male-identified performers *publicly* situate themselves within a dominant heterosexual framework and decry any suggestion of possible effeminacy offstage. For example, most of the brahmin male performers I spoke with were married and had children, and the possibility of nonnormative sexuality was never directly broached by any of them.[43] The only hint at sexuality arose when I asked my interviewees the following question: "If you take on the *strī-vēṣam*, do you feel like a woman?" Although my question was directed toward onstage performance, all of the dancers responded by describing their offstage experiences and insisting that they only act like women onstage and never off, a point that seems to extend across other cases of gender impersonation in South Asia (Morcom 2013, 87).[44]

Impersonation in the Kuchipudi village is not simply a heterosexual practice, but a heteronormative one. Specifically, the brahmin cis male dancers who don the *strī-vēṣam* reside at the epicenter of village life and differ starkly from urban transgender *hijṛā*s or *koṭhī*s in South Asia, who are marginalized for their illicit practices of gender guising (Reddy 2005; Morcom 2013; Dutta and Roy 2014).[45] For example, nonbrahmin men who impersonate outside the village context can be interpreted as effeminate or even, in certain cases, as *hijṛā*s, a point I return to later in the book. However, within the village context, male dancers achieve a heteronormative ideal of brahmin masculinity by donning the *strī-vēṣam*. But, these claims to normativity are themselves tenuous, particularly as Kuchipudi dance spills from village to urban and transnational contexts. Kuchipudi impersonation expresses a simultaneity of possibility: it enables hegemonic brahmin masculinity within the village and is concurrently indexical of nonnormative, deviant forms of gender in cosmopolitan spaces. The convergence of these idiosyncratic expressions of gender and caste makes the Kuchipudi village and Kuchipudi dance a unique starting point to explore the construction of hegemonic brahmin masculinity and its contingencies.

KUCHIPUDI AS VILLAGE, KUCHIPUDI AS DANCE

The village of Kuchipudi is located in the Krishna district of the Telugu-speaking state of Andhra Pradesh, approximately thirty miles from Vijayawada, the closest metropolitan center (see Map 1). Like most of my interlocutors, I traveled to and from Kuchipudi by public transportation, catching the public bus at the crowded Vijayawada bus station and traveling southeast along a local highway, finally reaching the village about an hour or so later. Unlike the faster and more scenic route by car along the Krishna River, the meandering bus ride is a dusty, bumpy, and far more economical means of travel that acquainted me with the local townships of the Krishna *jilla* (district) of Andhra Pradesh. The bus driver would rarely call out stops to passengers, so I quickly learned to read the signage outside and memorize the order of the neighboring towns—Vuyyuru, Pamarru, and then Kuchipudi—after my first, rather confusing, bus ride to the village.

The public bus lets passengers off near the main crossroads of the village, which is lined with small shops and carts that sell a range of food items and knick-knacks. Walking under the main gate of the village's commercial center, one soon arrives at the Siddhendra Kalakshetra, the sprawling state-run dance institute in the village that served as my stay during my fieldwork. A short walk from the Kalakshetra is the heart of the village's *agrahāram,* or brahmin quarters, which is centered around a temple dedicated to Ramalingeshvara and Balatripurasundari, the local forms of the Hindu deities Shiva and the goddess, respectively (see Figure 3). In front of the temple is a wide platform that serves as a stage for the many open-air dance festivals hosted in the village throughout the year. Walking along the streets adjacent to the temple, one finds rows of whitewashed houses inhabited by hereditary Kuchipudi brahmin families with distinct surnames, such as Vempati, Vedantam, and Chinta. Aside from festivals days when the village is bustling with visiting dancers and their families, the *agrahāram* is relatively unremarkable and similar, in many ways, to the nearby villages and towns that one passes during the bus ride from Vijayawada to Kuchipudi. Despite its dusty, unpaved streets and rather sleepy atmosphere, this village is home to a transnationally recognized "classical" Indian dance form. Dancers across the globe, spanning from Australia to France to the United States, learn and perform Kuchipudi, even if they have never visited the birthplace of the dance form in the fertile coastal region of Andhra Pradesh.

In this section and the following section, I will explore the contentious history of Kuchipudi as both a village and the eponymous dance form arising from this village. While much of the history of Kuchipudi dance is obscured by lack of reliable records, four scholars provide the most comprehensive research on Kuchipudi to date: Arudra, Anuradha Jonnalagadda, Davesh Soneji, and Rumya Putcha.[46] Arudra's (1989, 1994) influential essays on Kuchipudi published in the arts journal *Sruti* offer scathing critiques of practitioner histories, particularly by interrogating the location of the Kuchipudi village and questioning the existence of Siddhendra,

FIGURE 3. Ramalingeshvara and Balatripurasundari temple in the center of the Kuchipudi village. Photo by author.

Kuchipudi's founding saint. Through detailed documentation of historical records and analysis of Kuchipudi's repertoire, Anuradha Jonnalagadda's extensive research (1993, 1996a, 1996b, 2006, 2016) traces the evolution of Kuchipudi from a regional performance form to a classical dance tradition, particularly through the efforts of well-known guru Vempati Chinna Satyam. Davesh Soneji's (2004, 2008, 2012) archival and ethnographic fieldwork with *devadāsīs* (courtesans) in Tamil- and Telugu-speaking South India point to the complicated relationship between Kuchipudi Smarta brahmins and *devadāsī* communities and performance.[47] His careful attention to the marginalized histories of *devadāsīs* provides an important corrective to practitioner histories of Kuchipudi dance, which overlook the significant role that courtesan women played in the construction of Kuchipudi as "classical" dance. Rumya Putcha's (2011, 2013, 2015) work analyzes the classicization of Kuchipudi dance in the mid-twentieth century, particularly in relation to the burgeoning South Indian film industry and key figures, such as Vedantam Lakshminarayana Sastry.[48] Indebted to and engaging the work of these four influential scholars, here I trace the transformation of Kuchipudi from a village in Telugu South India to a "classical" Indian dance tradition.

The history of the Kuchipudi village, particularly as it is described by practitioners of Kuchipudi dance, prominently mentions the gift of the Nawab of Golconda Abul Hassan Qutb Shah, also known by his Sufi name Tana Shah. It is said that in 1678, during a tour of his kingdom, Tana Shah saw a troupe of brahmin men

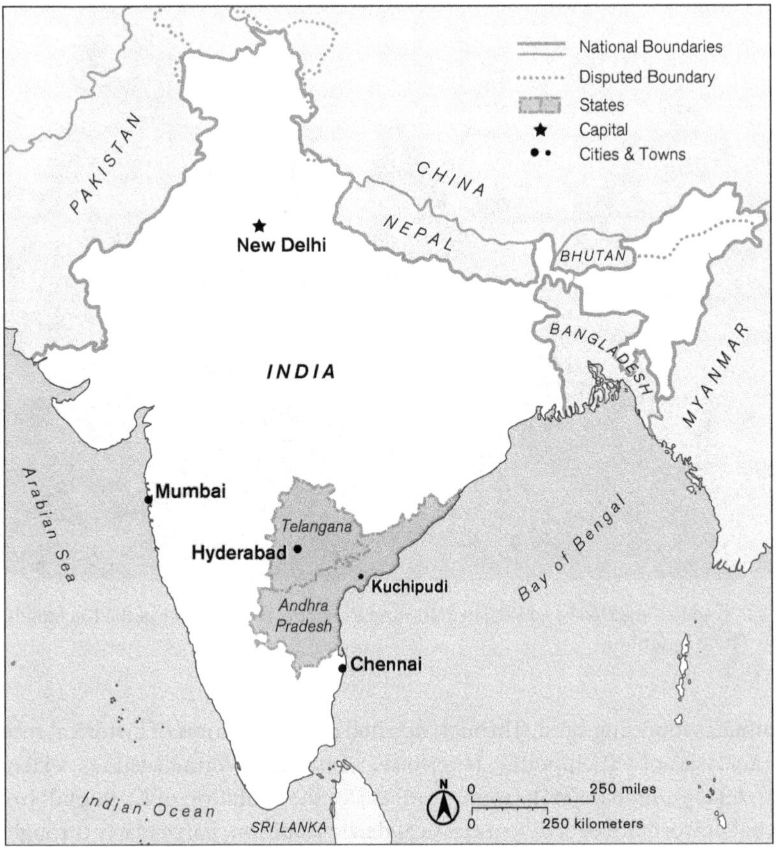

MAP 1. Map of India (2018). Image by Ben Pease.

performing a dance drama in the village of Kuchipudi. He was thought to be so enthralled by the performance that he gave away the village as an *agrahāram* (brahmin quarters) to the brahmin families who dedicated their lives to this art (Jonnalagadda 1996b, 39). Despite the lack of historical record of Tana Shah's gift (Arudra 1994), this story is still told in the village of Kuchipudi to this day, and it is a point of legitimation for its brahmin inhabitants, who repeatedly invoke the image of their powerful Muslim patron.

An important historical record of the Kuchipudi village is the 1763 property dispute that arose among the families living in the village at the time. Members of these brahmin families attempted to resolve the dispute legally by appealing to the Nizam, the then-current ruler, who appointed Mosalikanti Kamoji Pantulu and Kandregula Jogipantulu as his agents. A settlement was reached, and a property division document was drafted on August 24, 1763, indicating that families

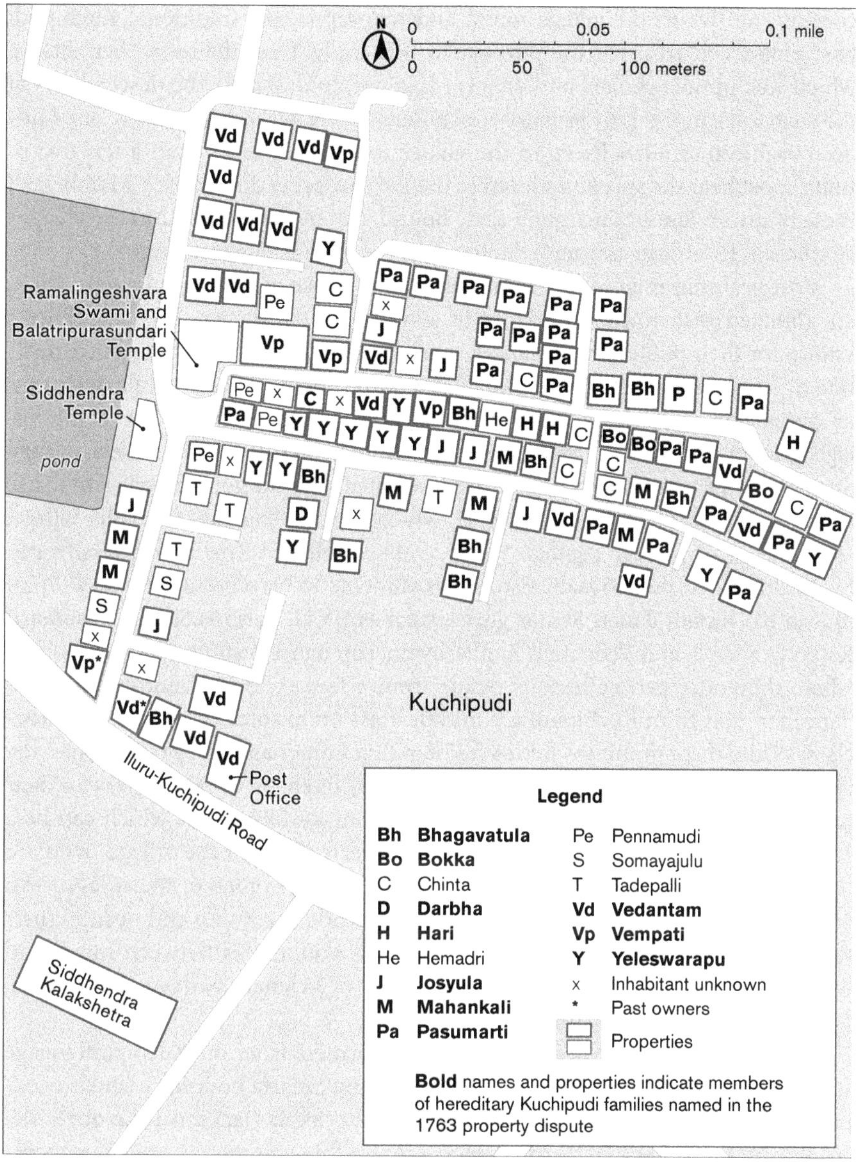

MAP 2. Map of the Kuchipudi village. Image by Ben Pease.

with the following fifteen surnames were legitimate residents of the Kuchipudi village: Bhagavatula, Bokka, Darbha, Hari, Josyula, Mahankali, Pasumarti, Peddibhatla, Polepeddi, Vallabhajosyula, Vedantam, Vempati, Vemu, Venukunti, and Yeleswarapu (Jonnalagadda 1996b, 40).[49] Descendants of these families continue to live in the village today, and many promote traditional Kuchipudi performance genres. For the purpose of this study, I use the term "hereditary," which Kuchipudi scholars and dancers also use, to designate the descendants of the surnames in the 1763 property document. There are approximately one hundred brahmin families living in the village today, and, aside from a few exceptions, most bear the surnames listed in the 1763 property document.[50] Members of these brahmin families maintain caste boundaries by residing within the village's *agrāharam* (brahmin quarters) depicted on the village map (see Map 2).[51]

Most brahmin men of this community, even those of the younger generation, are affiliated with Kuchipudi dance in some capacity, whether they are dancers known for their public performances, teachers who train students at a dance institute or home studio, musicians skilled in South Indian classical vocals or drums, or organizers of festivals and performances. Prominent dancers from the village, namely Vedantam Ramalingasastry, Chinta Ravi Balakrishna, Yeleswarapu Srinivas, and Pasumarti Haranadh, are associated with the government-run dance institute, the Siddhendra Kalakshetra, which attracts students from the village, as well as nearby urban centers. The recently established Krishna University, run by Pasumarti Keshav Prasad, also draws students to earn certificates and diplomas in Kuchipudi dance. Senior gurus, such as P.V.G. Krishna Sarma, Pasumarti Rattayya Sarma, and Vedantam Radheshyam, run dance institutes in their homes, where they offer private lessons. Aside from a few exceptions, most hereditary dance families from Kuchipudi are middle-class or, in some cases, lower middle-class. While these brahmins live in freestanding homes and carry cell phones, the income earned from dance is limited. Organizers often fail to pay dancers for their travel expenses or accommodations to and from performances, which can be a source of frustration for the brahmin male performers of the village, who are the primary earners of family income. The brahmin women of the village, who are the focus of chapter 5, generally remain inside the home and occupy their time with cooking and housework. The rigid boundaries between men's and women's occupations mirror the observations of Velcheru Narayana Rao (1991, 116) regarding Telugu brahmin households.

As already noted, the hereditary male performers from the Kuchipudi village self-identify as Vaidiki, a sect of Telugu-speaking Smarta brahmins whose occupational practices traditionally focus on priestly rituals (Jackson 1994, 207). The Vaidiki brahmin male performers who inhabit this community consider themselves the exclusive bearers of "tradition," or *sāmpradāyam*.[52] For most Kuchipudi brahmin male dancers, *sāmpradāyam* connotes the early elements of the Kuchipudi repertoire, namely *kalāpa*s and *yakṣagāna*s, which used to be performed (and are occasionally still performed) by village dance troupes. *Kalāpa*s are the earliest elements of the Kuchipudi repertoire dating to approximately the eighteenth century (Soneji 2012, 267n12). *Kalāpa*s, such as *Bhāmākalāpam*, involve approximately two or three characters and alternate between dramatic dialogues and dance items performed by one or more characters. By the nineteenth century, the Kuchipudi repertoire expanded to include *yakṣagānas*, which are dramatic performances that include a broader array of characters, usually heroes, heroines, and antiheroes (Jonnalagadda 1996b; Nagabhushana Sarma 2009).[53] Performances of *kalāpas* and *yakṣagānas* include a mixture of dance pieces interspersed with dialogues between characters, conveying a theatrical mode akin to Tamil Special Drama outlined by Susan Seizer (2005). In fact, early *kalāpas* and *yakṣagānas* express more drama than dance, an aesthetic feel that changed with the influence of well-known guru Vempati Chinna Satyam in the mid-twentieth century (see chapter 4).

Kuchipudi male dancers from the village are skilled at donning a wide variety of *vēṣams*, ranging from the young girl Usha in the *yakṣagāna Uṣā-pariṇayam* to the demon king Balicakravarti in the *yakṣagāna Bhakta-prahalāda*. Among these various roles, the donning of Satyabhama's *strī-vēṣam* in *Bhāmākalāpam* is most significant because of its associations with Siddhendra, the founding saint of Kuchipudi dance (see chapter 1). In the early periods of Kuchipudi history (ca. eighteenth and nineteenth centuries), all-male troupes comprising a troupe leader, dancers, and accompanying musicians would travel to nearby villages and towns and enact *kalāpas* and *yakṣagānas* on makeshift open-air stages (Jonnalagadda 1996b, 43–46). With the influence of Parsi theatre from western India and the advent of modern theatrical techniques such as lighting, sound amplification, and sets, Kuchipudi performances shifted to the proscenium theatre in the twentieth century (Jonnalagadda 1996b, 46; Bhikshu 2006, 251). Despite these changes, in the Kuchipudi village today there is an outdoor stage adjacent to the Ramalingeshvara temple where most dance festivals and performances are conducted, retaining the dramatic feel of early Kuchipudi performance.

While anyone, regardless of gender or caste, can take classes at one of the village's numerous dance institutes, not everyone is encouraged to embody the traditional elements of the Kuchipudi repertoire, specifically donning Satyabhama's *strī-vēṣam*. In particular, brahmin women from the Kuchipudi village and non-brahmin men (both within and outside the village) are restricted from such traditional forms of performance in the village. In the case of the former, Kuchipudi brahmin women primarily occupy domestic roles and, aside from a few notable exceptions, rarely participate in dance. This practice of gender exclusion is justified by Kuchipudi male dancers with the following reasons: women have monthly periods that prevent them from regular performance; previously, women were not allowed to travel unaccompanied by male relatives; and journeys to performance locales are often very difficult and women cannot cope with such strenuous conditions.[54] Over the course of the twentieth century, the gender composition of Kuchipudi dance outside the village has drastically shifted, and through a number of postcolonial transformations, female dancers now dominate the Kuchipudi stage. Although women from outside the village are now encouraged to dance, brahmin women from the Kuchipudi village continue to be excluded from public performance, a trend that I explore in detail in chapter 5.

The Kuchipudi village dance community is exclusive not only in terms of gender, but caste as well. As a point of comparison, I spoke with Ajay Kumar, a talented younger nonbrahmin impersonator and teacher from Vijayawada, the major urban center near Kuchipudi. Ajay related that although he has trained in the Kuchipudi village and even completed his MA in Kuchipudi dance at the Siddhendra Kalakshetra, the village gurus were reluctant to teach him the practice of impersonation because he does not belong to a hereditary Kuchipudi brahmin family. As a result of this reluctance, Ajay dons the *strī-vēṣam* to perform solo items and modern dance dramas, rather than enacting female characters in the traditional *kalāpa*s and *yakṣagāna*s of the Kuchipudi repertoire.[55] When such traditional dance dramas are staged in the Kuchipudi village by hereditary families, they are always enacted by brahmin men.

In the contemporary context, Kuchipudi is a transnational dance form performed by both men and women from a variety of caste backgrounds, nationalities, and even religious identities (Jonnalagadda 2008). Throughout the book, I opt to use the term "transnational," as opposed to "global," to identify contemporary Kuchipudi dance, particularly as it exists outside the village context. In doing so, I take a cue from Priya Srinivasan's *Sweating Saris* (2012), which makes a case for envisioning Indian dance as a form of transnational labor.[56] The dancers of this book (both men and women) are wage earners who straddle transnational contexts, often traveling from India to the United States and Canada over the summer to give workshops and stage performances for diaspora audiences. Likewise, the increasing popularity of online platforms such as YouTube and Skype makes it possible to take lessons and learn choreographed dance pieces within the comfort of one's own home. Even village brahmin men often travel abroad to host workshops and give performances; for example, younger brahmin dancers (and brothers) Vedantam Venkata Naga Chalapathi Rao and Vedantam Raghava now permanently reside in Canada and the United States, respectively, and return to India over summer and winter breaks, thereby reversing the flow of transnational labor.

Given these recent transformations, it may come as a surprise that within the village, Kuchipudi is still considered a brahminical and male-only dance form in which only brahmin men don the *strī-vēṣam*. The insularity of the village's brahmin *agrahāram* coupled with the expansion of Kuchipudi as a transnational dance form affords a particularly fruitful starting point to trace the transformation of gender and caste norms from village to urban and transnational spaces. The significance of impersonation in the Kuchipudi village provides a unique case study through which to examine the construction of hegemonic brahmin masculinity within a highly confined space, while tracing the contingency of gender and caste norms beyond the village.

KUCHIPUDI AS CLASSICAL

Today, Kuchipudi is nationally recognized in India as one of eight "classical" dance forms, along with Bharatanatyam, Kathakali, Odissi, and Kathak, among others (Satkunaratnam 2012).[57] However, the appellation "classical" is a title bestowed on Kuchipudi in the mid-twentieth century in the wake of the Indian dance "revival" in South India. In this section, I draw on the growing body of scholarship on South Indian dance to outline the historical background that enabled the classicization of Kuchipudi and other Indian dance forms in the early to mid-twentieth century.[58] In chapter 1, I expand on this discussion to foreground the ways in which the hagiography of Siddhendra, the founding saint of Kuchipudi dance, and the role of the impersonator are dually integral to this classicization process.

Twentieth-century India witnessed immense political upheaval in the wake of the fall of the British empire, an upsurge of Indian nationalist sentiments, and the creation of a new nation-state in 1947. The nationalist push to transform India from a colony of the British empire to an independent nation-state with its own political agenda significantly impacted India's artistic and performance styles, particularly in relation to the figure of the *devadāsī*. Arthi Devarajan (2012, 1182) aptly defines *devadāsīs* as "creative and contentious figures who have worked as temple dancers, courtesans, entertainers, and key participants in social rituals, political campaigns, and diplomatic events in South Asia." In his extensive research with courtesan communities, Soneji (2012) is careful to outline the complex definitions associated with the term *devadāsī*. He notes that "today the term '*devadāsī*' is used to index a vast number of communities of women who are generally glossed by English phrases such as 'sacred prostitute' or 'temple dancer.' It collapses a number of regional practices under a singular sign, and the literal translation of the word ('slave of god') is all too often taken as a closed definition of the category" (6). The *devadāsī* women that Soneji works with in Telugu South India refer to themselves as *kalāvantulu* (lit., "receptacles of the arts").[59]

Comparable to the figure of the *satī* in colonial discourses, the *devadāsī* became the grounds upon which issues of sexuality, gender, performance, caste, and nationhood were debated and reconstructed (Spivak 1988; Mani 1998; Arondekar 2012; Soneji 2012). The anti-nautch movement against *devadāsīs* gained traction in late nineteenth-century South India, particularly through the efforts of social activists Kandukuri Viresalingam (1848–1919) and S. Muthulakshmi Reddi (1866–1968) (Viresalingam 1970, 59; Soneji 2012, 120–21; Thobani 2017, 31). In 1927, Reddi, the first female doctor in the Madras Presidency, drafted a resolution to the Madras Legislative Council that critiqued the practice of dedicating *devadāsī* girls to temples (Soneji 2010, xxi). Reddi's recommendations materialized into legislation, namely "A Bill to Prevent the Dedication of Women to Hindu Temples" in 1930 and "Madras Devadasis (Prevention of Dedication) Act of 1947," the latter of which criminalized the dedication of a girl to an image or deity in a temple (Soneji

2010, xxi; Soneji 2012, 119–23). *Devadāsī* dance continued in nontemple contexts until 1956 when an amendment to the 1947 act banned *devadāsī* dancing at marriages and other social occasions, thereby ending public *devadāsī* performance altogether (Soneji 2012, 191). Nonetheless, the embodied memory and ritual significance of *devadāsī* women has continued into the contemporary period, as evident in the ethnographic accounts of Soneji (2012) and Lucinda Ramberg (2014).[60]

In conjunction with the anti-nautch movement in the early twentieth century, dance performance in Tamil-speaking South India witnessed a "revival" as "the hereditary community of devadasi dancers was replaced by a new community of upper-caste dancers" (Allen 1997, 65). Traditional *devadāsī* performers did not fit into the elite nationalist vision of "classical" Indian dance and were therefore replaced by middle-class and upper-caste (mostly brahmin) women dancers who abandoned the erotic (*śṛṇgāra*) repertoire for less sexually suggestive themes (Meduri 1988; Allen 1997). *Devadāsī* dance was renamed from *sadir* to Bharatanatyam (lit., "the dance of Bharata"), which clearly forges connections with Bharata's *Nāṭyaśāstra* and a presumed glorious Hindu golden age (Allen 1997, 79; Putcha 2013, 96).[61] *Devadāsī* dance became the basis for the first nationally recognized "classical" Indian dance form, Bharatanatyam, while the *devadāsī* herself was all but forgotten (Meduri 1988, 6).

Alongside the development of anti-nautch reform, the establishment of institutions such as the Music Academy (est. 1928) prompted what became known as a dance "revival" in colonial South India (Allen 2008). As Matthew Harp Allen (1997, 63–64) succinctly describes:

> The term "revival" is a drastically reductive linguistic summary of a complex process—a deliberate selection from among many possibilities—which cries out to be examined from more than one point of view. While the "revival" of South Indian dance certainly *involved* a re-vivification or bringing back to life, it was equally a re-population (one social community appropriating a practice from another), a re-construction (altering and replacing elements of repertoire and choreography), a re-naming (from *nautch* and other terms to *bharata natyam*), a re-situation (from temple, court, and salon to the public stage), and a re-storation (. . . a splicing together of selected 'strips' of performative behavior in a manner that simultaneously creates a new practice and invents an historical one). The discourse on South Indian dance has to date privileged the term "revival" over other equally descriptive ones, obscuring the complexity of the process, focusing attention onto a simple, celebrative vision of the giving of new life.

Integral to the so-called South Indian "revival" of *devadāsī* dance were the efforts of Tamil brahmin dancer Rukmini Arundale. Inspired by the Orientalist leanings of the international Theosophical Society, Arundale repackaged courtesan performance to suit elite middle-class and upper-caste sensibilities and resanctified the stage as the temple. In Bharatanatyam, Arundale sought to construct a dance repertoire that rivaled Euro-American classical dance, while departing from traditional solo *devadāsī* performance (Peterson 2011/12, 26). Arundale's dance institution, the Kalakshetra (established in Madras in 1936), became the veritable locus for a Bharatanatyam empire that reshaped the trajectory of all Indian dance forms for decades (Meduri 1988; Allen 1997). *Devadāsī* performers, by comparison, were disenfranchised and overtly excluded from the performative sphere. They became, in the words of Srinivasan (2012, 151–52), the hidden laborers of Indian dance, akin to the contemporary weavers and sari salesmen whose embodied labor (or memory of embodied labor in the case of the *devadāsī*) is overlooked and ultimately forgotten during the moment of public performance. In other words, the "*devadasi* were thus rudely dismissed, while the dance itself, like the mythical phoenix, rose from the ashes" (Meduri 1988, 6).[62]

The ostensible revival and performative repackaging of the *devadāsī* repertoire into Bharatanatyam catapulted a national transformation of the Indian arts scene. Mid-twentieth-century dancers and scholars began to employ the language of "classical" Indian dance, an appellation given to dance forms grounded in the *Nāṭyaśāstra* (ca. fourth century CE) and other Sanskrit manuals on dramaturgy and the arts. In the words of Kathak dance scholar Pallabi Chakravorty (2010, 276):

> During the nationalist phase in the early twentieth century, the revival of Indian classical dance came to be associated intimately with the construction of India's national identity. The concept of a common heritage provided an umbrella under which all the different regional dance styles were assembled. The dances came to embody the 'spiritual' roots of the past.

In the process of Sanskritizing Indian dance, the technical elements of Sanskrit aesthetic theory merged with the philosophical commentary of Abhinavagupta (ca. eleventh century CE) to uplift "classical" dance from dramatic art to ultimate spiritual experience (Meduri 1988, 8; Coorlawala 2004, 53–54). Today, the path forged between Indian classical dance and religion is encapsulated in the phrase *bhakti rasa,* a term that describes a heightened aesthetic mood for "experiencing a moment of intimate connection deepening the relationship between a devotee and the divine that is embodied on stage" (Zubko 2014a, 2).[63] The coupling of dance with the discourse of *bhakti* further theologizes Bharatanatyam as a religiously based upper-caste dance form, while also distancing it from the more sensuous performance repertoire of *devadāsī* dancers.[64]

Notably, Soneji (2012) reminds us that the success of "classical" Indian dance is still palpable for contemporary *devadāsī*s despite anti-nautch legislation. He writes:

> Women in contemporary *kalāvantula* communities reflect on loss and aesthetics in a manner that takes, for example, the success of "classical" Indian dance, cinema dance, and other elite cultural practices into account; these provide the foil for their own experiences. Their narrations reveal an acute awareness of their social location

> outside the middle class and enable them to mark their fractured identities within a historically determinate framework. (221)

For Soneji's interlocutors, performance serves as a form of "reflective nostalgia" that allows them to both embody and remember an untenable past (214).

In the years following the ostensible "revival" of dance and music in Tamil South India, elite scholars and patrons from Telugu South India proposed their own version of "classical" dance that rivaled the status of Bharatanatyam in Tamil Nadu. Among the various regional dance styles of Telugu South India, Kuchipudi was selectively chosen and promoted on the national stage and soon became synonymous with the category of "classical." Soneji (2012, 201) notes that "nationalists and elite philanthropists in Andhra Pradesh accorded a parallel status to a reworked version of the *smārta* Brahmin male dance tradition from Kuchipudi village, and not to the dance of the *kalāvantulu*." As both Soneji (2012) and Putcha (2015) argue, Kuchipudi paradoxically became a classical Indian dance tradition in the twentieth century through the simultaneous inclusion and erasure of *devadāsī* identity.

Although rarely mentioned in Kuchipudi circles today, it is evident that Kuchipudi brahmins frequently interacted with and borrowed from *devadāsī* dancers (Appa Rao 1958; Putcha 2013).[65] One of the most influential figures responsible for reshaping Kuchipudi dance through the framework of *devadāsī* performance is Kuchipudi village brahmin Vedantam Lakshminarayana Sastry (1886–1956). Most Kuchipudi dancers and scholars credit Lakshminarayana Sastry for transforming Kuchipudi from an ensemble, exclusively male theatrical tradition (*nāṭyamēḷam*) to a solo dance style featuring female dancers (*naṭṭuvamēḷam*) (Jonnalagadda 1996b, 47 and 2016, 1067; Shah 2002, 133; Putcha 2015, 9). What many Kuchipudi dancers and scholars fail to recognize is that this reframing of Kuchipudi dance is a direct result of Lakshminarayana Sastry's engagement with *devadāsī* performers. As Putcha (2015, 12–13) argues: "At a time when *kuchipudi* repertoire revolved around theatrical ensemble genres, Sastry fashioned a solo repertoire, most likely based on interactions with female dancers and in the spirit of oriental dance popularized by contemporaries such as Uday Shankar (1900–1977)." The effects of Lakshminarayana Sastry's efforts are enormously influential on Kuchipudi as it is practiced today; most solo dance pieces performed by contemporary Kuchipudi dancers are a direct byproduct of Lakshminarayana Sastry's efforts in repackaging solo female dance.[66]

Another important factor in the classicization of Kuchipudi was the state-based performing arts organization Andhra Pradesh Sangeet Natak Akademi (APSNA), established in 1957, just one year after the creation of the newly named Telugu-speaking state of Andhra Pradesh (Jonnalagadda 2006, 271).[67] In 1958, the Central Sangeet Natak Akademi (the national branch of APSNA) organized an All-India Dance Seminar in New Delhi. Vissa Appa Rao, a notable Telugu scholar and Niyogi brahmin, and Maranganti Kanchanamala, an English-educated female student of Vedantam Lakshminarayana Sastry, were sent as delegates from Andhra Pradesh to attend the seminar as representatives of Kuchipudi dance (Putcha 2013, 91). Despite the fact that both Appa Rao and Kanchanamala were not from the class of hereditary brahmin dancers from the Kuchipudi village, they were sent as representatives of Kuchipudi dance on account of their ability to speak in English and converse with non-Telugu audiences (Putcha 2013, 101).[68] According to Kuchipudi public memory, the 1958 seminar failed to acknowledge Kuchipudi as a "classical" dance tradition when dancer Kanchanamala was relegated to performing in a daytime slot and the stalwart Bharatanatyam guru Rukmini Arundale referred to Kuchipudi as a subset of Bharatanatyam (Jonnalagadda 1996b, 48 and 2016, 1063; Putcha 2013, 94). Slighted by the Central Sangeet Natak Akademi, proponents of Kuchipudi publicly announced its classical status the following year (1959) in the "Kuchipudi Nritya Sadassu" (Seminar on Kuchipudi Dance) hosted by APSNA. These two successive seminars—1958 and 1959—function as critical historical markers for the formation of Kuchipudi as classical dance, a point that Putcha (2013) explores further in her work.[69]

The attempts to classicize Kuchipudi did not end with the 1958 and 1959 seminars but continued in subsequent years as Kuchipudi practitioners and proponents worked to popularize the dance form and expand its reach beyond Telugu South India through the auspices of APSNA. In 1959, All India Radio in Vijayawada recorded several Kuchipudi dance dramas, including *Bhāmākalāpam* (Jonnalagadda 2016, 1064). In October 1960, APSNA initiated a tour of a troupe from the Kuchipudi village led by Kuchipudi artist Chinta Krishna Murthy and managed by Telugu brahmin Banda Kanakalingeshwara Rao (Jonnalagadda 2016, 1063). The tour included performances in Madras, Tanjavur, and Madurai (all urban centers in the South Indian state of Tamil Nadu) and incorporated elaborate explanations of the history and legacy of Kuchipudi by Kanakalingeshwara Rao.[70] Following the success of the tour, APSNA, encouraged by Kanakalingeshwara Rao, established the Siddhendra Kalakshetra in Kuchipudi in 1961 and satellite institutions in urban centers across Andhra Pradesh (Jonnalagadda 2016, 1064).[71] APSNA was dissolved in 1983 and replaced by Potti Sreeramulu Telugu University in 1985, which in the following years took over the Siddhendra Kalakshetra in the Kuchipudi village and significantly expanded its syllabus (Jonnalagadda 2006, 272–73; 2016, 1069). Today, students can earn various degrees in Kuchipudi dance, including a diploma, certificate, MA, and PhD, at the Siddhendra Kalakshetra, which is a satellite campus of Potti Sreeramulu Telugu University in Hyderabad, Telangana. The institutionalization of the dance form in recent decades has been further buttressed by the commercialization of the village through state- and locally sponsored arts festivals. Now a tourist destination for visitors from all over the world, the Kuchipudi village is recognizably home to Kuchipudi "classical" dance.[72]

The emergence of Kuchipudi as a "classical" Indian dance tradition was an iterative process that occurred during the years leading up to and following the creation of the Telugu-speaking state of Andhra Pradesh (Shah 2002). The formation of the state-level arts organization APSNA, coupled with the efforts of elite brahmin proponents such as Banda Kanakalingeshwara Rao, propelled Kuchipudi as "classical" Telugu dance into the national limelight. Additionally, the repackaging of the solo female dance repertoire by Kuchipudi guru Vedantam Lakshminarayana Sastry and the prominence given to middle-class and English-educated female dancers like Kanchanamala paved the way for a cosmopolitan vision of Kuchipudi dance beyond the village (Putcha 2013). In the mid-twentieth century, Kuchipudi dancers and proponents publicly asserted the significance of Kuchipudi as classical dance and not simply an obscure geographical locale. Mirroring and competing with the dance "revival" of Bharatanatyam in Tamil Nadu, Kuchipudi became *the* dance form of Telugu South India and one of the classical dance traditions of the nascent Indian nation-state. As the works of scholars Arudra, Jonnalagadda, Soneji, and Putcha demonstrate, any discussion of Kuchipudi as dance needs to be preceded by a careful interrogation of Kuchipudi's contentious past. And, as I will argue in chapter 1, the hereditary brahmin men of Kuchipudi's *agrahāram* are important players in the classicization of Kuchipudi dance, particularly on account of the practice of impersonation. The brahmin male body donning a woman's guise became the central script for fashioning Kuchipudi into a nationally recognized "classical" Indian dance form.

DANCING IN THE FIELD

"You don't move like one of us," said a voice from behind me as I walked from the Siddhendra Kalakshetra's main building to the adjacent dormitory after a morning dance class. The voice belonged to Pasumarti Haranadh, the *mṛdaṅgam* player at the dance institute who became a close contact during my stay in the village. Startled by his direct assertion, I asked him to explain why—what made me so different? Hari, as he is commonly known, responded simply by saying that he had watched me rehearse Satyabhama's *pravēśa daruvu* in class that morning, and my movements seemed out of sync. Although exasperated by this assertion, I had to admit that he was correct; there was something about Satyabhama's character that I could never quite capture, whether it was in the dance halls in the Siddhendra Kalakshetra or in a back room of the Hindu Temple of Atlanta, where I first learned the piece from my teacher, Sasikala Penumarthi, nearly fifteen years earlier. Satyabhama's lilting walks and proud looks always seemed to elude me in the moment of performance, and I could never discipline my body to enact her character to the satisfaction of my teachers, either in the United States or in India.

In her work on transnational Indian dance, Priya Srinivasan (2012) raises the concept of the "unruly spectator" that helps to reframe my failure in performance. In first-person voice, Srinivasan (2012, 8–9) writes:

> In one respect, my body is involved in the research through the act of practicing the dance and through my kinesthetic responses to the information gathered. In another respect, I am restless as I find it imperative to unpack multiple points of view to reveal Indian dance within a broader political economy. For these reasons, throughout the book, I participate as the "unruly spectator." The unruly spectator offers a feminist perspective on spectatorship and takes an active role in uncovering the ways that power can be negotiated by examining dance mistakes such as a slipping sari, a bleeding foot, or sweaty sari blouses.

Envisioning Hari's comments through the lens of the "unruly spectator" allows me to rethink my performance of Satyabhama's *pravēśa daruvu;* perhaps the reason that I could never quite capture Satyabhama's gait or glances is not entirely due to a failure in my skills in dance, but rather on account of a restriction placed on the character herself. From the start of Kuchipudi's contentious past, Satyabhama has always been envisioned through the brahmin male body, thereby delimiting the female dancer from ever fully inhabiting her character. As I was told repeatedly by my interlocutors, to see Satyabhama in performance, one must watch the brahmin male body in *vēṣam.*

I begin with this vignette to note that dancing in the field, however unsuccessfully, serves as an underlying ethnographic method in this study, thus in line with a host of scholars who both study and embody Indian performance.[73] Having participated in dance classrooms in India and the United States since 1997, I am deeply familiar with the profuse amounts of sweat that dance labor entails, particularly in the muggy context of Chennai, which often drenches the sari *and* the sari blouse in sweat (Srinivasan 2012). Although I do not often insert myself as the "unruly spectator," in the manner of Srinivasan, to read and disrupt the performances around me, my familiarity with disciplining my body in dance and very often failing at this disciplinary practice undergirds my analysis in this book.

In fact, dancing was my primary entrance into the field. Sidestepping the initial embodied awkwardness of fieldwork underscored by Gloria Goodwin Raheja and Ann Grodzins Gold (1994) and Tulasi Srinivas (2018), I was able to build relationships with my interlocutors by dancing in their classrooms. This choice, however, was not simply a utilitarian avenue of introduction; rather, dance became the means to attain what Deidre Sklar (1994) refers to as *kinesthetic empathy.* Sklar defines kinesthetic empathy as a method of qualitative movement analysis that builds the "capacity to participate with another's movement or another's sensory experience of movement" (15). In the context of my fieldwork, dance became my avenue to kinesthetic empathy. It is by dancing that I was able to participate with and sometimes even against the stories and histories of the dancers who fill the pages of this book.

Building on Sklar's notion of kinesthetic empathy, I specifically requested to learn to dance *Bhāmākalāpam*, the hallmark dance drama of the Kuchipudi brahmin male tradition. In every dance classroom, whether at the University of Hyderabad campus, the Siddhendra Kalakshetra in the village, or the Kuchipudi Art Academy in Chennai, I learned bits and pieces of the *Bhāmākalāpam* dance drama, ultimately learning the entirety of Satyabhama's role by the end of my fieldwork stay. The goal was not to excel in performing Satyabhama, which is difficult for most dancers in India and an impossibility for an American-raised South Asian woman (Devarajan 2011). Rather, the point was to move beyond "objective" observation to project myself into another's moving body (Sklar 1994, 15). By learning both the movements and the dialogues of *Bhāmākalāpam*, "I put my body on the line while training and otherwise engaging other dancers" (Srinivasan 2012, 18). Even in moments when I failed in dance (or perhaps dance failed me), such as the vignette mentioned previously, I built my capacity for kinesthetic empathy; as any dancer knows, failure is a certainty in both practice and performance.

There were several instances, however, in which dance stepped in the way of my "real" work. In the Kuchipudi village, for example, I was interrupted in the middle of a recorded interview to dance an item for a large group of Scandinavian tourists who were visiting the Siddhendra Kalakshetra. On another occasion, I was asked by the principal of the Siddhendra Kalakshetra to abandon my weekend interview plans and travel by train with his troupe to Bengaluru to perform. Another time, I was asked to video-record basic Kuchipudi movements with the principal's eleven-year-old son for a dance teacher visiting from the United States. While frustrating at the time, in hindsight, these interruptions were integral to building my relationship with the Kuchipudi community and gaining insight into the world of dance beyond the interview context. Notably, this method of performance ethnography permeates the interdisciplinary fields of dance studies, ethnomusicology, and the anthropology of sport.[74] As a dancer-ethnographer, I combine performance analysis and ethnographic method to analyze the practice of impersonation in the context of the Kuchipudi village and in transnational Kuchipudi dance. While I do not always foreground my dancing body, my experiences of dancing in the field inform my analysis of Kuchipudi as village and Kuchipudi as dance.

To be clear from the outset, this study is not an ethnography of a single village in the manner of many seminal ethnographies of South Asia (Gold 2000; Prasad 2007; Flueckiger 2013). Rather than spending my entire fieldwork stay in the Kuchipudi village, I chose to divide my time among three separate fieldwork sites—Hyderabad, the Kuchipudi village, and Chennai—because the historical trajectory of Kuchipudi dance brought me to these locales. I conducted fieldwork from 2009 to 2010, followed by several return visits to all three sites over the following eight years (2010–18).[75] During this time, I interviewed approximately forty Kuchipudi dancers and scholars, in addition to conducting archival research at the Sangeet Natak Akademi archives in New Delhi. Most of my interviews with Kuchipudi dancers were conducted in Telugu. In the chapters to come, all direct quotations from interviews are translated from Telugu to English unless otherwise noted. Alongside formal interviews, I observed, recorded, organized, and participated in several Kuchipudi performances.

Initially, I conceived the project as an ethnography of the village, particularly focusing on the village's community of brahmin male dancers. However, after beginning fieldwork, it quickly became clear that staying within the boundaries of the village would paint a lopsided picture of Kuchipudi dance by reifying the authority of Kuchipudi brahmin men over and above all the other dancers across the globe who describe themselves as Kuchipudi artists. In choosing to move beyond the village to urban sites of Kuchipudi dance, including Chennai, Hyderabad, and Atlanta, I observed both the authority and contingency of Kuchipudi brahmin masculinity, which is challenged through the expansion of Kuchipudi as a transnational dance form. The shift from village to urban and transnational enabled me to envision a broader geography of masculinities in which the hegemonic masculinity of brahmin men on the village stage is displaced in global contexts (Connell and Messerschmidt 2005, 849). Consequently, this book is a multisited ethnographic study of practice, particularly as the practice converges and disrupts the legacy of normative and hegemonic forms of brahmin masculinity in Kuchipudi dance.[76]

The material analyzed here, especially in chapters 2, 3, and 4, arises from *Bhāmākalāpam* performances in Hyderabad and Atlanta that I organized and in which I participated. In January 2011, I collaborated with Hyderabad-based dance scholars Anuradha Jonnalagadda and Modali Nagabhushana Sarma to stage a three-day symposium on *kalāpa* traditions. The symposium included performances and lecture-demonstrations by artists from the Kuchipudi village, courtesan communities from coastal Andhra Pradesh, and Turpu Bhagavatam performers (a regional theatrical style from Vijayanagaram that also performs *Bhāmākalāpam*).[77] In September 2011, I organized a performance of *Bhāmākalāpam* at Emory University performed by Sasikala Penumarthi, an Atlanta-based artist trained by Vempati Chinna Satyam, and Vedantam Raghava, a Dallas-based guru whose family is from the Kuchipudi village. While I attended dozens of performances during my fieldwork in India, the pictures reprinted in the book are based on the performances I organized and had explicit permission to photograph and record. Given the public nature of Kuchipudi performance, I also requested permission to include the real names of all the dancers quoted and pictured in this book.

The politics and privilege of caste also frame my fieldwork experiences. During my initial encounters with the brahmin inhabitants of the Kuchipudi village, the first question usually posed to me regarded the issue of caste. Unable to distinguish my caste from my style of dress or surname (*iṇṭipēru*), my village interlocutors usually posed the question in a fairly straightforward manner: "Are you one of us?" (Telugu: *mana vāllā?*). I was first asked this question during my introductory meeting with the principal of the Siddhendra Kalakshetra, the village's dance institute that served as my home during my fieldwork stay. Seeing my apparent confusion at what seemed to be a simple question—"Are you one of us?"—the principal began to laugh. A student standing in the doorway framed the inquiry more clearly, "Are you Vaidiki or Niyogi?" It suddenly dawned on me that the question was not simply about community or belonging, but a question of caste, one that had never been directly posed to me in urban dance settings, either in India or the United States. Although irritated by his direct inquiry and deeply conscious of the long history of patriarchal and caste-based oppression that comes with my brahmin status, I was forced to answer truthfully: "Yes, I am one of you." As the daughter of a Vaidiki father and Niyogi mother, I was aware of the long-standing rivalry between these Telugu sectarian brahminical groups and thus quickly decided to identify as Vaidiki in an attempt to integrate myself with my Vaidiki interlocutors.[78] Upon hearing of my caste affiliation, and specific subcaste, my questioner relaxed at the thought that I was, indeed, one of them.[79]

I feel a deep-seated discomfort that my acceptance into the Kuchipudi village was based, in part, on my privileged status within the folds of the Vaidiki brahmin community. Given my interactions with the brahmins of the Kuchipudi village, I would argue that their willingness to answer my questions, support my research, teach me dance, and feed me as one of their own would not have been possible if my caste had been different. Although it is not my intention to imply that I would have been treated poorly if my caste status had been different, my caste identity was an important factor that legitimized my presence as an "insider" during the course of my ethnographic fieldwork, a point documented by other brahmin scholars working with brahmin communities (Prasad 2007, 23; Fuller and Narasimhan 2014, 24–25; Putcha 2015, 21).[80] My caste alignment allowed me to partake in a position of privilege *along with* my interlocutors. While there is no way to circumvent this privileged status, I take a cue from the work of Ayesha Chaudhry (2017, 26) to center my own positionality among my brahmin interlocutors in order to divest myself from my own privilege.[81]

Despite my seemingly insider position, I present a critical history of impersonation and brahmin masculinity in Kuchipudi dance from the mid-twentieth century to the present context. The methodologies of this book reflect the paradoxical dialectic of the scholar of dance who must struggle with the inherited histories of the very dance form she both critiques and embodies. I must contend with my own intersecting identities as Kuchipudi dancer, Telugu Vaidiki/Niyogi brahmin woman, and American scholar, while simultaneously divesting power from the narratives, traditions, and discourses I have learned to embody (Chaudhry 2017, 27). In raising these questions of dancing in the field, I hope to mark the unsettling disquiet of critiquing the very dance form that grounds my embodied knowledge and shapes my aesthetic insights.

OUTLINE OF THE BOOK

The chapters of this book are progressively arranged: the earlier chapters establish the power of hegemonic brahmin masculinity in the Kuchipudi village, while the later chapters expose its contingency in village, urban, and transnational forms of Kuchipudi dance. The book begins in the Kuchipudi village, focusing on its hereditary community of upper-caste brahmin men who are expected to don the *strī-vēṣam* to impersonate characters from dance dramas based on Hindu religious narratives. In the first chapter, I trace the role that impersonation plays in the constructed genealogy of Kuchipudi as "classical" dance. Addressing a longstanding lacuna in scholarship on Indian dance, I argue that the dancing male body is integral to the classicization of Kuchipudi as distinct from other "classical" dance forms, namely Bharatanatyam. By examining instances of vocal guising in the narrative of Siddhendra, the founding saint of Kuchipudi dance, and sartorial guising in Kuchipudi performance, the chapter analyzes the mechanisms by which the brahmin impersonator came to occupy center stage.

In the second chapter, I draw on ethnographic fieldwork and performance analysis to examine the practice of impersonation in the contemporary Kuchipudi village, as well as urban and transnational spaces. Focusing on the case of well-known impersonator Vedantam Satyanarayana Sarma, I argue that impersonation appeals to a brahminical tradition of authority (*sāmpradāyam*) that sanctions village brahmin men, while excluding all others from performance. Impersonation onstage spills into personation offstage as Kuchipudi brahmin men don the *strī-vēṣam* to achieve normative and even hegemonic masculinity both in village dance performance and everyday life.

The picture of brahminical authority painted in the opening chapters is questioned in the second half of the book, particularly through the introduction of the seminal theoretical concept of constructed artifice (*māyā*). Chapter 3 analyzes the village enactments of the *vidūṣaka* (clown) character Madhavi, who parodies the constructed artifice (*māyā*) of brahmin masculinity through comedic gesture and verbal discourse. Chapter 4 explores the intersections of sexuality and impersonation, particularly how the sexually ambiguous enactments of Madhavi in urban and transnational performance interrogate the heteronormative framework underlying the artifice of brahmin masculinity. Chapter 5 foregrounds the voices of village brahmin women who are marginalized from Kuchipudi dance by their brahmin male counterparts.

Like any ethnographic study, the material analyzed in this book is temporally limited in that it reflects a snapshot of the Kuchipudi village's brahmin community from a selective period of time, in this case 2009–18. Through the course of writing this book, many performers and scholars have passed away, including Vedantam Satyanarayana Sarma, whose enactment of Satyabhama's *pravēśa daruvu* is featured in the opening of this introduction. The death of these interlocutors, the shifting trends in Kuchipudi performance, and the urbanization of the areas around the Krishna district, among a host of other factors, will invariably change the landscape of the Kuchipudi village in the years to come. Despite its temporal constraints, *Impersonations* asks perennial questions, such as: Which bodies get to dance and why? And, what happens when brahmin men dance? In thinking through the intersection of gender, caste, and performance, I envision constructed artifice (*māyā*) as a theoretical category to examine not only the contingency of brahmin masculinity in the Kuchipudi context, but also the mutability of gender and caste norms across South Asia. A hermeneutics of constructed artifice is not simply gender theory arising from vernacular context, but rather aims to articulate a truly global perspective on gender in its many *vēṣams* (guises).

1

Taking Center Stage

The Poet-Saint and the Impersonator of Kuchipudi Dance History

Impersonation in Kuchipudi dance is grounded in a moment of divine inspiration. According to popular hagiography, the founding saint of Kuchipudi dance, Siddhendra, had a revelatory vision of Krishna and his consort Satyabhama, after which he abandoned all worldly ties and dedicated his life to singing the praises of his god. Envisioning himself as Satyabhama, Siddhendra composed *Bhāmākalāpam* (lit., "the lyrical drama of Bhama"), which features Satyabhama's love and separation from Krishna. Siddhendra taught this dance drama to all the brahmin boys of the village Kuchelapuram (now Kuchipudi), prescribing that they continue to don Satyabhama's *vēṣam* for generations to come.

This popular narrative is often cited as the critical starting point of Kuchipudi dance history, whether in dance classrooms in India or the United States. Although practitioners and scholars disagree about the exact period of Siddhendra's lifetime, assigning him dates that span from the fourteenth to the seventeenth centuries, the existence and the influence of Siddhendra on Kuchipudi dance is accepted as unequivocal fact.[1] The common belief in the hagiography of Siddhendra, however, must be framed against the backdrop of broader colonial and postcolonial interventions that gave rise to Kuchipudi as "classical" dance. Elite Telugu proponents in the mid-twentieth century significantly expanded the life story of Siddhendra into a devotional hagiography of religious significance. By imagining Siddhendra as the ultimate male devotee who speaks through the female voice of Satyabhama pining for her god/husband Krishna, Telugu elite and later Kuchipudi dancers locate the life story of Siddhendra within the broader framework of vernacular *bhakti* traditions. Through these mid-twentieth-century innovations and expansions, Siddhendra transforms from the reported author of *Bhāmākalāpam* into a paradigmatic *bhakti* poet-saint and, arguably, the first Kuchipudi impersonator.

Alongside this discursive rewriting is the performative ecology of colonial and postcolonial South India. Although borrowing from the *devadāsī* repertoire, Kuchipudi—an ostensibly brahminical, male-only dance form from a single village—skirted the anti-nautch sentiments that plagued the development of Bharatanatyam, the major "classical" dance form of South India, in the early twentieth century. Additionally, a national fascination with sartorial guising in Indian theatre propelled the hereditary brahmin impersonator to a position of prominence on the Kuchipudi stage.[2] By virtue of his caste status and gender identity, the brahmin impersonator from the Kuchipudi village became the face of Kuchipudi classical dance in postcolonial South India. In what follows, I examine the significance of impersonation in Kuchipudi dance history, as both vocal guising in narrative and sartorial guising in performance, to trace the constructed genealogy of Kuchipudi dance and foreground the mechanisms by which the poet-saint Siddhendra and the brahmin impersonator came to occupy center stage.

THE DANCING MALE BODY

By focusing on the figure of the Kuchipudi brahmin impersonator, this chapter contributes to the field of Indian dance historiography that often overlooks the critical role that the dancing male body, particularly the dancing brahmin male body, played in shaping South Indian dance as classical. While men are certainly present in histories of South Indian dance, particularly as dance masters (*naṭṭuvaṉārs*) and relatives of hereditary female performers (Srinivasan 1985; Soneji 2012), men who dance are often missing from these broader discussions. The most sustained discussion of South Indian male dancers appears in Hari Krishnan's essay, "From Gynemimesis to Hypermasculinity" (2009), which discusses Muvvanallur Sabhapatayya, Chinnaiya, and Krishnasvami Ravu Jadav, three male dancers who performed in the nineteenth-century Tanjavur court. Among these male dancers, Sabhapatayya is said to have performed in the guise of a *devadāsī* before King Serfoji II, who ruled Tanjavur from 1798–1833 (Krishnan 2009, 380). Chinnaiya (1802–1856), the eldest brother of the famous Tanjavur Quartet, is also said to have given performances in a woman's guise in Tanjavur and Mysore (381–82).[3]

Mirroring the trends observed by Kathryn Hansen (2002) in the context of Parsi theatre in western India, impersonation, a practice Krishnan (2009, 383) refers to as gynemimesis, existed alongside the presence of female dancers in nineteenth- and early twentieth-century South India.[4] This trend is also attested to by Muthukumar Pillai, an early twentieth-century male dance master who performed in *strī-vēṣam* as early as 1888 (Meduri 1996, 43). Even E. Krishna Iyer, Tamil brahmin lawyer and one of the founders of the famous Madras Music Academy (est. 1928), is known to have performed in *vēṣam* from 1923–29 (Krishnan 2009, 378).[5]

However, the male dancing body in *strī-vēṣam* soon became displaced in the newly revived dance form of Bharatanatyam. According to Krishnan:

> The emergence of the new nationalized form of dance called bharata natyam in the 1930s reflected not only a concern for sexual and aesthetic propriety on the part of its upper-class women performers . . . but also a parallel concern for the nurturing of a new masculine identity for its male performers. This new masculinity, a reaction to colonial constructions of South Asian men as "effeminate" (Sinha 1995), was also affected by Gandhian nationalism that was rooted in the ideas of self-control, discipline, and sexual abstinence . . . This new, state-endorsed invention of the male performer of dance could not accommodate the slippery representations of gynemimetic performance. (384)

In place of impersonation, the athletic and bold movements of Kathakali dance were adapted for the Bharatanatyam male dancer, particularly in Rukmini Arundale's dance school Kalakshetra (est. 1936) (Krishnan 2009, 284). Kathakali, similar in many ways to Kuchipudi, is an exclusively male dance form from the South Indian state of Kerala that combines dramatic enactments and elaborate guises of both male and female characters (Zarrilli 2000). In the mid-twentieth century, male Bharatanatyam dancers began to increasingly rely on "the histrionics of kathakali, which involved bold, strong, almost athletic movements of the face, torso, arms, and lower limbs" (Krishnan 2009, 384–85). Thus, male Bharatanatyam dancers enacted a "new Indian masculinity" that reinterpreted the athletic repertoire of Kathakali within the framework of the newly invented dance form of Bharatanatyam.

In chapter 3 of *Unfinished Gestures,* Davesh Soneji (2012) also examines the role of men in the trajectory of South Indian dance, particularly focusing on legal debates surrounding *devadāsī* performance. Male relatives of hereditary female performers promulgated the creation of new caste identities—*icai vēḷālar* in Tamil-speaking regions and *sūryabaḷija* in Telugu-speaking regions—in reaction to the growing stigmatization of *devadāsī* identities (114–15). New nonbrahmin caste associations headed by men supported the anti-nautch movement and sought to outlaw professional dancing by women in their communities, while positioning these men as "authentic" dance masters and artists (115, 143). Like the debates on *satī* (Mani 1998), the debates about *devadāsī* identity remained within the purview of male actors: "The key promise of *devadāsī* reform for women—namely, 'respectable' citizenship in the emergent nation—was never actualized, primarily because ultimately the movement itself was monopolized by men, and it was transformed into a project for men" (Soneji 2012, 115).[6] Adding further complexity to this picture is the relationship between brahmin male patrons and hereditary female performers (129, 267n11).[7] The sustained relationships between *devadāsī*s and their brahmin male patrons resulted in some brahmin men, like S. Satyamurti (1887–1943), taking a stance against the anti-nautch movement (130). Soneji's archival and ethnographic research points to the complicated relationships between *devadāsī* performers, their male relatives, and their brahmin male patrons.

Integral to the landscape of *devadāsī* reform and the classicization of Indian dance was the growing repertoire of "Oriental" dance, which opened up space for the male dancing body in transnational performance. Along with well-known female dancers Ruth St. Denis and Anna Pavlova, male dancers Ted Shawn (1891–1972), Uday Shankar (1900–1977), and Ram Gopal (1912–2003) are particularly prominent in scholarly discourses on both Indian and American dance (Erdman 1987; Coorlawala 1992; Allen 1997; Srinivasan 2012; Sinha 2017). For example, Russian ballerina Anna Pavlova teamed up with novice Indian dancer Uday Shankar to perform two ballets with Indian themes—*A Hindu Wedding* (a piece for twenty-two dancers) and *Radha-Krishna* (featuring Pavlova and Shankar as Radha and Krishna, respectively)—that toured the United States in 1923–24 (Erdman 1987, 72–73; Allen 1997, 93). Shankar, who at the time was not formally trained in Indian dance, soon made it his mission to present Indian dance to Western audiences. Notably, Shankar's brown body gave him the legitimacy to perform his vision of Indian "authenticity," even as he lacked a nuanced knowledge of Indian dance. As Joan Erdman (1987, 73) notes: "Being born and raised in India gave [Shankar] a natural genuineness, but he still lacked a 'text' to translate." Shankar's ability to translate across contexts developed after his early performances with Pavlova, and by the end of his career he was heralded as India's first modern dance choreographer (79).[8]

Ted Shawn and Ram Gopal have equally transnational pasts that blend Hindu religious imagery with an Orientalist aesthetic (Gopal 1957; Allen 1997; Sinha 2017). In the case of the former, Ted Shawn partnered with Ruth St. Denis in 1915 to form the Denishawn company (Desmond 1991, 30; Srinivasan 2012, 99).[9] Denishawn's early choreography included *Nautch* (1919) and *Dance of the Black and Gold Sari* (1923), pieces performed by St. Denis, Shawn, and eight other dancers throughout various regions of Asia in 1925–26 (Coorlawala 1992, 123; Allen 1997, 88). During the segment of the Asia tour in India (January–May 1926), Shawn developed a solo piece, *Cosmic Dance of Siva,* inspired by Ananda K. Coomaraswamy's (1918) influential essay "The Dance of Shiva" (Allen 1997, 90).[10] *Cosmic Dance of Siva* debuted at the Grand Opera House in Manila in 1926 after the India tour and featured Shawn himself as the embodiment of Nataraja, the lord of dance:

> As the Hindu sculpture of Nataraja or the dancing Siva, [Shawn] wore only body paint, brief trunks, and a towering crown and stood on a pedestal within a huge upright metal ring that haloed his entire body . . . The dynamics of the solo ranged from still balances on half-toe to violent twists of the torso and furious stamping of the feet, all confined within the hoop that represented the container of the universe. (Shelton 1981, 213, as cited by Allen 1997, 91)

Given that much of American modern dance traces its roots to St. Denis and Shawn, the appropriation of Hindu iconography for the purposes of Shawn's syncretic dance piece is not inconsequential. Just as Nataraja was revived to become the patron saint of Indian dance (Allen 1997, 83–85), Indian dance itself was repurposed to become the foundations of modern American dance, as evident in Shawn's choreography. A similar synthesis of Orientalist taste and Indian iconography may be seen in the arresting photographs of Ram Gopal by American photographer Carl Van Vechten in his New York apartment-turned-studio in 1938 (Sinha 2017).[11] Collectively, male dancers such as Ted Shawn, Uday Shankar, and Ram Gopal underscore Sitara Thobani's (2017, 37) suggestion that Indian dance was produced in the "contact zone" instantiated by British colonialism, Indian nationalism, and Euro-American Orientalism. Simply put, "this dance has always been performed on Empire's stage" (26).

Beyond these singular male figures, however, the discussion of the dancing male body is more limited in scholarship on Indian dance. In *Kathakali Dance-Drama,* Phillip Zarrilli (2000) provides a robust analysis of the embodied techniques of male Kathakali dancers. Margaret Walker's (2016) discussion of the history of Kathak analyzes the role of hereditary Kathak male dance gurus, particularly the well-known Birju Maharaj. In the context of Malaysia, Premalatha Thiagarajan (2017) examines male dancers in Odissi and Bharatanatyam, particularly the Muslim-Malay male dancer Ramli Ibrahim.[12]

However, no scholarship to date seriously considers the role of the dancing male body in the twentieth-century "revival" of classical Indian dance. Instead of envisioning male dance through the lens of exceptional figures of the nineteenth-century Tanjavur court, the colonial revival, or the twentieth-century transnational dance scene, this chapter posits the brahmin male community of dancers from the Kuchipudi village as integral to the classicization of South Indian dance. By virtue of their gender and caste status, the village's hereditary brahmin male community was able to sidestep the anti-nautch politics of colonial India and emerge as the symbol of the Telugu arts scene. Impersonation, in this case the brahmin male body donning a woman's guise, became the central script for fashioning Kuchipudi into a nationally recognized "classical" Indian dance form.

SIDDHENDRA: THE FIRST KUCHIPUDI IMPERSONATOR

While Kuchipudi practitioners may point to Sanskrit textual sources, namely Bharata's *Nāṭyaśāstra,* as the foundations of Kuchipudi dance, the history of the dance is a narrative that typically begins with Siddhendra. As the reported author of *Bhāmākalāpam,* the earliest recorded dance drama of the Kuchipudi repertoire, Siddhendra is thought to have both established and propagated Kuchipudi as a dance form. While Kuchipudi dancers may accept Siddhendra's life story as undeniable fact, the lack of substantive historical evidence has caused scholars to question the historicity of *Bhāmākalāpam*'s ostensible author (Arudra 1994; Jonnalagadda 1996b).[13]

In palm-leaf manuscripts from the Tirupati Oriental Research Institute and the Government Oriental Manuscripts Library in Chennai, Siddhendra is unceremoniously mentioned as the composer of the *Bhāmākalāpam* dance drama, often in a single sentence.[14] For example, in the palm-leaf *Bhāmākalāpam* R. 429 from the Tirupati Oriental Research Institute, dating to approximately the late nineteenth century, there is a single mention of a figure known as Siddhendra: "This is Siddhendra Yogi's composition" (*Bhāmākalāpam* R. 429, palm-leaf 11b).[15] No additional reference is made to Siddhendra's family background, patronage, or training, all of which constitute pertinent information the Telugu poet usually includes in the colophon of his or her poetic text.[16]

Adding to this complexity is the fact that the *Bhāmākalāpam* dance drama is not solely under the purview of the brahmins of the Kuchipudi village. As several scholars have noted, *Bhāmākalāpam* (also known by other names, including *Pārijātanāṭaka, Navajanārdana Pārijātam,* and *Bhāmāvēṣakatha*) is a dance drama that was performed by a wide array of caste communities in Telugu South India from the eighteenth century onwards (Jonnalagadda 1996a; Soneji 2012; Putcha 2015). The brahmins of the Kuchipudi village, the female *kalāvantulu* (courtesans) of the east and west Godavari districts, and the male Turpu Bhagavatam practitioners from the goldsmith communities in eastern Andhra all performed and continue to perform *Bhāmākalāpam* under various titles (Ramakrishna 1984; Jonnalagadda 1996a, 1996b; Nagabhushana Sarma 1996; Soneji 2012; Putcha 2015).[17] Furthermore, many palm-leaf manuscripts housed in public library archives, including *Bhāmākalāpamu* R. 429, likely belonged to Telugu courtesan communities rather than to the brahmins of the Kuchipudi village.[18] The fact that *Bhāmākalāpam* belongs to the repertoires of multiple Telugu performance communities raises critical questions regarding the historicity of *Bhāmākalāpam*'s reported author.[19] It is not my intention to reconcile the debate regarding Siddhendra's existence, a task that appears to be historically difficult if not impossible. While it may not be possible to determine who exactly Siddhendra *was* in the premodern period, we can ascertain who he *became* in the course of the twentieth century: the paradigmatic *bhakti* poet-saint of Kuchipudi dance. As I will now argue, Siddhendra's hagiography, told in varying iterations by scholars and practitioners of Kuchipudi dance, appears to be a mid-twentieth-century act of innovation and expansion.

In postcolonial Andhra Pradesh, we find a remarkable expansion of Siddhendra's identity beyond the simple reference found in *Bhāmākalāpam* palm-leaves to a lengthy hagiography of divine import. Drawing on printed accounts that first emerged in the mid-twentieth century, Siddhendra's hagiography can be summarized as follows:

> There was once a young orphaned brahmin boy named Siddhappa, who used to travel from village to village living off the charity of others. Fond of music and drama,

he used to watch performances whenever he could. After all-night performances, he would spend the night at the *maṭha* [religious institution] established by Narahari Tirtha in Srikakulam.[20] The head of the *maṭha* took kindly to the boy and sent him to Udupi for Vedic study.

Siddhappa returned to Srikakulam as an erudite scholar versed in Vedic and Śāstric texts, including the *Nāṭyaśāstra,* and was renamed with the honorific title Siddhendra. Upon his return, the elders of the village encouraged Siddhendra to fulfill the marriage vows that he had made to a girl living on the opposite banks of the Krishna River.[21] As Siddhendra set out across the river to meet his new bride, he was caught midstream in a torrential storm. Siddhendra prayed to Krishna, promising that he would renounce worldly ties if he safely arrived on the opposite banks of the river.

Siddhendra survived as a result of his prayers to Krishna and successfully arrived on the other side of the river, where his in-laws were waiting. When his new bride lifted her eyes to see Siddhendra for the first time, she screamed "*Sannyāsi!* [Renunciant!]" and fell faint. Siddhendra then had a divine vision of Krishna with his consort Satyabhama and realized that his future could only be one of devotion. He envisioned himself as Satyabhama, the devotee and beloved of Krishna. Soon, his songs, which featured Satyabhama's love and separation from Krishna, came to be known as *Bhāmākalāpam.*

He traveled to the nearby town of Kuchelapuram and taught his dance drama to a group of talented young brahmin boys. Siddhendra then took a vow from all the boys of Kuchelapuram that they would continue to enact *Bhāmākalāpam* at least once every year. They assured him that they would continue to enact the dance drama for generations to come. Thus, it is until this day that *Bhāmākalāpam* continues to survive in the village of Kuchelapuram, now known as Kuchipudi.[22]

The life story of Siddhendra is unremarkable when examined in the broader context of vernacular *bhakti* (devotional) traditions in which the employment of vocal guising is a common literary trope (Ramanujan 1989b; Narayanan 2003; Pechilis 2012; Clooney 2014).[23] Here, I define *vocal guising* as a literary convention in which the poet, either male or female, impersonates the voice of a lovesick female heroine. Karen Pechilis (2012, 796) identifies a diverse list of *bhakti* poets, spanning from male poet-saints such as Manikkavacakar and Nammalvar (both Tamil saints from ca. ninth century) to female poet-saints such as Andal (Tamil Alvar saint ca. ninth century) and Mirabai (Hindi saint ca. sixteenth century), who use the image of the lovesick heroine to speak to god.[24]

When discussing North Indian Vaishnava (Vishnu-centered) poets from the sixteenth and seventeenth centuries, John Stratton Hawley (2000, 240) writes:

> When they speak of lovesickness, they project themselves almost exclusively into the voice of one of the women who wait for Krishna—before lovemaking or, even more likely, afterward . . . Whether one conceives of it in the secular or religious sense (and because these are not entirely separable), longing has a definite gender: it is feminine.

Siddhendra's hagiography, which collapses the identity of Siddhendra with Satyabhama, builds on the long-standing trope of vocal guising conventional to vernacular *bhakti* traditions. Disavowing corporeal human love, Siddhendra, like the long line of male *bhakti* saints before him, envisions himself as Satyabhama, the devotee and beloved of Krishna, and pens *Bhāmākalāpam* as an allegorical drama of love and separation from his god.

These allegorical iterations of Siddhendra's hagiography are historically questionable. While it is possible that versions of Siddhendra's life story circulated as part of the oral tradition among the brahmins of Kuchipudi, perhaps even as early as the eighteenth or nineteenth century, there is little textual evidence to support the presence of these earlier oral narratives (Jonnalagadda 1996b, 45). Siddhendra's hagiography, at least the devotional version presented above, was only popularized in the mid-twentieth century by Telugu elite through speeches, printed articles, and books. As an example, we can turn to Vissa Appa Rao's (1958) address at the Dance Seminar in Delhi in 1958 that, as discussed in the introduction, was a critical turning point for the classicization of Kuchipudi. The speech, titled "Kuchipudi School of Dance," was given before an elite audience of scholars and dancers, including noted Sanskritist V. Raghavan and Bharatanatyam proponent Rukmini Arundale, the latter of whom infamously contested Kuchipudi's purported classical status (Putcha 2015). Leaving the ensuing classicism controversy aside, it is noteworthy that in his speech, Appa Rao (1958) positions Siddhendra in a long line of Vaishnava (and mostly North Indian) *bhakti* saints including Jayadeva, Chaitanya, Mirabai, Kabir, and Tulsidas, clearly invoking the imagery of a unified "*bhakti* movement" coalescing in North India in the early modern period (Hawley 2015). Appa Rao (1958, 8) also points to *bhakti* concepts, namely *jīvātma*/*paramātma* (individual soul / divine soul) and *madhura-bhakti* (devotion of love), and Sanskrit aesthetic imagery to frame Siddhendra's life story. In the first-ever national address given about Kuchipudi dance, Appa Rao, himself a Niyogi brahmin and Telugu scholar, unequivocally paints Siddhendra as a paradigmatic *bhakti* poet-saint.[25]

The *bhakti*-cization of Siddhendra's life story is further apparent in the writings of Telugu brahmin and Kuchipudi proponent Banda Kanakalingeshwara Rao. In an English article, Kanakalingeshwara Rao (1966) provides an elaborate hagiography of the orphaned boy Siddhappa who had a divine vision of Krishna at a young age, traveled to Udupi to learn the *śāstra*s, and ultimately penned *Bhāmākalāpam* to express his *madhura-bhakti* (devotion of love) to Krishna through the voice of Satyabhama. Kanakalingeshwara Rao (1966, 33) carefully justifies Siddhendra's choice to promote Kuchipudi dance among the brahmin community:

> The Devadasis of the village requested Siddhendra to teach them *Bhama Kalapam*. The songs of *Bhama Kalapam* were already of sensuous love. The Devadasi were already adept in such gestures. Siddhendra thought that they would still more demoralize society if they presented Bhama Kalapam dances. So he induced good-looking

young Brahmin boys to learn *Bhama Kalapam.* Till then the Brahmins had never danced, though they were Gurus.

Kanakalingeshwara Rao's overtly apologist tone is clearly implicated in the broader anti-nautch discourses of colonial and postcolonial India. Likely worried that brahminical Kuchipudi dance could be subject to the same critiques as *devadāsī* performance, Kanakalingeshwara Rao weaves together what poet-scholar Arudra (1994, 29) later dismisses as an "unauthenticated account" of Siddhendra, who selectively chooses to teach brahmins over *devadāsī*s. The Siddhendra of Kanakalingeshwara Rao's essay is portrayed as both an erudite brahmin scholar learned in the Sanskrit *śāstra*s and the arts, as well as the ideal *bhakti* saint who expresses ultimate devotion to Krishna. This reformulation of Siddhendra as brahmin scholar–cum–*bhakti* saint works to ground Kuchipudi dance in both Sanskrit textual tradition and Vaishnava devotional discourse. The availability in print of Kanakalingeshwara Rao's writings, which are cited extensively in the publications of Kuchipudi dancer-scholars (Rama Rao 1992; Acharya and Sarabhai 1992; Usha Gayatri 2016), popularized his version of Siddhendra's story. Kanakalingeshwara Rao's extensive efforts in promoting Kuchipudi dance, as previously discussed in the introduction, also established him as an important authority on Kuchipudi and its founding saint. Also dovetailing with these mid-twentieth-century writings, printed texts within the past few decades replicate the *bhakti* sentiments of Siddhendra's hagiography, further positioning him as an erudite brahmin scholar turned *bhakti* poet-saint.[26]

The aforementioned narratives of Siddhendra's hagiography are not grounded in historical fact or archival evidence, nor are they even mentioned in early palm-leaf texts of *Bhāmākalāpam.* Rather, I suggest they are mid-twentieth-century acts of innovation and expansion by Telugu elite scholars and dancers that function to legitimize the history of Kuchipudi through the religious discourse of *bhakti.*[27] Perhaps the clearest admission of narrative invention appears in a booklet by M.A. Naidu, published in 1975 on the occasion of the World Telugu Conference. In this booklet, *Kuchipudi Classical Dance,* Naidu (1975, 8) begins a discussion of Siddhendra's life story by acknowledging the historical uncertainty of the account:

> There is a very interesting incident about how 'Siddhayya', or Siddhappa became Siddhendra Yogi. *There is no recorded evidence about this incident. So, I am narrating the incident as I comprehend it to be reasonable.* [Emphasis added]

Naidu then outlines the portion of the narrative which recounts that Siddhendra, on his return to Kuchipudi, became stranded in the middle of the Krishna River and prayed to his lord Krishna to save him. After being saved from drowning, Siddhendra renounced earthly ties and "diverted all the amorousness in him into creating 'Bhamakalapam'" (Naidu 1975, 9). Naidu's straightforward admission that, despite the lack of recorded evidence, he is narrating the incident of Siddhendra's life as *he comprehends it to be reasonable* provides insight into the background of most hagiographies of Siddhendra. According to Arudra (1994), Siddhendra's biographical details are mired in "lingering questions and some fashionable fallacies," giving pause for concern when examining the hagiography of Kuchipudi's founding saint.[28]

Despite historical uncertainty, Siddhendra's life story is now ubiquitously accepted throughout Kuchipudi circles in India and abroad. During the course of my fieldwork in the Kuchipudi village, my brahmin interlocutors invariably invoked *bhakti* imagery, namely the image of the *jīvātma* (individual soul) in search of the *paramātma* (divine soul), when discussing Siddhendra's life story. For example, village resident and hereditary brahmin Pasumarti Keshav Prasad, observed the following about Siddhendra's heroine Satyabhama: "For that kind of woman, in order to reduce her pride, the *jīvātma* [individual soul] and the *paramātma* [divine soul] have to combine. The *jīvātma* has to go into the *paramātma.* The *paramātma* is Krishna. [Satyabhama] has to be absorbed into Krishna." Chinta Ravi Balakrishna, a younger brahmin dancer from the Kuchipudi village, mapped the story of Siddhendra onto that of Satyabhama:

> The whole story of *Bhāmākalāpam* is Siddhendra Yogi's creation. Siddhendra has taken the beauty of the character and molded his own life experiences of *viraham* [separation] onto Satyabhama . . . Siddhendra's life story is that he got separated from his wife at sixteen years old. The major concept is how to unite *jīvātma* with *paramātma.* That *jīvātma* is the soul within the human . . . Krishna is *paramātma.*

In addition to these observations, many other brahmin men from the Kuchipudi village invoked the figure of Siddhendra and the imagery of the *jīvātma* (individual soul) and the *paramātma* (divine soul) when describing Satyabhama and Krishna, respectively.[29] The invocation of *jīvātma/paramātma* terminology is commonplace in published texts on Kuchipudi history by dancers and scholars alike.[30]

The broadly resonant themes of vernacular *bhakti,* particularly the invocation of *jīvātma/paramātma* terminology, enabled the expansion and popularization of Siddhendra's hagiography in the mid-twentieth century. By employing a version of the modernist, pan-Indian discourse of *bhakti* (Hawley 2015), Kuchipudi scholars and dancers envision Siddhendra as the ideal *bhakti* poet-saint whose longing for his god materializes in his poetic production. For Kuchipudi dancers and scholars alike, Siddhendra is the male devotee (*jīvātma*) who speaks through the voice of the female character Satyabhama, who is pining for her god/husband Krishna (*paramātma*). The implication of Siddhendra's gender identification with Satyabhama not only influences the reception of his hagiography but also sets the stage for the practice of impersonation through the *Bhāmākalāpam* dance drama. If we read the practice of impersonation capaciously, vocal guising can also be envisioned as an act of impersonation. As a male poet impersonating a female voice, Siddhendra is not only the paradigmatic *bhakti* saint, but also arguably the first impersonator of Kuchipudi dance history.

SIDDHENDRA AND KSHETRAYYA: HAGIOGRAPHIES FROM KRISHNA DISTRICT

Siddhendra's hagiography, one of a local villager–turned–*bhakti* saint, bears a striking resemblance to the mid-twentieth-century hagiographies of Kshetrayya, the seventeenth-century Telugu composer whose *padams* (short lyrical compositions) were and continue to be performed by *devadāsī* communities across South India (Ramanujan, Narayana Rao, and Shulman 1994; Soneji 2012).[31] While historical documentation remains unclear, Kshetrayya is said to have been born in the village of Muvva in Krishna district, located less than three miles from the Kuchipudi village. In an edited volume of Kshetrayya's *padams* printed in 1963, Appa Rao, the scholar who also spoke at the aforementioned Delhi seminar in 1958, describes Kshetrayya as an illiterate cowherd from Muvva who, like Siddhendra, has a divine vision of Krishna and decides to abandon all worldly ties.[32] In his preface to *Kṣētrayya padamulu*, Appa Rao (1963, 11–12) suggests that Kshetrayya even traveled to the neighboring village of Kuchipudi and learned music, dance, and Indian aesthetic theory from the community of brahmin male performers residing there. Appa Rao is careful to note that Kshetrayya is likely to have had association with *devadāsī* women who were affiliated with the Muvva temple and learned music and dance from the brahmins of the Kuchipudi village (11–12). Other Kuchipudi scholars forge connections between Siddhendra and Kshetrayya, usually citing the proximity of Kuchipudi and Muvva as an indication of the thriving "cultural heritage" of Andhra Pradesh state (Kanakalingeshwara Rao 1966, 30).[33]

The emergence of two regionally proximate hagiographies—Siddhendra from Kuchipudi and Kshetrayya from Muvva—in mid-twentieth-century writings of elite proponents of Telugu language and arts such as Appa Rao, Kanakalingeshwara Rao, and others is no coincidence. In fact, Siddhendra and Kshetrayya are often cited together by scholars who explicitly point to the proximity of Kuchipudi and Muvva, as if the presence of one *bhakti* poet-saint in the region justifies the existence of a second (Appa Rao 1963, 11–12; Vatsyayan [1974] 2007, 57). In her study of Telugu language politics in colonial and postcolonial South India, Lisa Mitchell (2009) notes the increased attention given to the lives (*caritramu*) of Telugu poets in the writings of Telugu language proponents such as Gurajada Sriramamurti (1878) and Kandukuri Viresalingam (1887). As Mitchell (2009, 86) suggests, "Texts like Sriramamurti's *Kavi Jīvitamulu* and Viresalingam's *Āndhra Kavula Caritramu* shift the emphasis from poets as authors to poets as central characters in novelized renditions of their own lives." A parallel shift from poets as authors to poets as the central characters in their own hagiographies occurs in the case of Siddhendra in the mid-twentieth century (Mitchell 2009, 86).[34] Within a few years of the creation of Andhra Pradesh state, Telugu elites and others working to promote the Telugu arts contributed to a printed corpus of hagiographies of Siddhendra and Kshetrayya, in both Telugu and English, available to wider audiences.

The devotionalization of Telugu poets Siddhendra and Kshetrayya into *bhakti* saints was quickly replicated in later print sources, film, and visual imagery, as evidenced by the recently commissioned images of Siddhendra at Tank Bund in Hyderabad.[35] In the Kuchipudi village, there is a temple in honor of Siddhendra at the center of the *agrahāram* that employs a full-time priest to attend to a black granite *mūrti* (image) of the Kuchipudi founding saint (see Figure 4). Festivals in honor of Siddhendra are held annually on the outdoor performance venue located adjacent to the Siddhendra temple.[36] These performative and artistic representations, coupled with his devotionalized hagiography, articulate Siddhendra's "visual theology" as one of great saintly devotion (Eck 1998, 41).

What prompted this mid-twentieth-century transformation of Siddhendra from reported author to paradigmatic *bhakti* poet-saint? I argue that the broader transformations of Kuchipudi into a classical dance form in postcolonial South India necessitated an elevation and subsequent rewriting of Siddhendra's life story into devotional hagiography. By casting Siddhendra as the ultimate devotee of Krishna, Kuchipudi practitioners and elite brahmin patrons, including Vissa Appa Rao, Banda Kanakalingeshwara Rao, and others, worked to endow Siddhendra and his life story with the religious weight befitting the founding saint of a classical dance tradition.

It is notable that Appa Rao and Kanakalingeshwara Rao—both Smarta brahmin men—promulgated the *bhakti* hagiographies of Siddhendra and Kshetrayya. The convergence of Smarta brahmins and *bhakti* is not solely a Telugu phenomenon. In the Sardar Vallabhbhai Patel Memorial Lectures in New Delhi in 1964, noted Sanskritist and Tamil Smarta brahmin V. Raghavan painted a sweeping picture of the *bhakti* movement as the offspring of a great integration of poet-saints from southern to northern India (Hawley 2015, 20).[37] Raghavan's characterization of a pan-Indian *bhakti* movement shaped not only Indian cultural sensibility, but also scholarly production, including the writings of Western anthropologist Milton Singer (1972) (Hancock 1999, 64–67; Hawley 2015, 25). When discussing the relationship between Singer and Raghavan, Mary Hancock (1999) clearly outlines the impact of Smarta brahmin intervention: "By contextualizing [Singer's] work . . . it is possible to see strategies by which Smārtas developed a discourse on national culture that has been influential in Indian cultural politics and in the production of scholarly knowledge about South Asia" (67). According to Hancock, urban elite cultural production in South India is a Smarta brahmin endeavor (64).

The role of the brahmin in Tamil-speaking South India must be situated against the backdrop of colonial and postcolonial language politics of what is referred to as *tamil̲ppar̲r̲u*, or Tamil devotion (Ramaswamy 1997, 194). Within this context, the Tamil brahmins of the late-nineteenth- and early-twentieth-centuries were

FIGURE 4. Siddhendra's *mūrti* (image) in a temple in the Kuchipudi village. Photo by author.

considered traitors of Tamil by their adherence to Sanskritic culture. Sumathi Ramaswamy (1997) writes:

> A question that was repeatedly raised in the discourses of many of Tamil's devotees from the turn of the century is "Are Brahmans Tamilian?" The answer, increasingly,

> was an emphatic "No." Brahmans are exclusionist and caste conscious; they identify themselves with the North, with Aryan culture, and with Sanskrit. Above all, and most sacrilegiously from the radical enthusiast's point of view, they disparage Tamil, treating its high literature and culture as derivative of Sanskrit. (194–95)

Situated within the broader matrix of anti-brahminical neo-Shaivism and Dravidianism, which crystallized in the early to mid-twentieth century, the Tamil brahmin was explicitly disavowed (140). Tamil brahmins during this period were viewed as incapable of Tamil devotion, *tamiḻppaṟṟu,* in the mode of their nonbrahmin counterparts (194).

For centuries, South India has been characterized by polyglossia and therefore it is difficult to delineate the boundaries of what constitutes Tamil- and Telugu-speaking areas (Narayana Rao 2003; Peterson 2011). Nevertheless, I would argue that the Telugu version of *tamiḻppaṟṟu* is not characterized by anti-brahminical sentiment in the same manner of both neo-Shaiva and the Dravidian movements of the colonial and postcolonial periods of Tamil-speaking South India. In the context of the arts, Smarta brahmins served as the architects of Telugu cultural production. For Kuchipudi, Smarta brahmins Appa Rao and Kanakalingeshwara Rao promulgated Siddhendra's hagiography, which prompted the canonization of Siddhendra as an ideal *bhakti* poet-saint. The commonplace *bhakti* trope of vocal guising and the invocation of *jīvātma/paramātma* further enabled the "mythopoetics" of Siddhendra and his life story (Putcha 2015, 3). The visual imagery of Siddhendra's saintly persona in the village temple, coupled with popular artistic renderings, also extended the devotional aura of Kuchipudi's founding saint. Like the *bhakti* saints before him, Siddhendra transformed from the attributed author of *Bhāmākalāpam* to the founding saint of a nationally recognized Indian classical dance form. The classicization of Kuchipudi thus rests on the *bhakti*-cization of Siddhendra by Smarta brahmin men, as mid-twentieth-century innovations paradoxically enabled the creation of classical tradition. The story of Siddhendra and his *Bhāmākalāpam,* promulgated by Smarta brahmins, became the imagined genealogical starting point for the history of Kuchipudi as classical.

THE BRAHMIN IMPERSONATOR: THE HALLMARK OF KUCHIPUDI CLASSICAL DANCE

Alongside the transformation of Siddhendra's hagiography, sartorial impersonation is critical to Kuchipudi's classicization process. For the remainder of this chapter, I discuss the ways in which the performative ecology of twentieth-century India, both in dance and theatre, propelled the Kuchipudi brahmin impersonator to center stage. Uniquely benefiting from elite Telugu propaganda and the national fascination with theatrical impersonation, while also sidestepping anti-nautch critique, the brahmin impersonator serves as the primary symbol of Kuchipudi as "classical" dance.

Impersonation and Indian Theatre

Impersonation has a lengthy history in South Asian textual, ritual, and performative contexts, and in the form of sartorial guising, it is most evident in the accounts of colonial Parsi, Marathi, and Gujarati theatre in western India. Although impersonation declined in Calcutta theatre in eastern India by the 1870s, the practice of male actors donning a woman's guise onstage was prevalent in western Indian theatre from the late nineteenth century until the 1930s, particularly on account of the social prescription against middle-class women performing in public (Singh 2009, 273).[38] Following the advent of professional Indian theatre companies, such as the Victoria Theatrical Company established in Bombay in 1868, a "premium was now placed on young men of pleasing figures and superlative voice, who would ensure company profits through their virtuosity in women's roles" (Hansen 1999, 132). These impersonators, as scholars of Indian theatre underscore, coexisted with actresses onstage but were uniquely sought after as men who embodied and represented an ideal notion of Indian womanhood (Hansen 1999; Singh 2009).[39]

Two impersonators—Jayshankar Sundari (1888–1967) and Bal Gandharva (1889–1975)—epitomize the national fascination with sartorial impersonation in Indian theatre. Kathryn Hansen's extensive research on both artists testifies to their skills in impersonation and their ability to shape ideals of Indian womanhood.[40] The former, Jayshankar Sundari, was a Gujarati stage impersonator who gained his epithet after performing the role of Sundari (a young wife) in the play *Saubhagya Sundari* in 1901. Sundari, as Hansen (1999, 134) notes, relied on a method of total identification with women, modeling specific roles on specific women he was acquainted with in his daily life. Sundari's success as an impersonator enabled him to shape ideals of Indian womanhood and, in fact, it was "a fashion for ladies in Bombay to imitate him in their daily lives" (135). In a paradoxical self-reflexive process, Sundari modeled his impersonation on society women who, in turn, modeled their presentation of womanhood on him (Hansen 2013, 209). Impersonation thus transcended the boundaries of the stage to shape everyday gender ideals, a point to which I return in the next chapter.

Bal Gandharva, an impersonator who dominated the Marathi stage from 1905 to 1955, was even more popular than Sundari in his presentation of an aesthetically idealized image of womanhood (Kosambi 2015, 268).[41] Gandharva even set fashions for women's dress and behavior and was responsible for popularizing specific styles of wearing saris, jewelry, and flowers. Medicinal tonic, soap, key chains, and toilet powder all displayed Gandharva's image in *vēṣam*, contributing to the commodification of gender guising more generally, while simultaneously normalizing the male body in a woman's guise (Hansen 1999, 135–36). Like Sundari, Gandharva had the ability to shape gender ideals offstage by donning a woman's guise onstage.[42] Although the practice of sartorial impersonation was ubiquitous in western Indian theatre from the late nineteenth century until the advent of film in the 1930s, Sundari and Gandharva stand apart from their contemporaries. In 1955 and 1957, Gandharva and Sundari, respectively, were honored with the Sangeet Natak Akademi Award, the highest national award given to a practicing artist.[43] In 1964 and 1971, Gandharva and Sundari were each awarded the Padma Bhushan, the third-highest civilian award bestowed by the Government of India (Hansen 2013, 174). These national honors codified the ability of Gandharva and Sundari to shape ideals of respectable Indian womanhood and pushed against colonial perceptions of masculinity in early twentieth-century India. As Hansen (1999, 140) argues:

> [T]hrough the institution of female impersonation, a publicly visible, respectable image of "woman" was constructed, one that was of use to both men and women. This was a representation that, even attached to the male body, bespoke modernity. As one response to the British colonial discourse on Indian womanhood—the accusations against Indian men on account of their backward, degraded females—the representation helped support men, dovetailing with the emerging counter-discourse of Indian masculinity. Moreover, women derived from these enactments an image of how they should present themselves in public. Female impersonators, by bringing into the public sphere mannerisms, speech, and distinctive appearance of middle-class women, defined the external equivalents of the new gendered code of conduct for women. That such tastes were crafted by men (albeit men allegedly imitating women) gave them the imprimatur of acceptability.

In short, the image of respectable Indian womanhood in late colonial and postcolonial India became visible through the male body of the stage impersonator.

The complex performative ecology of Parsi, Gujarati, and Marathi theatres is reflected in Telugu performance, particularly Telugu theatre and Kuchipudi dance. In the case of Telugu theatre, the most recognized impersonator from Telugu-speaking South India is Sthanam Narasimha Rao (1902–1971). First known for performing the role of Candramati in the play *Satya Hariscandra* in 1921, Sthanam (as he was commonly known) became enormously popular for his enactment of *strī-vēṣam* onstage (Nagabhushana Sarma 2013, 27). His notable performances include the role of Satyabhama in Muttaraju Subba Rao's play *Śrī Kṛṣṇa Tulābharam* and Madhuravani in Gurajada Appa Rao's play *Kanyāśūlkam* (Nagabhushana Sarma 2013, 46–50, 54–57).[44] The vice president of India, Sarvepalli Radhakrishnan, remarked after watching Sthanam perform Satyabhama in 1954:

> I had seen the play "Sri Krishna Tulabharam" some 30 years ago in Andhra and am glad to find that even today veteran actor Sri Sthanam maintained his body, poise and grace. He excelled in Satyabhama despite his advanced years and he still makes women blush and has now lived up to his reputation. (Nagabhushana Sarma 2013, 47)

Women watching Sthanam, according to Radhakrishnan, blushed at his abilities at donning a woman's guise, thereby underscoring the broader implications of impersonation beyond the context of staged performance. Like Sundari and Gandharva, Sthanam was nationally recognized for his skills in donning a woman's guise on the Telugu stage and presumably helped shape ideals of womanhood offstage.[45] As evidenced by the accounts of Sundari, Gandharva, and Sthanam, the ability to approximate an ideal image of womanhood onstage was highly valued in Indian theatre and dance; however, when this act of approximation bordered on effeminacy, impersonation became subject to critique.

Impersonation and Colonial Constraints

The enormous popularity of impersonators in twentieth-century Indian theatre must be situated in conversation with transforming perceptions of masculinity in colonial India. As Mrinalini Sinha (1995) has documented in detail, in late nineteenth-century colonial India an overdetermined opposition was constructed between the so-called "manly Englishman" and the "effeminate Bengali *babu*," the latter being a pejorative term used to characterize elite Bengali men.[46] When describing the development of the notion of the effeminate *bābu*, Sinha (1995, 2) further explains:

> In this colonial order of masculinity, the politically self-conscious Indian intellectuals occupied a unique place: they represented an 'unnatural' or 'perverted' form of masculinity. Hence this group of Indians, the most typical representatives of which at the time were middle-class Bengali Hindus, became the quintessential referents for that odious category designated as 'effeminate *babus*'.

By the late nineteenth century, effeminacy had evolved from characterizing the entire population of Bengal to specifically highlighting middle-class Indian elites, who at the time were beginning to challenge the colonial order (Sinha 1995, 16–17). A growing self-perception of effeminacy burgeoned among Bengali elite, and consequently, they attempted to redeem their own masculinity by appropriating the ideology of so-called "martial" traditions (Sinha 1995, 91–92).[47] The appropriation of colonial masculinity by Indian elites was particularly noticeable in the case of the well-known Bengali religious leader Vivekananda, who exhorted his countrymen to inculcate an ideal ascetic masculinity (Roy 1998, 105–10; Chakraborty 2011, 54).[48]

Alongside the voyeuristic pleasure of witnessing an impersonator pass as a woman onstage, there was an underlying uneasiness about male actors donning a woman's guise, both from colonial and Indian perspectives. *Scinde, or The Unhappy Valley,* a semi-biographical travelogue written by Orientalist writer Richard F. Burton in the mid-nineteenth century, includes the following passage describing northern Indian male Kathak performers dressed in a woman's guise:

> Conceive, if you can, the unholy spectacle of two reverend-looking grey-beards, with stern, severe, classical features, large limbs, and serene, majestic deportment, dancing opposite each other dressed in woman's attire; the flimsiest too, with light veils on their heads, and little bells jingling from their ankles, ogling, smirking, and displaying the juvenile playfulness of "—limmer lads and little lassies!" (1851, 247).

Margaret Walker (2016, 64) notes the "unconcealed scorn" present in Burton's description of the impersonators.[49] She goes on to state that although male Kathak dancers were relatively rare in both colonial travel writings and iconography, there was an underlying connection between these male Kathak performers who danced as women and vernacular theatre forms such as Nautanki, in which impersonation is prominent (64–65).

Similarly, in nineteenth- and twentieth-century Bengali and Maharashtrian theatre, impersonators began to be critiqued for their obscenity and ridiculous appearance (Singh 2009, 274). Anxieties around Indian masculinity contributed to these concerns:

> The whole issue of masculinity and effeminacy also came into the nationalist discourse. Female impersonators appeared to threaten the construction of masculinity; bringing it into the limelight seemed to reinvigorate stereotypes of weakness and inferiority among the male population, a bitter legacy of colonial domination. (275)

Theatre actors themselves expressed self-consciousness for donning a woman's guise onstage, worried that this sartorial mimicry might threaten their masculinity (Kaur 2013, 196; Kosambi 2015, 274–75). A push toward realism in Indian theatre and the growing presence of stage actresses also subtly contributed to the growing ambivalence of impersonators onstage.[50]

These competing notions of effeminacy and masculinity point to an evolving and ambivalent understanding of sartorial impersonation in colonial and postcolonial India. Within the context of staged performance, impersonation was (and continues to be) lauded as a highly stylized mimetic practice that manifests nationalist ideals of womanhood. However, beyond the circumscribed realm of performance, impersonation became subject to critique by broader colonial and postcolonial discourses on gender and sexuality. These tensions, as I outline in the chapters that follow, are not limited to mid-twentieth-century India, but continue to characterize the practice of impersonation on the contemporary Kuchipudi stage.

Impersonation in Kuchipudi Dance

Impersonation functions as the significant rite of passage for the village's brahmin male community, who today envision themselves as the "cultural brokers" (Hancock 1999, 64) of Kuchipudi's inherited tradition of authority (*sāmpradāyam*) through the practice of impersonation. Grounded in the life story of Siddhendra, the practice of impersonation most notably appears in the vow taken by young brahmin inhabitants of Kuchelapuram (current Kuchipudi) to perform *Bhāmākalāpam* for generations to come. When describing this vow, Indian dance scholar Mohan Khokar (1957, 28) states:

> [Siddhendra] went to the village of Kuchelapuram and gathered a group of Brahmin boys who were prepared to assist him. With their help he produced and presented the play written by him. Lord Krishna was immensely pleased with Siddhendra Yogi who, in gratitude of this acknowledgement, took a vow from all the boys of Kuchelapuram who participated in his play that they would continue to enact [*Bhāmākalāpam*] at least once every year. They in turn further assured him that they would continue to see that their sons and grandsons continue to act the same play in the same way at the same village of Kuchelapuram. Thus it is that to this day the tradition of [*Bhāmākalāpam*] survives in the village of Kuchelapuram.

In continuing to perform *Bhāmākalāpam*, particularly the lead role of Satyabhama, Kuchipudi brahmin men envision impersonation as integral to the imagined cultural history of the Kuchipudi village and its eponymous dance form.

In the village today, all men from hereditary brahmin families must don Satyabhama's *strī-vēṣam* at least once in their lives, irrespective of their skill or ability to perform. In fact, my interlocutors would often repeat the prescription—"Every man born in Kuchipudi must wear Satyabhama's *vēṣam* at least once in his life"—in everyday conversations. My interlocutors in the village would also proudly show me professional photographs of themselves in *vēṣam*, which were prominently displayed in their homes, thereby mirroring the interactions Joyce Flueckiger (2013, 69–70) had with male participants in *vēṣam* during the Gangamma *jātara* in Tirupati. Even nonbrahmins from outside of the village, such as the Hyderabad-based dancer Haleem Khan, raised to me Siddhendra's injunction to impersonate as the primary reason for donning Satyabhama's *strī-vēṣam*. For these dancers, impersonation is viewed as a religious fulfillment to Siddhendra, who himself adopted a female voice in his devotional writings. Impersonation thus operates on two levels in the Kuchipudi imaginary: the poet speaking to his god through the voice of the female lover, and the dancer fulfilling his religious vows by impersonating the female character. The dual resonances of impersonation, on the level of narrative and staged performance, make it a uniquely significant practice for the brahmins of the Kuchipudi village.

The prominence of impersonation is further apparent in the historical biographies of dancers from the village. In a survey of notable performers and gurus in Kuchipudi dance from the late nineteenth century onwards, Jonnalagadda (1993) outlines the biographies of over thirty brahmin male dancers from the village known for donning the *strī-vēṣam*. While there may have been popular impersonators from the eighteenth and early nineteenth centuries, there are no surviving historical records of these earlier generations of Kuchipudi performance history. In fact, only two impersonators—Vempati Venkatanarayana (1871–1935) and Vedantam Satyanarayana Sarma (1934–2012)—are particularly noteworthy in Kuchipudi dance memory. The former was a mythic guru credited for his performances of Satyabhama in *Bhāmākalāpam* (Jonnalagadda 1993, 165–66; Usha Gayatri 2016, 186).[51] The latter was a mid-twentieth-century performer who is undoubtedly the most popular impersonator from the Kuchipudi village (Jonnalagadda 1993, 131). While little is known about Venkatanarayana, far more documentation exists for Vedantam Satyanarayana Sarma, who was and continues to be wildly popular for his skills of impersonation, a point that I will discuss in detail in the next chapter.

Handpicked by well-known Kuchipudi guru Chinta Krishna Murthy (1912–1969), Satyanarayana Sarma was an instant success due to his skills in impersonation, particularly his enactments of Satyabhama in *Bhāmākalāpam* and Usha in the *yakṣagāna Uṣā-pariṇayam* (Nagabhushana Sarma 2016, 154). The village troupe, Venkatarama Natya Mandali, which was led by Krishna Murthy and featured Satyanarayana Sarma in *strī-vēṣam*, was chosen to represent Kuchipudi in national dance festivals, seminars, and tours, including those sponsored by the state-based arts organization Andhra Pradesh Sangeet Natak Akademi (APSNA) (Nagabhushana Sarma 2016, 154–59). For example, the "Kuchipudi Nritya Sadassu" (Seminar on Kuchipudi Dance) hosted by APSNA in 1959, in which dancers and scholars publicly asserted Kuchipudi's "classical" status, featured a performance by Satyanarayana Sarma in *Gollākalāpam* (lit., "the lyrical drama of Gollabhama") (Putcha 2013, 104).[52] Recipient of several national awards, Satyanarayana Sarma was later selected to tour nationally throughout Europe and the United States in the 1980s (see chapter 2). Through the support of village elders and elite patrons, Satyanarayana Sarma was quickly promoted as the face of Kuchipudi dance in the mid-twentieth century, mirroring Bal Gandharva, Jayshankar Sundari, and Sthanam Narasimha Rao before him.

Disentangling the imagined authority given to the practice of impersonation from the critical history of that practice is a complicated process. On the one hand, impersonation appears simply as a rite of passage required by the hagiography of Siddhendra and, therefore, it would seem that all village brahmin men must, at the very least, attempt to impersonate. However, this relatively straightforward injunction is implicated in the broader historical processes traced thus far, namely the mid-twentieth-century expansion of Siddhendra's life story and the concurrent classicization of Kuchipudi dance. Dovetailing with the enormous popularity of impersonation in Indian theatre, the brahmin impersonator of the Kuchipudi village was accorded a position of prominence in state-sponsored public appearances in the mid-twentieth century. At the same time, elaborate hagiographies of Siddhendra, which provided the religious grounding for the practice of impersonation, were disseminated in printed sources. In other words, the Kuchipudi impersonator gained national prominence in Kuchipudi dance at the same time that elite Telugu proponents began vocalizing a highly devotionalized version of Siddhendra's hagiography.[53]

It is noteworthy that impersonation is also a distinguishing element of Kuchipudi dance that sets it apart from Bharatanatyam, the dance form that is said to be a "revival" of the *devadāsī* performance repertoire (Allen 1997). While the history of Bharatanatyam is firmly entrenched in the quagmire of anti-nautch sentiments of colonial South India, Kuchipudi—an ostensibly brahminical, male-only dance form from the heart of Telugu South India—was able to sidestep controversies of courtesan involvement in order to gain its classical status. Despite the fact that *devadāsī* women had long-standing interactions with South Indian brahmins and despite the fact that the female solo repertoire was discreetly adopted into the Kuchipudi fold, particularly through the efforts of guru Vedantam Lakshminarayana Sastry, the history of the *devadāsī* performer herself is lost in the broader classicization of Kuchipudi (Soneji 2012, 267n11; Putcha 2015, 12–13, 19). In her place, the brahmin impersonator from the Kuchipudi village became the face of Kuchipudi classical dance in postcolonial South India. The nexus of performance, religion, gender, caste, and patronage thereby converge upon the body of the brahmin impersonator to create the central script for Kuchipudi as classical dance. In sum, impersonation is not only a prescriptive act required for all Kuchipudi brahmin men but also the central practice that distinguishes Kuchipudi as classical.

• • •

The genealogy of Telugu dance is grounded in a paradoxical landscape that silences the *devadāsī* performer while legitimating the male body in *strī-vēṣam*. Scholarly histories of South Indian dance interrogate popular narratives of revival and respectability to underscore the explicit marginalization of *devadāsī* communities in colonial and postcolonial formations of Indian dance and music (Srinivasan 1985; Meduri 1988; Allen 1997; Soneji 2012; Putcha 2015). Yet, aside from the few notable exceptions discussed above, scholarship on South Indian dance forms overlooks the key role of the male dancer in contributing to and shaping the revival of South Indian dance. This chapter contributes to the growing body of scholarship on South Indian performance by analyzing the twentieth-century processes that enabled the construction of Siddhendra as the *bhakti* saint and the concurrent prominence bestowed upon the brahmin impersonator. My intention, however, is not to authorize the brahmin male dance as somehow more legitimate than the *devadāsī* performer in the landscape of South Indian dance. Rather, by interrogating the inherited narrative of Kuchipudi hagiography and performance, I call into question the processes by which Siddhendra, the poet-saint, and the village brahmin impersonator came to occupy center stage.

It is also important to note that the contested history described in this chapter is mostly unknown among Kuchipudi practitioners in the contemporary period. While scholarly debates revolve around lingering questions underlying Kuchipudi's history, many practitioners I encountered during fieldwork spoke of Kuchipudi without raising these issues. Rather than focusing on topics of classicization, courtesans, or statehood, practitioner accounts rested on a different set of themes, primarily the hagiography of Siddhendra, the evolution of Kuchipudi performance genres (from *Bhāmākalāpam* to solo items), and the legacy of twentieth-century dancers and gurus who helped shape the artistry and performance techniques of Kuchipudi today.

The competing visions of Kuchipudi dance may be reconciled by suggesting that scholarly histories are more "accurate" while practitioner accounts are "constructed" in the contemporary period. However, as a scholar and practitioner of Kuchipudi dance with investments in the ethnographic enterprise as a form of feminist practice (Abu-Lughod 1990), I am reluctant to overlook the ways in which Kuchipudi dancers speak about their dance, however recent such discussions may be. In the ethnographic study and performance analysis of Kuchipudi that follows, I focus primarily on the contemporary context of Kuchipudi dancers, for whom Siddhendra is a significant persona, the village of Kuchipudi a historic place, and Kuchipudi dance an uncontestably classical tradition. My ethnographic accounts of the practitioners from the village give voice to their perspectives, and I ground my analytical work in their words. My theoretical approach, however, is framed by Kuchipudi's contentious past, particularly the ways in which the brahmin male body is scripted as the authoritative vehicle to express its classical status. This dual attentiveness to historical processes and to present sensibilities shapes my theorizations of both Kuchipudi as village *and* Kuchipudi as dance.

2

"I am Satyabhama"

Constructing Hegemonic Brahmin Masculinity in the Kuchipudi Village

The melodious voice of D.S.V. Sastry, a brahmin male singer raised in the Kuchipudi village, resounded across the D.S.T. Auditorium at the University of Hyderabad on the evening of January 20, 2011.

> *Bhāmanē Satyabhāmanē.* I am Bhama, I am Satyabhama.
> *Bhāmanē Satyabhāmanē.* I am Bhama, I am Satyabhama.

Seated on stage right along with senior Kuchipudi guru Pasumarti Rattayya Sarma playing the cymbals (*naṭṭuvāṅgam*) and accompanied by an orchestra, Sastry filled the spaces of the auditorium with the lyrics of Satyabhama's introductory song. The stage lights began to rise, and a veiled figure appeared from behind the orchestra and moved to stage left, his swinging gait synchronized with the rhythms of the item's seven-beat time-measure (*misra-chāpu*): *ta-ki-ṭa-ta-ka-dhi-mi.* Once across the stage, the dancer cast off his veil and grasped the long braid hanging down his back, deftly pulling it over his shoulders in front of him. As the dancer slowly turned around, the audience finally caught a glimpse of Vedantam Venkata Naga Chalapathi Rao, or Venku as he is commonly referred to, in Satyabhama's *vēṣam* (guise).

Although I had gone backstage to photograph Venku's makeup session prior to the start of the performance, I was still surprised to witness his onstage transformation. Backstage Venku was casually dressed in a white undershirt (*banyan*) lined by dark chest hairs, a floor-length cotton garment (*luṅgi*) wrapped around his waist. Now wearing a white and red silken costume, Venku shone under the spotlights onstage, his face completely altered by layers of makeup that had been carefully applied by a professional makeup artist. For the three-hour *Bhāmākalāpam* performance, Venku captivated the audience with his skills of impersonation, expressed not only through his costume and gait, but also through affectations of his voice when he spoke as Satyabhama during dramatic conversations. As I sat watching Venku enact Satyabhama that evening, I could feel the palpable energy of the auditorium, which was filled with three hundred raucous university students and members of the Hyderabad dance community. They laughed at Satyabhama's glib remarks to her confidante Madhavi and applauded her final union with Krishna, all while relishing the aesthetic pleasure of watching Venku's cis male body in *strī-vēṣam* (woman's guise).

That evening's *Bhāmākalāpam* performance reminded me of my interview with Venku nine months earlier in his urban Vijayawada apartment. A cup of milky chai in hand and his daughter playing at his feet, Venku spoke earnestly about his journey as a dancer and impersonator. Venku is the most skilled impersonator of the younger generation of brahmin performers from the village and he has worked hard over the years to distinguish himself from Vedantam Satyanarayana Sarma, the most famous Kuchipudi impersonator of the twentieth century. Despite Venku's challenges of supporting his family while making a name for himself as a male dancer and impersonator, he adheres to a rather rigid notion of tradition (*sāmpradāyam*). When I asked him what he thought about the increasing presence of women dancing Kuchipudi, Venku was straightforward in his response:

> First we must uphold the tradition (*sāmpradāyam*). From what I know, it's in order for the tradition to not get lost. I mean changes might come and the tradition must change . . . But first Siddhendra had a rule that men should dance . . . Up until this point, men have been mostly enacting *Bhāmākalāpam*. Nowadays, there's a few more women performing. But the ones you see, you can count on your fingers. Because there have been so many men who have been upholding the tradition, I think it's better if men continue on with it.

I found Venku's answer unsettling, especially given his warm demeanor and openness toward my research. As I have come to learn, Venku's observations regarding Kuchipudi tradition reflect a broader sentiment within the village's brahmin community. For my interlocutors, the *Bhāmākalāpam* dance drama and Satyabhama's role, more specifically, is only rendered legible through the brahmin male body, even in the context of transnational Kuchipudi dance in which female dancers outnumber their male counterparts. Despite the transnational Kuchipudi landscape, within the village, hereditary brahmin men hold power as bearers of tradition (*sāmpradāyam*), both in the domains of performance and everyday life.

This chapter explores the technologies of power undergirding the practice of impersonation in the Kuchipudi village, particularly in relation to the production of hegemonic brahmin masculinity. Due to an originary prohibition against female performers in early forms of Kuchipudi dance, brahmin dancers from the village would don elaborate costume and makeup to enact both male and female roles from Hindu religious narratives. The enactment of Satyabhama's role is undoubtedly the most important *vēṣam* for the brahmins of the village due to the prescription of Siddhendra described in the previous chapter. The earliest village performances of the introductory item in which Satyabhama declares, "I am Bhama [woman], I am Satyabhama [True Woman]," were danced by brahmin men. Although all brahmin men are required to dance Satyabhama once in their lives, impersonation as a rite of passage is not its only social function. Rather, impersonation is a practice of power that creates normative ideals of gender and caste in village performance and everyday life, particularly as the practice of impersonation onstage spills into personation offstage (Mankekar 2015).

To set the stage, the chapter begins with the mechanics of impersonation. Drawing on the Kuchipudi lexicon, I focus on three embodied techniques of impersonation: costume (*āhārya*), speech (*vācika*), and bodily movement (*āṅgika*). In each technique, Kuchipudi brahmin male dancers draw on idealized understandings of "real" women's bodies while, paradoxically, limiting their female counterparts from performance. The latter half of this chapter focuses on Vedantam Satyanarayana Sarma, the most famous impersonator of the twentieth century. By excelling in the one factor central to traditional Kuchipudi performance—the donning of Satyabhama's *strī-vēṣam*—Satyanarayana Sarma establishes the norm that epitomizes hegemonic brahmin masculinity in the Kuchipudi village (Connell 1995). Satyanarayana Sarma's mythic practices of impersonation create the paradigmatic ideal for his gender and caste community, an ideal that is ultimately illusory and impossible for any other performer to fully embody. In their failure to impersonate in the manner of their famous predecessor, younger performers like Venku adhere to *normative* brahmin masculinity, an emergent form of hegemonic masculinity that is always in process but never fully hegemonic (Inhorn 2012). To be a successful impersonator in the Kuchipudi village, one must impersonate Satyanarayana Sarma impersonating Satyabhama.

SARTORIAL TRANSFORMATIONS: THE EMBODIED TECHNIQUES OF IMPERSONATION

Impersonation in the Kuchipudi village most commonly involves a sartorial transformation of the brahmin male dancer into a given female character. Kuchipudi dancers, such as Venku described in the opening vignette, not only wear elaborate jewelry and makeup, but also alter the pitch of their voice and the swing of their gait to don the *strī-vēṣam*. When discussing the practices of impersonation, Kuchipudi dancers often raise the concept of *abhinaya* (mimetic mode of expression), particularly as it is referenced in Sanskrit texts on dramaturgy and aesthetics, namely Bharata's *Nāṭyaśāstra* (ca. 300 CE) and Nandikeshvara's *Abhinayadarpaṇa* (ca. tenth to thirteenth centuries CE).[1] In the eighth chapter of the *Nāṭyaśāstra,* Bharata describes four types of *abhinaya*: bodily gesture (*āṅgika*), speech and dialogue (*vācika*), makeup and costume (*āhārya*), and temperament (*sāttvika*) (*Nāṭyaśāstra* VIII.9).[2] These four categories of *abhinaya,* as postulated by Bharata and elaborated by Nandikeshvara, were frequently referenced in my interviews and conversations with Kuchipudi performers and scholars, even more often than Bharata's well-known theory of *rasa* (aesthetic taste).

The appeal to premodern Sanskrit texts, namely Bharata's *Nāṭyaśāstra* and Nandikeshvara's *Abhinayadarpaṇa,* on the part of my interlocutors is reflective of what Uttara Asha Coorlawala (2004) refers to as "Sanskritized dance." According to Coorlawala, texts such as Bharata's *Nāṭyaśāstra* became the Sanskrit framework of Indian dance, particularly in the context of the newly revived South Indian dance form, Bharatanatyam:

> This linking of dance with continuous lineages of oral practice and recovered authoritative texts—acceptable to newly embraced western scholarship—has come to be recognized as a characteristic of Sanskritized dance . . . "Sanskritization" had come to denote a deliberate self-conscious return to ancient Vedic and brahminical values and customs from a new intellectual perspective, (often but not necessarily in response to "Westernization"). The term is often used synonymously with brahminization, because Sanskrit had been the exclusive preserve of brahmin males. In dance, [S]anskritization has become a legitimizing process by which dance forms designated as "ritual," "folk," or simply insignificant, attain social and politico-artistic status which brings the redesignation, "classical." (53–54)[3]

The convergence of Sanskrit texts, brahminical tradition, and classical dance is certainly evident in the context of Kuchipudi, a dance form that became Sanskritized and classicized over the course of the twentieth century.[4] Although my interlocutors unequivocally accept Kuchipudi as an ancient dance form rooted in the *Nāṭyaśāstra* and other Sanskrit texts, it is important to underscore the twentieth-century-processes of classicization as noted by Coorlawala and others (see introduction). In this chapter, I draw on the Sanskrit lexicon of Kuchipudi dance to analyze the techniques of impersonation, while also recognizing the social-historical contexts that enabled Kuchipudi to become a Sanskritized classical dance form. Although I am fully aware of the problematic attempts to Sanskritize Kuchipudi, as an ethnographer of dance, I also take seriously the words that my interlocutors use to describe their dance practices. In the discussion that follows, I analyze three embodied techniques of impersonation: costume (*āhārya*), speech (*vācika*), and bodily movement (*āṅgika*). In each of these cases, Kuchipudi impersonators transform their physical appearances to approximate an idealized understanding of "real" women's bodies within the context of staged performance.

Āhārya abhinaya

Āhārya abhinaya, which refers to costume and makeup, is a critical feature of any performance given by a Kuchipudi impersonator. The application of makeup, donning a wig, putting on ornaments, and wearing a silk costume are crucial embodied techniques of impersonation. Chinta Ravi Balakrishna, a young brahmin dancer from Kuchipudi, described to me the importance of costume (*āhārya*): "Once I put on the hair bun, bangles, and the rest of the costume, I think to myself: 'I am not Ravi Balakrishna. I am that female dancer. I am Satyabhama.' Thinking that, I get onto the stage."

The impact of sartorial guising on Ravi Balakrishna's experience parallels the words of early twentieth-century Gujarati theatre impersonator Jayshankar Sundari. When describing the first time he wore a woman's blouse, Sundari writes in his autobiography (alternating between third-and first-person voice):

> At the moment when Jayshankar first attired himself in a *choli* and *lahanga* [blouse and full skirt], he was transformed into a woman, or rather into the artistic form that expresses the feminine sensibility. A beautiful young woman revealed herself inside me. Her shapely, intoxicating youth sparkled. Her feminine charm radiated fragrance. She had an easy grace in her eyes, and in her gait was the glory of Gujarat. She was not a man, she was a woman...and for that instant I felt as though I was not a man. (Hansen 2015, 266)[5]

Both Ravi Balakrishna's and Sundari's observations regarding the transformative processes of impersonation bear resemblance to Saba Mahmood's (2005) analysis of the embodied practices of prayer and veiling for the women's mosque movement in Egypt. For Mahmood's female mosque participants, external bodily acts such as prayer and veiling are "the *critical markers* of piety as well as the *ineluctable means* by which one trains oneself to be pious," thereby serving as a form of *habitus* (158).[6] In the case of Kuchipudi, the pre-performance steps of donning the *strī-vēṣam* initiate gender transformation; the elaborate process of applying makeup, donning a wig, and wearing a silk costume transform not only the external appearance of the impersonator but also his internal gender identification. External bodily acts, in this case costume and makeup, are said to inculcate an internal ideal of womanhood in the body of the impersonator.[7]

Mirroring Ravi Balakrishna's words is a description of the legendary Vedantam Satyanarayana Sarma. A 1973 documentary by the India Films Division featuring Satyanarayana Sarma describes the importance of costume and makeup for his practice of impersonation:

> No sooner did [Satyanarayana Sarma] wear a female wig, ornaments, and *pāyal* [bells, that he acquired] feminine traits. That state of mind used to last for quite some time. After he removed the female makeup and wore *dhoti* and *kurta,* the original masculinity of Satyanarayan used to set in again. Until then, he used to feel like a female.[8]

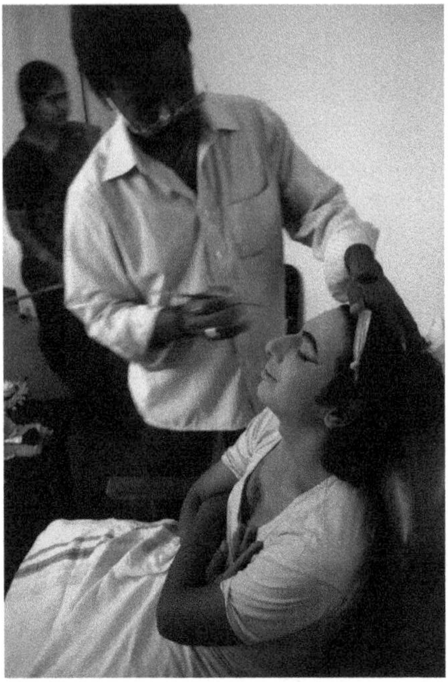
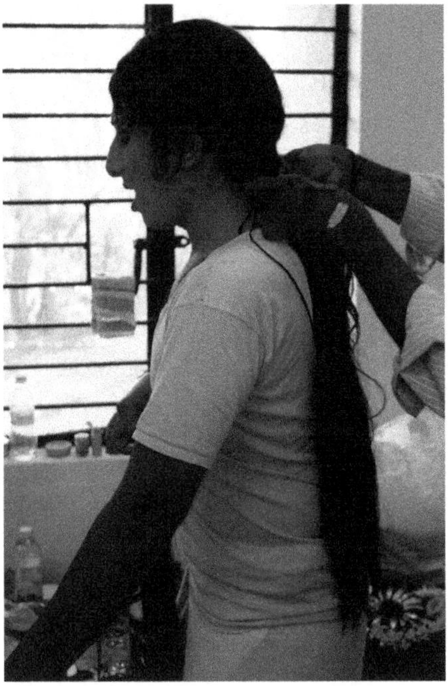
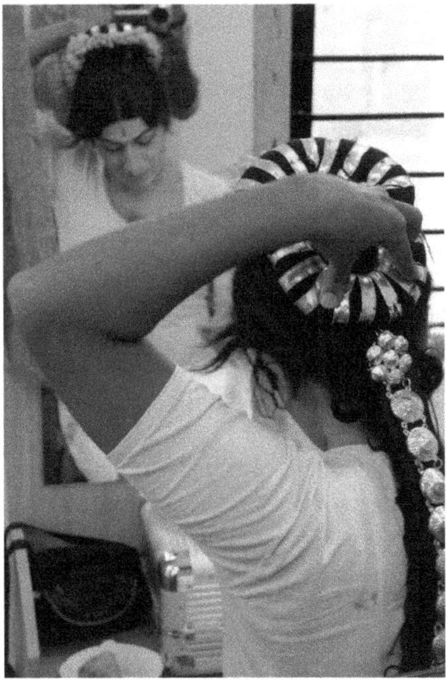

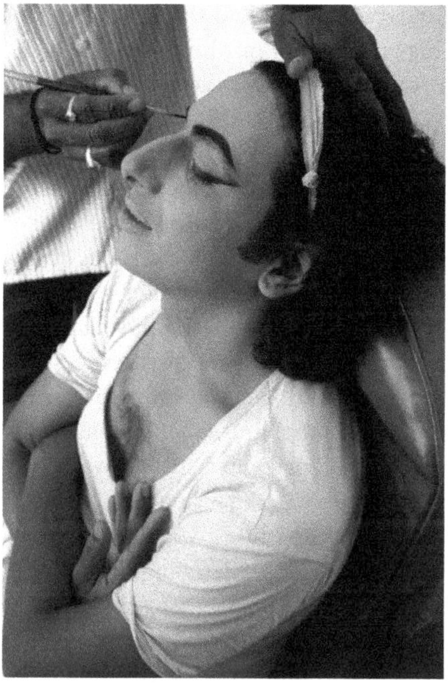

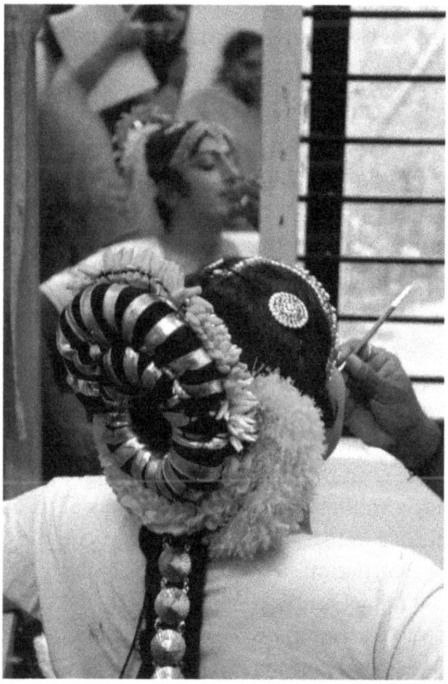

FIGURES 5–11. Vedantam Venkata Naga Chalapathi Rao donning Satyabhama's *strī-vēṣam.* Photos by author.

Avinash Pasricha, a noted Indian dance photographer, has had the opportunity of photographing Satyanarayana Sarma in his green room in Mumbai while the dancer spent his usual three hours getting ready for a performance. The series of photographs depict Satyanarayana Sarma applying his makeup, adjusting his wig, plaiting his hair, and putting on his costume (Kothari and Pasricha 2001, 58–59).[9] Pasricha described to me that while photographing Satyanarayana Sarma, he witnessed a step-by-step metamorphosis of the stalwart impersonator into Satyabhama.

In an attempt to replicate Pasricha's series, I photographed Vedantam Venkata Naga Chalapathi Rao donning the guise of Satyabhama prior to the *Bhāmākalāpam* performance in January 2011 discussed in the opening vignette of this chapter (see Figures 5–11). The second photograph of the series shows Venku leaning back in his chair, dressed casually in a white *banyan* (undershirt) and *luṅgi* (traditional garment worn around the waist), as a professional makeup artist draws the graceful shape of a feminine eyebrow, paintbrush in hand. After applying liberal amounts of spirit gum, the makeup artist secures a long black wig on Venku's head and braids the hair into place. The braid, which is particularly important for Satyabhama's character, is overlaid with a long golden ornament representing the sun, moon, and twenty-seven stars (Kapaleswara Rao 1996, 83).[10] With the help of special U-shaped bobby pins, Venku secures a circular bun and half-ring bun on the crown of his head, wrapping the two buns with rows of white and orange paper flowers. After a final round of makeup, Venku wears the silken red and white costume of Satyabhama's character. The entire process takes approximately two hours, beginning with makeup and ending in Satyabhama's *vēṣam*.[11]

In "The Art of Female Impersonation," Andhra Natyam impersonator Kalakrishna (1996) describes the corporeal requirements of donning the *strī-vēṣam*.[12] Although not belonging to a hereditary Kuchipudi brahmin family, Kalakrishna's observations in this article are useful for analyzing the embodied practices of impersonation in the Kuchipudi village. In particular, Kalakrishna outlines the various practices of body padding, which my interlocutors were often reluctant to discuss outright with me:

> One who wants to personify a female role in [a] dance drama or in [a] solo dance item must necessarily practice the various movements of neck, extremities and his body according to the structure of his body to bring out the delicate feminine movements suitable to the role he plays. Sufficient care must be taken so that the muscles do not develop like that of an athlete. Generally a youth between 14 and 24 years of age will be able to bring out the delicate nuances of a woman in his movements. So he can play female roles up to 25 years of age. He can continue to play the female roles as long as he has control over his body, if he should not retire . . .
>
> A man who takes up female roles must be very careful in his make-up, selection of dress, ornaments, hair dressing etc., according to his height and weight. Only then would his getup suit well the role he is to depict. To make his body appear like that

> of a woman he must use necessary padding wherever it is required in the dress. In particular a solo dancer should practice at least 5 times with full costume so that he gets accustomed to the extra heaviness during movements of the body, leg, and hand.
>
> Earlier the male artists who played female roles used to grow their natural hair long just like that of women. Even then they took care to cover their masculine features with a wooden ornament called '*Ganiyam*.' Now female impersonators can select suitable wigs to suit the structure of their head and face. (67)

Kalakrishna delineates an ideal age and body composition for the male dancer impersonating a female character. Regulatory practices of the body, akin to the techniques discussed by Phillip Zarrilli (2000) in Kathakali dance, mold the impersonator's body to portray "delicate feminine movements." Particular kinds of ornamentation, along with body padding to cover "masculine features," also enable the practice of sartorial impersonation.

In line with Kalakrishna's observations, Pasumarti Rattayya Sarma, a senior guru from the Kuchipudi village, also emphasized the importance of observing differences in bodily appearance:

> Kuchipudi artists need to do so much research to enact a female character. They need to research how to wear the wig and how to do the makeup. They need to do research on how the female hairline is, in order to put the wig on in the right way. Some women have even hairlines, and some women have curls on their faces. So you have to observe those things and make the curls in the right way. That's why those people who do female impersonation need to do research.

Rattayya Sarma's emphasis on "research," which he referenced using the English language term rather than its Telugu equivalent, suggests that Kuchipudi male dancers draw on real-life examples when impersonating a female character. Similarly, aforementioned Gujarati impersonator Jayshankar Sundari is said to have studied young women from elite families and modeled his stage personas based on these observances (Hansen 2015, 266). Anuradha Kapur (2004) notes an anecdote from Sundari's life when he was introduced to a young woman, Gulab, at his uncle's home. Later, when her parents went to see Sundari's new play, they remarked: "But this is our daughter, Gulab!" (100).

As discussed in chapter 1, all brahmin men from hereditary Kuchipudi families are required to don Satyabhama's *vēṣam* at least once in their life, thereby fulfilling a vow made to their founding saint Siddhendra. Despite this vow, not all Kuchipudi brahmin men are adept at impersonation. Pasumarti Keshav Prasad, an expert at organizing festivals and performances in the village of Kuchipudi, described his own one-time experience of taking on the *strī-vēṣam:*

> We all learned Kuchipudi and had to take on a female role at least once. I also wore it once, but just for fun. I wasn't a professional performer when I wore it, but I wanted

> to have that experience of donning a female role at least once. The reason is because Siddhendra Yogi had a vow for all of the Kuchipudi people. Every man who is born in Kuchipudi needs to wear Satyabhama's *vēṣam* at least once in his life . . . Otherwise, why would I do it? My face doesn't suit a female role. I look like a *rākṣasa* [demon].

The success of Kuchipudi impersonation is not simply dependent upon the artistic skill of a given performer, but also his appeal in female makeup and costume. The more appealing (and convincing) a performer looks donning the *strī-vēṣam*, the more likely he is at being a successful impersonator.[13] In all of these discussions, Kuchipudi impersonators draw on their own idealized perceptions of gendered bodies when approaching the practice of impersonation. Impersonators must not only wear appropriate padding to cover up "masculine" features, but also regulate their bodily appearance to prevent the growth of unwanted musculature, thereby effecting a "delicate feminine" appearance onstage. Keshav Prasad mirrors this sentiment when suggesting that his "face doesn't suit a female role." By likening his own impersonation to a demon in a woman's guise, Keshav Prasad positions himself outside of this normative gender ideal.

Rattayya Sarma draws on his own "research" of women in everyday life when approaching the embodied techniques of *āhārya*, particularly with respect to wearing a wig and applying makeup. Rattayya Sarma's "research" of hairlines, however, is not simply an observation of the women around him, but also a prescription for how male dancers should impersonate variations across women's bodies. For Rattayya Sarma, there is a "right way" of wearing curls on the face, and the successful impersonator is one who observes women's hair in daily life and replicates this "research" onstage. Underlying Rattayya Sarma's suggestions is an idealized perception of "real" women's bodies as they are presented within staged performance.

Vācika abhinaya

In contemporary Kuchipudi performances enacted by village brahmin men, such as the one described at the beginning of this chapter, dancers are accompanied by a professional orchestra seated on stage right. The main orchestra members, who are also from village brahmin families, include a senior guru playing the cymbals (*naṭṭuvāṅgam*), a lead vocalist trained in Karnatak music, and a percussionist playing the double-barrel drum (*mṛdaṅgam*).[14] The vocalist sings the dance items of a given performance, such as Satyabhama's introductory song, while the dancer lip-synchs the song to give the effect of singing the piece himself. When the performance shifts to a dramatic scene between characters, such as a conversation between Satyabhama and her confidante Madhavi, the dancers speak their dialogues in front of a microphone (or sometimes two microphones) positioned toward the front of the stage.[15] Notably, the use of microphones and the staging of performances in a proscenium theatrical context is a twentieth-century transformation in Kuchipudi dance (Jonnalagadda 1996b, 46; Bhikshu 260–61).

The Kuchipudi impersonator performing roles such as Satyabhama must modulate his voice to be soft and high-pitched. Rattayya Sarma described how male performers must modulate the pitch of their voice to fit a particular female character's age and context. Rattayya Sarma referred to two Sanskrit categories of heroines when discussing *vācika:* Satyabhama is a mature heroine (*prauḍa-nāyikā*), so her voice must sound different from the character of Usha, a naive heroine (*mugdha-nāyikā*) and lead character of the *yakṣagāna Uṣā-pariṇayam. Vācika* (voice), as prescribed by these dancers, must also vary within a single character. For example, the voice modulation of Satyabhama describing herself with pride should be different from the voice modulation of the same Satyabhama telling Madhavi she is too shy to speak her husband's name in public. Ravi Balakrishna observed:

> When Satyabhama is doing her introductory song, she speaks with pride about her beauty, and with *gambhīram* [strength], so you cannot have a soft modulation. But in the next item *Siggāyanōyamma daruvu,* you need to speak softly because she is shy . . . In the item *Madana daruvu,* [when Satyabhama describes her pains of separation], there must be a trembling voice when speaking . . . With this trembling voice, the *Madana daruvu* comes properly . . . The voice modulation needs to be based upon what is the character, what is the situation, and what is the context.

As Ravi Balakrishna's comments suggest, the Kuchipudi male artist does not simply project a falsetto voice to perform *strī-vēṣam,* but rather manipulates *vācika* based on the identity, situation, and context of a given character.

Yeleswarapu Srinivas, a younger dancer and instructor at the Siddhendra Kalakshetra, outlined the process of learning *vācika* from his gurus:

> Our gurus taught us that however women talk, you should talk like that. The gurus used to teach us how to talk when acting as female characters . . . When you are talking as a female, the voice should come from your throat. When you are talking as a male, it should come deeper . . . When you are using a female voice, you compress the tracts of your throat. When it comes to a male character, you should open the throat.

I had the opportunity of watching Srinivas teach *Bhāmākalāpam* to two female students pursuing an MA in Kuchipudi dance from the Siddhendra Kalakshetra. When teaching the students the dialogue before the *Siggāyanōyamma daruvu,* a solo item in which Satyabhama states that she is too shy to speak her husband's name, Srinivas insisted that one of the female students, whose voice was naturally low in vocal register, modulate her voice to make it softer and higher in pitch. Srinivas demonstrated the lines for her by modulating his voice in a higher pitch and suggested that she follow his example. When describing the voice of early twentieth-century impersonator Bal Gandharva, Kathryn Hansen (1999) notes that Gandharva's voice was not falsetto, but rather between male and female registers, like many stage actors at the time. Gandharva's spoken voice onstage "is said to have been an idealized version of (presumably upper-caste) women's speech" (Hansen 1999, 136). A comparable idealized understanding of women's speech frames Srinivas's approach to *vācika* in his classroom. Much like Rattayya Sarma in the discussion of costume, there is a "right way" to speak as a female character, and dancers, both male and female, must modulate their voices to achieve an ideal "feminine" pitch. In Srinivas's classroom, it was the male teacher rather than the female students who articulated and achieved this ideal.

Āṅgika abhinaya

Along with dress and voice, movements of the body, or *āṅgika abhinaya*, are crucial to the practice of impersonation. Kuchipudi dancers observe the bodily movements of women around them in order to portray the *āṅgika* of a female character. Satyanarayana Sarma, for example, "carefully observe[s] how a woman walks, talks, shows anger, love, indifference, etc. And he trie[s] to incorporate such movements in delineating the character" (Nagabhushana Sarma 2012, 22). Venku observes differences in women's movements based on age when performing the characters of Satyabhama and Usha, respectively:

> My guru [Pasumarti Rattayya Sarma] told me, "This is how Usha should be and this is how Satyabhama should be." Usha is actually a young girl, right? He used to tell me to observe. He would tell me to observe girls studying in middle school or girls studying in the tenth grade. They have a type of humility and shyness that they don't even realize. There's a difference between a twenty-eight or twenty-nine-year-old girl [like Satyabhama] and a fourteen- or fifteen-year-old girl [like Usha]. Once they have gotten to twenty-nine, their mind is matured. When they talk or walk, they have a certain freeness either in their body or their speech. But with fourteen-year-old girls, there is some shyness inside that they don't even realize.

Following the example of his guru Rattayya Sarma, Venku watches the girls around him to refine his bodily movements across female characters of different ages. Like Rattayya Sarma in the case of *āhārya*, both Satyanarayana Sarma and Venku research the movements of women in daily life to portray *āṅgika* within the context of staged performance.

What are the specific bodily gestures (*āṅgika*) performed by Kuchipudi impersonators? Based on observations of both archival performance videos at the Sangeet Natak Akademi in New Delhi and live performances of Kuchipudi impersonators in Hyderabad, Bangalore, Chennai, and the Kuchipudi village, I compiled a list of stylized gestures of the body used by the male Kuchipudi performer donning the *strī-vēṣam*. The gestures include batting the eyelashes, casting shy sideways glances, turning the mouth, biting the finger, shaking the hands, rotating the shoulders, adjusting the top pleats of the sari, holding the bottom pleats of the costume, and standing with the toe pointed in a position called *sūcī-pādam*. Not all Kuchipudi impersonators employ all these gestures; rather, some of these gestures occur as trademark features in the performances of particular impersonators. For example, Satyanarayana Sarma is known for casting shy sideways glances when playing a female character, while Venku usually holds the bottom pleats of his costume and stands with his toe pointed in *sūcī-pādam* when donning the *strī-vēṣam* (see Figure 11). All of the aforementioned gestures, except for perhaps turning the mouth and casting shy sideways glances, are exaggerated by male Kuchipudi dancers but downplayed by female dancers from outside the village.[16]

This difference in male versus female performance was made apparent to me when I learned the majority of *Bhāmākalāpam* from Vedantam Radheshyam, a guru from a hereditary Kuchipudi brahmin family and instructor at the Siddhendra Kalakshetra in the Kuchipudi village. The one pedagogical instance I found most challenging and most informative in Radheshyam's classroom was learning the *Raṅgugā nā meḍa daruvu,* an item in which Satyabhama asks how Krishna could have forgotten the marriage necklace he tied around her neck. In the second and third stanzas of the item, Satyabhama recalls her first night of lovemaking with Krishna, particularly the ways in which he kissed her and placed his hands upon her breasts. Learning this item was challenging for me, not because of the explicit sexual content of the lyrics, but rather because of the ways in which the lyrics were visualized through embodied performance. Radheshyam's version of this *daruvu* fully used the gestures of *āṅgika abhinaya* listed above, particularly excessive movement of the shoulders and biting of the lower lip, which I had never learned from my female Kuchipudi teachers in India or the United States. I had clearly embodied the restrictions on erotic expression (*śṛṅgāra*) imposed on Indian classical dance by Rukmini Arundale in the mid-twentieth century (Meduri 1988, 8; Coorlawala 2004, 55). As a Telugu brahmin woman dancing in the village, I struggled to express eroticism in the manner demanded by my brahmin male teacher. Radheshyam, by contrast, seemed entirely unconcerned with such restrictions on female bodily comportment and encouraged me to exaggerate my gestures further.

The paradox of bodily gestures and gait (*āṅgika*) is that while female dancers rarely employ exaggerated gestures, Kuchipudi impersonators use them to effect an ostensibly "feminine" appearance onstage. When the impersonator turns his mouth, moves his shoulders, or holds the pleats of his costume, he affirms to the witnessing audience that he is, in fact, a woman.[17] But what kind of woman? The female characters that Kuchipudi impersonators perform onstage are not everyday women but idealized perceptions of "real" women's bodies enacted through stylized costume, voice, and movement. By adjusting his curls, modulating the pitch of his voice, and biting his lip, the impersonator approximates an idealized understanding of what it means to appear as a woman. Implicit in this approximation is a standard of realness, or the attempt to effect a gender ideal onstage that cannot be construed as artifice (Butler [1993] 2011, 88). In donning a woman's guise, the Kuchipudi impersonator must observe real women around him, and then transform his physical appearance to effect this realness within performance. The ultimate impersonator, therefore, is one for whom "the approximation of realness appears to be achieved, the body performing and ideal performed appear indistinguishable" (88). When the impersonator can *pass* as a woman, both onstage and off, only then is the approximation of realness truly achieved.

SATYANARAYANA SARMA AS SATYABHAMA

The single performer synonymous with the practice of impersonation in the Kuchipudi village, and the Kuchipudi dance context more broadly, is Vedantam Satyanarayana Sarma (1935–2012). Although Kuchipudi guru and impersonator Vempati Venkatanarayana (1871–1935) is thought to have promoted *Bhāmākalāpam* during the late nineteenth and early twentieth centuries, it is Satyanarayana Sarma who is more frequently associated with the character of Satyabhama (Jonnalagadda 1993, 131, 165–66). As described in the opening vignette of this book, Satyanarayana Sarma exhibits an ease in donning Satyabhama's *strī-vēṣam* and his skills of impersonation enable him to achieve a standard of realness that far surpasses his counterparts in the Kuchipudi village.

In fact, the rhythm of life in Kuchipudi seems dictated by Satyanarayana Sarma's presence, or absence, in the village. His occasional appearance to conduct morning rituals at the Ramalingeshvara temple during my fieldwork was illustrative of his authoritative status. The first time I saw him at the temple during my extended stay in the village, the priest of the adjacent Siddhendra temple rushed to my side, proclaiming as if he had spotted a celebrity, "Satyanarayana Sarma has come!" Clad in carefully ironed silk garments with three distinctive strokes of sacred ash covering his forehead, Satyanarayana Sarma marked his status through his fine attire, which was distinct from the often unkempt, white cotton garments of many of my other elder brahmin male interlocutors. Through his dress alone, Satyanarayana Sarma established himself as the paragon of brahminical and upper-class masculinity.

When I approached Satyanarayana Sarma to conduct a formal interview, he politely declined, stating that his health was fragile due to a recent illness, and he was unable to speak at length about any subject. Disappointed, particularly because Satyanarayana Sarma had assured me a few months prior to my stay in Kuchipudi that he would speak with me, I became resolved to obtain an interview which, according to my remaining interlocutors, was crucial for any good research project on *Bhāmākalāpam*. I begged Ravi Balakrishna, Satyanarayana Sarma's only direct disciple living in the village, to help me obtain an interview; he tried, but Satyanarayana Sarma resolutely refused. Frustrated, I left for Chennai to complete the rest of my fieldwork but returned to find Satyanarayana Sarma's insistence upon silence unwavering. My interlocutors, particularly those dancers and instructors centered around the Siddhendra Kalakshetra where I was staying, knew of my frustrations and empathized with my situation. Yet no one was willing to intervene on my behalf. It was clear that Satyanarayana Sarma resided at the peak of the power hierarchy within the brahmin performance community and was impervious to influence by anyone. Although I was finally able to get a formal interview with him in January 2011 during a return visit, the purpose of this vignette is to highlight his authoritative status within the Kuchipudi village. This status is directly tied to Satyanarayana Sarma's exceptional skills in the practice of impersonation, particularly his abilities in donning Satyabhama's *strī-vēṣam*.

Born on September 9, 1935, Vedantam Satyanarayana Sarma began learning dance at a very young age from his elder brother, Vedantam Prahlada Sarma. By the age of fourteen, he had learned most of Satyabhama's character in *Bhāmākalāpam* from his brother, but the elders of the village felt that he was not ready for public performance. According to a biographical article written by Modali Nagabhushana Sarma, one day when Satyanarayana Sarma was accompanying his uncle, Vedantam Lakshminarayana Sastry, to a neighboring village, he felt that someone was following him. He looked back and saw a sage smiling at him; the sage then said to Satyanarayana Sarma, "You are worried, aren't you? You will have better opportunities in your nineteenth year and you will carry the Kuchipudi mantle far and wide" (Nagabhushana Sarma 2012, 11).

The sage's words soon proved to be true when Satyanarayana Sarma received the opportunity to perform the role of goddess Parvati in the dance drama *Uṣā-pariṇayam* in New Delhi in 1954. This performance earned him acclaim in the eyes of his elders, and he was given the chance to play the lead female character of Usha in *Uṣā-pariṇayam* the following year (Nagabhushana Sarma 2012, 11–12). Just as Satyanarayana Sarma was gaining recognition for his abilities in impersonation, the gurus of the Kuchipudi village decided to consolidate disparate performance groups (*mēlams*) into Venkatarama Natya Mandali, a troupe that gained prominence under the leadership of Chinta Krishna Murthy (1912–1969) (Nagabhushana Sarma 2016, 153). Krishna Murthy groomed Satyanarayana Sarma as the lead impersonator of his troupe, and together they performed extensively across South India, as well as on the national stage (Nagabhushana Sarma 2012, 12). Satyanarayana Sarma soon gained fame for his adeptness at impersonation and came to be known as "*kali yuga* Satyabhama" ("an incarnation of Satyabhama for our age") outside the village (15).

Notably, the height of Satyanarayana Sarma's career coincided with the classicization of Kuchipudi dance in the mid-twentieth century. As discussed in the previous chapter, following the creation of the state of Andhra Pradesh in 1956, Kuchipudi was catapulted onto the national stage and came to be recognized as *the* "classical" dance form of Telugu South India (Putcha 2013). Patronage by elite brahmin scholars coupled with state pride in Telugu arts positioned the exclusively brahmin male dance form of Kuchipudi as critical to the endeavors of the newly formed performing arts organization Andhra Pradesh Sangeet Natak Akademi (APSNA) (Jonnalagadda 2016, 1063). Integral to APSNA's efforts was the promotion of Kuchipudi dance outside of the village through public tours and national radio recordings. In October 1960, for example, APSNA initiated a tour across South India led by Chinta Krishna Murthy and managed by Kuchipudi proponent Banda Kanakalingeshwara Rao (Nagabhushana Sarma 2016, 158–61). Performances featured Satyanarayana Sarma enacting the lead female characters in the dance dramas *Bhāmākalāpam* and *Uṣā-pariṇayam* (159). According to Jonnalagadda (2016, 1063–64), "this is one of the most successful tours of any Kuchipudi group till then as it earned the appreciation of the already renowned scholars and artistes of Tamil Nadu like, V. Raghavan, E. Krishna Iyer, Rukmini Devi Arundale, Indrani Rehman, Ramayya Pillai and others."

Performances such as these propelled Satyanarayana Sarma into the spotlight, while also enabling the national recognition of Kuchipudi as a classical Indian dance form. Over the course of the mid-twentieth century, Satyanarayana Sarma's exceptional skills of impersonation became symbolic of the Kuchipudi dance that emerged in postcolonial Andhra Pradesh. As testimony to his state and national recognition, Satyanarayana Sarma was the first Kuchipudi recipient of the Sangeet Natak Akademi Award in 1961. He was later elected into the Sangeet Natak Akademi Fellowship in 1967 and also received the prestigious national title of Padma Shri in 1970. This national fame soon shifted to global promotion; in 1986, he toured across the United States, Europe, and Russia, and descriptions of his performances are archived in the *New York Times, Los Angeles Times,* and even the conference notes of a program in Denmark.[18] Satyanarayana Sarma's numerous awards and international fame positioned him as the face of Kuchipudi classical dance in the mid-twentieth century. Beyond the Kuchipudi context, a national fascination with men impersonating women in the twentieth century, as evidenced by impersonators in Parsi, Gujarati, and Marathi theatre discussed in the previous chapter, further propelled Satyanarayana Sarma's popularity.

When describing Satyanarayana Sarma's skills of impersonation, Nagabhushana Sarma (2012, 8) states: "This exceptional performance skill challenging all the norms of credibility was the mainstay of Vedantam Satyanarayana Sarma's virtuosity of impersonating women; a virtuosity that beguiles both men and women." In a personal interview, Nagabhushana Sarma relayed to me that he has seen Satyanarayana Sarma perform *Bhāmākalāpam* at least fifty times since his childhood. He reported that during these performances, there was not a single time that he did not cry when Satyanarayana Sarma enacted the *lēkha* scene of *Bhāmākalāpam,* in which Satyabhama writes a letter to Krishna begging for his return. As Nagabhushana Sarma recalled:

> Our experiences with Vedantam Satyanarayana Sarma were very fine moments in our lives where we wept with him. When he finished his letter, there was no occasion when people did not weep . . . And so, I have seen him about fifty times. Fifty! In my younger days we had a craze for going and seeing Satyam's *Bhāmākalāpam* wherever he performed. And he used to perform in a fifty-mile radius. He used to

> perform almost once a week. I studied near Vijayawada, which is hardly twenty-five kilometers to Kuchipudi. And they used to perform in the villages. And whenever he did the letter, you were lost.

This praise of Satyanarayana Sarma's performance of Satyabhama is not unique, but rather reflective of a general tenor of admiration when discussing his particular skills of impersonation. Every Kuchipudi dancer I interviewed regarding the practice of impersonation invariably named Satyanarayana Sarma as the singular person capable of donning the *strī-vēṣam*.[19] Further testimony to this national approbation is the Central Sangeet Natak Akademi archives in New Delhi, which hosts a sizeable collection of videos and photographs of Satyanarayana Sarma in *vēṣam*. In the eyes of the dancers and scholars who witnessed this legendary figure, Satyanarayana Sarma *is* Satyabhama.

Satyanarayana Sarma's other important performative skill is his reported ability to deceive his audiences by "passing" as a woman.[20] In an autobiographical article, Satyanarayana Sarma describes that once, while in the town of Nagpur, he performed the role of the young heroine Usha. When he went into the dressing room to change his costume between scenes, a wealthy patron entered and began making amorous advances. In order to return to the stage in time for his next scene, Satyanarayana Sarma had to reveal his identity to his prospective suitor, who was evidently unaware of Satyanarayana Sarma's skills in impersonation. Satyanarayana Sarma (1996, 86) described the moment: "[My suitor] felt embarrassed and returned to his seat after saying that had I really been a lady, he would have bequeathed his entire property to me, but unfortunately I happened to be male."[21]

As another example, Satyanarayana Sarma relates a story when he was staying in the house of a wealthy landowner in the Duvva village of the east Godavari district. During the performance, the landowner purchased a large garland and then gave it to Satyanarayana Sarma onstage while he was still in costume. The man's wife, who also appeared to have been unaware of Satyanarayana Sarma's impersonation, became upset that her husband had garlanded an unknown woman, and immediately left the performance. A fight erupted between the couple after they went home, and Satyanarayana Sarma (1996, 87) described the events that followed:

> Meanwhile, I removed the make-up and went to see them. Their fight was almost reaching the climax when I explained to her that it was none other than me who played the role of Satyabhama and showed her the garland. She was shocked and went inside the house with an embarrassed look.

Satyanarayana Sarma undoubtedly delights in these stories of passing as a woman. He told me similar stories when I first met him in the summer of 2006 and again in December 2007. During both of these informal visits, he relayed the story of the rich landlord in his dressing room, as well as an incident when the screenwriter for the 1967 film *Rahasyam* mistook him for a woman, even though he was dressed in male attire and cast to play the role of the male Hindu love god, Manmatha. In fact, Satyanarayana Sarma seems to be most comfortable before his audiences garbed in female attire. In a lecture demonstration at the Sangeet Natak Akademi's *Nrityotsava* festival in 1995, available in the New Delhi Sangeet Natak Akademi archives, Satyanarayana Sarma repeatedly refers to his "bald head" and male attire and indicates to the audience that he might look better in *strī-vēṣam* with flowers in his hair.

As evidenced by his repeated invocation of such accounts, Satyanarayana Sarma takes great pride in his ability not only to impersonate but to pass as a woman in offstage encounters. These moments of passing designate Satyanarayana Sarma as an impersonator capable of achieving a standard of realness, both on- and offstage. One can never be certain of the actual circumstances of the oral accounts, especially because Satyanarayana Sarma's skills in impersonation were likely known by many of the audience members who came to witness his performances during the height of his career. Nevertheless, Satyanarayana Sarma employs these incidents of passing to construct his own hagiography as *the* impersonator of the Kuchipudi village. The hagiographic quality of Satyanarayana Sarma's biography is also evident in the aforementioned narrative of the sage who appears earlier in his professional career and can be interpreted as a vision of Siddhendra himself. Like the *bhakti*-cization of Siddhendra's hagiography discussed in the previous chapter, Satyanarayana Sarma elevates his own life history from personal reflection to performative hagiography through these accounts of passing.

Satyanarayana Sarma's skills in impersonation have gained him critical acclaim in national dance circuits, as well as performative and financial status in the Kuchipudi village. As the most talented dancer in the performance practices that are the hallmark of the Kuchipudi brahmin male tradition, Satyanarayana Sarma wields performative power onstage. As the recipient of significant financial wealth from his nationally recognized dance skills, he exhibits financial and social power offstage. During my walks through the village, it was difficult to overlook Satyanarayana Sarma's towering multistoried home, which was extensively renovated before his death in 2012 (see below). There are several pieces of property in the Kuchipudi village in his name, including his house near the Ramalingeshvara temple, as well as buildings opposite the Siddhendra Kalakshetra (see Map 2 in the introduction). Satyanarayana Sarma's class status differs starkly from many of his counterparts in the village, who live by more modest means.

On November 17, 2012, Vedantam Satyanarayana Sarma passed away from a lung infection, and his death invoked mourning in the global Kuchipudi community. While he was an acclaimed Kuchipudi impersonator, Satyanarayana Sarma was not readily willing to impart the secret of his skills to the next generation of dancers. Despite the fact that all Kuchipudi brahmin men are bound by the vow of donning the *strī-vēṣam,* only a select handful are successful at doing so, and even fewer are capable of imparting their skills to future generations. By leaving no one to carry forth his legacy, Satyanarayana Sarma retains his place as the most acclaimed Kuchipudi impersonator of the present day even after his death. As evident in the title of the 2012 documentary *I am Satyabhama,* Satyanarayana Sarma is, and perhaps will always be, Satyabhama.

APPROXIMATING THE NORM: FAILURES OF IMPERSONATION

Following in the footsteps of Vedantam Satyanarayana Sarma has proven to be a difficult task for the younger generation of village brahmins, particularly because the legendary dancer himself, as mentioned above, was reluctant to part with the secrets of his skills and trained only a handful of students through the course of his career. One dancer who has surmounted these odds and made a name for himself as an impersonator is Vedantam Venkata Naga Chalapathi Rao (aka Venku), described in the opening vignette of this chapter. Trained by his father Vedantam Rattayya Sarma and village guru Pasumarti Rattayya Sarma, Venku is a talented artist known for enacting both female and male roles. Like Satyanarayana Sarma, Venku has received national recognition for his performance skills and was the 2006 recipient of the prestigious Sangeet Natak Akademi's Bismillah Khan Yuva Puraskar Award. However, unlike his more famous predecessor, Venku's practices of impersonation have been subject to critique. For example, after Venku's performance of Satyabhama at the University of Hyderabad described and depicted earlier in this chapter, a few scholars and dance critics remarked that Venku's performance, albeit impressive, was too "masculine." I was surprised by these observations, especially given the enthusiasm of the audience around me when watching the performance. In her review of the performance for the arts magazine *Nartanam,* dance critic Madhavi Puranam (2011b, 83) underscored this sentiment:

> The Bhamakalapam performance in the classical Kuchipudi tradition by Vedantam Venkatanagachalapati Rao was neat and virtuous but the dancer could not attain finesse in impersonating Satyabhama, as he veered to more masculine mannerisms, exaggerated vigorous footwork and torso movements in dance playing to the gallery.

When I relayed some of these impressions to Venku in the days following the performance, he insightfully remarked that when enacting Satyabhama, he was not attempting to replicate the expressive techniques of Satyanarayana Sarma, but rather trying to do something different and, therefore, should not be limited to the boundaries of his legendary predecessor. Venku also stated that he was performing *Bhāmākalāpam* in the style (*bāṇi*) of his guru Pasumarti Rattayya Sarma, which requires more vigorous foot movements in comparison to the style usually performed by Satyanarayana Sarma.

While Venku may not have been trying to replicate Satyanarayana Sarma's practices of impersonation, it is clear that some members of the audience, particularly those familiar with Kuchipudi dance, expected him to do so. By incorporating ostensibly "masculine" (i.e., vigorous) footwork into his performance of *Bhāmākalāpam,* Venku departed from the impersonation techniques established by Satyanarayana Sarma. Venku's enactment of Satyabhama resonates with the failed performance of the oral epic *Candaini* as discussed by Joyce Flueckiger (1988). When analyzing a regional performance of *Candaini* in the Chhattisgarh town of Dhamtari, Flueckiger describes how the lead performer Devlal failed to meet audience expectations, resulting in a mass exodus of audience members halfway through the performance. Audience members later attributed the failure in performance to Devlal's lack of *vēṣam* on stage: "He should have worn a sari" (163).[22] Failure, nonetheless, can still tell us something valuable about the performance context, and according to Flueckiger: "analysis of the 'failure' reveals an innovative, nontraditional performance setting that elicited contradictory expectations on the part of the performers, patrons, and various groups within the audience—expectations which could not all be fulfilled" (159). Similar to Devlal's failed performance of *Candaini,* the critiques of Venku in *strī-vēṣam* reveal the underlying expectations of the Kuchipudi community: in order to enact Satyabhama successfully, one must replicate the performance style of Vedantam Satyanarayana Sarma. In other words, when donning the *strī-vēṣam,* the Kuchipudi brahmin man must successfully impersonate Satyanarayana Sarma impersonating Satyabhama. Venku's failure to impersonate Satyabhama in the manner of his famous predecessor thus positions Satyanarayana Sarma as the ideal impersonator of the Kuchipudi village, one who is ultimately impossible for any other performer to emulate.

Male dancers from the Kuchipudi village are not the only ones incapable of following in Satyanarayana Sarma's footsteps. Female Kuchipudi dancers from outside the Kuchipudi village also fail to approximate Satyanarayana Sarma's standard of impersonation. Dance scholar Jivan Pani (1977, 38) underscores this point:

> Leave aside [Satyanarayana Sarma's] exquisite dance-movements, if he merely walks on the stage as Satyabhama, the sensuousness, delicacy and grace of gait delight the eyes and remains as an experience for life. There are now many female *Kuchipudi* dancers. None equals [Satyanarayana Sarma]; at least the many I have seen. At best they appear to be imitating him. Does he imitate any particular woman? Perhaps none except Satyabhama, who is not an historical person, but a myth; a symbol.

Satyanarayana Sarma thus outperforms female dancers who find themselves in the position of imitating the impersonator to perform Satyabhama, a character whose name literally translates as "True Woman."

Paradoxically, Satyanarayana Sarma himself could never fully embody the norm he created. While he continued to impersonate well into his sixties and seventies, these later performances failed to capture audiences' attention in the manner of those staged during the height of his career.[23] The lasting impression of Satyanarayana Sarma's skills in donning the *strī-vēṣam,* however, remained, and he continued to be invited to impersonate both within and outside the Kuchipudi village, despite the availability of younger impersonators such as Venku.[24] Satyanarayana Sarma's death in 2012 entrenched his authoritative status in the Kuchipudi village and rendered true the claim that "gender norms are finally phantasmatic, impossible to embody" (Butler [1990] 2008, 192). Even after his death, Satyanarayana Sarma continues to be the norm for impersonating Satyabhama, thereby positioning him as the embodiment of hegemonic masculinity for the Kuchipudi village.

HEGEMONIC MASCULINITIES: A LOCAL APPROACH

Raewyn Connell, one of the pioneering scholars of masculinity studies, defines the term "hegemonic masculinity" as the form of masculinity that legitimates hierarchal relations between men and women, between masculinity and femininity, and among various forms of masculinities (1987, 183–90).[25] In response to later challenges to this theory, Connell and her colleague James W. Messerschmidt (2005, 849) call for an expansion of the notion of hegemonic masculinity to account for outstanding gaps, including recognizing the plural geographies shaped by three organizing locations: (1) local (constructed in arenas involving face-to-face interactions of families, organizations, and immediate communities); (2) regional (constructed at the level of culture or nation-state); and (3) global (constructed in transnational arenas involving transnational world politics, business, and media).[26] Multiple, interlinking, and even conflicting forms of hegemonic masculinities exist across all three levels, countering the assumption of a hierarchal flow of power from global to regional to local.

Connell and Messerschmidt's distinctions of hegemonic masculinities are important for highlighting the nuance of masculinities and power across spatial locations. However, we must be wary of conflating hegemonic masculinity with global conceptions of hypermasculinity or machismo. In his discussion of South Asian American basketball leagues, Stanley I. Thangaraj (2015, 14) describes the call to "man up" and "be a beast" on the American basketball court, where "'manning up' is a process of engaging with mainstream dictates of masculinities mixed in with South Asian American experiences of emasculation." Masculinity conveyed through toned musculature and athletic skill on the basketball court characterizes the process of "manning up" for Thangaraj's South Asian American interlocutors (14). In a similar vein, Jasbir Puar (2007, 181) describes the dialectal images of the turbaned Sikh man in the American diaspora: "the turbaned man is the warrior leader of the community, the violent patriarch, and at the same time, the long-haired feminized sissy, a figure of failed masculinity in contrast to (white) hegemonic masculinities."[27] The range of South Asian American masculinities as expressing effeminacy, hypermasculinity, and even terror recapitulate Orientalist logics of colonial masculinities in South Asia, which alternate between effeminate and martial visions of masculinity (Sinha 1995).

The dialectical stereotypes of the hypermasculine terrorist versus the effeminate "model minority" limit the scope of hegemonic masculinity by eclipsing the everyday realities and flows of power for South Asian and South Asian American men. Marcia C. Inhorn (2012, 45) notes a similar limitation to the concept of hegemonic masculinity in her ethnographic study of infertility among Arab men:

> While the theory is designed to account for masculine relationality, as well as fluid and shifting power between men, its ethnographic applications often seem to reify specific masculinities as static manly types, which hold particular positions within a set social hierarchy. Namely, the pigeonholing of ethnographic participants as examples of "hegemonic" or "subordinated" males casts them as static subjects and serves to solidify the types themselves. This obscures the lived reality of different forms of masculinity as *ever-changing social strategies* enacted through practice. [Emphasis in original]

Inhorn addresses the limitations of hegemonic masculinity by introducing the concept of emergent masculinities, a term that points to the myriad processes that men must navigate when adapting to social changes in the world around them (60).

In the Kuchipudi village, hegemonic masculinity also takes on a uniquely local form. Village brahmin men are, for the most part, unconcerned with global (and primarily American) conceptions of hegemonic masculinity, as evident from the embodied techniques of impersonation surveyed in this chapter.[28] Instead of sporting muscular chests and bulging biceps, like the basketball players of Thangaraj's study, Kuchipudi brahmin men cultivate an ideal conception of womanhood through their male bodies. The threat of effeminacy becomes apparent only when impersonation moves from the village to urban and transnational spaces (see chapter 4). Within the context of the village, effeminacy is secondary to formulations of hegemonic masculinity achievable only through the donning of the *strī-vēṣam*. The myriad expressions of masculinity are also ever-changing, or *emergent* in the words of Inhorn (2012), particularly as the newer generation of impersonators inherit the mantle of their predecessors. In this vein, one can delineate hegemonic masculinity as achieved by Satyanarayana Sarma from the emergent forms of masculinity expressed by younger brahmin dancers. This latter group adheres to standards of what I refer to here as *normative masculinity*—the processual or emergent form of hegemonic masculinity that is never fully actualized. Constrained by norms of caste, gender, and community, younger brahmin men like Venku regulate their staged performances and quotidian practices through a standard of normative masculinity that is always in process but never fully hegemonic. Through their continuous attempts and failures in impersonation, Venku and his counterparts express the impossibility of hegemonic masculinity, thus foreshadowing the concept of constructed artifice (*māyā*) discussed in the next chapter.

To understand the formulations of hegemonic masculinity, it is useful to outline three overarching norms of gender and caste in the Kuchipudi village, underscored here in italics. At the most basic level, impersonation is a normative practice in the Kuchipudi village: *the norm in the Kuchipudi village is to see the brahmin male body performing a woman's guise.* Moreover, because all brahmin men from the Kuchipudi village are bound by the prescriptive code of donning Satyabhama's guise, this portrayal works to create their normative gender and caste identities. In other words, *to achieve hegemonic masculinity in the Kuchipudi village, a brahmin man must impersonate.* Impersonation onstage spills into personation offstage as Kuchipudi brahmin men don a woman's guise in the context of performance in order to articulate their gender and caste status in everyday life (Mankekar 2015).

The norms of Kuchipudi village performance, however, do not affect brahmin male performers alone. As evidenced by the embodied techniques of impersonation—costume (*āhārya*), speech (*vācika*), and gait (*āṅgika*)—Kuchipudi impersonators observe women's bodies in their everyday lives and alter their physical appearance to approximate an idealized image of womanhood onstage. The underlying paradox of these embodied practices is that while Kuchipudi brahmin men can impersonate "real" women onstage, Kuchipudi brahmin women are excluded from performance altogether. Kuchipudi female dancers outside the village who have begun to dance in recent decades are also deemed incomparable to Satyanarayana Sarma's stalwart skills of gender guising (Pani 1977). The practice of impersonation in the Kuchipudi village stands in contrast to the ritual guising practices of the Gangamma *jātara,* in which ultimate reality is envisioned as female through the ritual *vēṣams* of the goddess (Handelman 1995; Flueckiger 2013). In comparison to the Gangamma *jātara*, which puts forth a female-centered world and challenges aggressive masculinity (Flueckiger 2013, 73), brahmin masculinity constructed through impersonation in the Kuchipudi village produces the ultimate form of authority.

This leads to the final and perhaps most significant norm of the Kuchipudi village: *Kuchipudi brahmin men assert that they can perform a woman's guise better than women themselves* (Hansen 1999, 140). This norm suggests that impersonation is not simply a performance tradition, but also a practice of power that shapes the gender and caste identities of the brahmin men *and* women of the village. By donning Satyabhama's guise to fulfill the prescription made by their founding saint, Kuchipudi brahmin men approximate their gender and caste norms in order to assert their power as the "cultural brokers" (Hancock 1999, 64) of Kuchipudi tradition (*sāmpradāyam*).

Impersonation is an authoritative practice of exclusion that lays the groundwork for hegemonic masculinity: to be a Kuchipudi brahmin man, one must impersonate, and, conversely, to impersonate, one must be a Kuchipudi brahmin man. The paradigmatic example of hegemonic masculinity is Vedantam Satyanarayana Sarma, a brahmin man with performative authority onstage and class status offstage. Satyanarayana Sarma epitomizes Connell's (1987, 183–90) earlier definition of hegemonic masculinity, which legitimates hierarchal relations between men and women, between masculinity and femininity, and among various forms of masculinities. When Satyanarayana Sarma becomes Satyabhama, he is not simply donning a woman's guise, but also asserting his authority to do so. For Satyanarayana Sarma, the line "I am Satyabhama" in Satyabhama's introductory song is a performative utterance of power that articulates the contours of hegemonic masculinity in both performative and quotidian contexts. However, with the death of Satyanarayana Sarma and the rise of a younger generation of performers like Venku, the ideal of hegemonic masculinity in the Kuchipudi village is increasingly reframed and perhaps ultimately unachievable. As I explore in the chapters to come, hegemonic brahmin masculinity unravels entirely the farther away we move from the village's exclusive brahmin community.

. . .

The brahmin enclave of the Kuchipudi village is not simply a cluster of upper-caste homes situated along unpaved streets, but also an imaginative space in which gender, caste, and performance intersect to create normative ideals for Kuchipudi brahmin men. In her research on colonial conceptions of brahmin masculinity, Mrinalini Sinha (1995, 11) draws attention to the intersections of caste and gender by suggesting that "since the experience of gender itself is deeply implicated in other categories such as caste/class, race, nation, and sexuality, an exclusive focus on gender can never be adequate for a feminist historiography."[29] This chapter builds upon Sinha's attention to gender within a broader matrix of categories such as class and caste by analyzing not only the corporeal theatrics of brahmin male performance, but also how gender and caste norms are constructed and reimagined through the body of the impersonator.

The practice of impersonation is crucial for understanding the construction of hegemonic brahmin masculinity in the Kuchipudi village. By wearing elaborate costumes or modulating the pitch of their voices, Kuchipudi brahmin men are not simply donning Satyabhama's *strī-vēṣam,* they are also articulating their gender and caste identities by fulfilling the vow made to their founding saint Siddhendra. The class and caste status of brahmin male dancers such as Vedantam Satyanarayana Sarma reveal the integral role of impersonation in the fabric of Kuchipudi village life. The case of Satyanarayana Sarma also illustrates the technologies of power of the Kuchipudi village, in which the embodied practices of a single brahmin impersonator create and sustain norms of gender, caste, and community. Yet, failures in impersonation define the limits of hegemonic masculinity and enable us to delineate normative masculinity as emergent, always in process but never fully complete. As this chapter demonstrates, gender impersonation in the Kuchipudi village is *not* gender trouble (Butler [1990] 2008); rather, gender impersonation is the means by which brahmin men exert power and craft hegemonic masculinity onstage and in their everyday lives.

3

Constructing Artifice, Interrogating Impersonation

Madhavi as Vidūṣaka *in Village* Bhāmākalāpam *Performance*

Satyabhama:	Dear Madhavi, a woman's life is a terrible life!
Madhavi:	What's that? A woman's life is the only life. You can wear necklaces and you can wear jewels. You can walk forward and you can walk backwards. You can say, "Oh!" and you can say "Ah!" A woman's life is the *only* life!
Satyabhama:	You think a woman's life is only about wearing necklaces and jewels?
Madhavi:	What's a woman's life to you?
Satyabhama:	A woman's life is like a tender banana leaf.
Madhavi:	Okay, but what's a man's life?
Satyabhama:	A harsh thorn!
Madhavi:	Well said! A man's life is like a harsh thorn. But what's the connection between the two?
Satyabhama:	If the banana leaf falls on the thorn, or if the thorn falls on the banana leaf, the leaf gets torn. Either way, it's bad for the leaf.
Madhavi:	Okay, if the banana leaf falls on the thorn, or the thorn falls on the banana leaf, the leaf gets torn. Can I ask you something else? If a *laḍḍu* [round sweetmeat] falls into ghee [clarified butter], or ghee falls on a *laḍḍu,* when both end up in my stomach, is it bad for me?

On the evening of January 20, 2011, the packed audience in the D.S.T. Auditorium at the University of Hyderabad erupted into laughter upon hearing this dialogue between Satyabhama and her confidante Madhavi, the primary characters of the *Bhāmākalāpam* dance drama. This humorous exchange, in which Satyabhama describes the terrible state of a woman's life and Madhavi pokes fun at her responses, is paradigmatic of Madhavi's role within *Bhāmākalāpam*. As Satyabhama's female confidante and primary conversation partner, Madhavi is not simply a patiently listening *sakhi* (girlfriend), but rather the dance drama's *vidūṣaka* (clown), whose witty remarks parody Satyabhama's angst of separation from her husband.

Madhavi's comedic role, however, extends beyond verbal jest to sartorial presentation. As discussed in the previous chapter, the Kuchipudi impersonator who portrays Satyabhama takes great pains to perform an idealized understanding of "real" women's bodies through elaborate sartorial guising, voice modulation, and bodily movement. In comparison, the brahmin male dancer portraying Madhavi does not impersonate a woman in the same manner. Instead, the performer triangulates across three distinct roles through the course of a single performance: the *sūtradhāra* (the director-cum-narrator of the dance drama), Madhavi (the female confidante of Satyabhama), and Madhava (the male confidant of Krishna). The male performer who plays these three characters—the *sūtradhāra*, Madhavi, and Madhava—does so with no shifts in costume, voice modulation, or gait. Instead, he transforms his character through subtler cues, such as the utterance of a single vocative or moving to a specific side of the stage. Unlike the case of Satyabhama, the brahmin man becomes the female character of Madhavi without the practice of sartorial guising.

This chapter and the next center on performance analysis of the *Bhāmākalāpam* dance drama, particularly focusing on the *sūtradhāra*, Madhavi, and Madhava. Drawing on the work of scholars of Indian theatre, including David Shulman (1985), Susan Seizer (2005), and Richard Schechner (2015) among others, this chapter provides detailed accounts of the dialogues and performance techniques of *Bhāmākalāpam*. The theoretical centerpiece of the chapter rests on reimagining the term *māyā*, commonly translated into English as "illusion." According to contemporary teachers and dancers within the village of Kuchipudi, it is through *māyā* that a single performer can become the *sūtradhāra* when speaking to the audience, Madhavi when seen through the eyes of Satyabhama, and Madhava when seen by Krishna. Drawing on the interpretations of my interlocutors, I translate *māyā* as "constructed artifice" to theorize the parodic gender enactments of *sūtradhāra*/Madhavi/Madhava in *Bhāmākalāpam* performance. Through the lens of constructed artifice, I analyze how Madhavi, a character serving the dual roles of friend (*sakhi*) and *vidūṣaka* (clown), interrogates both Satyabhama's gender portrayal onstage and the brahmin male body donning her *strī-vēṣam*.

THE *SŪTRADHĀRA* IN *BHĀMĀKALĀPAM* PERFORMANCE

In contemporary performances of *Bhāmākalāpam* by hereditary brahmin dancers from the village, the *sūtradhāra* is the first character who audiences meet. Standing at the center of the stage, he calls for the audience's attention as a prelude to the start of the performance:

> Listen, assembled people! Listen to this story of *Bhāmākalāpam,* which will be a delight and fill your ears with a nectar of sounds. This is a composition of the great Siddhendra. We will present it now. Please enjoy.[1]

The *sūtradhāra* (lit., "one who holds the strings") traditionally leads the supporting orchestra by playing the *naṭṭuvāṅgam* (cymbals) and directs the audience's attention by narrating key events in the drama. While the *sūtradhāra* exists in Sanskrit drama and is referenced in the *Nāṭyaśāstra,* the character develops regional subtleties in various folk theatrical forms (Varadpande 1992).[2] In the case of *Bhāmākalāpam,* the *sūtradhāra* is visually portrayed as a brahmin through distinctive markers in dress. Importantly, the *sūtradhāra* functions as a catchall character who transforms into the female Madhavi when speaking with Satyabhama and into the male Madhava when speaking with Krishna. While potentially confusing to the untrained eye, the *sūtradhāra*'s seamless ability to transform into Madhavi and Madhava is a convention understood by Telugu-speaking audiences, particularly from the village of Kuchipudi.[3]

This convention also extends to other South Indian performance traditions, namely Kutiyattam, in which the method of *pakarnaṭṭam* (lit., "acting with shifting roles") allows "an actor to impersonate multiple roles in a dramatic situation without any change in makeup and costume" (Gopalakrishnan 2006, 141). These shifts in multiple roles can extend across gender boundaries; for example, an actor portraying Hanuman can also enact Sita and other roles in Kutiyattam drama to convey the story of the Hindu epic *Rāmāyaṇa* (141). In the case of *Bhāmākalāpam,* the *sūtradhāra* (director/narrator) enacts the roles of Madhavi, Satyabhama's *sakhi* who is also the drama's *vidūṣaka* (clown), and Madhava, Krishna's male confidant (*sakha*).

How does the *sūtradhāra*'s transformation happen, and how are audiences able to understand it? In this section, I highlight specific sequences in the *Bhāmākalāpam* dance drama to analyze the ways in which a single brahmin male performer transitions across these three distinct roles. I draw primarily on the *Bhāmākalāpam* performance staged as part of the International Symposium on *Kalāpa* Traditions at the University of Hyderabad in January 2011, in which Vedantam Venkata Naga Chalapathi Rao played Satyabhama and Chinta Ravi Balakrishna played *sūtradhāra*/Madhavi/Madhava. As a point of comparison, I also reference a recording of the *Bhāmākalāpam* performance at the annual

FIGURE 12. Chinta Ravi Balakrishna as the *sūtradhāra*. Photo by author.

Siddhendra Mahotsav festival staged in the Kuchipudi village in March 2006, in which Vedantam Satyanarayana Sarma played Satyabhama and Chinta Ravi Balakrishna played *sūtradhāra*/Madhavi/Madhava.[4] All the performers I discuss in this chapter are hereditary brahmin men from the Kuchipudi village.

THE *SŪTRADHĀRA* BECOMES MADHAVI

The *Bhāmākalāpam* performance at the International Symposium on *Kalāpa* Traditions opens with the sole figure of the *sūtradhāra*, who stands center stage and calls the audience to attention by announcing the commencement of *Bhāmākalāpam*, specifically Satyabhama's entrance (see Figure 12). Once Satyabhama enters onstage and begins her introductory song (*pravēśa daruvu*), the *sūtradhāra* moves to stage right to sit with the orchestra and play the *naṭṭuvāṅgam* (cymbals). Upon completion of Satyabhama's *pravēśa daruvu*, the *sūtradhāra* gets up from his seated position in the orchestra and comes again to the center of the stage, but this time as the female character Madhavi. Upon seeing Madhavi, Satyabhama beseeches her friend, calling out to her with vocative titles such as *kundara-dana* (woman with teeth as white as jasmines), *sarōjānana* (woman with a face like a lotus), *takkaka-māyalāḍi* (woman who is clever), and *nīrēja-patrēkṣana* (woman with eyes like lotus petals). By calling out to her friend using these vocatives, Satyabhama establishes the gender identity of her companion to the audience (see Figure 13).

FIGURE 13. Satyabhama (right) addressing Madhavi (left). Photo by author.

Satyabhama then questions her confidante as to the whereabouts of her husband, but Madhavi feigns ignorance as to Krishna's identity. Satyabhama, too shy to speak her husband's name in public, avoids naming Krishna directly and, instead, refers to him as *śaṅkhamu-dharincina-vaṇṭivāḍu* (one who holds the conch), *cakramu-dharincina-vaṇṭivāḍu* (one who bears the discus), and *makara-kundanamulu-dharincina-vaṇṭivāḍu* (one who wears earrings shaped like crocodiles). Madhavi cleverly pokes fun at each one of her friend's responses by suggesting that the descriptions of the conch, discus, and earrings indicate a caste status different from Krishna, who belongs to a *jāti* (caste) of cow-herders.

Satyabhama then attempts to identify her husband as the person in between her elder and younger brothers-in-law. A quick gender shift occurs in this part of the conversation as Madhavi briefly switches back to the role of the *sūtradhāra* by addressing a supporting member of the orchestra and asking if he knows the identity of Satyabhama's husband. The switch from Madhavi to the *sūtradhāra* was most clear in the March 2006 *Bhāmākalāpam* performance staged in the Kuchipudi village. In the dialogue regarding the identity of Satyabhama's husband, the male dancer enacting the dual roles of *sūtradhāra*/Madhavi simultaneously converses with Satyabhama and the orchestra. The shifts in their conversation proceed as follows:

Satyabhama:	My husband is in the space (*sandhi*) between my elder brother-in-law and my younger brother-in-law.
Sūtradhāra/Madhavi:	[*Addressing Satyabhama as Madhavi*]: In the space between your elder brother-in-law and younger brother-in-law?
	[*Addressing the orchestra as the* sūtradhāra]: Hey, Sastry Garu![5] Do you know what this space is?
Orchestra Member:	Please tell me.
Sūtradhāra/Madhavi:	[*Addressing the orchestra as the* sūtradhāra]: In this village, there's the Pasumarti space. There's the Bhagavatula space. There's the Darbha space.[6] So what's this space between her elder and younger brothers-in-law that she's talking about? You don't get it, do you?
	[*Satyabhama exits the stage*].
Orchestra Member:	No, I don't.
Sūtradhāra/Madhavi:	[*Addressing the orchestra as the* sūtradhāra]: I'll tell you. Her elder brother-in-law is Balarama.
Orchestra Member:	Oh ho!
Sūtradhāra/Madhavi:	[*Addressing the orchestra as the* sūtradhāra]: Her younger one is Satyaki.
Orchestra Member:	Aha!
	[*Satyabhama re-enters onstage*].
Sūtradhāra/Madhavi:	[*Addressing the orchestra as the* sūtradhāra]: Her husband is the one in between these two. He's not too tall. He is not too short. He's not too fat. He's not too skinny. He's very dark like a black plum.
	[*Addressing Satyabhama as Madhavi*]: What do *you* want with him?

During this conversation between the *sūtradhāra* and the orchestra, Satyabhama exits the stage briefly, which clearly signals that the onstage discussion is between the male *sūtradhāra* and a male member of the orchestra, not between the female Madhavi and the orchestra. These humorous asides between the *sūtradhāra* and the orchestra are similar to direct addresses found in Tamil Special Drama (Seizer 2005) and Shakespearean theatre (Cohen 2016).[7] By shifting the conversation toward the orchestra and away from Satyabhama, the male Kuchipudi performer transforms his character from the female Madhavi into the male *sūtradhāra* by speaking to the male orchestra member.

The humorous nature of the conversation is carried forth in later dialogues between Satyabhama and Madhavi. When Satyabhama requests that her friend go in search of Krishna, Madhavi insists that Satyabhama must give her something for her efforts. This evolves into an elaborate conversation regarding Satyabhama's jewels, a section of the dance drama commonly referred to as *sommulapaṭṭu:*

Satyabhama: What do you want me to give you?

Madhavi: Tell me what you have.

Satyabhama: I've got jewels for every day of the week.

Madhavi: So you've got jewels for every day of the week, do you? I also have jewels in my house.

Satyabhama: Oyamma Madhavi, having jewels for every day of the week means that I have one entire jewelry box for each and every day.

Madhavi: So you've got seven boxes? Should I tell you the boxes I have in my house? I have a box for black lentils. A box for yellow lentils. A box for salt. A box for tamarind. A box for cumin. I even have a pantry box to put all those boxes in! Since you have jewels for every day of the week, then give me your Sunday jewels and I'll be happy.

Satyabhama: Hari, Hari, Hari, Hari! My Sunday jewels are dedicated to the sun god.

Madhavi: Shiva, Shiva, Shiva, Shiva! Isn't your husband sitting around with his other wife Rukmini?

Satyabhama: Oyamma Madhavi, she's not letting him come, is she?

Madhavi: So I'll go and bring him. Just give me what I ask.

Satyabhama: I'll give you whatever you want if you bring my husband. Please go and bring him. [*Musical interlude*].

Madhavi: Oyamma Satyabhama! You've given me your Sunday jewels, but there's one more piece of jewelry that I want.

Satyabhama: What's that?

Madhavi: I don't remember the name of it, but I can tell you its shape. Look here, it looks like this. [*Displays index finger in the shape of a hook*].

Satyabhama: [*Looking puzzled*]: Oh ho! Is it tamarind?

Madhavi: What? I said it was a piece of jewelry! What do I want with a pregnancy craving like tamarind at this age? Look at it again. [*Displays index finger in the shape of a hook*] . . .

Satyabhama: Is it my golden belt?

Madhavi: Do you think your belt will fit me? That's not it. It's like this. [*Displays index finger in the shape of a hook*] . . .

Satyabhama: Is it my sun and moon hair ornaments?

Madhavi:	What do I need with sun and moon hair ornaments? I see the sun and moon every day when I get up and go to sleep. There's no roof on my house so I can pray to the sun and moon whenever I want. That's not it!
Satyabhama:	Is it my earrings?
Madhavi:	No, that's not it. It's right next to those. Just right next to those.
Satyabhama:	Is it my anklets?
Madhavi:	What? You went from your head to your foot! I said it looks just like this. [*Displays index finger in the shape of a hook*]. It's right next to your earrings.
Satyabhama:	Is it my nose stud?
Madhavi:	Good, at last you've come to the right place. It's right next to that.
Satyabhama:	[*Shocked*]. Is it my nose ring? I can't give you that![8]

In this dialogue, Madhavi playfully puns on Satyabhama's words by transforming boxes of jewelry into boxes of lentils, and sun- and moon-shaped hair ornaments into the rising sun and moon, which, as Madhavi states, are visible from her roofless house. This dialogue not only makes evident Madhavi's comedic role, but also establishes her gender and class status. While Satyabhama is a woman with boxes of jewels, Madhavi is a woman with boxes of grain. In positioning her class status as inferior to Satyabhama's, Madhavi uses this dialogue to poke fun at Satyabhama's endless riches, which are thought to arise from her possession of the wealth-giving *syamantaka* gem. Madhavi's specific request for Satyabhama's nose ring, however, takes on further significance, as this particular ornament is indicative of her identity as an auspicious married woman. In asking for her nose ring, Madhavi paradoxically forces Satyabhama to abandon all the ornamental signifiers of her identity as a married woman in exchange for her husband's return. Satyabhama reluctantly agrees and then writes a letter pleading for her husband's quick return; she asks Madhavi to journey to Krishna's palace and deliver the letter, thereby concluding the first and longest scene of the *Bhāmākalāpam* dance drama.

THE INTRODUCTION OF MADHAVA

The delivery of Satyabhama's letter marks a change in scenes in *Bhāmākalāpam* from Satyabhama's abode to the palace of Krishna. After both Satyabhama and Madhavi exit the stage, Krishna enters and introduces himself in his *pravēśa daruvu*. The performer who enacts the roles of the *sūtradhāra* and Madhavi then reenters the stage, but this time as the character of Madhava, the confidant of Krishna. Madhava comes to the center of the stage and calls out to Krishna:

Salutations to the one who is the entire universe.
Salutations to Hari whose eyes are like lotus petals.

Salutations to the one who is the source of all compassion.
Salutations to you, Krishna!

Madhava then prostrates completely on the ground in a sign of respect to Krishna. The act of full prostration, typically performed by men in the Indian context, signals to the audience the gender shift of this character from Madhavi to Madhava, that is, from female character to male character. This gender shift is further established in the following dialogue, in which Krishna explicitly addresses the character as "Madhava," the male equivalent of the name "Madhavi."[9] The dialogue between Krishna and Madhava from the 2011 *Bhāmākalāpam* performance proceeds as follows:

Krishna: Hey, Madhava! How are you?

Madhava: I'm fine.

Krishna: How's Satyabhama?

Madhava: Since the day that you abandoned Satyabhama, sitting on her cot made of swan feathers, she's stopped eating and drinking altogether. She's eating her clothes and dressing herself in food.

Krishna: What?

Madhava: Forgive me! My mind is distracted since seeing you. Satyabhama has stopped eating and drinking altogether. She's become so thin that she's wearing her waist belt as a ring on her finger.

Krishna: [*Looking surprised*]: Madhava, has Satyabhama become that fat?

Madhava: [*Realizing his mistake*]: Forgive me! She's stopped eating and drinking. She's become so thin that she is wearing her ring as a belt around her waist. You can read all of her troubles in this letter. [*Hands the letter to Krishna*].

Akin to the character of Madhavi, Madhava's role serves a comedic purpose in the *Bhāmākalāpam* dance drama. The clearest example of such humor is when Madhava suggests that Satyabhama has gained so much weight as a result of her separation from Krishna that she is now wearing her waist belt as a ring on her finger. According to Indian literary convention, a woman's waist should be so thin it is unseen between her large breasts and curving hips (Dehejia 2009, 30). Madhava creatively flips this idealized image by envisioning Satyabhama as a woman who is so large that she wears her belt as a ring on her finger and not the other way around. Notably, Madhava is careful in this conversation to poke fun only at Satyabhama and never direct his jokes toward Krishna; Madhavi and Madhava thus both engage in humorous exchanges but only at Satyabhama's expense.

After reading the letter, Krishna and Madhava journey back to Satyabhama's palace for the third and final scene, in which the three characters—the *sūtradhāra*, Madhavi, and Madhava—all appear onstage together. When entering Satyabhama's palace, Madhava transforms back into Madhavi and notifies Satyabhama of Krishna's arrival. Then the characters (Madhavi and Madhava) attempt to mediate between Satyabhama and Krishna, who are positioned at opposite ends of the stage and initially avoid speaking to each other. In this mediation, the performer goes to stage left to address Satyabhama as her female confidante Madhavi, and then moves to stage right to speak to Krishna as his male confidant Madhava.

In the context of Tamil Special Drama, Susan Seizer (2005, 208) maps out a complex system of spatial organization in the scene of the buffoon's duet with a teenage girl dancing on the road. Specific parts of the stage are gender-coded in this scene, with downstage left being exclusively used by the male buffoon and downstage right being the place where the dancing girl is confined (222). This gendering of space is equally present in *Bhāmākalāpam* in which spatial movement and proximity to the lead character (either Satyabhama or Krishna) signals a gender shift from Madhavi to Madhava. When the two lead characters finally come together, the male *sūtradhāra* reappears and sits down with the orchestra on stage right to play the *naṭṭuvāṅgam.*

Then, at center stage, Satyabhama and Krishna engage in a lover's quarrel, in which Satyabhama angrily accuses her husband of flirtatious behavior, and Krishna attempts to defend himself. During this exchange, the *sūtradhāra* continues to play the *naṭṭuvāṅgam* with the orchestra. When Satyabhama tries to hit Krishna with her braid, the *sūtradhāra* gets up from his seated position in the orchestra and transforms back into Madhavi. Pulling Satyabhama aside, Madhavi questions Satyabhama's pride and underscores Krishna's divine status. Satyabhama finally repents of her anger and asks Madhavi to bring golden flowers so that she can pray at the feet of her husband. The *Bhāmākalāpam* dance drama ends with Satyabhama and Madhavi offering flowers at Krishna's feet (see Figure 14).

MADHAVI'S *MĀYĀ*: PRACTITIONER ACCOUNTS OF *SŪTRADHĀRA*/MADHAVI/MADHAVA

In an attempt to understand the gender shifts of the characters *sūtradhāra*/Madhavi/Madhava, I asked my interlocutors in the Kuchipudi village a simple question: Is Madhavi a female character or a male one? I found that this single question, more than any other, generated the most discussion among the performers and teachers I interviewed. Among the many answers I received, the most evocative responses regarding this question were given by individuals known for their performances in the roles of *sūtradhāra*/Madhavi/Madhava, namely senior gurus Pasumarti Rattayya Sarma and Pasumarti Venugopala Krishna Sarma, as well as rising Kuchipudi performer Chinta Ravi Balakrishna. All three Kuchipudi performers attributed Madhavi's gender shifts to the Indian philosophical concept of *māyā,* commonly translated into English as illusion.

FIGURE 14. Madhavi and Satyabhama offer flowers to Krishna (performed by Yeleswarapu Srinivas). Photo by author.

The first person to raise the concept of *māyā* to me was Pasumarti Rattayya Sarma, a senior guru from the village who has played the character of Madhavi opposite seasoned artists such as Satyanarayana Sarma, as well as younger performers such as Venku (see chapter 2). According to Rattayya Sarma, *māyā* explains how a single performer can be the *sūtradhāra* when speaking to the audience and orchestra, Madhavi when seen through the eyes of Satyabhama, and Madhava when seen by Krishna. Rattayya Sarma states:

> Do you know this character of Madhavi? She's a kind of *māyā*. What is *māyā?* This *māyā* is what Krishna has sent. When she comes near Satyabhama, she actually appears like a woman. But when she goes to Krishna, she becomes Madhava. The difference is clear. This is unique to Kuchipudi and is not found elsewhere. If Satyabhama sees her, she says, "Oyamma Madhavi."
>
> The person who does this role is very pure. He is very powerful. He appears like a woman to Satyabhama. That is his talent. It's a gift from god. And when he goes near Krishna, he becomes Madhava. There he appears as a man and here he appears as a woman. For the people who are watching, he appears as the *sūtradhāra.*

For Rattayya Sarma, *māyā* underlies the transformative gender capabilities of *sūtradhāra*/Madhavi/Madhava, a trait bestowed by Krishna, god himself.

Similar to Rattayya Sarma's observations regarding *māyā* are the sentiments of Pasumarti Venugopala Krishna Sarma (commonly referred to as P.V.G. Krishna

Sarma), a senior guru from Kuchipudi famous for portraying the roles of *sūtradhāra*/Madhavi/Madhava. Krishna Sarma is a disciple of the late Chinta Krishna Murthy, the most well-known *sūtradhāra* in recent Kuchipudi memory, and has played opposite Satyanarayana Sarma in many performances prior to his retirement from the stage. Krishna Sarma also raises *māyā* when discussing Madhavi's character:

> For the *paramātma* [divine soul] of Krishna, Madhavi is a manifestation of *māyā*. She is teasing Satyabhama. It's *māyāvaram* [the gift of *māyā*]. When you can win over Krishna with *bhakti* [devotion], why do you need Madhavi? She has to be there for the sake of the drama . . . Madhavi is *māyā*, right? Since Madhavi is *māyā*, she is actually testing Satyabhama to measure how much Krishna-*bhakti* she has. Like you put a measuring stick to measure petrol, that's how she's measuring. That character is *māyā*, and occasionally in the middle, she is teasing. She's Satyabhama's dearest friend, right? . . . That's how Madhavi's character is a manifestation of *māyā* and the *sūtradhāra*. The *sūtradhāra* has to be able to experience all of the characters' emotions.

Krishna Sarma emphasizes the devotional nature of Madhavi's *māyā* by depicting her character as a measuring stick used to measure the amount of Krishna-*bhakti* that Satyabhama has. Both Rattayya Sarma and Krishna Sarma situate *māyā* within a broader devotional discourse, in line with the Sanskritization of Indian dance (Coorlawala 2004). According to both dancers, the ability to transform genders is infused with religious significance. Krishna Sarma also highlights the humorous aspects of Madhavi's character by suggesting that her teasing is what drives the plot of *Bhāmākalāpam* forward.[10]

Chinta Ravi Balakrishna, a younger performer from the Kuchipudi village who usually portrays the roles of *sūtradhāra*/Madhavi/Madhava in contemporary performances of *Bhāmākalāpam*, mirrors the sentiments of Rattayya Sarma and Krishna Sarma by also raising the concept of *māyā*. For Ravi Balakrishna, the *māyā* of *Bhāmākalāpam* is an innovation of Siddhendra himself:

> [Siddhendra] created a story between Satyabhama and Krishna, and in the middle is *māyā*, which is Madhavi. He created the character of Madhavi . . . You might ask whether this character is a man or a woman. It is *māyā*. When she's near Satyabhama, she's Madhavi. When the character is near Krishna, he's Madhav[a]. When going near Satyabhama, she acts like a woman and tries to bring her closer to Krishna. And when she is near Krishna, she acts like a man and coaxes him by telling him, "Satyabhama's a young girl and doesn't know what she's doing." That's how Siddhendra created this character.

Ravi Balakrishna, like Rattayya Sarma and Krishna Sarma, employs *māyā* to justify the gender transformations of the characters *sūtradhāra*/Madhavi/Madhava. It is through the workings of *māyā* that this character becomes Madhavi when approaching Satyabhama and Madhava when going near Krishna.

The fact that all three performers skilled in enacting the roles of *sūtradhāra*/Madhavi/Madhava invoke the concept of *māyā* marks its significance. What is *māyā,* and why is it, opposed to any other Sanskrit term, raised in this context? Modern contemporary interpretations often confine *māyā* to the English term "illusion," but its evolution in Indian thought expands beyond such a limited definition. The concept of *māyā* is a philosophical category that expresses a range of connotations that span from magic to illusion to deception to creative power. In the Vedas, the earliest canonical Sanskrit texts, *māyā* connotes both positive aspects such as artistic power, marvelous skill, or wisdom, as well as negative aspects such as cunning or trickery (Doniger 1984, 117–18; Pintchman 1994, 88).[11] Later interpretations of *māyā,* namely the Indian philosophical school of Vedanta, interpret it as illusion (Radhakrishnan [1927] 2008, 418).[12]

More recently, performance studies scholar Richard Schechner (2015) forges a connection between *māyā* and the related Sanskrit term *līlā.* Drawing on Wendy Doniger's (1984) interpretations of *māyā* as the artistic power of creation, Schechner (2015, 134) connects *māyā* with the term *līlā,* which he defines as "a more ordinary word, meaning play, sport, or drama." For Schechner, the dual concept of *māyā-līlā* is a "theory of play and performance" (92) that can be used to understand *rām-līlā,* which are the annual enactments of Tulsidas's *Rāmcaritmānas* performed, among other places, in Ramnagar, the fort town across the river from Varanasi.[13] *Māyā-līlā,* as it appears in the context of *rām-līlā* in Ramnagar, is "the playful manifestation of the divine, an ongoing enactment of the convergence of religion and theatre" (81). The *māyā-līlā* of Ramnagar *rām-līlā*s, according to Schechner, bridges the mundane and the divine, as humans have the potential to transform into gods during the moment of performance.

My Kuchipudi interlocutors similarly forge a connection between *māyā* and performance. These dancers interpret *māyā* to mean illusion, more generally, likely alluding to popular interpretations of the term.[14] Rattayya Sarma and his counterparts in the village also draw on *māyā* to ground Kuchipudi dance within a religious framework similar to the employment of *jīvātma* (individual soul), *paramātma* (divine soul), and *bhakti* (devotion), as outlined in chapter 1. In comparison to these other Sanskrit terms, however, *māyā* is the only one that is invoked by Kuchipudi dancers to explain an explicitly gendered phenomenon. In fact, the malleability of *māyā* makes it particularly suitable for understanding the complex gender transformations of *sūtradhāra*/Madhavi/Madhava in *Bhāmākalāpam.* Although I am fully aware of the problematic attempts to Sanskritize Kuchipudi dance (Coorlawala 2004), I also take seriously the words that my interlocutors use to describe their dance, particularly when these dicourses focus on gender practices. Rather than entirely dismissing the views of Rattayya Sarma and his counterparts as another means of Sanskritizing and/or devotionalizing Kuchipudi, I believe that their invocation of *māyā* to explain the gender shifts of *Bhāmākalāpam* has theoretical possibility. The Kuchipudi performers are on to something when suggesting that gender can be read through the lens of *māyā*, a term that both means illusion and eludes any single definition. Given *māyā*'s hermeneutic potential, I will dedicate the remainder of this chapter to theorizing *māyā* as a lens for interpreting the artifice of gender in the *Bhāmākalāpam* dance drama.

CONSTRUCTING ARTIFICE, INTERROGATING IMPERSONATION

Drawing on the observations of Kuchipudi practitioners Rattayya Sarma, Krishna Sarma, and Ravi Balakrishna, as well as Schechner's (2015) interpretations of Ramnagar *rām-līlā* performance, I foreground *māyā* as a theoretical lens for interpreting brahmin masculinity, in particular, and gender performativity, more broadly, in Kuchipudi dance. To distinguish my use of *māyā* from its lengthy inherited history of Advaita Vedanta interpretations, I translate *māyā* not as illusion, but as "constructed artifice."[15] Envisioning *māyā* as constructed artifice highlights the Indian philosophical resonances of the term, while also forging a connection with Judith Butler's ([1990] 2008, [1993] 2011) theories on gender performativity, which interrogate the presumptive reality of gender. In the 1999 preface to her seminal work *Gender Trouble*, Butler ([1990] 2008, xxiii–xxiv) writes:

> If one thinks that one sees a man dressed as a woman or a woman dressed as a man, then one takes the first term of each of those perceptions as the 'reality' of gender: the gender that is introduced through the simile lacks 'reality,' and is taken to constitute an illusory appearance. In such perceptions in which an ostensible reality is coupled with an unreality, we think we know what the reality is and take the second appearance of *gender to be mere artifice, play, falsehood, and illusion* [emphasis added] . . . When such categories come into question, the *reality* of gender is also put into crisis.

Like Butler's theorizations on the illusory nature of gender, my reading of constructed artifice (*māyā*) is also disruptive in that it seeks to reimagine the gender performance of the characters on the Kuchipudi stage and, more importantly, to interrogate brahmin masculinity articulated through the body of the impersonator. I juxtapose the enactments of Satyabhama and Madhavi to analyze two fields in which the artifice of gender emerges in *Bhāmākalāpam* performance: speech and parody. By reading gender as constructed artifice, on the levels of both speech and parody, I interrogate not only idealized enactments of "real" women's bodies in Kuchipudi dance, but also hegemonic brahmin masculinity constructed through the processes of sartorial impersonation.

The Artifice of Gender through Speech

"Oyamma Madhavi." With the utterance of these two simple words, Satyabhama not only beckons her confidante, but also genders her into existence. Vocative addresses such as this one are a critical means through which gender is created and re-created in the *Bhāmākalāpam* dance drama. The female Madhavi becomes the male Madhava, who in turn transforms into the male *sūtradhāra,* through the speaking of names. This power of speech, which often goes unseen in the context of a highly stylized theatrical tradition such as Kuchipudi, is critical to the gender transformations of the *sūtradhāra,* Madhavi, and Madhava.

How does speech work to construct the artifice of gender in *Bhāmākalāpam*? Through the citational power of language (Butler [1993] 2011), names connote gender identities in South Asian languages. In Sanskrit, for example, a name ending in a short *-a* indicates a male-identified gender, and a name ending in a long *-ā* or *-ī* indicates a female-identified gender. In Telugu, a name ending in *-uḍu* indicates a male-identified gender, and a name ending in a short *-a* or *-i* indicates a female-identified gender.[16] *Bhāmākalāpam,* which is performed in Telugu, a language that draws heavily on Sanskrit linguistic convention, employs "Mādhavi" (Telugu) or, less frequently, "Mādhavī" (Sanskrit) for the name of Satyabhama's confidante. The names "Mādhavuḍu" (Telugu) or "Mādhava" (Sanskrit) are used interchangeably to refer to Krishna's confidant.[17] Audiences hearing "Mādhavi" or "Mādhavī" associate the name with a female-identified character, and "Mādhavuḍu" or "Mādhava" with a male-identified character. When Satyabhama calls to her friend by saying "Oyamma Mādhavi," she constructs the impression of a female-identified character for the audience. Similarly, when Krishna addresses his confidant as "Hey, Madhava!" it creates the impression of a male-identified character onstage.

The use of vocatives to establish gender becomes even more complicated in the case of the *sūtradhāra.* In the *Bhāmākalāpam* performance (referenced above) staged in the Kuchipudi village in 2006, the performer portraying Madhavi shifts back to the role of the *sūtradhāra* by addressing a supporting member of the orchestra in the middle of a dialogue with Satyabhama. This shift is indicated when the *sūtradhāra* calls out to a member of the orchestra, "Hey, Sastry Garu!" and even has a conversation with the orchestra member, despite the fact that Satyabhama is still.

The *sūtradhāra*'s direct address parallels the stage aside, or technique of "theatrical footing," commonplace in the buffoon's monologue in the opening act of Tamil Special Drama (Seizer 2005, 178). As Seizer notes, the buffoon's monologue in Tamil Special Drama is intended to be a humorous, lewd, and gender-segregated conversation between the male actor portraying the buffoon and the male musicians seated on stage right. The direct address, therefore, "allows the Buffoon the ruse of confiding his more intimate thoughts and feelings to these men's familiar ears alone, rather than to an entire village audience full of unknown persons, women and children included" (179). The direct address works similarly in *Bhāmākalāpam,* in which the *sūtradhāra*'s theatrical aside to the male orchestra member creates a gender-segregated conversation between the male performers onstage, while excluding Satyabhama. However, unlike Tamil Special Drama, the audience members (presumably both men and women) can be incorporated into the conversation, as is evident in the previous dialogue about the various families (Pasumarti, Bhagavatula, Darbha) in the village.

The transformation of Madhavi to the *sūtradhāra* is evident through gender cues embedded in the context of the dialogue. When calling out, "Hey, Sastry Garu!" the female character onstage, Madhavi, transforms into the male *sūtradhāra* who is speaking to a fellow male member of the orchestra. This gender transformation from female Madhavi to male *sūtradhāra* is also apparent in pronoun use. When Madhavi speaks to Satyabhama, she uses the second-person singular and addresses her as "you." When the *sūtradhāra* speaks to the orchestra member *about* Satyabhama, he uses third-person singular and addresses Satyabhama as "she." The audience is signaled to the shift of the *sūtradhāra* back into Madhavi when the performer returns to referencing Satyabhama in the second person. Here, it is not the vocative alone, but the context in which it is uttered that enables the gender transformation of Madhavi into the *sūtradhāra*.[18]

Another complex situation arises when both Satyabhama and Krishna are present onstage. In the example of the *Bhāmākalāpam* performance at the International Symposium on *Kalāpa* Traditions cited previously, Satyabhama calls out to Madhavi from stage left while Krishna addresses Madhava from stage right. The spatial movement from stage left to stage right is accompanied by a gender transformation of Madhavi into Madhava, again indicated through the vocative addresses employed by Satyabhama and Krishna. When Satyabhama calls out "Oyamma Madhavi," she creates the "female" Madhavi onstage; similarly, when Krishna beckons to his friend, "Hey, Madhava!" he creates the "male" Madhava. Speech, in this case the vocative and grammatical gender of the Telugu language, has the power not only to identify a character but also to gender her.

Vocative address and dialogue are crucial particularly for interpreting the character of Madhavi, more so than Madhava or the *sūtradhāra*. While the audience may experience the presumed male gender of Madhava or the *sūtradhāra* through the employment of male-identified costume and gait, comparable external markers of gender are noticeably lacking in the case of Madhavi. Audiences witnessing *Bhāmākalāpam* performances by Kuchipudi village dancers must interpret Madhavi's gender based on how she is referred to and not how she appears.[19] This creates a disconnect between gender visually performed through the body of the performer and gender linguistically created through the dialogue of the performance. Madhavi's gender is ephemeral and can be transformed through the utterance of a vocative directed at another character ("Hey, Sastry Garu!"). Here, the vocative can both create and deconstruct gender, thereby rendering gender itself illusory, a form of constructed artifice. The utterance "Oyamma Madhavi" is not simply Satyabhama's vocative address to her confidante, but also a transformative statement that showcases the artifice of gender through speech.[20]

The Artifice of Gender through Parody

Although usually interpreted as Satyabhama's female confidante (*sakhi*) enacted by the *sūtradhāra,* Madhavi closely parallels the role of the *vidūṣaka* (clown or jester) of Sanskrit dramatic texts and vernacular theatrical performance. Envisioning Madhavi as a female *vidūṣaka* reframes her gender performance as distinct from the *sūtradhāra* and Madhava, whose humor lacks the disruptive quality of her parody. As a female *vidūṣaka,* Madhavi unmasks the artifice of gender by parodying both the character of Satyabhama and the brahmin male body donning her guise.

The male *vidūṣaka,* or clown, is a stock character in Sanskrit dramatic texts and performances. According to the opening chapter of the *Nāṭyaśāstra* (ca. 300 CE), the seminal text on Sanskrit dramaturgy, the *vidūṣaka* is one of the primary characters of the drama, along with the *nāyaka* (hero) and *nāyikā* (heroine) (*Nāṭyaśāstra* I.96).[21] The *vidūṣaka* is invariably present in most Sanskrit plays, including notable works such as Kalidasa's *Vikramorvaśīya* (ca. fifth century CE) and Shudraka's *Mṛcchakaṭikā* (ca. seventh century CE).[22] In terms of characteristics, the *vidūṣaka* serves a comedic (and often parodic) role in drama through humorous appearance and playful dialogues. The *Nāṭyaśāstra* elaborates on the comic and even grotesque attributes of the *vidūṣaka:* "The Jester (*vidūṣaka*) should be dwarfish, should possess big teeth, and be hunch-backed, double-tongued, baldheaded and tawny-eyed" (*Nāṭyaśāstra* XXXV.79).[23] The *vidūṣaka* is also considered, for the most part, a brahmin man who is clumsy and forgetful of how to be a good brahmin.[24] Also notable is the *vidūṣaka*'s strong penchant towards food, as most of his conversations are focused on gastronomic affairs:

> In the Vidūṣaka's bag of verbal tricks, the most worn and predictable is his attempt to channel any conversation (but especially a high-flown lyrical speech by the hero) into purely gastronomic lines: his similes, more often than not, are taken from the world of kitchen and table, and he is certain to interpret any statement or query as referring to matters of food. He sees the world with the eyes of Tantalus, except that his focus is more narrow, for the Vidūṣaka's true craving is for cakes and sweetmeats, *modakas* (Shulman 1985, 158).

In converting metaphors on love to conversations on food, the *vidūṣaka* redirects the erotic aesthetics of the drama, *śṛṅgāra,* to the *rasa* of humor and laughter, *hāsya* (157).[25]

The *vidūṣaka* is not limited to premodern Sanskrit texts but is a stock character in contemporary vernacular theatre including the aforementioned Kerala theatrical form Kutiyattam, which bases its performances on the texts of Sanskrit plays (Shulman 1985, 174–75).[26] In Kutiyattam, the *vidūṣaka* speaks in the vernacular language Malayalam and serves as translator of the Sanskrit and Prakrit dialogues uttered by the other characters onstage. By speaking in direct address to the audience in Malayalam, the *vidūṣaka* fulfills a split function in Kutiyattam performance: he is both a comedic actor within the play *and* an interpreter of the play to the audience. Moreover, the *vidūṣaka* of Kutiyattam satirically inverts the main characters through parodic counter-verses, or *pratiślokas*, delivered in Malayalam that scornfully mock the elevated speech of the Sanskrit verses (*ślokas*) spoken by the drama's hero, *nāyaka* (177–78). The parallels between the *vidūṣaka* in Sanskrit drama and Kutiyattam and Madhavi's character in *Bhāmākalāpam* are remarkable. The *vidūṣaka*'s counter-verses in Kutiyattam are mirrored in Madhavi's verbal puns of Satyabhama's dialogues. In the opening scene of the dance drama, for instance, Madhavi reimagines Satyabhama's epithets of Krishna into descriptions of a wandering ascetic or a potter's son. Later on, Madhavi's puns transform Satyabhama's sun- and moon-shaped hair ornaments into the rising sun and moon, visible from Madhavi's roofless house.

The *vidūṣaka*'s gastronomic inclinations are evident in Madhavi's playful refiguring of Satyabhama's boxes of jewels into boxes of grains:

Satyabhama: Oyamma Madhavi, having jewels for every day of the week means that I have one entire jewelry box for each and every day.

Madhavi: So you've got seven boxes? Should I tell you the boxes I have in my house? I have a box for black lentils. A box for yellow lentils. A box for salt. A box for tamarind. A box for cumin. I even have a pantry box to put all those boxes in! Since you have jewels for every day of the week, then give me your Sunday jewels and I'll be happy.

This penchant towards food also features prominently in the dialogue between Satyabhama and Madhavi presented in the opening of this chapter:

Satyabhama: If the banana leaf falls on the thorn, or if the thorn falls on the banana leaf, the leaf gets torn. Either way, it's bad for the leaf.

Madhavi: Okay, if the banana leaf falls on the thorn, or the thorn falls on the banana leaf, the leaf gets torn. Can I ask you something else? If a *laḍḍu* [sweet] falls into ghee [clarified butter], or ghee falls on a *laḍḍu,* when both end up in my stomach, is it bad for me?

Just like the *vidūṣaka,* whose "true craving is for cakes and sweetmeats, *modakas*" (Shulman 1985, 158), Madhavi twists Satyabhama's metaphor of the leaf torn by the thorn into one about clarified butter and *laḍḍus*, a sweet very similar in shape to a *modaka.*

The comedic weight of the drama is not carried by Madhavi alone, but also extends to Madhava and the *sūtradhāra.* By employing the mode of direct address and stage asides to the audience/orchestra, the *sūtradhāra* jokes with the orchestra member about Satyabhama by reimaging the word "space" (*sandhi*), not as a relationship between Satyabhama's brothers-in-law, but as lanes named after the families of the Kuchipudi village:

Satyabhama:	My husband is in the space (*sandhi*) between my elder brother-in-law and my younger brother-in-law.
Sūtradhāra/Madhavi:	[*Addressing Satyabhama as Madhavi*]: In the space between your elder brother-in-law and younger brother-in-law?
	[*Addressing the orchestra as the* sūtradhāra]: Hey, Sastry Garu! Do you know what this space is?
Orchestra Member:	Please tell me.
Sūtradhāra/Madhavi:	[*Addressing the orchestra as the* sūtradhāra]: In this village, there's the Pasumarti space. There's the Bhagavatula space. There's the Darbha space. So what's this space between her elder and younger brothers-in-law that she's talking about? . . .

Similarly, Madhava also parodies Satyabhama to Krishna by suggesting that she has gained so much weight that her waist belt is being worn as a ring on her finger. The respective conversations between the *sūtradhāra* and the orchestra, and Madhava and Krishna, are humorously targeted at Satyabhama, who is not present during the dialogues and is referred to indirectly in the third person. Madhavi, by contrast, *directly* interacts with Satyabhama and pokes fun at the heroine's unending wealth, her outward appearance, and her lovesick emotions. This direct interaction clearly positions Madhavi as the parodic foil to Satyabhama, comparable to the relationship between the *vidūṣaka* and the hero (*nāyaka*) in Sanskrit drama. Reading Madhavi as the female *vidūṣaka* of *Bhāmākalāpam* extends her role beyond simple verbal jest to one of parody, and it is through this parody that the artifice of gender becomes apparent.

The single distinguishing factor that separates the *vidūṣaka* of Sanskrit drama and the characters of *sūtradhāra*/Madhavi/Madhava is gender. While the *vidūṣaka* is portrayed, for the most part, as a male character in Sanskrit dramatic texts and regional theatre, the enactment of a *female* clown/jester through Madhavi expands the scope of the *vidūṣaka* beyond Sanskrit dramatic and vernacular performative contexts. A comparable example of a comedic female character akin to Madhavi is Kuli in the Kerala ritual drama known as *muṭiyēṯṯu* (lit., "carrying the crown"). As Sarah Caldwell (2006, 194) notes, "Kūḷi's character is a grotesque caricature of a 'tribal' female who is often shown in advanced states of pregnancy." Kuli functions as a foil to the dark goddess Kali, who is at the center of ritual *muṭiyēṯṯu* performance.

A similar contrast is posited between Madhavi-as-*vidūṣaka* and Satyabhama-as-*nāyikā* (heroine) in *Bhāmākalāpam*. Gendered female through discourse,

Madhavi's comedic function in the drama is not only to parody Satyabhama's lovesick dialogues, but also to parody the idealized image of womanhood portrayed by Satyabhama, whose name literally translates as "True Woman." This meta-parody is apparent in the opening conversation of this chapter in which Madhavi proclaims that a woman's life consists of wearing necklaces and jewels, walking forward and backward, and saying "Oh!" and "Ah!" It is further compounded in the dialogue of the nose ring, in which Madhavi fashions her index finger into the shape of a hook and demands that Satyabhama guess what she is asking for.

> Madhavi: I don't remember the name of it, but I can tell you its shape. Look here, it looks like this. [*Displays index finger in the shape of a hook*].
>
> Satyabhama: [*Looking puzzled*]: Oh ho! Is it tamarind?
>
> Madhavi: What? I said it was a piece of jewelry! What do I want with a pregnancy craving like tamarind at this age? Look at it again. [*Displays index finger in the shape of a hook*] . . .

Satyabhama continues to guess what Madhavi is asking for, pointing to all her ornaments from her head to her feet, alluding to the Sanskrit literary trope in which the various features of a divine figure or human being, often a woman, are described either from head to toe (*śikha-nakha*) or toe to head (*nakha-śikha*). Satyabhama is shocked when she finally realizes that Madhavi desires her nose ring, the one ornament that signifies her marital status. In demanding Satyabhama's nose ring, Madhavi implicitly subverts the idealized image of Satyabhama as an auspicious married woman.

Madhavi's parody, however, does not end with Satyabhama's character onstage, but also extends to the brahmin male body donning the *strī-vēṣam*. As we recall from the previous chapter, the Kuchipudi brahmin must painstakingly alter his guise, voice, and bodily movement to impersonate *as precisely as possible* the age and appearance of Satyabhama's character. The impersonation of Satyabhama is an act of *approximation* of an idealized vision of womanhood made exclusively possible through the brahmin male body. By interrogating Satyabhama's character in the context of the drama, Madhavi-as-*vidūṣaka* also parodies the idealized womanhood enacted by the brahmin male performer. The lack of visual guising of the performer enacting Madhavi further heightens this parody; as a woman who has become a woman through discursive rather than visual means, Madhavi-as-*vidūṣaka* calls into question the very need for sartorial impersonation onstage.

The parody extends further if we examine the issue of caste. The *vidūṣaka* in Sanskrit drama is generally considered to be a brahmin ignorant of proper brahminhood, and is even referred to in some contexts as a Brahmabandhu or "low" brahmin (Shulman 1985, 165).[27] Compounding this is the *vidūṣaka*'s "ineffable gluttony," which serves as a direct critique of the insatiability of brahmins, a theme commonplace in Indian literatures (Siegel 1987, 199). Through his ignorance of correct brahminhood and his penchant for eating, the *vidūṣaka* implicitly critiques brahminical appeals to authority by positioning upper-caste brahmins as both unlearned and insatiable. Madhavi, the female *vidūṣaka* of *Bhāmākalāpam*, also interrogates brahminical identity through her food-based conversations, which flip Satyabhama's metaphor of the torn leaf into an image of sweetmeats. When Satyabhama is too shy to utter Krishna's name aloud and identifies him as *makara-kundanamulu-dharincina-vaṇṭivāḍu* (one who wears earrings shaped like crocodiles), Madhavi quickly retorts by mimicking the Vedic chants of brahmins, who are also imaged as wearing crocodile-shaped earrings. In doing so, she reminds both Satyabhama and the audience that Krishna, god himself, is *not* a brahmin.

When taken together, Madhavi's parody of gender and caste in the *Bhāmākalāpam* dance drama works as an implicit critique of not just brahminhood, but specifically of brahmin masculinity constructed through impersonation. Through her humorous dialogues and lack of sartorial guising, Madhavi-as-*vidūṣaka* parodies both the character of Satyabhama as an auspicious married woman and also the brahmin male body donning her *strī-vēṣam*. In doing so, Madhavi interrogates the very means by which brahmin men achieve, or at least aspire to achieve, hegemonic brahmin masculinity within the Kuchipudi village. The juxtaposition of Madhavi alongside Satyabhama further underscores this parody of impersonation: that a brahmin man can become Madhavi with the utterance of a single vocative interrogates the extensive efforts made by the impersonator to enact Satyabhama's character. In *Bhāmākalāpam* performance, therefore, we find two starkly different enactments of gender on a single stage: the impersonation of a gender ideal in the case of Satyabhama, and the parody of that ideal in the case of Madhavi.

Madhavi's role in *Bhāmākalāpam* must be situated in relation to Christian Novetzke's (2011) notion of the "Brahmin double." According to Novetzke's examination of literary and performative materials from the Marathi-speaking Deccan of the thirteenth to eighteenth centuries, the notion of the "Brahmin double" became an important way for brahmins to criticize their own caste authority while also maintaining their authoritative status in public arenas of performance:

> The Brahmin double [is] a rhetorical strategy deployed *by Brahmin performers* in public contexts. This 'double' is a result of a very specific context where a Brahmin performer or public figure (real or imagined) performs for an audience, the majority of which are likely not Brahmins. The Brahmin double consists of the character of a 'bad Brahmin', who is portrayed as foolish, greedy, pedantic or casteist, and who serves as a 'double' for a 'good' Brahmin. This 'bad Brahmin' is thus a 'body double', receiving abuse and deflecting polemical attack from the performer, giving legitimacy to a Brahmin performer standing before a largely non-Brahmin audience. (235) [emphasis in original][28]

Madhavi-as-*vidūṣaka* certainly presents the image of the "bad brahmin," particularly in her ineffable gluttony and parodic dialogues. The "good brahmin," in this case, is the male dancer donning Satyabhama's *strī-vēṣam,* adding a layer of gender complexity to the doubling act. Reading Madhavi as the "bad brahmin" double to the "good brahmin" performer enacting Satyabhama interrogates the efficacy of Madhavi's parody of gender and caste norms. Such a reading suggests that Madhavi's role does not, in fact, critique Satyabhama, but rather reinforces brahminical power through her public discursive performance. In other words, Madhavi, the "bad brahmin," upholds rather than subverts the power of the "good brahmin" male body in Satyabhama's *vēṣam.*

I acknowledge this ambiguity in Madhavi's role. Like drag performance, Madhavi-as-*vidūṣaka* "is a site of a certain ambivalence, one which reflects the more general situation of being implicated in the regimes of power by which one is constituted and, hence, of being implicated in the very regimes of power that one opposes" (Butler [1993] 2011, 85). Nevertheless, Madhavi expresses the potential for subversion through her parody of gender, which operates on three distinct levels: (1) the parody of the character of Satyabhama in the context of the *Bhāmākalāpam* dance drama; (2) the parody of an idealized womanhood enacted by the brahmin impersonator in *strī-vēṣam* onstage; and (3) the parody of hegemonic brahmin masculinity that ensues in everyday village life. It is on this third level—the interrogation of hegemonic brahmin masculinity in the everyday—that gender and caste norms are rendered as constructed artifice, or *māyā,* through Madhavi's play. In concluding his discussion of the *vidūṣaka,* Shulman (1985, 213) describes the brahmin clown as imbued with the powers of *māyā:*

> In a word, [the *vidūṣaka*] exemplifies the world's status as *māyā,* at once tangible and real, and immaterial; entirely permeable by the imagination, always baffling, enticing, enslaving, and in the process of becoming something new and more elusive. The essence of *māyā* is contradiction—the incongruous wonder of the absolute transformed into sensible form; the innate, mysterious, dynamic contradiction of the clown.

The *vidūṣaka*'s *māyā* extends to the character of Madhavi, whose gender parody onstage works to expose the constructed artifice of gender and caste norms implicit in Kuchipudi performance and everyday village life. Through Madhavi, we are reminded of the ineffable gluttony of brahmins, the humor hidden beneath a woman's lovesickness, and the possibility of gender transformation through the utterance of a single vocative. The extent of Madhavi's critique only becomes fully apparent in the next chapter, which moves from the heteronormative spaces of the Kuchipudi village to queer enactments of *Bhāmākalāpam* in urban and transnational Kuchipudi dance.

. . .

Impersonation, as the previous chapter attests, is not simply a sartorial practice circumscribed to the Kuchipudi stage, but also a performance of power that creates hegemonic brahmin masculinity in the everyday life of the village's brahmin *agrahāram*. Yet, this gender and caste ideal is itself a form of artifice, rendered unstable through the shifting use of the vocative or the parodic interplay of words. Through humorous words, gestures, and acts, Madhavi, the female *vidūṣaka* of *Bhāmākalāpam*, exposes the constructed artifice, or *māyā* in the words of my Kuchipudi interlocutors, of Satyabhama's character and the brahmin male body impersonating her.

Interpreting Madhavi's character as a subversive critique of Satyabhama alludes not only to the relationship between these two characters, but also the broader performative and political economy of the Kuchipudi village, which gives legitimacy to particular dancers over others. This ambivalent authority is most apparent when examining the figure of Pasumarti Rattayya Sarma, a brahmin guru from the village. A contemporary of Vedantam Satyanarayana Sarma and a disciple of the same guru, Chinta Krishna Murthy, Rattayya Sarma has been teaching generations of students in the Kuchipudi village, both in the state-run Siddhendra Kalakshetra and in his home (Jonnalagadda 1993, 117). Although skilled in impersonation, Rattayya Sarma could never match the reputation of his counterpart Satyanarayana Sarma and was always relegated to playing supporting female characters, including Madhavi, while Satyanarayana Sarma ubiquitously performed the lead heroine of a given dance drama, particularly Satyabhama. Some of my interlocutors implied to me that this disparity was on account of Rattayya Sarma's lack of appeal in *strī-vēṣam,* particularly in comparison to the stalwart impersonator Satyanarayana Sarma.

Rattayya Sarma's financial status was also far more precarious than Satyanarayana Sarma's. As Satyanarayana Sarma continued to garner public and financial attention for his impersonation, even in the years following his retirement, Rattayya Sarma had no such following. In fact, after my fieldwork, Rattayya Sarma was forced to retire from the Siddhendra Kalakshetra due to budgetary restrictions and only occasionally teaches students at home, which severely limits his source of income to himself and the family members he supports. Now in his seventies, Rattayya Sarma remains as one of the last gurus of the Kuchipudi village skilled in traditional elements of the Kuchipudi repertoire, namely *kalāpa*s and *yakṣagāna*s, but he does not receive the opportunities or recognition given to his more famous counterpart.[29] Eclipsed from impersonation for decades, Rattayya Sarma is also prevented from achieving the authoritative status of Satyanarayana Sarma, who will always be Satyabhama in the eyes of most villagers. Rattayya Sarma is therefore a critical example of a brahmin man who does not actively participate in the broader economy of hegemonic masculinity in the Kuchipudi village (Messerschmidt and Messner 2018, 41–43).[30] Although Rattayya Sarma may adhere to normative brahmin masculinity, which I defined in the previous chapter as an emergent form of hegemonic masculinity that is always in process, he will never achieve the hegemonic status of Satyanarayana Sarma. Yet, in his failure to impersonate in the manner of his predecessor, Rattayya Sarma opens the possibility for the contingency of brahmin masculinity, particularly through his enactment of *sūtradhāra*/Madhavi/Madhava.

By positing Madhavi as central to interpreting *Bhāmākalāpam* performance, this chapter gives voice to Rattayya Sarma, a Kuchipudi dancer who has resided in the shadows of his performance community. Unlike Satyanarayana Sarma, whose allure in *vēṣam* depends on a visual aesthetics of impersonation, Rattayya Sarma's rapid gender transformations as *sūtradhāra*/Madhavi/Madhava rest on nonsartorial techniques of verbal craft and parodic gesture. By parodying Satyabhama, Rattayya Sarma as Madhavi as *vidūṣaka* calls into question the authoritative status of Satyabhama and the impersonator performing her. The relationship of Madhavi and Satyabhama in the context of *Bhāmākalāpam* can thus be envisioned as a metaphoric foil for on-the-ground realities of Kuchipudi village life where impersonation is awarded with performative and financial power and the parody of impersonation is awarded with boxes of lentils. Nevertheless, when read as constructed artifice, Madhavi's character provides us with the theoretical means for displacing hegemonic brahminical masculinity through the utterance of a single vocative or playful pun. Taken together, Madhavi-as-*vidūṣaka,* the character, and Rattayya Sarma, the brahmin performing her, foreground the playfulness of artifice, or *māyā-līlā* in the words of Schechner (2015), on the Kuchipudi stage.

4

Bhāmākalāpam beyond the Village

Transgressing Norms of Gender and Sexuality in Urban and Transnational Kuchipudi Dance

Today, Kuchipudi is an Indian dance form practiced across transnational contexts, spanning from Australia to Paris to the United States. Kuchipudi's transnational reach is attributed to a single figure from the mid-twentieth century: Vempati Chinna Satyam (1929–2012). A brahmin from the Kuchipudi village, Chinna Satyam left his hometown in the late 1940s to move to the Tamil-speaking urban center of Madras (present-day Chennai), where he would soon establish the Kuchipudi Art Academy (hereafter KAA), an institution referred to as the "Mecca for all aspirants who wanted to learn Kuchipudi" (Nagabhushana Sarma 2004, 7).[1] Paralleling the ostensible "revival" of Bharatanatyam a few decades beforehand (Allen 1997), Chinna Satyam began to experiment, innovate, and reimagine Kuchipudi from an insulated dance style solely performed by village brahmin men to a transnationally recognized "classical" Indian dance form.

Chinna Satyam's experiments with Kuchipudi abandoned many key elements of the dance form as it was practiced in his natal village: he began to teach both women and men from a variety of caste backgrounds; he choreographed elaborate dance dramas featuring both mythological and social themes; and, most significant for this study, he eliminated the practice of male dancers donning the *strī-vēṣam*. There is an extensive body of literature about Chinna Satyam's various innovations with performance and pedagogy by practitioners and scholars of Kuchipudi (Pattabhi Raman 1988/89; Andavalli and Pemmaraju 1994; Jonnalagadda 1996b; Nagabhushana Sarma 2004; Bhikshu 2006; Chinna Satyam 2012). However, these discussions are, for the most part, silent on Chinna Satyam's experiments with impersonation, particularly as it pertains to Siddhendra's *Bhāmākalāpam* and the character of Madhavi.[2] In his rechoreographed version of *Bhāmākalāpam* (ca. 1970s), Chinna Satyam entirely transformed the gender composition of the dance drama by recasting the roles of Satyabhama *and* Krishna to be enacted by female dancers and by altering Madhavi to a gender-variant character enacted by a male performer.[3] Chinna Satyam's decisions regarding *Bhāmākalāpam* are certainly pragmatic insofar as they arise from the demands he faced to craft choreography legible to both non-Telugu-speaking performers and non-Telugu-speaking audience members. However, the implications of his *Bhāmākalāpam* are far more transgressive than scholars and practitioners of Kuchipudi dance readily admit. Chinna Satyam countered the village's caste and gender norms, particularly Siddhendra's long-standing prescription to impersonate, by casting a woman to portray Satyabhama and by introducing gender ambiguity on the Kuchipudi stage, a decision that ultimately subjected him to critique by his village counterparts.

Focusing on Chinna Satyam's *Bhāmākalāpam* staged in the cities of Madras in 1981 and Atlanta in 2011, this chapter traces the transformations of Kuchipudi dance across a number of distinct performative and lived spaces: village to urban to transnational, male to female to gender-variant, brahmin to nonbrahmin, normative to queer. I juxtapose Chinna Satyam's *Bhāmākalāpam,* which includes both female and male performers from various caste backgrounds, alongside the traditional version of *Bhāmākalāpam* presented in the village, in which all performers are hereditary brahmin men. While the previous chapters have envisioned village performance practices, particularly donning the *strī-vēṣam,* as upholding normative views on gender, caste, and sexuality, this chapter explores the disruptive possibilities of urban and transnational Kuchipudi dance, in which broader discourses on gender and sexuality call into question the utility of the brahmin male body in *strī-vēṣam.*

I signal the expansiveness of Chinna Satyam's experiments with Kuchipudi by referring to his style as both an urban and transnational dance form. After establishing the KAA in 1963, Chinna Satyam fashioned an urban dance style colloquially referred to as "Madras Kuchipudi" (Thota 2016, 140). By the 1980s, Chinna Satyam and his students increasingly began performing across global contexts, including North America and Europe. In the 1990s and early 2000s, Chinna Satyam and students of the KAA toured the United States every few years, performing a compilation of his dance dramas for South Asian American audiences. Today, particularly through online platforms such as Skype and YouTube, Chinna Satyam's choreography truly exists across transnational spaces. For example, during one of my return visits to the KAA, I watched Chinna Satyam's son, Vempati Ravi Shankar, teach a Skype lesson to a student in Australia after he had spent the day training a dancer visiting from Paris.

In referring to Chinna Satyam's Kuchipudi as both urban *and* transnational, I take a cue from Priya Srinivasan's *Sweating Saris* (2012), which makes a case for envisioning Indian dance as a form of transnational labor. I also recognize the importance of Sitara Thobani's (2017, 24–25) claim that the production of Indian classical dance was, at the very outset, a transcultural affair that must be envisioned as "always already global," articulated at the "contact zone" between Indian nationalism and colonial imperialism. Like my interlocutors, I distinguish between Kuchipudi village performance, which is exclusively enacted (and controlled) by the village's brahmin male community, and Chinna Satyam's Kuchipudi, which was first performed at the KAA and now extends across transnational spaces. Nevertheless, I recognize the exchanges across these seemingly distinct geographical sites of dance production. Today, the Kuchipudi village is inextricable from Chinna Satyam's style of Kuchipudi, a point to which I return in the conclusion of this study.

In moving from village *agrahāram* performance to urban and transnational Kuchipudi dance, I am indebted to the extensive scholarship of Anuradha Jonnalagadda (1996b, 2004, 2012, 2016), whose research traces the transformation of Kuchipudi dance under Chinna Satyam's tutelage. Notably, I do not discuss the impacts of the South Indian film industry on cosmopolitan Kuchipudi dance, a point that is documented in the works of Rumya Putcha (2011) and Katyayani Thota (2016).[4] Rather, my attention in this chapter is limited to Chinna Satyam's experiments with *Bhāmākalāpam* to consider what happens to the practice of impersonation and the ensuing construction of brahmin masculinity as Kuchipudi moves beyond the village and its circumscribed brahmin community to the urban and transnational stage. Drawing on the language of Gayatri Gopinath (2005) and E. Patrick Johnson (2001), I envision Chinna Satyam's urban and transnational form of Kuchipudi as a site of queer diaspora that exposes the heteronormative anxieties undergirding Kuchipudi village life. By dislodging impersonation from the purview of the brahmin male body, Chinna Satyam's *Bhāmākalāpam* engenders the capaciousness of *vēṣam*, a practice that holds the power to simultaneously subvert and re-signify hegemonic norms.

VEMPATI CHINNA SATYAM: EXPERIMENTS WITH *BHĀMĀKALĀPAM*

Born on October 15, 1929, to a hereditary Kuchipudi brahmin family, Vempati Chinna Satyam began his dance training with village guru Tadepalli Perayya Sastry. At the age of eighteen, he left the confines of his natal village to travel to Madras and join his elder cousin, Vempati Pedda Satyam, who was already working in the city's burgeoning cinema industry (Thota 2016, 137). Chinna Satyam worked with Pedda Satyam and Vedantam Raghavayya, another relative from the Kuchipudi village, to choreograph dance sequences for South Indian films (Nagabhushana Sarma 2004, 7). Chinna Satyam soon began learning from Vedantam Lakshminarayana Sastry, the well-known exponent of solo Kuchipudi dance who, as mentioned in the introduction, interacted with and adapted from *devadāsī* performers (Chinna Satyam 2002, 28; Putcha 2015, 12–13).[5] Then, in 1963, Chinna Satyam started his own school, the Kuchipudi Art Academy (KAA) (Nagabhushana Sarma 2004, 7). Paralleling the institutionalization of Bharatanatyam through Rukmini Arundale's Kalakshetra, Chinna Satyam's KAA became the locus for a veritable Kuchipudi empire in the decades to come. By 1986, Chinna Satyam inaugurated Kuchipudi's global presence with a tour of the United States, along with Vedantam Satyanarayana Sarma (Nagabhushana Sarma 2012, 18). Such tours abroad, now a staple for Kuchipudi dancers based in India, can be viewed as examples of transnational labor characteristic of twentieth- and twenty-first-century Indian dance (Srinivasan 2012).

Chinna Satyam's particular brand of Kuchipudi that developed from the 1960s onwards can best be characterized under the rubric of *heteroglossia*. Citing Mikhail Bakhtin (1981), Indian dance scholar Ketu Katrak (2011, 14) defines heteroglossia as follows:

> [Heteroglossia] asserts multiplicity over unitary meanings . . . Heteroglossia also includes "multiple social discourses" that include varying ideological and class positions. Bakhtin's notion of language as inherently hybrid enables layers of meaning generated in the interaction between text and reader, or speaker and listener, and I would add, of performer and audience.

In a similar vein, Chinna Satyam worked to adapt Kuchipudi to the heteroglossia of a cosmopolitan context: his style of Kuchipudi is attentive to a multiplicity of spaces (village, urban, and transnational), linguistic registers (Telugu, Tamil, and Sanskrit), and movement vocabularies (traditional and contemporary).[6] In the early years of the KAA, it is likely that Chinna Satyam's cosmopolitan audiences were deeply familiar with Indian dance movements (through Bharatanatyam) and Telugu language (through Karnatak music). Nevertheless, Chinna Satyam was still faced with the challenge of "modernizing" village Kuchipudi for a cosmopolitan aesthetic sensibility, a point that is readily apparent in the title of N. Pattabhi Raman's article, "Dr. Vempati Chinna Satyam: Modernizer of a Tacky Dance Tradition" (1988/89), published in the popular dance magazine *Sruti*. Chinna Satyam molded Kuchipudi to appeal to a cosmopolitan context of heteroglossia, particularly through his "modern" dance dramas, a genre that builds on yet differs from the *kalāpa*s and *yakṣagāna*s performed by the village's brahmin dance community (Jonnalagadda 1996b, 137–43; Putcha 2015, 10).

The first example of such a dance drama is *Sri Krishna Parijatam*, which Chinna Satyam adapted to the Kuchipudi stage in 1959. The eponymous play, which was wildly popular in Telugu theatre in the early twentieth century, is based on the Telugu retelling of Krishna's theft of the *pārijāta* tree from the garden of Indra, the king of the gods, for his wife Satyabhama.[7] Chinna Satyama's *Sri Krishna Parijatam* integrated the plot of the stage play along with several pieces from the village

Bhāmākalāpam dance drama, which were choregraphed in line with his uniquely cosmopolitan aesthetic. With the help of scriptwriter S.V. Bhujangaraya Sarma and Karnatak music aficionado Patrayani Sangeetha Rao, Chinna Satyam choreographed several other dance dramas, including those focusing on social themes, such as a Kuchipudi reworking of Rabindranath Tagore's play *Chandalika* (Chinna Satyam 2012, 38–39).[8] Chinna Satyam's proclivity for experimenation is apparent throughout his repertoire, which makes use of theatrical lighting, stage décor, and sets, as well as showcasing different methods of technique and presentation (Bhikshu 2006, 260–62). Chinna Satyam's productions are palpably distinct from the long-standing performances of the Kuchipudi village, which are typically enacted on an outdoor stage without the aid of elaborate sets, stage props, or lighting. Through Chinna Satyam, Kuchipudi dance became firmly entrenched on the proscenium stage or, perhaps more accurately, in the Chennai *sabha* (Rudisill 2007, 2012).[9]

Chinna Satyam's innovations of Kuchipudi dance were not only restricted to the genre of "modern" dance dramas, but also touched upon elements from the preestablished repertoire of *kalāpas*, namely *Bhāmākalāpam* attributed to Siddhendra. Although it is difficult to ascertain the exact date, Chinna Satyam set out to rechoreograph *Bhāmākalāpam* in the 1970s, likely following the success of his dance drama *Sri Krishna Parijatam* mentioned above.[10] Chinna Satyam's *Bhāmākalāpam,* which adapts wholesale pieces from his earlier dance drama *Sri Krishna Parijatam,* is a loosely construed amalgamation of the village's traditional *Bhāmākalāpam* interspersed with innovative elements of his distinctively "modern" repertoire. Abandoning the long-standing practice of brahmin men in *strī-vēṣam,* Chinna Satyam, who at the time was teaching a great number of female students, cast nonbrahmin and brahmin women to enact Satyabhama and Krishna, respectively. Most notably, he rechoreographed Madhavi into a gender-variant character who is performed "neither as a woman nor as a man" (Jonnalagadda 1996b, 138).

Building on the analysis of village *Bhāmākalāpam* performance in chapter 3, here I focus on Chinna Satyam's experiments with *Bhāmākalāpam* in urban and transnational Kuchipudi dance. I draw on the following source material: (1) Vempati Chinna Satyam's handwritten script of *Bhāmākalāpam*; (2) a 1981 video of Chinna Satyam's *Bhāmākalāpam* staged in Madras and directed by Chinna Satyam himself; and (3) a production of Chinna Satyam's *Bhāmākalāpam* directed by his student Sasikala Penumarthi at Emory University in Atlanta, Georgia, in September 2011.[11] While most of the images included in this chapter come from the 2011 performance of *Bhāmākalāpam,* it is Chinna Satyam's 1981 video recording that provides the most compelling evidence for the radical nature of his choreographic interventions, particularly in the case of Madhavi. I also incorporate interviews with Kuchipudi performers trained in Chinna Satyam's KAA, including Chinna Satyam's son, Vempati Ravi Shankar, and his daughter, Chavali Balatripurasundari, both of whom became close contacts during my time in India and in the years following. Chinna Satyam himself, who passed away two years after my fieldwork, was present during my time at the KAA, but advanced in age and not able to give sustained interviews.[12] Finally, my own embodied experiences of learning Kuchipudi dance under Chinna Satyam's student, Sasikala Penumarthi, for the last twenty years and performing the role of Krishna in the 2011 performance of *Bhāmākalāpam* in Atlanta inform my discussion. Although I do not directly employ the reflexive methodology of auto-ethnography (Adams and Holman Jones 2008, 375), my experiences of learning to dance and perform the roles of Satyabhama and Krishna invariably leak into my analysis in this chapter.

SATYABHAMA

One of the most notable innovations of Chinna Satyam's KAA was the introduction and institutionalization of women into Kuchipudi dance. When establishing the KAA in 1963, Chinna Satyam followed the trend begun by his guru Vedantam Lakshminarayana Sastry and opened the doors of his institution to women, an act that must have been viewed as radical to the circumscribed community of brahmin men he left behind in the village. Attracting middle- and upper-class women, particularly those already versed in the movement vocabulary of Indian dance and/or trained to perform in South Indian films, Chinna Satyam soon amassed a contingent of female students, such as the actress Hema Malini and dancers Sobha Naidu and Manju Bhargavi (Kothari and Pasricha 2001, 205).[13] In fact, there were so many female students learning at the KAA that Chinna Satyam was often bereft of male dancers to play lead characters in his dance dramas (Venkataraman 2012, 77). Occasionally, Chinna Satyam imported male dancers from the Kuchipudi village, and a handful of village dancers have played supporting male roles in the academy's dance drama productions, including Vedantam Rattayya Sarma, the father of Venku, the impersonator described in chapter 2. More often, however, Chinna Satyam cast female dancers to play both female *and* male roles and, in the case of *Bhāmākalāpam*, the characters of Satyabhama and Krishna are both played by women (see Figures 15 and 20).

Apart from Vedantam Satyanarayana Sarma in the Kuchipudi village, the single name that has become synonymous with Satyabhama's role in *Bhāmākalāpam* is Sobha Naidu. A senior nonbrahmin disciple of Chinna Satyam's since 1969, Sobha Naidu gained a reputation for performing the lead characters in KAA's productions, particularly the role of Satyabhama in the dance dramas *Bhāmākalāpam* and *Sri Krishna Parijatam*.[14] When describing her experience portraying this character, Naidu states:

> Right from my childhood, my fascination for Satyabhama continued. The impact of the programme *Srikrishna Parijatam* was so much on me that I decided to join the Academy on the very next day. After a few years of training, I got the opportunity to portray this wonderful character . . . When it comes to performance, I start feeling

FIGURE 15. Sasikala Penumarthi enacts Satyabhama. Photo by Uzma Ansari.

> that I am Satyabhama, when I sit to start getting ready. Once I enter the stage I forget my identity and try to put my heart and soul into the character.[15]

Naidu goes on to distinguish her performance of Satyabhama from the brahmin impersonators from the village, who must put in an "extra effort" to enact the character:

> When male dancers portray the character of Satyabhama, they have to certainly put extra effort in the sense they should take special care and every minute they should be conscious of what they are doing. Otherwise it might create an odd impact on viewers. The art lovers have a particular image of the character. If the artist is a woman, whether she does full justice or not, if she puts her own efforts, it would leave an impact on the audience. But if it is the male artist doing any female character, he has to put extra effort and at the same time should be conscious of his every movement lest it would spoil the image of the character.[16]

When I spoke with Venku, a younger brahmin from the village known for his skills in impersonation, he explicitly downplayed the enactment of Satyabhama by a female dancer:

> Satyabhama is a female character. If a woman does a female character, there's nothing there . . . There's no greatness there. A man doing a female role is great. Like that, a female doing a male role is great . . . It's good if a man does a female role or if a woman does a male role. That's because there's a difference there. If a woman normally does a female role, what is the big difference? There's nothing.

While Venku's statements are certainly contentious and arise from his particular standpoint as an aspiring impersonator, they do hint at one important impact of Chinna Satyam's KAA: the noticeable lack of the brahmin male body in Satyabhama's *vēṣam*. The unequal gender ratio of female to male dancers, which prompted Chinna Satyam's casting of women to enact female characters like Satyabhama, rendered moot the long-established practice of impersonation in the village. As Vijayawada-based impersonator Ajay Kumar succinctly remarked to me, "There is no need for men to dance as women when women are dancing themselves." The absence of the brahmin man in *strī-vēṣam* distinguishes Chinna Satyam's *Bhāmākalāpam* from village *Bhāmākalāpam* performances. Chinna Satyam's rechoreographed Satyabhama, enacted by a female dancer, must also be positioned alongside his gender-variant rendering of Madhavi.

SŪTRADHĀRA/MADHAVI/MADHAVA

To understand the radical nature of Chinna Satyam's *Bhāmākalāpam*, we must look beyond Satyabhama to the characters of *sūtradhāra*/Madhavi/Madhava, which are

FIGURE 16. Vedantam Raghava as the *sūtradhāra*. Photo by Uzma Ansari.

uniquely different from village performances. Chinna Satyam's *Bhāmākalāpam* opens in a manner similar to Kuchipudi village performances as the *sūtradhāra*, played by a male dancer, comes onstage to announce the commencement of the drama. The *sūtradhāra* is dressed like his village counterpart, wearing a turban on his head, an upper cloth to cover his bare chest, and a stitched silk costume below the waist (see Figure 16). Along with two female accompanying dancers, the *sūtradhāra* performs benedictory prayers, stage consecration, and description of Satyabhama's braid, known as the *jaḍa vṛtāntam* (lit., "story of the braid") (Kapaleswara Rao 1996).[17] After this introduction, the *sūtradhāra*, along with the two dancers, exits the stage and does *not* reappear throughout the course of the drama. The *sūtradhāra*'s role as the "one who holds the strings" through playing the cymbals (*naṭṭuvāṅgam*) is modified in Chinna Satyam's *Bhāmākalāpam* and, in the case of the 1981 recording, Chinna Satyam played the *naṭṭuvāṅgam* himself. By downplaying the *sūtradhāra*'s onstage presence, Chinna Satyam positions Madhavi (as opposed to the *sūtradhāra* or Madhava) as centrally important to his *Bhāmākalāpam*.

When Satyabhama finishes her character introduction and calls out to her confidante, the performer cast as the *sūtradhāra* returns onstage with his costume significantly altered to portray Madhavi. The dancer enacting Madhavi is dressed in a long shawl covering his bare chest in the manner of the upper part of a woman's sari. Below his waist, he either wears a stitched silk costume (as pictured in Figure 17) or sometimes the bottom part of a sari, which is wrapped through the legs

FIGURE 17. Madhavi (left) and Satyabhama (right). Photo by Uzma Ansari.

in what appears to be a Vaishnava style of dress.[18] Finally, and perhaps most distinctively, the male performer wears a wig of black hair adorned with flowers. At the end of the dance drama, when Madhava approaches Krishna, the performer changes once again back into the male costume initially worn by the *sūtradhāra* at the beginning of the drama. Thus, *sūtradhāra*/Madhavi/Madhava are distinguished through changes in sartorial appearance. When the male performer wears flowers in his hair, the audience recognizes his enactment of the female character Madhavi; when the performer wears a turban, the audience recognizes the male roles of the *sūtradhāra* or Madhava.[19]

In addition to these alterations in costume, there are significant changes in bodily movement, particularly with respect to Madhavi's character. In both the 1981 recording and the 2011 performance of *Bhāmākalāpam,* the male performer enacting Madhavi moves with a "feminine" gait (*āṅgika*), particularly through exaggerated hand gestures and a swaying of the hips. The same male performer does not employ such movements when enacting the *sūtradhāra* or Madhava in other parts of the dance drama. This bodily comportment contrasts with the village enactments of *sūtradhāra*/Madhavi/Madhava, in which the movements (*āṅgika*) are gendered masculine for all three characters.

This distinction in bodily movement is most evident during the scene in which Madhavi asks Satyabhama for her nose ring. After Madhavi demands the nose ring, Satyabhama attempts to appease Madhavi by bringing her jewelry box and decorating her friend with a number of her own ornaments, including her bangles, waist belt, and anklets, while Madhavi looks into a mirror approvingly. Although adorned with Satyabhama's jewels, Madhavi is still dissatisfied and forces Satyabhama to give up her own nose ring. Satyabhama reluctantly removes her nose ring, touches it to her eyes in a gesture of respect, and gives it to Madhavi. Finally in possession of her prize, Madhavi dramatically casts off her own nose ring and mimetically adorns herself with Satyabhama's new one (see Figure 18).

Madhavi's mimetic donning of Satyabhama's nose ring and other ornaments is a feature noticeably absent in village performances of *Bhāmākalāpam.* In village *Bhāmākalāpam* performances, while Madhavi might *ask* for Satyabhama's ornaments, including her nose ring, she never *wears* the jewels. Instead, she takes them by hand, thereby reasserting the disconnect between the performer's external gender performance and the character's presumed gender identity. In Chinna Satyam's *Bhāmākalāpam,* by comparison, Satyabhama carefully dresses Madhavi with her ornaments, while the musicians repeat the verse, *Vāda mēla pōve* ("Go and get my lord"). Through each repetition of the line, the embodied movements of both performers situate Madhavi as a female-identified character. Here, I use the language of female-identified and male-identified to indicate the overtly constructed nature of the performance of *sūtradhāra*/Madhavi/Madhava. For ease of reading, I do not use similar terminology to discuss other characters of *Bhāmākalāpam,* but such language could be employed in all cases. For example, a male dancer donning the

FIGURE 18. Madhavi wears Satyabhama's nose ring. Photo by Uzma Ansari.

strī-vēṣam is performing a female-identified character in the same manner that a female dancer donning Satyabhama's guise is also performing a female-identified character.

Notably, Madhavi's bodily movements contrast with the character's dialogues, which are voiced by a male vocalist. One of Chinna Satyam's innovations was to excise verbal dialogues delivered by the characters onstage. Rather than having the performers stand in front of a microphone and deliver the dialogues themselves, the vocalists in the orchestra (seated on the far end of stage right), sing the dialogues into a microphone (accompanied by music), while the dancers onstage lip-synch these dialogues. Stylized lip-synching characterizes all of Chinna Satyam's dance dramas, and the excision of dialogues enables performers from a wide variety of linguistic backgrounds to participate in his cosmopolitan vision of Kuchipudi dance (Chinna Satyam 2012, 41). The adaptation of lip-synching also shifts the focus of the dance drama from voiced dialogues to mimetic gesture and vigorous dance movements. In the words of one of my village interlocutors, "How can Chinna Satyam's students speak their own dialogues when they're jumping all over the stage?" This contrasts with village performances of *Bhāmākalāpam,* in which the stage-right vocalist sings a *daruvu,* such as Satyabhama's introductory song, but only the performer enacting Satyabhama will speak her lines using an affected high-pitched voice. Such affectations of voice, *vācika abhinaya,* are entirely absent from Chinna Satyam's style of Kuchipudi, in which dancers never learn dialogue delivery in their years of training.

The shift from dialogue delivery in the context of village *Bhāmākalāpam* to stylized lip-synching in the context of Chinna Satyam's *Bhāmākalāpam* results in a gender-incongruous presentation of Madhavi's character. For example, when Madhavi demands jewels for every day of the week, the male vocalist voices her lines while never once altering the pitch of his voice to *sound* like that of a woman's. This results in a curious situation in which the male performer lip-synchs dialogues voiced by a male vocalist to speak as a female-identified character. This is particularly apparent in the 2011 performance in which the female vocalist voiced Satyabhama's dialogues and the male vocalist voiced Madhavi's. Madhavi speaks as a woman within the context of the dialogue, yet lip-synchs the voice of the male vocalist, seated at the edge of stage-right.

Important also to Madhavi's portrayal are both sartorial presentation (*āhārya*) and gait (*āṅgika*): the female-identified character of Madhavi is performed by a male dancer dressed in a male-identified costume (i.e., stitched silk costume) but who also wears flowers in his hair, drapes his chest with a shawl, and moves in a feminine manner (similar in certain ways to the bodily gestures of Satyabhama discussed in chapter 2). By changing Madhavi's costume and bodily movements to partially male- and partially female-identified, Chinna Satyam alters the performance of the character itself into a gender-variant role, particularly in comparison to its village counterpart. And, as I will discuss in the next section, audiences viewing Chinna Satyam's rendering of Madhavi also view her, or perhaps more accurately *them,* as a gender-variant character. A juxtaposition of Chinna Satyam's *Bhāmākalāpam* alongside its Kuchipudi village counterpart is helpful for understanding the distinctions across these two performance contexts (see Table 1).

As this table makes clear, the gender roles of Madhavi's character are enacted differently across village and urban/transnational spaces: in the Kuchipudi village,

TABLE 1. *Sūtradhāra*/Madhavi/Madhava across *Bhāmākalāpam* Performance Contexts

Bhāmākalāpam Performance Context	*Sūtradhāra*	Madhavi	Madhava
Kuchipudi village:	*Character:*	*Character:*	*Character:*
	Brahmin male-identified character serving a benedictory function; reappears throughout the performance; speaks to the audience and orchestra and plays the *naṭṭuvāṅgam* (cymbals)	Satyabhama's female-identified confidante; appears in Satyabhama's presence and with Satyabhama and Krishna in the final scene	Krishna's male-identified confidant; appears in Krishna's presence and with Satyabhama and Krishna in the final scene
	Performance:	*Performance:*	*Performance:*
	Brahmin male dancer with male-identified costume and gait; dialogue voiced by male dancer	Brahmin male dancer with male-identified costume and gait; dialogue voiced by male dancer	Brahmin male dancer with male-identified costume and gait; dialogue voiced by male dancer
Chinna Satyam's *Bhāmākalāpam*:	*Character:*	*Character:*	*Character:*
	Male-identified character serving a benedictory function; appears only in the beginning of the performance; does not play the *naṭṭuvāṅgam* (cymbals)	Satyabhama's female-identified confidante; appears in Satyabhama's presence and with Satyabhama and Krishna in the final scene	Krishna's male-identified confidant; appears only in Krishna's palace; does not reappear in the final scene with Satyabhama and Krishna
	Performance:	*Performance:*	*Performance:*
	Male dancer with male-identified costume and gait; dialogues voiced by male vocalist (seated stage-right)	Male dancer wearing a combination of male-identified and female-identified costume; "feminine" gait; dialogues voiced by male vocalist (seated stage-right)	Male dancer with male-identified costume and gait; dialogue voiced by male vocalist (seated stage-right)

there is an incongruity between the external gender performance of Madhavi in male-identified costume, gait, and speech, and the character's gender identity as Satyabhama's female-identified confidante. *Outward gender performance is enacted as distinct from gender identity.* By contrast, in Chinna Satyam's *Bhāmākalāpam,* there is synchronicity across Madhavi's external gender performance and the character's gender identity, both of which are read as reflecting some form of gender ambiguity. *Outward gender performance parallels gender identity.*

Relevant here is Judith Butler's ([1990] 2008, 187) distinction between three contingent dimensions of corporeality: anatomical sex, gender identity, and gender performance.[20] Like Butler, I recognize both gender identity and gender performance as *contingent* dimensions that are performatively construed through "corporeal style," rather than reflective of an internal gender essence or core (190). The incongruity or synchronicity of gender identity and gender performance across *Bhāmākalāpam* contexts signals the contingency of gender itself, which can be entirely reimagined through simple changes in costume, gait, and speech. This is perhaps most apparent in the case of Chinna Satyam's rechoreographed version of Madhavi: the male dancer enacting Madhavi is not donning the *strī-vēṣam*, as in the case of the village brahmin man in Satyabhama's guise, but instead portraying a gender-variant *vēṣam* never before seen on the Kuchipudi stage.

"NEITHER AS A WOMAN NOR AS A MAN": INTERPRETING MADHAVI'S GENDER VARIANCE

Madhavi's gender-variant performance in Chinna Satyam's *Bhāmākalāpam* is a source of ongoing speculation and criticism by practitioners and scholars of Kuchipudi dance. Here, I will examine the discourses of scholars, students, and village practitioners to analyze Chinna Satyam's experiments with Madhavi's character. Anuradha Jonnalagadda, a dance scholar and longtime student of Chinna Satyam's, highlights the historical context of Madhavi's gender portrayals by suggesting that previously in royal courts, a eunuch figure was often found within women's domestic spaces, a point that likely draws on textual sources, including the *Nāṭyaśāstra* and Sanskrit drama.[21] Jonnalagadda reads Madhavi not as a female character in the manner of village Kuchipudi performances, but rather as a eunuch who can move across public and domestic space. Jonnalagadda (1996b, 138) also highlights the character's comedic import:

> In the traditional practice, *sutradhara* conducted the show as *nattuvanar*, singer, and also played the role of Madhavi, the *ishtasakhi* [beloved friend] of Satyabhama. He enters into a dialogue with her and plays a major role in eliciting information from her. He becomes Madhava, the *sakha* [friend] of Krishna, when he goes to him with the letter of Satyabhama. Thus, *sutradhara* helps in the continuation and development of the story. As different from this, Chinna Satyam introduced a separate character who becomes *sutradhara* in *Venivrittanta* (*Jadavrittanta*) [the opening benediction], Madhavi while in the company of Satyabhama and Madhava in the presence of Krishna. A change even in the attire and portrayal could be observed. He is attired *neither as a woman nor as a man* [emphasis added] and his movements are such that they evoke humour and thus provide a comic relief.

Jonnalagadda's suggestion that Chinna Satyam reimagined the character of Madhavi as "neither as a woman nor as a man" is reflected in the sentiments of several of Chinna Satyam's students. For example, Manju Bhargavi, one of Chinna Satyam's senior students, described Madhavi as belonging to a "third gender" (using the English term):

> Madhavi is a third gender. When he, when Madhavi is with Satyabhama, the third gender becomes she. But when she goes to Krishna, she becomes he. So, wherever, whomever, Madhavi is enacting with, then it becomes that. When he is enacting with a male, then he becomes a male. When it's with a female, then it becomes a female.

Implicit in this analysis is a distinction between gender identity and gender performance. Bhargavi reads Madhavi's gender identity as belonging to a "third gender," but Madhavi's gender performance emerges differently depending on the character's proximity to Satyabhama or Krishna. The emergent nature of gender performance is reflected in the various pronouns employed by Bhargavi, including "she" to describe Madhavi near Satyabhama, "he" to describe Madhava near Krishna, and "it" to describe the character's gender-variance. This interpretation of Madhavi's gender performance mirrors, in a way, the discourse of village dancers who attribute the *sūtradhāra*/Madhavi/Madhava's unique shape-shifting ability to *māyā*. However, Bhargavi's characterization of Madhavi's identity as "third gender" differs starkly from my village interlocutors, who never employed such gender-variant terminology to describe village *Bhāmākalāpam* performances. Similar to Bhargavi, Chinna Satyam's son and student Ravi Shankar described Madhavi as a "third gender" character that was created by his father to bring about the humorous aspects of *Bhāmākalāpam*. Sasikala Penumarthi, a senior student of Chinna Satyam's, characterized Madhavi as "acting in between, not a boy and not a girl."

In addition to discussing Chinna Satyam's *Bhāmākalāpam* with his students, I also asked the brahmin performers of the Kuchipudi village. While my interlocutors in the village were reluctant to express criticism of Chinna Satyam in any other case, especially considering his globally recognized status as a stalwart Kuchipudi guru, several of them expressed outright disapproval at Chinna Satyam's *Bhāmākalāpam*, specifically his changes to the character of Madhavi. As an example of this critique is the observation of Venku, who described to me the portrayal of Madhavi in Chinna Satyam's *Bhāmākalāpam* by his late father, Vedantam Rattayya Sarma, in the Kuchipudi village:

> That same Madhavi character, [Chinna Satyam] Garu did with my father. My father wore the wig and wore the *aṅgavastram* [upper cloth] and did it. When did he do it? It was when Manju Bhargavi [quoted above] did Satyabhama, and my father did Madhavi. I remember that time very well. When they did it in the Kuchipudi village, Vedantam Parvatisam Garu was an elder Kuchipudi guru. He came onstage and

> scolded [my father]. He scolded him onstage ... That's because he was my father's guru. My father learned from Parvatisam Garu.

When Rattayya Sarma performed Chinna Satyam's Madhavi in the village, he was overtly critiqued by local gurus, including well-known village teacher Vedantam Parvatisam. By shifting the character of Madhavi from a brahmin male *vēṣam* to attired as neither a woman nor as a man, Chinna Satyam, and Rattayya Sarma by extension, were subject to outright criticism by their Kuchipudi village counterparts. Evincing this critique, Jonnalagadda (1996b, 138n132) writes: "This particular portrayal of Madhavi did attract criticism from traditionalists. They feel that the character degenerated with such portrayal."

Rattayya Sarma, along with his two sons Raghava and Venku, are (to my knowledge) the only brahmin men from the village of Kuchipudi skilled in enacting Madhavi's role in Chinna Satyam's version of *Bhāmākalāpam*. Although Raghava had previously enacted Madhavi in Chinna Satyam's *Bhāmākalāpam*, he was reluctant to portray the role in the September 2011 performance staged at Emory University in Atlanta, specifically stating that he did not want to enact Chinna Satyam's gender-variant Madhavi. Raghava finally agreed to perform the role in line with the visual appearance of Chinna Satyam's Madhavi *and* the discursive register of the Kuchipudi village Madhavi. Raghava visually enacted Chinna Satyam's Madhavi through costume and bodily movement *and* discursively constructed the village Madhavi through dialogue, which sets apart the Atlanta performance as an amalgamation of village and urban/transnational *Bhāmākalāpams*. Aware of the critique leveled by village gurus against his father years before, Raghava blended together both styles of enacting Madhavi, perhaps in an effort to avoid further critique.

As these disparate voices demonstrate, there is a range of terms employed by Kuchipudi practitioners to describe Chinna Satyam's re-envisioned version of Madhavi. Despite this breadth, there appears to be an underlying thread when interpreting Chinna Satyam's alterations to Madhavi: this character is read as expressing some form of gender variance, although the nature of this ambiguity is subject to interpretation. Whether Madhavi is described as a eunuch or "third gender," it seems clear that Kuchipudi practitioners have come to interpret Madhavi in Chinna Satyam's *Bhāmākalāpam* as a gender-variant role.

RESISTANT VERNACULAR PERFORMANCE AND QUEER DIASPORA

While Chinna Satyam's students turned to the *Nāṭyaśāstra*, Sanskrit drama, and even humor to justify his choices in rechoreographing Madhavi as a gender-variant character, the brahmins of the Kuchipudi village expressed outright disapproval. Their critiques of Chinna Satyam's *Bhāmākalāpam* expose two overarching concerns about the drama more broadly, and the characters of Satyabhama and

Madhavi, in particular. First, the brahmins of the village are anxious about the movement of traditional elements of the Kuchipudi repertoire, namely *kalāpa*s and *yakṣagāna*s, outside of the village into cosmopolitan spaces in which caste and gender restrictions are obsolete. Siddhendra's prescriptions that all village brahmin men must impersonate Satyabhama is threatened in the event that non-brahmin and non-male bodies perform *Bhāmākalāpam,* particularly the role of Satyabhama. If there is no need for men to dance as women when women are dancing themselves, then how can village brahmin men attain their gender and caste ideals *without* impersonation?

Although my interlocutors rarely criticized Chinna Satyam for training women, the effects of his KAA are palpable for village brahmins. The concern about the influx of nonbrahmin and non-male dancers performing Kuchipudi is evident in the words of Vedantam Rajyalakshmi, the mother of dancers Venku and Raghava mentioned before. Rajyalakshmi said to me during an interview in 2014:

> Ever since my childhood, it always used to be the case that men would take on the *strī-vēṣam* to perform. From what I know, it was never the case that women would put on a costume and perform onstage. Nowadays, people are performing their own *pātra*s [characters]. Even now, in my village, our men still perform in *strī-vēṣam.* Outsiders also may be performing, but none of us like it. It's only appealing if men from our village take on the role . . . People might ask the question why? Who should perform? Only our people [i.e., people from the Kuchipudi village]. Who should be appreciated? Only our people. Hundreds of people have danced. We villagers may go and watch. But we all think that whoever may be performing, only people from our village who have our blood should dance. No one else has that. That's the mind-set of all our people.

While I will discuss Rajyalakshmi and other Kuchipudi brahmin women further in chapter 5, it is important here to underscore the gender critique implicit in her words. According to Rajayalakshmi, there is a linear decline in performance from the past to the present: village brahmin men used to impersonate but nowadays "people are performing their own *pātra*s," that is dancers are performing their own gender roles. Like many of my interlocutors, Rajyalakshmi avoided naming Chinna Satyam directly, but the effects of his KAA are certainly evident in her comments. By pragmatically doing away with Siddhendra's prescription to impersonate and also by introducing "outsiders" to the Kuchipudi stage, Chinna Satyam's urban and transnational style of Kuchipudi eclipses the possibility for brahmin men to don the *strī-vēṣam,* thus undermining the village's long-standing gender and caste norms.

Second, the critiques of Chinna Satyam's Madhavi stem from the anxieties of the village's brahmins, who are concerned about the intrusion of nonnormative discourses on gender and sexuality from urban and transnational spaces. These anxieties were apparent in the invocation of *kojja,* the Telugu equivalent for the term *hijṛā*.[22] For example, when I first asked one brahmin male performer about whether he would ever perform Madhavi's character in Chinna Satyam's *Bhāmākalāpam*, he expressed outright distaste, insisting that he would never take on "that *kojja-vēṣam*." In another case, the term *kojja* was invoked by a brahmin performer to describe a nonbrahmin male Kuchipudi dancer who dons the *strī-vēṣam* in urban performances. *Kojja*, for these brahmin performers, functions as a thinly veiled signifier to indirectly speak about issues of nonnormative sexuality, a topic that my brahmin interlocutors never broached directly in conversation. Because I was never able to discuss issues of sexuality outright with the brahmin men of Kuchipudi, the mention of *kojja* alerted me to the anxieties that brahmin men may harbor about the practice of impersonation. For my interlocutors, impersonation enacted by village brahmins is seen as adhering to a brahminical tradition of authority (*sāmpradāyam*) handed down by their founding saint Siddhendra. By comparison, impersonation by those *outside* the village is deemed inauthentic, at best; at worst, it is considered exemplary of nonnormative *hijṛā/kojja* sexual practice (Reddy 2005).[23]

The discernible tenor of anxiety evident in the voices of Kuchipudi village brahmins regarding Chinna Satyam's *Bhāmākalāpam* signals the subversive possibility of his gender-variant Madhavi. Although Chinna Satyam's choices in rechoreographing Madhavi appear to be contextual, arising from his streamlined vision of Kuchipudi as cosmopolitan dance, the aesthetic effects of his *Bhāmākalāpam* are, I would argue, undeniably *queer*. Taking a cue from black queer theory and South Asian American studies, including the works of E. Patrick Johnson (2001, 2003), Gayatri Gopinath (2005, 2018), Shaka McGlotten (2016), and Kareem Khubchandani (2016), among others, I employ a queer of color critique to read Chinna Satyam's *Bhāmākalāpam*.

Most broadly, I read the urban and transnational spaces of Madras (present-day Chennai) and Atlanta as extensions of *queer diaspora*, in the words of Gopinath (2005, 2018). As spaces outside the boundaries of the Kuchipudi village, the urban and transnational contexts of Madras/Chennai and Atlanta function as sites of *diaspora*, a term that as Gopinath (2005, 6) notes in its most literal definition, "describes the dispersal and movement of populations from one particular national or geographic location to other disparate sites." In moving from the Kuchipudi village to Madras in the mid-twentieth century, Chinna Satyam inaugurated Kuchipudi on the diasporic stage, if we can read diaspora broadly as the spaces beyond the boundaries of the Kuchipudi *agrahāram* (brahmin quarters).

But how does Chinna Satyam's *Bhāmākalāpam* exist within spaces of *queer* diaspora? Gopinath (2005, 11) brings together the terms *queer* and *diaspora* to critique both the heteronormative and nationalist frameworks that cast diaspora within a Hindu nationalist imaginary:

> Suturing "queer" to "diaspora" thus recuperates those desires, practices, and subjectivities that are rendered impossible and unimaginable within conventional diasporic

> and nationalist imaginaries . . . If within heteronormative logic the queer is seen as the debased and inadequate copy of the heterosexual, so too is diaspora within nationalist logic positioned as the queer Other of the nation, its inauthentic imitation. The concept of a queer diaspora enables a simultaneous critique of heterosexuality and the nation form while exploding the binary oppositions between nation and diaspora, heterosexuality and homosexuality, original and copy. (11)

Relatedly, Jisha Menon (2013, 101) argues for the importance of urban theatre in shaping the emergence of queer selfhoods: "Theatre, as a social, expressive practice, lies at the intersection of discourse and embodiment and so provides a particularly fecund site to consider the emergence of queer selfhoods at the nexus of representation and desire." Aesthetic practices that engage the visual, in this case staged performance, serve as critical sites for what Gopinath (2018, 8) more recently refers to as a *queer optic*, which "brings into focus and into the realm of the present the energy of those nonnormative desires, practices, bodies, and affiliations concealed within dominant historical narratives."

Chinna Satyam's urban and transnational reframing of Kuchipudi certainly participated (and continues to participate) in the dominant historical narrative of Indian dance, namely the classicization of Kuchipudi that mirrors the mid-twentieth-century "revival" of Bharatanatyam. Nevertheless, through his female Satyabhama and gender-variant Madhavi, Chinna Satyam opens the possibility of reading his cosmopolitan Kuchipudi within a visual aesthetics of queer diaspora. Uninhibited by the constraints of hegemonic brahmin masculinity entrenched in the Kuchipudi village, Chinna Satyam was able to experiment with alternative bodies—non-male-identified and even gender-variant—in his newly synthesized vision of Kuchipudi dance in the urban and transnational diaspora. By rechoreographing *Bhāmākalāpam,* the most religiously significant dance drama of Kuchipudi village tradition, Chinna Satyam opens the possibility for disruptive performance. To extend Gopinath's (2005, 11) argument, Chinna Satyam's *Bhāmākalāpam,* with its female Satyabhama and gender-variant Madhavi, functions as the inauthentic imitation or queer Other to the village's *sāmpradāyam,* or its brahminical tradition of authority.

In addition to envisioning Chinna Satyam's *Bhāmākalāpam* as an aesthetic practice of queer diaspora, I also read the dance drama as a "resistant vernacular performance" (Johnson 2005, 140), one that counters the long-standing norms of the Kuchipudi village, which position the brahmin impersonator as front and center. My understanding of resistant vernacular performance directly draws on the work of E. Patrick Johnson, who brings together discourses of blackness and performance to enable new readings of both black American culture and performance studies (2003, 7). In an article on black queer studies, Johnson (2001) critiques the persistent whiteness that informs the work of queer theorists beginning with Butler's ([1990] 2008) *Gender Trouble.* Rejecting Butler's eschewal of subjectivity, Johnson calls upon black "quare" studies to suture the gap between performativity and performance in order to open the space for agency through the performance of identity.[24] For Johnson (2001, 12), queer vernacular performances serve as sites of resistance that "work on and against dominant ideology," a process that José Esteban Muñoz (1999, 11) famously refers to as *disidentification*. Johnson (2001, 13) also imagines the scope of black queer performance beyond the stage to the everyday:

> Theorizing the social context of performance sutures the gap between discourse and lived experience by examining how quares use performance as a strategy of survival in their day-to-day performances . . . Moreover, queer theory focuses attention on the social consequences of those performances. It is one thing to do drag on the club stage, yet another to embody a drag queen identity on the street. Bodies are sites of discursive effects, but they are sites of social ones as well.

Theorizing the social context of performance indicates that it is not simply circumscribed to the stage, but spills into and shapes quotidian life.

Related to Johnson's analysis, it is helpful to turn to the practices of reading and throwing shade in drag performance.[25] In the context of drag balls, such as those portrayed in Jennie Livingston's film *Paris Is Burning* (1990), parody occurs through verbal and nonverbal techniques of insult, namely the practices of "reading" and "throwing shade."[26] Reading, as Shaka McGlotten (2016, 265) succinctly notes in their discussion of *Paris Is Burning*, "is an artfully delivered insult." Also, in the context of the film, Butler ([1993] 2011, 88) links the practice of reading to a failure of impersonation:

> For "reading" means taking someone down, exposing what fails to work at the level of appearance, or insulting or deriding someone. For a performance to work, then, means that a reading is no longer possible, or that a reading, an interpretation, appears to be a kind of transparent seeing, where what appears and what it means coincide. On the contrary, when what appears and how it is "read" diverge, the artifice of the performance can be read as artifice; the ideal splits off from its appropriation.

While reading is grounded in the verbal, throwing shade is a nonverbal gesture of insult. Throwing shade, according to McGlotten (2016, 279), "does not require any specific enunciation to deliver an insult; rather, it uses looks, bodily gestures, and tones to deliver a message." As Dorian Corey, a stalwart drag queen interviewed by Livingston in *Paris Is Burning*, states: "Shade is, 'I don't tell you you're ugly, but I don't have to tell you because you know you're ugly.' And that's shade" (McGlotten 2016, 265). Throwing shade—a term now popular in the American vernacular—is, at least in the context of *Paris Is Burning*, a nonverbal form of insult that parodies the practice of drag.

Chinna Satyam's Satyabhama and Madhavi participate in the performative economy of reading and throwing shade through what Esther Newton (1979, 106) refers to as incongruous juxtaposition. Madhavi's visual appearance in Chinna Satyam's *Bhāmākalāpam* provides a concrete example for this analysis. In both the 1981 and 2011 *Bhāmākalāpam* performances, the performer portraying Madhavi wore a silk upper cloth, or *aṅgavastram,* covering his bare, hairy chest. This upper cloth was not pinned in place, a stark contrast to the prodigious use of safety pins by contemporary Kuchipudi performers to ensure correct costuming. Instead, dancers—Dharmaraj in the video recording and Raghava in the staged performance—continuously fidgeted with their upper cloth by adjusting it over the shoulder, tucking the end into the waistband, and tying the entire cloth around the waist in the manner of the end of a woman's sari. At one point in the 2011 performance, Raghava-as-Madhavi adjusted his purple *aṅgavastram* by tying it around his waist and then fanned himself with it in a sign of fatigue from Satyabhama's excessive demands.

By playfully adjusting his *aṅgavastram,* Raghava-as-Madhavi visually parodies idealized womanhood, particularly as it is enacted by the character (Satyabhama) *and* performer (Penumarthi) onstage. The sartorial juxtaposition of the performer's hairy chest and the silken shawl (*aṅgavastram*) not only draws attention to Madhavi's gender-variance, but also throws shade at the character of Satyabhama, whose name literally translates as "True Woman." Raghava-as-Madhavi not only throws shade on Satyabhama, but Penumarthi as well, as is evident in the image in which Satyabhama is forced to comb through Madhavi's hair (see Figure 19). These performative acts are arguably queer gestures that challenge the heteronormative script of Kuchipudi dance; as Kareem Khubchandani (2016, 82) writes, dance has the capacity to free "movements and affects that have been repressed in our muscles by scripts of caste, racial, (post)colonial, heteronormative, and homonormative respectabilities." In Figure 19, for example, the male performer in gender-variant guise forces the female performer in Satyabhama's guise to do the menial task of combing their hair.

We can, in fact, envision Madhavi as a gender-variant *vidūṣaka* whose role, like the drag performer, serves to elicit humor through sartorial incongruity. This parody is made explicit through incongruous juxtaposition of Madhavi alongside Satyabhama. While the female performer enacting Satyabhama portrays the paradigmatic woman in love, the male performer enacting Madhavi parodies this gender portrayal, particularly by mixing outward gender signs. The presence of such parody, or what Fabio Cleto (1999) refers to as camp aesthetics, is absent in the performances of the Kuchipudi village. Although Madhavi-as-*vidūṣaka* in village *Bhāmākalāpam* parodies Satyabhama and the brahmin impersonator, particularly by poking fun at Satyabhama's ongoing lovesickness and the ineffable gluttony of brahmins, the parody remains, for the most part, circumscribed to the realm of discourse and not the visual field. Chinna Satyam's Madhavi, by contrast, exceeds the limits of discourse, both on the level of the staged dialogues *and* on the level of the heteronormative discursive regime underlying Kuchipudi

FIGURE 19. Satyabhama combs Madhavi's hair. Photo by Uzma Ansari.

village life. Madhavi-as-gender-variant *vidūṣaka* embodies an aesthetic practice of queer diaspora that counters this discursive regime through their outward visual signs (Gopinath 2018, 7). While on the discursive level of the drama, Madhavi might be Satyabhama's female friend (*sakhi*), on the visual level, Madhavi is Satyabhama's (and Penumarthi's) queer foil. And, if we juxtapose Chinna Satyam's *Bhāmākalāpam* alongside village performance, the female dancer guised as Satyabhama can be read as the queer foil to the brahmin male body in *strī-vēṣam*.

The disruptive possibilities of a gender-variant Madhavi and female Satyabhama are not lost on the community of brahmin men in the village of Kuchipudi. Chinna Satyam's choreography is interpreted by brahmins from his natal village as countering the long-standing tradition of authority ascribed to *Bhāmākalāpam*, a drama imbued with religious significance. Following Siddhendra's mandate, impersonating Satyabhama's *vēṣam* is a religious rite of passage that enables the construction of hegemonic brahmin masculinity in the village, evident in the case of Vedantam Satyanarayana Sarma (see chapter 2). By contrast, Chinna Satyam's *Bhāmākalāpam* features a female Satyabhama and a gender-variant Madhavi. Within the binary logic of the village's brahmin male community, the queer diaspora enacted through Chinna Satyam's *Bhāmākalāpam* is envisioned as an "inauthentic imitation" of traditional village performance (Gopinath 2005).

Notably, Chinna Satyam's experiments with Kuchipudi must be situated against the backdrop of the urban revival of Indian classical arts and dance, which is dominated by South Indian Smarta brahmins (Hancock 1999; Rudisill 2007; Peterson and Soneji 2008).[27] Although many of Chinna Satyam's well-known female dancers, including Sobha Naidu, Bala Kondala Rao, and Kamala Reddy, belong to dominant nonbrahmin Telugu castes (such as Kamma, Reddy, etc.), Chinna Satyam continued to express preference for brahmin dancers, including Manju Bhargavi and Sasikala Penumarthi, in his choreography. Chinna Satyam may have flouted village gender norms, but he still upheld the long-standing reliance on "Brahmin taste" in performance (Rudisill 2007, 103; Soneji 2012, 224). In other words, Chinna Satyam's experiments with Kuchipudi can never be divorced from the upper-caste, middle-class dance revival of South India in which the brahmin female body was (and continues to be) deemed aesthetically suitable to dance.

Despite Chinna Satyam's continued preference for brahmin female dancers, the brahmin men of the Kuchipudi village are, in many ways, secondary to his urban and transnational vision of Kuchipudi. In particular, the brahmin man in *strī-vēṣam* is entirely peripheral to Chinna Satyam's *Bhāmākalāpam*, which features a female dancer in Satyabhama's *vēṣam* and a male dancer in Madhavi's gender-variant role. This glaring absence has real effects; namely, it destabilizes the possibility for achieving dominant ideals of gender, sexuality, and caste that undergird quotidian Kuchipudi village life. The dramatic enactments of a female Satyabhama or gender-variant Madhavi reframe the practice of impersonation beyond the brahmin male body in *strī-vēṣam*, thereby exemplifying the strategy of "working on and against" dominant frameworks (Muñoz 1999, 11–12). In divesting *Bhāmākalāpam* from the brahmin male body, Chinna Satyam's dance drama not only breaks from tradition, but also exposes the contingency of hegemonic brahmin masculinity, which is rendered remarkably fragile in the wake of transnational change. Chinna Satyam's *Bhāmākalāpam* also engenders the capaciousness of *vēṣam*, a performative practice that holds the power to simultaneously subvert and re-signify hegemonic norms.

IMPERSONATING KRISHNA

Although the KAA was replete with female students, Chinna Satyam was often bereft of male dancers to play lead characters in his religiously themed dance dramas, particularly those staged in the seventies and eighties. While Chinna Satyam tapped into his resources in the Kuchipudi village by importing many brahmin men to enact secondary roles in his dance dramas, such as sages, demigods, antigods, and kings, he shied away from such imports for his lead male characters, particularly the role of Krishna. Rather than using village male dancers to enact Krishna and other male leads, Chinna Satyam instead instituted the reverse trend of donning a man's guise (Telugu: *maga-vēṣam* or *puruṣa-vēṣam*) by casting his female dancers to perform these roles.[28] In fact, it was the norm for Chinna Satyam's female students to portray all the male leads in his dance dramas, including

Krishna in the dance dramas *Bhāmākalāpam, Sri Krishna Parijatam,* and *Rukmini Kalyanam,* Vishnu in *Padmavati Srinivasa Kalyanam,* and Shiva in *Haravilasam.* Chinna Satyam instituted a reverse trend in the KAA: although women were given the opportunity to play lead male characters, men were not given the opportunity to don the *strī-vēṣam* to enact female roles like Satyabhama, thereby eclipsing the long-standing tradition of the Kuchipudi village.[29]

Despite his practical reasons for establishing a trend of donning a man's guise, *maga-vēṣam,* Chinna Satyam was selective in the kinds of male roles he allowed his female dancers to enact. He cast only female dancers to portray the Hindu deity Vishnu and his manifestations such as Krishna or Srinivasa, but he cast both male and female dancers to play the role of Shiva. Akin to the detailed process of donning Satyabhama's guise, there is a highly stylized process that transforms the dancer into the role of Krishna or Vishnu, who in visual imagery is commonly depicted with a blue-gray tinge across his body (Dehejia 2009, 193). For both Chinna Satyam's female dancers and village brahmin male dancers, donning the Krishna/Vishnu *vēṣam* is a transformative process that can take over two hours and involves the application of blue makeup covering the entire body, as well as wearing a wig, ornaments, and costume (see Figures 14 and 20). Dancers enacting Krishna or Vishnu must also wear a blue vest to cover their chest area. In addition to costume and ornamentation, bodily movement (*āṅgika*) is also a crucial aspect of this form of impersonation. The dancer enacting the role of Krishna or Vishnu must maintain an upright bodily posture, while also expressing elements of amorous charm and boyish mischievousness.

In the case of dancer Manju Bhargavi, whose towering height and broad figure made her easily capable of donning the *maga-vēṣam,* she was so adept in her ability to impersonate male roles that she almost never portrayed female characters onstage during her twenty-plus years under Chinna Satyam's tutelage (Venkataraman 2012, 76–77). In a published interview, Bhargavi states: "Master [Chinna Satyam] told me that I looked like a 'Hij[r]a' when I did a female role and that it did not suit me one bit" (Venkataraman 2012, 78–79). In order to convince her guru otherwise, Bhargavi had to perform Satyabhama in *Bhāmākalāpam* and he finally agreed that she could, in fact, enact female roles. Nevertheless, dance critic Leela Venkataraman (2012, 79) observes: "for persons who watch Manju Barggavee, the inevitable feeling which cannot be avoided is that her body, so set to male roles, still needs to be more malleable in adjusting to enacting female roles in Kuchipudi." For Venkataraman, Bhargavi is only aesthetically appealing in *maga-vēṣam.*

When I interviewed Bhargavi in March 2010, she insisted that enacting Shiva, not Krishna or Vishnu, was the most difficult role she had ever portrayed:

> As long as I performed for [Chinna Satyam], I only did the male characters. He didn't find somebody taller than me to perform a male role. I did justice to whatever male

FIGURE 20. Author impersonates Krishna. Photo by Uzma Ansari.

characters I performed. The Shiva in *Haravilasam* was the toughest I did. It was the toughest. For the female to do justice one hundred percent as a male, it was not easy. So, I had to put in a lot of effort.

In addition to emphasizing the difficulty of enacting Shiva's role "one hundred percent as a male," Bhargavi also suggested that Krishna is not as performatively challenging because of his "feminine" attributes (i.e., boyishness). Such interpretations of Krishna are characteristic of scholarship and popular perceptions of the Hindu deity, in which he is often considered more "feminine" in artistic and visual representations. Religious studies scholar Graham Schweig (2007, 442) explicitly makes this claim:

> Krishna is usually depicted as an eternally youthful male adolescent, yet his masculine body appears to possess many feminine attributes. The significance of such feminine aspects of the visage and bodily appearance of Krishna have yet to be fully appreciated by Western scholars. It is no accident that most Westerners, unfamiliar with the deity of Krishna, take artistic renderings of Krishna's form to be that of a woman!

In a similar vein, pointing to the paintings of artist Raja Ravi Varma in the late nineteenth century, art historian Cynthia Packert (2010, 24–25) highlights the fusion period of European modernism and Indian subject matter as "the beginning of a genre that continues in full measure today—presenting Krishna as a dewy-eyed, gender-bending poster boy."[30] While not dealing with the subject of gender directly, Karline McLain (2009, 28) notes in her study of the *Amar Chitra Katha* (*ACK*) comic books that because Krishna is described in classical Indian texts as a "slim, beautiful, blue-tinged or dark skinned adolescent, [Anant Pai, the creator of *ACK*] balked at images of a fair-skinned Krishna with bulging muscles." In fact, when it came to the illustrations of his initial comic book, Pai insisted that Krishna remain a "blue boylike figure" while allowing the other male characters in the story to be portrayed "with an overdeveloped musculature, holding their exaggerated upper bodies in postures reminiscent of Tarzan" (28). Krishna, unlike his hypermasculinized counterparts, retains a wistful youthfulness on the cover of the *ACK* comic book *Krishna* (26).[31]

The reading of Krishna as somehow more "feminine" or less "masculine" is predicated upon a Euro-American binary framework of gender (Sinha 2012), which does not take into account the alternative gender configurations ubiquitous in South Asia. Kuchipudi performance, both within the village and in urban and transnational spaces, demands a rereading of gender categories more broadly, and masculinity in particular. As is evident from the embodied techniques of impersonation surveyed in chapter 2, village brahmin men are, for the most part, unconcerned with global (and primarily American) conceptions of hegemonic masculinity (Thangaraj 2015). Instead of sporting muscular chests and bulging biceps, Kuchipudi brahman men cultivate an ideal image of womanhood through their male-identified bodies. Hegemonic brahmin masculinity is possible only by enacting Satyabhama's *vēṣam* onstage. By contrast, Chinna Satyam's Kuchipudi refigures the masculinities of divine characters. By repeatedly casting female dancers to enact Krishna, even during times when he could have used male dancers, Chinna Satyam suggests that Krishna's masculinity is *most legible through a woman's body.* Thus, the phenomenon of impersonation in Chinna Satyam's dance dramas reinterprets masculinity by detaching it from the sole domain of the brahmin male body.

Disengaging masculinity from the male body parallels the work of queer theorist Jack Halberstam (1998), who suggests that we reject normative, naturalizing modes of masculinity found in American contexts by separating masculinity from the male body. For Halberstam, "masculinity becomes legible as masculinity where and when it leaves the white-middle-class male body" (2). In short, Halberstam calls for masculinity without men. In a chapter discussing drag performances among black and Latinx queer communities in New York City, Halberstam argues that in comparison to drag queens, there is a noticeable dearth of the drag queen's counterpart, the drag king (231). As Halberstam points out, the history of public recognition of the drag king, and what he calls *female masculinity* more broadly, is most frequently characterized by stunning absences.[32] Halberstam goes on to attribute this distinction to the nonperformativity of masculinity; while femininity "reeks of the artificial," masculinity "adheres 'naturally' and inevitably to men [and thus] masculinity cannot be impersonated" (234–35). Thus, while drag queen performances are exaggerated parodies that expose the artificiality of femininity, drag king performances emphasize "a reluctant and withholding kind of performance" (239).[33] When interpreting the acts of drag kings, Halberstam notes: "the drag kings, generally speaking, seemed to have no idea of how to perform as drag kings . . . The drag kings had not yet learned how to turn masculinity into theater" (245).

A parallel de-emphasis on impersonating masculinity prevails in the Kuchipudi context. In comparison to village practices of donning the *strī-vēṣam,* donning the *vēṣam* of Krishna or Shiva lacks analogous authority in Chinna Satyam's KAA, despite the extensive efforts of sartorial and bodily guising that must ensue. While the male roles in Chinna Satyam's dance dramas are, for the most part, divine characters present in Hindu epic and Purāṇic narratives, impersonating them does not carry the same religious weight as impersonating Satyabhama. Even the terminology—the use of *maga-vēṣam* or *puruṣa-vēṣam* (man's guise)—lacks the frequency of usage of *strī-vēṣam* in the discursive registers of my interlocutors. Like American drag performance, impersonating masculinity is devoid of the pageantry of performing femininity on the Kuchipudi stage.

Brahminical authority and appeals to tradition, *sāmpradāyam,* also shape the importance bestowed on impersonation in the village context, as opposed to Chinna Satyam's urban and transnational locales. In the case of the Kuchipudi village, donning Satyabhama's *vēṣam* functions as a religious rite of passage for the village's hereditary brahmin male community, one that, according to village brahmins, is sanctioned by their founding saint Siddhendra himself. Upholding impersonation in this manner is not only an appeal to tradition, but also an attempt by brahmin men at maintaining power, particularly given the globalization of Kuchipudi dance beyond the boundaries of its natal village. By contrast, the women who impersonate Krishna or Shiva in Chinna Satyam's KAA exist in urban and transnational spaces in which the upper-caste and/or upper-class female dancing body is now ubiquitous. To impersonate Krishna in the urban setting of the KAA is a pragmatic act of necessity; by contrast, to impersonate Satyabhama in the village is simultaneously a fulfillment of a religious prescription and an act of maintaining power. Simply stated, donning the *strī-vēṣam* is ritually far more significant to Kuchipudi tradition than the more recent phenomenon of *maga-vēṣam*. This difference across *strī-vēṣam* and *maga-vēṣam* ultimately suggests that not all acts of impersonation are the same. Yet, taking a cue from Halberstam's (1998) work, I argue that the aesthetic effects of Chinna Satyam's *Bhāmākalāpam* divest masculinity from the brahmin male body; through his female Krishna, female Satyabhama, and gender-variant Madhavi, Chinna Satyam makes possible alternative configurations of masculinity *and* impersonation beyond the purview of village brahmin men.

• • •

While I will never know for certain, it seems likely from my interviews that when rechoreographing *Bhāmākalāpam*, Chinna Satyam gave no thought to the subversive possibilities of his creative vision. Instead, he was faced with on-the-ground realities of recasting his village's traditional dance drama for the heteroglossia of a cosmopolitan context (Katrak 2011, 14). Chinna Satyam often choreographed with his dancers in front of him, a point that was repeatedly relayed to me by his students during my fieldwork at the KAA.[34] In the case of *Bhāmākalāpam*, Chinna Satyam choreographed the dance drama drawing on the memories of his earlier dance drama, *Sri Krishna Parijatam*, and the stylized enactments of the two (non-brahmin) dancers in front of him—Sobha Naidu as Satyabhama and Dharmaraj as Madhavi. In fact, Chinna Satyam's student Sasikala Penumarthi and his daughter Chavali Balatripurasundari both noted that Dharmaraj, a stage actor by training, was likely responsible for Madhavi's humorous movements, rather than Chinna Satyam himself. According to these dancers, Chinna Satyam provided basic guidance to enact Madhavi, but Dharmaraj filled in the lines and fleshed out the humorous nature of the character.

Whatever the reasons may have been, the result is remarkably disruptive, particularly for the brahmins of the village. Flouting the prescription of Siddhendra himself, Chinna Satyam cast a female Satyabhama and reversed the long-standing trend of impersonation to cast a female Krishna. Moreover, Madhavi, described variously as a eunuch or "third gender," is performatively queer in the character's ability to be neither here nor there. Madhavi's sartorial incongruity and humorous appearance positions them as the drama's gender-variant character whose role pokes fun at both Satyabhama and the female dancer donning Satyabhama's *vēṣam*. If we juxtapose Chinna Satyam's *Bhāmākalāpam* alongside village performance, the presence of a female Satyabhama further critiques the brahmin male body in *strī-vēṣam*. When taken together, the playful possibilities of a female Satyabhama, female Krishna, and gender-variant Madhavi open new avenues for resistant vernacular performance (Johnson 2001) on the Kuchipudi stage.

It is the critique of the brahmin men of the Kuchipudi village, rather than the drama alone, that bestows Chinna Satyam's *Bhāmākalāpam* with its full disruptive potential. The vocal condemnation expressed by my village interlocutors regarding Chinna Satyam's Madhavi, coupled with the subtler critique of a female dancer enacting Satyabhama, underscore the heteronormative anxieties within the village's brahmin community. Chinna Satyam's *Bhāmākalāpam*, enacted on the urban and transnational stages of queer diaspora (Gopinath 2005), reveals the artifice of both brahmin identity and hegemonic masculinity. Shifting *Bhāmākalāpam* beyond the village to queer diaspora exposes sites of resistance to the configuration of Kuchipudi dance as village brahmin male tradition. By introducing a gender-variant Madhavi, female Satyabhama, and female Krishna on the Kuchipudi stage, Chinna Satyam's *Bhāmākalāpam* reveals not only the artifice of gender but also the artifice of caste and sexuality. To paraphrase Halberstam (1998, 2), the capaciousness of *vēṣam* can only become fully possible where and when it leaves the brahmin male body. The scope of Chinna Satyam's resistant vernacular performance, however, does not extend to his domestic life, which, as I explore in the next chapter, is circumscribed by his natal village's gender and caste norms.

5

Longing to Dance

Stories of Kuchipudi Brahmin Women

The Hyderabad-based Kuchipudi dance teacher Balatripurasundari learned to dance in secret. As the youngest daughter of internationally acclaimed Kuchipudi dance guru Vempati Chinna Satyam, Baliakka (as she is commonly called) was never encouraged by her father to dance. In fact, she was overtly discouraged from dancing on the basis that it might diminish her marriage prospects in the future and cause unnecessary hardships. Nonetheless, Baliakka learned by watching her father train hundreds of girls in his Madras-based dance institution, the Kuchipudi Art Academy (KAA). Likening herself to Ekalavya, the outcast student of Drona from the epic *Mahābhārata,* who learned archery in secret, Baliakka would sneak into the back of her father's dance classroom, practice facial expressions in front of the bathroom mirror, and fashion Kuchipudi gestures (*mudras*) underneath her blanket at night. Baliakka *longed* to dance like the other girls at her father's dance school, but her desire never won her father's approval because, according to Kuchipudi *sāmpradāyam* (tradition), brahmin girls from the Kuchipudi village cannot and do not dance.

This chapter focuses on the narratives of brahmin women belonging to hereditary Kuchipudi village families who have been overtly excluded from the embodied labor of performance. Unlike the brahmin men of the Kuchipudi village who are all associated with dance in some capacity, Kuchipudi brahmin women have no such performative roles to play. Kuchipudi brahmin women's bodies are deemed unsuitable for the labor of Indian dance and are, therefore, proscribed from the "sweat, blood, tears, slipping or stained saris, callused feet, missteps, or familiar gestures" that dance entails (Srinivasan 2012, 8). Kuchipudi brahmin women are neither the bearers of *sāmpradāyam* in the manner of their fathers, brothers, and sons, nor are they the embodiments of an idealized middle-class Indian womanhood in the manner of their dancing female counterparts. But, as upper-caste brahmin women, they retain a position of privilege, particularly in comparison to *devadāsīs* who have been overtly marginalized in postcolonial South India (Soneji 2012; Ramberg 2014). As a result, they occupy an uneasy interstice as brahmin women whose caste and gender enable their position of exclusion.

The women described in this chapter exemplify a range of relationships with Kuchipudi dance. While some find meaning in alternate forms of symbolic capital (Bourdieu 1977, 1989) such as religious ritual, others long to participate in dance as students, teachers, or even observers. These aspirations often remain unfulfilled within the brahminical and patriarchal model of Kuchipudi village life, which precludes brahmin women's bodies from entering the performative sphere. In contrast to impersonating elaborate *vēṣams* on stage like the brahmin men of the village, Kuchipudi brahmin women are cast as figures with wooden faces, *cekka mohālu,* who must struggle to articulate a recognizable sense of self, or personation (Mankekar 2015, 190). Yet, the stories of Kuchipudi brahmin women like Baliakka reveal the contingency of hegemonic brahmin masculinity in the urban and transnational landscape of Kuchipudi dance.

KUCHIPUDI BRAHMIN WOMEN: DISCOURSES OF EXCLUSION

As already noted in earlier chapters of this book, the village of Kuchipudi is home to a community of Vaidiki brahmin families who have been associated with the eponymous dance form of Kuchipudi for several generations. According to a property dispute in 1763, fifteen brahmin families with surnames such as Bhagavatula, Vedantam, and Vempati were named as the legitimate residents of the Kuchipudi village, and their descendants continue to live in the village today (Jonnalagadda 1996b, 40). Citing reasons of female menstruation and women's restricted movement in the public sphere, Kuchipudi brahmin men have overtly excluded women from hereditary brahmin families from participating in dance. This practice of exclusion continues in the Kuchipudi village today, and I found no example of a Kuchipudi brahmin woman who dances professionally in public in the contemporary period. The omission of Kuchipudi brahmin women's voices and bodies goes beyond dance performance; all scholarly accounts, from both Indian and American academic contexts, also overlook the roles and lives of Kuchipudi brahmin women in studies of Kuchipudi dance.

I too was susceptible to such oversight. Initially, I conceived of this project as an ethnography of the hereditary brahmin men of the Kuchipudi village with a particular focus on the practice of impersonation. However, during my fieldwork, I developed and sustained a close relationship with Chavali Balatripurasundari

(Baliakka), the third daughter of well-known Kuchipudi guru Vempati Chinna Satyam. I first met Baliakka in her Hyderabad flat in September 2009 when I asked her to review dance items from her father's repertoire. New to Hyderabad and in the process of establishing fieldwork contacts, I wanted to keep up with my dance practice, especially before moving to the Kuchipudi village later that year. When she came to know that I was a student of Sasikala Penumarthi, a well-known Atlanta-based dancer who trained under her father in the 1980s, Baliakka expressed hesitation. "What can I teach you?" she asked nervously. Despite her initial reluctance, I found Baliakka to be an exceptionally talented teacher. She would spend countless hours correcting each movement and every expression until she was satisfied that I performed an item exactly in the style of her father's choreography.

After morning classes, Baliakka always invited me to her flat to share a meal and watch videos of items and dance dramas from her extensive VHS and VCD archive. Sitting comfortably on the living room couch with cups of strong filter coffee in hand, Baliakka and I spent countless afternoons watching and talking about dance. Baliakka shared with me her love of her father's choreography, her admiration for my Atlanta-based teacher Sasikala, and her regret that she had never been formally trained. I grew to cherish these moments and found myself making excuses to return to Baliakka's house whenever possible. My great-aunt, with whom I usually stay in Hyderabad, learned not to expect me home for lunch and sometimes even dinner. "You'll be at Baliakka's, right?" my great-aunt would often ask with exasperation. These afternoon conversations with Baliakka continued anytime I came to Hyderabad, whether it was for weekend visits from the Kuchipudi village or many years later to introduce Baliakka to my children.

Relevant to this discussion is Joyce Flueckiger's (2013) analysis of the guising practices of the Gangamma *jātara*, a weeklong festival in honor of the regional goddess Gangamma in the temple town of Tirupati, Andhra Pradesh. The Gangamma *jātara* centers around the public guising practices of men: male members of the Kaikala family of weavers ritually don the guises of the goddess during the Gangamma *jātara*, while lay male participants publicly don the *strī-vēṣam* to "get a corner on women's *shakti* [power]" (Flueckiger 2013, 65). Rather than focusing solely on these public guising practices, Flueckiger decenters the male body in *vēṣam* by also examining how lay women participate in the Gangamma festival, whether it is through applying turmeric (*pasupu*) on their faces or cooking a dish of rice and lentils (*poṅgal*) in the temple courtyard (18–19, 50).

Although I was influenced by Flueckiger's research on the Gangamma *jātara*, as well as the work of anthropologists Gloria Raheja and Ann Gold (1994), I initially did not conceive of my time with Baliakka as part of my "real" fieldwork. However, the more I learned of Baliakka's story, the more I realized that there was a "hidden transcript" (Raheja and Gold 1994, 26) of brahmin women's speech that is unaccounted for in broader scholarship on Kuchipudi dance. Tulasi Srinivas (2018) notes that through the course of her interactions with women at Hindu temples in the Malleshwaram neighborhood in contemporary Bangalore, she came to understand new perspectives on gender and caste. Srinivas writes, "My appreciation of these women grew as time passed and I was privy to the multiplicity of roles and subjectivities they inhabited. I came to understand from them all the hierarchies, including caste and gender, were capable of being upturned, or 'adjusted'" (23). In a similar vein, during the course of my fieldwork I came to realize that to understand village brahmin masculinity in all its constraints, I needed to decenter the male body in *vēṣam* and account for the experiences of the women from hereditary village families. And, perhaps more importantly, Baliakka's was a story that needed to be told.

In 2014, I returned to India to conduct follow-up interviews with ten Kuchipudi brahmin women living in the Kuchipudi village and the urban centers of Vijayawada, Hyderabad, and Chennai. During this follow-up visit, I recorded a formal interview with Baliakka, in which she shared her experiences of learning to dance in secret at the KAA. In what follows, I have selected the accounts of four women: Vedantam Rajyalakshmi and Vedantam Lakshminarasamma, who reside in the village, and Vempati Swarajyalakshmi and Vempati Balatripurasundari (Baliakka), who reside in the urban centers of Chennai and Hyderabad, respectively. Baliakka's story is both the impetus and centerpiece of this chapter.

VEDANTAM RAJYALAKSHMI

Vedantam Rajyalakshmi is an energetic woman in her sixties living in the village of Kuchipudi.[1] She is the wife of the late Kuchipudi guru Vedantam Rattayya Sarma and the mother of younger professional dancers Venku and Raghava discussed in chapters 2 and 4, respectively. Rajyalakshmi, like many of her female counterparts living in the village, was born in Kuchipudi and married into a Kuchipudi brahmin family, a practice idiosyncratic to marital customs in northern India where village exogamy is dominant (Raheja and Gold 1994).[2] In southern India, more broadly, kinship systems usually follow a model of cross-cousin marriage: a man can marry a woman who is his father's sister's daughter, his mother's brother's daughter, or in rarer cases, his own sister's daughter (Trawick 1992, 118).[3] Kuchipudi's *agrahāram*, or brahmin enclave, has maintained an endogamous kinship system in which cross-cousin marriage is preferred; marriage to women outside the village is relatively uncommon, although this practice is changing in recent years.[4] This closed system of marriage results in women having multiple connections to dance; many of the women I interviewed not only have husbands who are professionally tied to dance in some capacity, but also fathers, uncles, brothers, and sons who are professional dancers, teachers, and/or musicians. These women would often take great pains to outline these associations to dance from their natal homes, noting whether their father or uncle were experts in dance.

The closed system of marriage also results in multiple layers of exclusion for the brahmin women of the Kuchipudi village. In childhood, as daughters and sisters of Kuchipudi brahmin men, girls are overtly excluded from learning dance, and in adulthood, as wives and mothers, they are not only restricted from dancing but also discouraged from watching dance performances. As evidence of this, Rajyalakshmi describes her childhood:

> None of my sisters learned to dance. I'm the only one who learned. Girls never used to learn in those days. My mother used to get angry, but I used to sneak out and learn. My mother beat me with a broomstick sometimes. Even then I went and learned. Krishna Sarma Garu [a Kuchipudi guru] shouted and told me not to come. And Parvatisam Garu [another Kuchipudi guru] beat me up. My father's younger brother Rajagopalam Babai and I went and learned to dance . . . After I kept getting beatings, I finally stopped.

Later in our conversation, Rajyalakshmi told me that Banda Kanakalingeshwara Rao, an elite Telugu proponent of Kuchipudi dance, began offering village brahmin girls five *paisa* (five cents) a day to learn. Despite this monetary incentive, no girls came forth to dance. Rajyalakshmi herself received money on two occasions, but her interest waned when her teacher shouted at her and asked her why she had come to dance. According to Rajyalakshmi, even one rupee would not be enough to motivate girls to learn in those days.

Although beaten for attempting to participate in dance, Rajyalakshmi still desired to perform the coveted role of Satyabhama in *Bhāmākalāpam:*

> After that, Chinta Krishna Murthy Garu used to teach outside on the street. He used to teach *Bhāmākalāpam* to Vedantam Satyanarayana Sarma. I learned by watching him. I used to come home and practice saying, "I am Bhama, I am Satyabhama." However, I didn't give any programs. I also used to get excited that I too could dance. In those days, in our village, girls were not allowed to go outside or perform on the stage. Even now, girls don't perform. Which girls in this village have performed on the stage? There's no girl among our people. Even though outsiders are now coming and learning, among our families, there are no girls who perform.

Rajyalakshmi's description of ongoing exclusion from dance is evidenced by the fact that during my follow-up fieldwork, I could find no example of a girl or woman from a hereditary Kuchipudi family who performs professionally in public. Although village girls may be encouraged to *learn* dance, which was the case during my experience of learning at the Siddhendra Kalakshetra (the village's government-run dance institute), no girls were ever encouraged to become professional dancers or dance teachers. Furthermore, no female dancers were ever promoted to enact the lead role of Satyabhama in village productions of *Bhāmākalāpam*. In the village, Satyabhama is always circumscribed to the brahmin male body.

FIGURE 21. Vedantam Rajyalakshmi in her home in the Kuchipudi village. Photo by author.

Rajyalakshmi was not only excluded from *learning* Kuchipudi as a young girl but was also restricted from *watching* Kuchipudi performances as a married woman. Rajyalakshmi's late husband Vedantam Rattayya Sarma was a stalwart performer in the Kuchipudi village and known for his enactments of lead male characters such as Balicakravarti and Banasura. When her husband was performing in the open-air stage in the center of the village, Rajyalakshmi would secretly go to watch his performances, hiding behind a pillar so that no one could see. As Rajyalakshmi relates:

> I used to sneak out and watch my husband perform from a secret place and come running home before he came back. When he came back, he would say, "You were there. You came to see my performance." When I said I didn't go, he would say, "No, I saw you from the stage." That's how he would fight with me as soon as he came home. But that's how I would sneak out and watch him. I used to watch from behind a pillar and come back before the last scene ended, before everyone left. After that, he used to finish the program, and I had to cook dinner for all of the performers.

By preventing his wife from attending his performances, Rattayya Sarma limited Rajyalakshmi to the domestic sphere, while coding public dance performance as exclusively male.

Spanning from the government-run dance institution, the Siddhendra Kalakshetra, near the entrance of the village to the open-air stage adjacent to the Ramalingeshvara temple in the heart of the village, most public spaces in Kuchipudi are intended for village brahmin men to teach classes and stage performances. Brahmin women, by comparison, are limited in their ability to freely interact with these spaces; even today, they might be present as audience members in a village performance, but they are rarely found in the Siddhendra Kalakshetra dance classrooms or other such public spaces, aside from the village temple. Like homosocial space in Moroccan society described by Fatima Mernissi (1987, 140), the gendering of space in the Kuchipudi village is drawn along the boundaries of public and private domains. Nevertheless, Rajyalakshmi's presence peeping from behind the pillar to watch her husband's performance demonstrates that the dichotomy between public and private is not always neatly defined (Lal 2005, 14–15).

VEDANTAM LAKSHMINARASAMMA

Vedantam Lakshminarasamma, also a resident of the Kuchipudi village, is the wife of Kuchipudi impersonator Vedantam Satyanarayana Sarma, who passed away in 2012 (two years before my interview with her).[5] Unlike Rajyalakshmi, who was eager to speak about her experiences of learning dance, Lakshminarasamma was far more reluctant. Her reticence surprised me, especially given her husband's fame and ongoing posthumous reputation in Kuchipudi dance circles. In our relatively short conversation, Lakshminarasamma noted that Satyanarayana Sarma had been trained not only by his older brother, Vedantam Prahlada Sarma, and another well-known village guru, Chinta Krishna Murthy, but also by her own father, Pasumarti Kondala Rao, thus demonstrating her interconnectedness with dance through multiple layers of kinship.

Like Rajyalakshmi, Lakshminarasamma also described that her husband never encouraged her to attend his performances, especially those occurring out of town, although she did attend his local performances:

> I never went anywhere if performances were happening outside the village. I only attended those performances that took place in our village, only those performances that took place in the Siddhendra Kalakshetra. Aside from that, he never used to take me anywhere, nor was I in the habit of going anywhere. That's how things were.

Lakshminarasamma's matter-of-fact and relatively terse responses again surprised me, especially in contrast to Satyanarayana Sarma's tendency to "breakthrough" into full performance (Hymes 2015, 31) in many of his formal and informal interviews (see introduction and chapter 2).

Notably, Lakshminarasamma's reluctance to speak may have been because Pasumarti Mrutyumjaya (Mutyam), a rising brahmin male performer in his mid-thirties from the Kuchipudi village, was present during the interview. Mutyam and I had become close friends during my fieldwork, and when he volunteered to introduce me to the women of the village in my return visit in 2014, I welcomed his presence, especially given his familiarity with the various brahmin households. Together, Mutyam and I conducted eight interviews with brahmin women from the village, including with Rajyalakshmi, Lakshminarasamma, and Swarajyalakshmi discussed in this chapter.[6] During the interviews we conducted together, I would begin by asking open-ended questions about a woman's family, domestic obligations, and experiences with dance. However, the more interviews we conducted together, the more Mutyam began to take over the role of interviewer, rapidly asking about a woman's knowledge of movement, pedagogy, and music. Mutyam would often conclude an interview by asking a woman to sing a line or two from a song she may have heard from watching and listening to the men around. Most women succinctly evaded his questions by simply stating, "I don't know anything."

These interview dynamics are apparent in the following conversation between Mutyam and Lakshminarasamma:

> Mutyam: When [Vedantam Satyanarayana Sarma] would practice singing for dance dramas, did you ever listen and sing along with him?

Lakshminarasamma: What do I know about that?
Mutyam: I mean, did you ever listen and learn?
Lakshminarasamma: I never used to sing. I don't know anything about that.
Mutyam: Can you sing a couple of lines from whatever you know?
Lakshminarasamma: There's nothing there. I don't know.
Mutyam: Did you ever learn dance or music?
Lakshminarasamma: I never learned anything. He used to come and go, but I never learned anything.
Mutyam: Did you ever want to learn dance or music?
Lakshminarasamma: I never had a desire to learn.

Mutyam repeated a similar set of questions at the end of our interview with Lakshminarasamma, entreating her to sing at least one line from *Bhāmākalāpam* or anything else she had heard while cooking in the kitchen. She responded again by simply stating, "I don't know anything." Lakshminarasamma's refusal to engage in the dance questions set forth by Mutyam contrasted with Rajyalakshmi, who was fully willing to outline her attempts and impediments in dance training.

Mutyam's presence as a village brahmin male dancer indisputably created a power dynamic in our interviews that seemed to have deterred many of the women from speaking freely. In their seminal ethnographic study of North Indian women's songs, Raheja and Gold (1994, 23) offer a relevant discussion about power relations in the interview context:

> [W]omen's speech, like all speech, is produced in specific historical and micropolitical contexts, and that what women will say reflects the power relationships implicit in the elicitation situation, and their own perceptions of what their speech will accomplish. If we rely only on women's interview statements, or on our observations of women's public adherence to the norms of silence and submission, we run the risk of assuming that women are incapable of using verbal strategies to oppose that dominant ideology.

Raheja and Gold instead focus on Indian women's expressive traditions—that is, songs and narratives—to examine modes of resistance implicit in the "hidden transcript" of women's speech (26). Aware of Raheja and Gold's robust examination of women's expressive traditions, I recognize the limitations of this interview conducted with Mutyam, which did not explore alternative forms of speech, like songs. By grounding the discourse in dance, Mutyam created a power dynamic in the interview that seemed to preclude Lakshminarasamma's participation. Lakshminarasamma's refusal to respond to Mutyam's questions also flags that the discursive framework of dance is not the only means by which these women construct meaning within quotidian Kuchipudi life, a point that is also apparent in the interview with Swarajyalakshmi.

VEMPATI SWARAJYALAKSHMI

I interviewed Vempati Swarajyalakshmi, the wife of renowned dance guru Vempati Chinna Satyam, in her home above the KAA in Chennai one year before her death in 2015. I also interacted with Swarajyalakshmi frequently during my fieldwork in the KAA in 2010, spending most afternoons in her upstairs residence in between morning and evening dance classes. While the direct quotations are from my 2014 interview with Swarajyalakshmi (conducted with Mutyam), my familiarity with her domestic life and daily routines from previous encounters during fieldwork also informs my discussion in this section.

Swarajyalakshmi's situation is, in many ways, different from those of her counterparts in the Kuchipudi village. Born to a brahmin family from a neighboring village, Swarajyalakshmi only came to the Kuchipudi village after her marriage in 1952. She resided there for three years while Chinna Satyam pursued his career in the burgeoning Madras film industry, and then moved to the city along with her mother-in-law, sisters-in-law, and nephew. When in Madras, Swarajyalakshmi lived with her extended family in a cramped apartment, which often housed many other relatives. A few years after her arrival to Madras, the whole family moved to Panagal Park, an area of the city where Chinna Satyam first established the KAA. At the time, the KAA functioned not only as a dance space, but also as Chinna Satyam's residence where he lived with his wife, five children, and other members of his extended family. The intermingling of the performative and the domestic extends to the current location of the KAA in R.A. Puram (another area in present-day Chennai), in which the bottom floor is the dance hall and the top floor serves as the residence for the Vempati family.

Living in an urban dance institute for most of her life, Swarajyalakshmi has had broad exposure to dance for decades. The rupture between domestic and performative spaces that characterizes the Kuchipudi village is absent in the KAA. Swarajyalakshmi and her sister-in-law were often responsible for feeding not only her family, but also the several dancers who resided in the KAA, including Kuchipudi village brahmins and any other visiting guests. In the Panagal Park location of the KAA, Swarajyalakshmi and other members of the Vempati family would sleep in the large dance hall at night, after Chinna Satyam conducted daylong lessons with scores of students. In other words, the KAA functioned as a dance institute by day and domestic space by night.

Swarajyalakshmi was thus surrounded by dance day in and day out, and although she herself did not learn to dance, she was able to articulate the details of her husband's career, including the names of dancers at the KAA, dates of performances, and locations of performances, to exactitude. Nevertheless, she was not always encouraged to attend these performances alongside her husband: "There was no reason to go. He never used to take me, nor did I ever want to go. I never used to ask him. My only job was to bow my head and say yes to whatever [my husband] said." Yet, despite this outright claim of exclusion and submission,

Swarajyalakshmi noted that later in her life, she did accompany her husband to performances, a shift that she credited to organizers who specially invited her to attend. She traveled with him to the Kuchipudi village and the urban centers of Mumbai, Mathura, Srirangam, and Trivandram (now Thiruvananthapuram) in India; she also traveled abroad with him, including trips to Sri Lanka and the United States.

Despite her attendance at some of her husband's performances, Swarajyalakshmi mirrored Lakshminarasamma in her reluctance to sing any elements from her husband's repertoire, particularly in response to questions posed by Mutyam.

Mutyam: Do you know any songs from his dance dramas? Normally, you would have been listening to the songs while cooking or sleeping.

Swarajyalakshmi: My songs are the ones that women sing in the house.

Mutyam: Women's songs are fine, but do you know any songs from [your husband's] dance dramas? Do you know any of those songs that he might have been humming during the day?

Author: Any songs are fine, like any woman's songs or a song from a dance item, perhaps.

Swarajyalakshmi: I don't know any songs used for dance items. I can't sing out loud. I'm not trained in *saṅgītam* [classical music]. I used to watch [my husband's] items, but never sing them. I only sing songs for god, or songs to be sung on Fridays, like *Lalitā Sahasranāma.* I used to sing those and cook.

Swarajyalakshmi deftly pointed to women's devotional songs, namely *Lalitā Sahasranāma* (One Thousand Names of Goddess Lakshmi), as a form of religious meaning, or symbolic capital (Bourdieu 1977, 1989), that subtly supersedes the value attributed to dance and music. Overtly excluded from the sphere of performance, Swarajyalakshmi turned to acts of religious devotionalism as forms of meaning-making in her everyday context (Pearson 1996).[7]

In her study of the Arangetram, the debut dance performance prominent in contemporary forms of Bharatanatyam in India and the American diaspora, Arthi Devarajan (2011, 5) draws on the work of Pierre Bourdieu (1977, 1989) to analyze the various threads of capital present in Indian dance performance: "The capital at work in this economy is composed of individual and collective prestige, Hindu and Indian cultural narratives, symbolic capital and material wealth, personal identity and performed characters, and insider and outsider status within cultural, practice-oriented interpretive communities." Devarajan (2011, 11) reads both training and performance as essential components in the pedagogical culture of dance as *habitus,* or "a social system wherein there are goals, *praxes,* priorities, social codes and hierarchies understood commonly by all members of the community (Bourdieu 1977: 72, 82–85)." The Arangetram provides an aspiring dancer with the symbolic capital that enables her to move upward in her dance community, while also training her body in the *habitus* that inculcates a particular embodied ideal envisioned in a particular character, such as Satyabhama (Devarajan 2011, 20, 28).[8]

Devarajan's interpretation of symbolic capital is helpful to frame the aforementioned narratives of Kuchipudi brahmin women. While some women from village brahmin families, such as Rajyalakshmi, desire to participate in the economy of dance and thus achieve a level of symbolic capital akin to their male counterparts, others like Swarajyalakshmi veer toward alternative expressions of meaning, namely religious capital through women's ritual songs. In his discussion of Telugu brahmin women's oral tradition of the *Rāmāyaṇa,* Velcheru Narayana Rao (1991, 133) notes that "[t]he women who sing these songs have not sought to overthrow the male-dominated family structure; they would rather work within it. They have no interest in direct confrontation with authority; their interest, rather, is in making room for themselves to move." Like the women of Narayana Rao's study, Swarajyalakshmi uses religious songs as a form of ritual capital that differs from the symbolic capital acquired through embodied dance performance. Swarajyalakshmi's responses to Mutyam's questions express a subtle form of resistance to the world of dance, suggesting alternative forms of meaning-making in quotidian Kuchipudi life. Such alternative modes of meaning are not present, however, in the perspectives of Swarajyalakshmi's daughter, Balatripurasundari. Baliakka, who flatly refused to have Mutyam present during our recorded interview, expressed a longing to participate in the embodied labors of dance training and performance.

CHAVALI BALATRIPURASUNDARI

Visitors to Chinna Satyam's KAA in Panagal Park in the 1970s and 1980s would have witnessed rows and rows of female dancing bodies, interspersed with a few male dancers, all replicating the neat lines and stylistic bends of Chinna Satyam's newly envisioned Kuchipudi aesthetics. What visitors would not have found, however, were Chinna Satyam's own daughters dancing alongside his female students. According to his third and youngest daughter Baliakka, Chinna Satyam vociferously discouraged his daughters and nieces from learning dance, worried that participation in public dance performance might interfere with their future marriage proposals. Although leaving the Kuchipudi village decades earlier, Chinna Satyam still adhered to the long-standing practice of excluding Kuchipudi brahmin women from performance. Chinna Satyam may have trained hundreds of female dancers for decades, but he never formally taught any female member of his family. Baliakka's mother Swarajyalakshmi articulated the reasons for her husband's choice not to teach the girls in his family:

Author: Why didn't Chinna Satyam Garu agree to teaching girls from his family?

Swarajyalakshmi: He would say, "We have to get our girls married. If they become crazy for dance, their future husband or future in-laws might not like it and cause trouble. What's the point of that?" Thinking all of these things, he always used to say that girls should not be taught to dance.

Author: But girls from other families could learn, right?

Swarajyalakshmi: Other girls might learn. They used to come and go, and we don't know if they had any troubles or not. But he never taught our girls. In the Kuchipudi village, women do not learn to dance.

Baliakka, whose perspectives on dance informed much of my knowledge of Kuchipudi brahmin women's experiences during my fieldwork, also noted similar reasons during our formal interview in 2014.[9] She speculated on her father's reasons for preventing her and her sisters from participating in dance:

> My father didn't teach us. He didn't encourage us. That's because he struggled ever since his childhood to get into this field. He struggled a lot, and everyone knows about that. Because he struggled, he didn't want his children to struggle. Even though he knew we were interested, he would avoid us. Also, because we're girls, and we would have to get married. He would think, "Will they get married? What troubles will other people give them?" and wouldn't encourage us. He knew that we really liked dance. That's why he thought if he cut our interest in the beginning, it wouldn't develop. Even though he didn't outwardly encourage us, our foundation fell there, near him [even after our marriage].

Chinna Satyam's responses seem particularly incongruous to the middle-class sentiment of Madras in the mid-twentieth century, in which middle-class and upper-caste women increasingly began to participate in South Indian dance (Meduri 1988). In fact, many of the prominent dancers in Chinna Satyam's academy were also from Telugu brahmin families, revealing the paradox underlying Chinna Satyam's refusal to teach his own daughters to dance. Although his institution enabled the rise of middle-class and upper-caste women's participation in urban Kuchipudi dance, he refused to teach his own daughters because of the very fact that they were technically considered to be Kuchipudi village brahmin women even in a cosmopolitan context.

This exclusion from dance was keenly felt by Baliakka. Growing up in the KAA in the 1970s, Baliakka was surrounded by an atmosphere of dance from morning until night. Whether it was watching her father's early morning choreography sessions or listening to the sounds of rehearsal upon coming home from school, Baliakka lived in a world immersed in dance. Although her father refused to teach her and her siblings, Baliakka did learn by intense observation and occasional practice. She spent most of her free time in her father's dance classrooms and would play the *tānpura* [stringed instrument] to accompany her father and Kanaka Durga, the Karnatak vocalist employed to sing dance items during classes. Baliakka describes these moments as follows:

> While my father was teaching, I'd play the *tānpura*, and watch him and listen to him. That's how I learned. It's like Ekalavya. Ekalavya also didn't learn from his guru. He learned the *vidyā* [knowledge] in secret. Like that, when my father was teaching his students, I'd sit on the side and observe how he was teaching . . . After the item was over, I would go upstairs into a room and close the door so that no one could watch and quickly practice the movements myself. I would only get satisfaction when I could do the movements correctly. Then, I'd sneak back downstairs without anyone knowing and sit again and play the *tānpura*.

Ekalavya, the son of the chief of the Nishadas (a clan of hunters), is a well-known character from the Sanskrit epic *Mahābhārata* who was rejected by Drona, the teacher of the Pandavas and Kauravas (the main protagonists of the epic). Mastering the skills of archery on his own, Ekalavya went before Drona, asking for his guidance once more. Drona agreed, demanding a seemingly impossible *dīkṣā* (fee) from Ekalavya:

> Droṇa replied, "Give me your thumb!" And hearing Droṇa's harsh command, Ekalavya kept his promise; forever devoted to the truth, with a happy face and unburdened mind, he cut off his thumb without a moment's hesitation and gave it to Droṇa. When thereafter the Niṣāda [Ekalavya] shot with his fingers, he was no longer as fast as he had been before (*Mahābhārata* 1(7)123.35–40).[10]

Baliakka's invocation of Ekalavya underscores her father's lack of approval; like Ekalavya, who famously cut off his thumb after he learned to master archery without his guru's help, Baliakka learned to dance without her father's consent. Also, like Ekalavya, Baliakka was never formally initiated in dance by her father, a point that she repeatedly references when comparing herself to his other female students.

The 1970s was likely the most generative period of Chinna Satyam's career, and he often spent many early mornings in the small hut behind the KAA complex in Panagal Park choreographing new dance items and dance dramas. Chinna Satyam never allowed anyone to directly watch these choreography sessions, a point that was reiterated to me by both Baliakka and her younger brother Vempati Ravi Shankar.[11] Baliakka recollects her furtive attempts to watch her father's choreography, along with her siblings:

> I used to watch when my father choreographed. Ever since we were little, we used to watch him teach, and watched how he choreographed . . . The hut [in the back of

> the academy where he did choreography] used to have thatched walls, kind of like a fence. There were holes in the walls. We would sit by those holes and watch him compose. He never wanted anyone sitting near him while he was composing because they might disturb him . . . It was just him and the student. He never liked it if anyone extra sat with him. That's why he never let anyone in to watch in case they would disturb him. But we really wanted to watch. So, we used to sneak on the paths and watch from those holes. If he heard any footsteps, he'd shouted, "Who's there?" and we'd quickly run away.

Baliakka could only watch her father's secret choreography sessions through holes in the hut left by rodents or, occasionally, when serving tea or water to her father and the student. Her body as a dancer, however, was never legitimated in this choreography space.

Occasionally, however, Baliakka did have the opportunity to dance alongside the other students by sneaking her way into the back of a crowded dance classroom so that no one would notice. If her father happened to see her standing at the end of the long line of students, he would stop the class at once and say with a mocking tone: "Is there anyone else? Are the pots and pans going to dance too? Go and call your mother. She'll also dance . . . Get out of here!" Baliakka would run crying to her mother, who would only admonish her for trying to dance in the first place:

> If I ever went inside and told my mother, she would say: "Are you going to do any programs? What's the point? Why do you want to make your father angry? Don't do it. Just watch." My mother would say that. But I was overcome with that desire to dance. I always thought we should dance. That's why sometimes when I was sleeping at night after eating, I'd pull the blanket all the way over my head, and move my hands, sing the songs, and do the expressions. I'd do actions inside my blanket. That's how. And no one should be able to see what I was doing. If they saw, my father might get angry that I was trying to dance.

These secret practices became the only way for Baliakka to discipline her body in the labors of Chinna Satyam's cosmopolitan Kuchipudi. In a similar vein, Baliakka relayed that sometimes she would lock herself in a dressing room and practice facial expressions in front of the mirror, pretending to be a student scolded by her father. Alternating between first-person singular ("I") and first-person plural ("we"), she states:

> There used to be a dressing room. We'd go there and shut the door so that no one could watch. In that room, there was a small mirror. Thinking of how he did the movements and how he did the expressions, we'd look into the mirror and do the movements. We'd remember how our father would get mad if a student didn't do a movement correctly, as he had envisioned it. We'd remember how he'd get irritated

> and how he'd get angry. We also used to hear all of those words. We used to listen to those conversations. Listening to them, we used to go to our room, and I'd pretend like I was like my father scolding a student. We could imitate our father, having watched him since we were young. He was who we would look at. He was our role model. He was the one who we admired.[12]

Although excluded from dance by her father, Baliakka clearly envisions Chinna Satyam as her role model; her attempts to *impersonate* him in the mirror enabled her to experience the student-teacher relationship from which she was excluded.

Although Chinna Satyam discouraged all his children from dancing, he eventually began teaching his younger son Ravi Shankar, whose exceptional talents suggested a promising future as a professional dancer. Seeing her younger brother encouraged to dance, Baliakka began to question her father as to why she could not also learn. Chinna Satyam responded with the same stock answers regarding marriage proposals and future hardships, noting that it was not Kuchipudi *sāmpradāyam* (tradition) to teach brahmin girls.

But he also discouraged Baliakka by simply saying about her and her sisters: "Why do you want to dance? You all have wooden faces (*cekka mohālu*). Your faces don't suit dance." Chinna Satyam's disapproving words regarding his daughters' expressionless, wooden faces, their *cekka mohālu*, shapes how Baliakka views herself as a dancer, even in her adult life. Although she now runs her own dance school in Hyderabad, Abhinayavani Nritya Niketan, she rarely performs in public or even practices in front of her students.[13] Proscribed from the "sweat, blood, tears, slipping or stained saris, callused feet, missteps, or familiar gestures" (Srinivasan 2012, 8) that dance entails, particularly the symbolic capital accrued through public performance, Baliakka limits herself to teaching students and only occasionally performs in *vēṣam* for her brother Ravi Shankar's dance dramas. She describes her hesitation when teaching and occasionally performing, again alternating between first-person plural and singular:

> We would feel nervous even to dance among four people. Even if we teach with great concentration and confidence, we feel very shy to dance, we feel embarrassed. Recently, my younger brother has been doing my father's ballets, and I've been doing some small, small roles. I have stage fear even to do those small roles. I'm very scared to get onstage.

During my fieldwork, Baliakka was often reluctant to demonstrate expressions or dance in front of me and her other students, despite her long-standing embodied knowledge of Chinna Satyam's style of Kuchipudi.

In fact, Baliakka stands alone as the sole Kuchipudi teacher who actively attempts to adhere with exactitude to Chinna Satyam's choreography. Most other dance teachers I have trained under in the United States and India draw on their own embodied memories of dancing under Chinna Satyam years beforehand, which results in a wide variety of interpretations even for a single movement. By contrast, Baliakka's lack of formal training under her father prompts her to seek out the "correct" rendering of a particular movement, and she spends most of her free time watching video recordings of Chinna Satyam's dance dramas and solo items. Baliakka's repertoire remains limited, for the most part, to Chinna Satyam's choreography as she maintains his legacy through her students, even after his death.

Although Chinna Satyam was aware of Baliakka's efforts in teaching, he never fully gave support to her in the way that he did to his sons, who took over running the KAA following his death in 2012. In the reported speech of Baliakka's mother, Swarajyalakshmi, Chinna Satyam stated that "if [Baliakka] likes teaching dance, then let her do it. If not, she shouldn't." Baliakka acknowledges the lack of her father's overt approval, especially in comparison to the degree of support given to her brother Ravi Shankar. Yet, she stands alone as one of the few examples of Kuchipudi brahmin women who participate in Kuchipudi dance professionally. The only other example is Baliakka's older sister Kameshwari, who also runs a nearby dance school in Hyderabad. Baliakka often aids Kameshwari in dance-related questions, and their students collectively perform together throughout the year. During my fieldwork, Baliakka's continued passion for dance was palpable, and she expressed an eagerness for detailing her experiences and knowledge of Chinna Satyam's oeuvre. Underlying her enthusiasm, however, was a distinct wistfulness; Baliakka had longed to be recognized by her father and her dance community in the manner of his other female students, including my own dance teacher of two decades, Sasikala Penumarthi.

As a Kuchipudi brahmin woman, however, Baliakka can never fully embody the idealized middle-class womanhood central to postcolonial forms of "classical" Indian dance (Srinivasan 2012, 36). Baliakka can never be like the other female dancers at the KAA who gained a reputation for public performance and then went on to establish their own globally recognized dance schools. Proscribed from performance since childhood, Baliakka's authority in dance remains limited to replicating as precisely as possible her father's choreography; it can never be achieved by performing herself. Baliakka's inherited vision of her *cekka moham*, her ostensibly wooden face, also prevents her from becoming the ideal Kuchipudi female dancer in the eyes of her father and the Kuchipudi brahmin community, thereby doubly excluding her from the symbolic capital of public dance performance. This double exclusion is characteristic not only of Kuchipudi brahmin women, but also of *devadāsīs* across South India.

FIGURE 22. Chavali Balatripurasundari in her home in Hyderabad. Photo by author.

SPEAKING FROM LIMINAL SPACES: *DEVADĀSĪ*S AND KUCHIPUDI BRAHMIN WOMEN IN SOUTH INDIA

Narratives of exclusion not only characterize the stories of Kuchipudi brahmin women, but also the lives of *devadāsī*s across South India who have been barred from performance due to extensive colonial and postcolonial reform efforts (see introduction). In his ethnographic work with *devadāsī*s in Tamil- and Telugu-speaking South India, Davesh Soneji (2012) describes *devadāsī* subjectivities as unfinished, caught between a nostalgic colonial past and an evolving postcolonial present. Although banned from dancing in temple or salon contexts due to state legislative reforms, *devadāsī* women's bodies still house the residual memories of performance. As an example, Soneji turns to R. Muttukkannammal, a *devadāsī* woman from the Tamil town of Viralimalai who performs, among other pieces, the long-forgotten *noṭṭusvaram,* or "note" song, based on Irish marching-band tunes, and *mōṭi,* a hybrid Hindi-Tamil "drinking song" (181).[14] For Muttukkannammal, performing the dance pieces *noṭṭusvaram* and *mōṭi* is not only a mode of remembering the past, but also an articulation of a sense of self. Drawing on the words of Muttukkannammal, Soneji argues that "mnemonic iteration through the act of performance is effective for *devadāsī*s at the level of individual identity" (188). In other words, remembering the past through embodied performance serves to construct selfhood in the present.

Soneji underscores the connection between memory, performance, and selfhood in his ethnographic work with Telugu-speaking *kalāvantulu* (Telugu for *devadāsī*) women from the East Godavari district:

> For some women in courtesan communities today, however, the [courtesan dance] repertoire is used as a mode of telling; it is mobilized to consolidate an identity they can live with. What is articulated by women in the Godavari delta is, I think, an alternative mode of being, an identity that uses the past in order to establish a relationship with themselves in the present. (190)

These accounts of *devadāsī/kalāvantulu* memory reveal a collective nostalgia which "serves as a mode of suspending the past in a way that makes it available and affective for the shaping of a contemporary selfhood" (213). For these *devadāsī*s, personation, in the words of Purnima Mankekar (2015, 190), is grounded in recollections of an embodied past of performance, a past they are prohibited from enacting in the present.

In her ethnographic work with *jōgati*s, South Indian Dalit women who are dedicated to the goddess Yellamma and refer to themselves as *devadāsī*s, Lucinda Ramberg (2014) further interrogates understandings of subjectivity and personhood, particularly in relation to broader discourses of *devadāsī* reform. Ramberg focuses on the embodied material practices of *jōgati*s, who, upon their initiation, become ritual caretakers of the goddess Yellamma (3). In considering the impact of colonial and postcolonial reform on *devadāsī* identity, Ramberg situates *jōgatis*' identities between the dialectic of marriage and prostitution:

> Within the symbolic and material economy surrounding Yellamma, devadasis are both *muttaide* (wife) and *randi* (prostitute, widow). Indeed, this double valence is precisely what makes them, and the devi [goddess] they embody, powerful and valuable. As wives of the devi, devadasis can and must transition from *muttaide* to *randi* and back again . . . Devadasis thus incorporate the status between wife and the non-wife, and threaten the distinction between them. (160)

Ramberg notes the complicated effects of state-imposed sanctions on the *devadāsī*'s dual identity. State legislation, such as the Karnataka Devadasis (Prohibition of Dedication) Bill, sought to foreclose the complexity of *devadāsī* identity to simply that of a prostitute (60–61). Ramberg, however, interrogates the assumption that *jōgati*s are exploited and without agency by arguing that through their affiliations with the goddess, *jōgati*s are empowered, on the one hand, to claim material resources of dominant-caste devotees and patrons and, on the other, to draw on their sexuality as a source of income for their families. These forms of material and symbolic capital, or value in Ramberg's words, add complexity to the role of *jōgati*s as women dedicated to the goddess (173). Like the brahmin women of Kuchipudi, *jōgati*s express divergent means of accumulating symbolic capital in their everyday lives.

These scholarly discourses reveal the marginalized position of *devadāsī*s in South India who have been overtly excluded through the effects of colonial and postcolonial reform. The *devadāsī/kalāvantulu* women described by Soneji (2012) were forced to reside on the margins as their repertoire was rewritten into "classical" Indian dance forms such as Kuchipudi and Bharatanatyam. The *jōgati*s featured in Ramberg's (2014) study must contend with the national rescripting of *devadāsī* identity as equivalent to prostitution, even as they navigate alternative religious and kinship networks. As nonbrahmin and marginalized women, *devadāsī*s can never appeal to forms of patriarchy and tradition in the manner of their brahmin counterparts. As a result, *devadāsī*s are doubly effaced, exemplifying Gayatri Spivak's (1988, 83) claim that if "the subaltern has no history and cannot speak, the subaltern as female is even more deeply in shadow."

It is important to underscore that although Kuchipudi brahmin women are proscribed from performance, they still participate in an economy of caste-based authority to which *devadāsī* women do not have access. As upper-caste women from hereditary Kuchipudi families, women such as Rajyalakshmi and Baliakka enjoy a degree of authority not accorded to the *devadāsī*s of contemporary South

India. Evincing this is the fact that women from hereditary Kuchipudi brahmin families often espouse a brahminical and patriarchal worldview that exclusively authorizes their fathers, husbands, and sons in the work of Kuchipudi dance. As cited in the previous chapter, Rajyalakshmi told me that only men from her village should take on the *strī-vēṣam*:

> Ever since my childhood, it always used to be the case that men would take on the *strī-vēṣam* to perform. From what I know, it was never the case that women would put on a costume and perform onstage. Nowadays, people are performing their own *pātras* [characters]. Even now, in my village, our men still perform in *strī-vēṣam*. Outsiders also may be performing, but none of us like it. It's only appealing if men from our village take on the role . . . People might ask the question why? Who should perform? Only our people [i.e., people from the Kuchipudi village]. Who should be appreciated? Only our people. Hundreds of people have danced. We villagers may go and watch. But we all think that whoever may be performing, only people from our village who have our blood should dance. No one else has that. That's the mind-set of all our people.

Despite having been beaten and shouted at for her attempts to dance, Rajyalakshmi continues to legitimate her brahmin male counterparts, including her husband and sons, as the rightful bearers of Kuchipudi *sāmpradāyam,* its brahminical tradition of authority. No one else, in Rajyalakshmi's own words, is aesthetically appealing.

The other women from the Kuchipudi village I spoke with also ascribed to a framework that legitimized their fathers, brothers, husbands, and sons in the profession of Kuchipudi dance. For example, most women began their interviews by telling me their family lineage, taking special pride in pointing out the various male dance professionals in their families. Similarly, Baliakka repeatedly deferred (and continues to defer) to her male counterparts, both in her childhood recollections and in her professional career as a Kuchipudi dance teacher. She positions her father and brother as the primary authorities in Kuchipudi dance techniques and presentation and mirrors their aesthetics as closely as possible when training her own students. This deference to her father's authority is evident in her own words:

> Even until this day, I'm afraid. Even for doing *naṭṭuvāṅgam,* because holding the cymbals and sitting onstage is my father's place. So that's one fear. My hands begin to sweat. Even now. If I look at the audience, I get nervous, so I don't look.

Playing the *naṭṭuvāṅgam* (cymbals), particularly in the context of Chinna Satyam's style of Kuchipudi, is usually reserved for a guru, often male, who directs a given performance. Baliakka expresses fear at even holding the cymbals and sitting onstage "in her father's place," even after his death. Further evincing this is the fact that Baliakka never acknowledges herself as a dance guru, a title she reserves solely for her father. As Baliakka's case makes evident, village brahmin women's bodies are not deemed aesthetically suitable mediums for expressing Kuchipudi dance, even as Kuchipudi brahmin men are authorized to don the *strī-vēṣam*. Kuchipudi brahmin women paradoxically reside at the interstice between the normative ideal of the Kuchipudi brahmin man (either performer or guru) and the marginalized figure of the *devadāsī* woman.

The experiences of Kuchipudi brahmin women mirror Narayana Rao's (1991) research of Telugu brahmin women's songs of the *Rāmāyāṇa*. According to Narayana Rao, "These songs are a part of the education Brahmin women receive, a part of brahminic ideology, which constructs women's consciousness in a way suitable to life in a world ultimately controlled by men" (133). By authorizing Kuchipudi brahmin men in the labor of dance performance, the women of hereditary Kuchipudi brahmin families paradoxically uphold normative conceptions of gender and caste that preclude their own participation in the sphere of dance. In the words of Uma Chakravarti (2003), Kuchipudi brahmin women serve as gatekeepers for brahminical patriarchy:

> The term 'brahminical patriarchy' is a useful way to isolate this unique structure of patriarchy, by now dominant in many parts of India. It is a set of rules and institutions in which caste and gender are linked, each shaping the other and where women are crucial in maintain the boundaries between castes. (34)

The experiences of women like Rajyalakshmi and Baliakka reflect the intersections of gender and brahminical patriarchy operative in the Kuchipudi village and Kuchipudi dance, more broadly. On the one hand, their upper-caste identities as *brahmin* women position them within a brahminical and patriarchal worldview that authorizes Kuchipudi brahmin performance as "classical," while delimiting *devadāsī* performance and identity as illegitimate. On the other hand, their gender identities as brahmin *women* from the Kuchipudi village place them in the margins of this normative ideal. These shifting negotiations across caste and gender illustrate the importance of a dynamic analysis of power and subordination when examining the intersectionality of caste, gender, and other axes of difference in South Asia (Thomas 2018, 8–9).

Kuchipudi as place also contributes to this narrative of exclusion. Although upper-caste and middle/upper-class female dancing bodies overwhelmingly populate the dance classrooms of urban and transnational forms of Kuchipudi, brahmin women from hereditary village families are prevented entry into this burgeoning sphere of cosmopolitan dance. Even brahmin women who reside in the urban centers of Chennai and Hyderabad, such as Swarajyalakshmi and Baliakka, still ascribe to the village's *sāmpradāyam*. Kuchipudi as *place* thus molds how village brahmin women interact with Kuchipudi as *dance*. These women can never fulfill the normative ideals they ascribe to, despite their desire to do so: they are neither Kuchipudi brahmin men who uphold a legacy of tradition in the village nor urban middle- or upper-class women who are authorized in the performative practices of "classical" Indian dance. As a result, all Kuchipudi brahmin women appear to metaphorically express *cekka mohālu*—wooden, expressionless, and voiceless faces—that proscribe their entry into performance, even as they function as gatekeepers for a brahminical worldview.

. . .

The landscape of Kuchipudi dance has entirely changed in the decade since I embarked on this project in 2009. In 2012, two years after the completion of the main portion of my fieldwork, Vedantam Satyanarayana Sarma and Vempati Chinna Satyam passed away. In the years following, other key figures interviewed in this book also passed away, including P.V.G. Krishna Sarma, Vedantam Lakshminarasamma, and Vempati Swarajyalakshmi. In January 2018, Vempati Ravi Shankar, Baliakka's younger brother, suddenly passed away after a failed kidney transplant.

All these changes in her family have resulted in some unintended consequences: Baliakka is now the apparent heir to her father's legacy. Aside from her sister-in-law, who is the primary teacher at the KAA, Baliakka is the only living member of her immediate family who teaches in a thriving dance school, and she is increasingly invited to attend functions and events in her father's memory.[15] Baliakka now has approximately fifty students, including a team of experienced dancers who perform every few weeks at festivals and other celebrations in Hyderabad and nearby urban locales. Notably, Baliakka's most outstanding student is a nonbrahmin young woman who serves as her right hand in the classroom.

When I returned to Baliakka's classroom in July 2018, I found it bustling with activity. Baliakka was in the midst of training a male student to perform solo items for an all-male dance festival while also reviewing items with a group of her most experienced female dancers, who were performing at another public festival that weekend. Baliakka suddenly stopped the practice in the middle of an item to shout at a younger dancer in the front row for not executing the three-beat step, *dhi-dhi-tai*. "What are you doing?" she yelled. "You're skipping a step by not striking *samam* [flat step]. Don't be lazy. *Dhi-dhi-tai*," she said sternly. As I watched the dancers practice a variety of items from Chinna Satyam's repertoire, I was struck by how much Baliakka's dance classroom resembled the main hall of the KAA in Chennai, with its rows of dancing bodies replicating the neat lines and stylistic bends of Chinna Satyam's unique Kuchipudi aesthetic. Except this time, Baliakka was not hiding in the back of the dance classroom, avoiding her father's gaze; instead, she was seated in the most authoritative position, underneath a portrait of her late father, watching keenly for any misstep.

More recently, Mutyam sent me a video recording of Baliakka dancing the Kshetrayya *padam, Vāḍaligite* (lit., "He's annoyed!") at a festival in the city of Guntur, Andhra Pradesh, in January 2019. Choosing not to wear the elaborate costume and makeup of contemporary Kuchipudi dancers, Baliakka was simply adorned in a red silk sari, reminiscent of older recordings of Vedantam Satyanarayana Sarma enacting Satyabhama.[16] Although she never formally learned the piece from her father, Baliakka danced with ease in this recording, skillfully portraying the angry heroine complaining to her girlfriend about her lover Krishna. When watching the video, I found a remarkable change in the dance teacher who told me five years earlier: "Even if [I] teach with great concentration and confidence, [I] feel very shy to dance, [I] feel embarrassed … I have stage fear even to do those small roles. I'm very scared to get onstage." Once reluctant to dance in front of her students in the confines of her classroom, today Baliakka performs in public to enact the very movements that have inhabited her body for decades.

Baliakka, the Ekalavya of Kuchipudi dance, has a remarkable story of hardship, longing, and ultimately triumph. As a Kuchipudi brahmin woman, she was forbidden from learning dance by her father, a world-renowned Kuchipudi guru who taught hundreds of women to dance, except Baliakka and her sisters. Nevertheless, she persevered and, through a series of unforeseen circumstances, the future of her father's legacy now rests on the shoulders of Baliakka, a Kuchipudi brahmin woman who, until very recently, has been proscribed from dance. And although she still turns to her father for legitimacy (as evinced by the numerous photographs of her father in her dance classroom), Baliakka is now the repository for Kuchipudi dance knowledge. While it is true that Baliakka has relied on her father and her younger brother to legitimize her role as a dance teacher, the landscape has shifted dramatically over the course of the last decade. Today, Baliakka is finally able to embody an authoritative position as a Kuchipudi guru, occupying the seat once reserved for village brahmin men like her father.

Baliakka's case illustrates not only the reshaping of her father's legacy, but also the contingency of hegemonic brahmin masculinity. As a result of the changes implemented by Chinna Satyam's KAA, men and women from a variety of caste backgrounds and nationalities can learn Kuchipudi dance. In the village, the brahmin man occupies the center of his performative and domestic world; but in the urban and transnational context, the brahmin male body is increasingly obsolete, particularly as an array of dancers, including hereditary brahmin women like Baliakka, begin to dance. The expansion of Kuchipudi from a village dance form to a transnational "classical" tradition not only expands the boundaries of Kuchipudi dance beyond the village, but also forecloses the possibility for achieving hegemonic brahmin masculinity through impersonation. To paraphrase the words of one interlocutor, there is no need for men to dance as women when women, even village brahmin women, are dancing themselves.

The expansion of Kuchipudi from village to urban/transnational dance form has, in a somewhat circuitous fashion, enabled Baliakka to become a Kuchipudi guru in her own right. In continuing to assert her right to dance, Baliakka is casting aside her *cekka-moham,* her supposed wooden face, to become the bearer of Kuchipudi *sāmpradāyam*. Baliakka is now the embodiment of her father's legacy, a position that I certainly did not anticipate her to inhabit when I met her for the first time nearly a decade ago. By decentering the brahmin male body in *vēṣam* and privileging the "hidden transcript" of women's speech (Gold and Raheja 1994, 26), this chapter positions Baliakka as the unexpected heroine of Kuchipudi dance history.

Conclusion

Rewriting the Script for Kuchipudi Dance

When I returned to the Kuchipudi village in July 2018, I found the grounds of the Siddhendra Kalakshetra buzzing with activity. A group of dancers were gathered on the front steps of the sprawling concrete building, gossiping in Telugu and sipping chai from white paper cups. Taking off my shoes and adding them to the piles of sandals scattered across the ground, I nervously walked inside and looked around expectantly for the familiar faces of the brahmin men—Vedantam Ramalingasastry, Yeleswarapu Srinivas, Chinta Ravi Balakrishna, and Pasumarti Haranadh—who normally conduct classes at the Kalakshetra. Used to being one among a handful of students during my fieldwork, I was surprised to see each classroom filled with hundreds of dancers, both men and women, their clothes dripping with sweat from the morning classes.

In the front dance hall, I found Chinta Ravi Balakrishna, a younger brahmin teacher, seated on a raised platform. Ravi Balakrishna's voice, amplified by the microphone in front of him, resounded across the room as he chanted out the syllabic beats for the *caturasra-jati*s, the combination of basic steps set to a four-beat time-measure, *ta-ka-dhi-mi*. Ravi Balakrishna's face broke into a wide smile when he saw me, and he beckoned me onto the platform. "We're running a three-day training for Kuchipudi teachers from all over the state of Andhra Pradesh," he said enthusiastically. I explained that I needed his signature to include his picture and interview in the book I was working on, and he readily agreed, even announcing my research project to the room of dancers before me. Reluctant to interrupt the class further, I watched from the front of the room as the rows of dancers practiced the movements in alternating batches.

As I wandered from room to room, I found the same setup: a brahmin male dance teacher seated in the front of the room, his voice amplified by a microphone, teaching basic steps and combinations of steps to rows of dancers drenched in sweat. In all the rooms, the movements were familiar; in fact, they were the exact same steps taught to me by my Atlanta-based dance teacher, Sasikala Penumarthi, who had been trained under Vempati Chinna Satyam at the Kuchipudi Art Academy (KAA) in the 1980s. Aside from some minor variations, the steps were also the same as those I had danced in institutes in urban India, including at the KAA in Chennai, the Kuchipudi Kalakshetram in Vishakapatnam, and Baliakka's classroom in Hyderabad.

Given the controversies of Chinna Satyam's *Bhāmākalāpam,* discussed in chapter 4, I was surprised by what I saw. Chinna Satyam's urban and transnational style of Kuchipudi, which is open to both male and female dancers from a range of caste backgrounds, was now being touted within the village as the standard form of pedagogy for dance teachers from all over the state of Andhra Pradesh. The ostensibly traditional elements of the Kuchipudi repertoire, including *Bhāmākalāpam,* seemed immaterial to the hundreds of dancing bodies before me. Instead, Chinna Satyam's cosmopolitan style of Kuchipudi was presented as a new tradition of brahminical authority, or *sāmpradāyam,* in the village. The reverse flow from urban/transnational to village demonstrates the porousness of these boundaries in the contemporary Kuchipudi landscape. As Chinna Satyam's Kuchipudi dominated the halls of the Siddhendra Kalakshetra in the village, the brahmin male body in *strī-vēṣam* was nowhere to be seen. Yet, the brahmin male teacher still retained his seat of power as the gatekeeper of Kuchipudi dance.

More than twelve years have passed since my initial visit to Kuchipudi in 2006, when I first encountered Vedantam Satyanarayana Sarma singing Satyabhama's *pravēśa daruvu* on the veranda of his house (see introduction). Over the years, it has become evident that despite its long-standing power in the Kuchipudi village, the donning of Satyabhama's *vēṣam* is not an enduring practice. Although impersonating Satyabhama remains a prescriptive mandate for all Kuchipudi brahmin men, only a select handful are successful at doing so. Changing perspectives on gender and sexuality outside the Kuchipudi village along with increased participation by women in Kuchipudi dance have altered the perception of impersonation in broader urban and transnational spaces.[1] In the current South Indian performance context, enactments of Satyabhama by brahmin male dancers often function as placeholders of "tradition" rather than displays of aesthetic and performative skill. Increasingly, such performances are displaced by the new *sāmpradāyam* of items from Chinna Satyam's repertoire. In dance classrooms in Atlanta, for example, the term "*Bhāmākalāpam*" usually only references Satyabhama's introductory item choreographed by Chinna Satyam. In fact, many of my fellow dancers, my teacher notwithstanding, have little knowledge of the full dance drama, including the lengthy spoken dialogues between Satyabhama and *sūtradhāra*/Madhavi/Madhava.

The arc of this book, which moves from village to urban and transnational spaces, examines the declining value ascribed to the brahmin male body in *vēṣam* from the mid-twentieth century to the contemporary context. Today, Kuchipudi is not simply a global dance form performed in various geographic locales; it is also a form of transnational labor (Srinivasan 2012), particularly as dancers and their choreographies move back and forth across global spaces with the aid of YouTube, Skype, and other online platforms. Professional Kuchipudi dancers, both men and women, often travel to the United States and Canada over the summer months to run workshops and give performances for local organizations. These lucrative opportunities are coveted, especially for male dancers who increasingly struggle to find avenues for performance, both in India and abroad. With transnational audiences, however, come transnational expectations. For example, when I approached a Seattle-based Telugu community member to organize a performance for Venku and his troupe, it was requested that the Kuchipudi artists perform a *yakṣagāna* such as *Bhakta-Prahalāda* (featuring the devotion of the young boy Prahalada to the god Vishnu), but nothing in *strī-vēṣam.* "Our audiences don't like to watch men dance as women," the organizer succinctly told me. *Strī-vēṣam,* which was once a normative practice in the Kuchipudi village, is now equated with nonnormative interpretations of gender and sexuality for South Asian American audiences. The shifting perceptions of impersonation, as evinced by this Seattle-based organizer, are certainly not lost on the brahmins of the village; while brahmin men may occasionally don the *strī-vēṣam* for local performances in and around Kuchipudi, they rarely perform in *strī-vēṣam* abroad.

The transformation of Kuchipudi from a village tradition to a "classical" Indian dance form in the mid-twentieth century initially relied on the brahmin male body in *strī-vēṣam,* as evident by the enormous popularity of Satyanarayana Sarma as Satyabhama in the 1960s and 1970s. However, the urbanization of Kuchipudi through Chinna Satyam's KAA has rendered obsolete the utility of the brahmin impersonator. Increasingly, nonbrahmin and non-male-identified bodies inhabit Kuchipudi tradition, particularly the *Bhāmākalāpam* dance drama, which was once circumscribed to hereditary brahmin men. Today, Kuchipudi dance no longer needs the brahmin male body in *strī-vēṣam,* thereby positing a challenge not only to village performance, but also hegemonic brahmin masculinity constructed in the process of that performance. The death of Satyanarayana Sarma, hailed as the greatest of all Kuchipudi impersonators and the paradigmatic example of hegemonic brahmin masculinity in the village, cements this decline. Adding to this is the growing influence of transnational discourses on gender and sexuality, which demarcate the practice of impersonation as nonnormative, or even a *kojja-vēṣam,* rather than an assertion of hegemonic masculinity. Once equivalent to white heteronormative masculinity (Connell 1995; Halberstam 1998), hegemonic brahmin masculinity is rendered remarkably fragile in the contemporary transnational landscape of Kuchipudi dance.

As an ethnography of practice, this study moves from village to urban and transnational spaces to trace the transformation of Kuchipudi impersonation with a particular attention to brahmin masculinity, both in its hegemonic and normative forms as illustrated by Satyanarayana Sarma and Venku, respectively (see chapter 2). Throughout this study, I interrogate the discursive narrative of Kuchipudi and its imagined tradition of authority (*sāmpradāyam*), particularly by questioning the dominant stories (Siddhendra's hagiography), figures (village brahmin men), and histories (classicization of Kuchipudi) that are taken for granted by many dance practitioners. In so doing, I foreground the perspectives of dancers residing in the liminal spaces of the village norms, including Pasumarti Rattayya Sarma, who could never impersonate in the manner of the famous Satyanarayana Sarma, and Chavali Balatripurasundari, who could only dance in secret without her father's consent. The invocation of constructed artifice, or *māyā* in the words of Rattayya Sarma and other village performers who enact the roles of *sūtradhāra*/Madhavi/Madhava, forges a connection between the lexicon of Kuchipudi as *dance* and the critique of Kuchipudi as *construct*. As this study illustrates, even hegemonic brahmin masculinity is rendered as artifice (*māyā*) as Kuchipudi transforms from the name of a village in coastal Andhra to the nationally (and even transnationally) recognized symbol of Telugu "classical" tradition.

The book also bridges feminist theory with studies of Indian performance by exploring the ways in which gender, sexuality, and caste are contingent categories. As a hermeneutical lens for reading gender, constructed artifice (*māyā*) addresses Mrinalini Sinha's (2012, 357) challenge that a "truly global perspective on gender—rather than merely the extension of an a priori conception of gender to different parts of the globe—must give theoretical weight to the particular context in which it is articulated." So, what then does a hermeneutics of constructed artifice (*māyā*) tell us about hegemonic brahmin masculinity, in particular, and gender and caste, more broadly?

As this study demonstrates, brahmin masculinity is highly contingent and inherently mutable. While it is undoubtedly hegemonic within the village, this caste-based power is quickly displaced in urban and transnational forms of Kuchipudi dance in which donning the *strī-vēṣam* is deemed superfluous and, in some cases, queer. Gender, by extension, is both fluid and fixed in the South Asian imagination; whether it is the guising practices of Venku as Satyabhama or the verbal jest of Ravi Balakrishna as *sūtradhāra*/Madhavi/Madhava, gender is portrayed as inherently mutable. And yet, gender is also incredibly rigid, as the narratives of Kuchipudi brahmin women demonstrate. Only men from village brahmin families can don *vēṣams* onstage; brahmin women, by contrast, should remain circumscribed to the domestic sphere. In urban spaces, performers are less constrained by such restrictive gender and caste norms, as women across caste lines begin to dance and even embody a range of masculinities by donning the *vēṣams* of Hindu deities such as Krishna and Shiva. Nevertheless, the ongoing influence of "Brahmin taste" (Rudisill 2007) in cosmopolitan Kuchipudi dance still privileges upper-caste, middle-class women as aesthetically suitable for the Kuchipudi stage. Gender is deeply connected not only to place, but also to caste, which legitimizes certain gender expressions—Kuchipudi village brahmin men and upper-caste/middle-class cosmopolitan women—while proscribing others, namely the *devadāsī* and her dance (Meduri 1988; Soneji 2012). Yet, as Baliakka's story from chapter 5 demonstrates, the narratives of brahmin women can also serve as sites for resistance.

Reading Kuchipudi dance through a lens of constructed artifice (*māyā*) also reframes the ostensible linkage of gender and sexuality that often goes hand in hand in Euro-American feminist thought. Sexuality, in the contexts observed in this study, is bound by heteronormative discourse, which itself is circumscribed by caste. Brahminical ideals are also heteronormative ones, and all those actors/dancers/persons falling beyond the sphere of brahminical patriarchy are rendered queer. The invocation of the terms *kojja/hijṛā* by some village brahmin men point to a rising discomfort at impersonation enacted by nonbrahmin dancers in cosmopolitan contexts and spaces. The presence of a female dancer enacting Satyabhama and a gender-variant Madhavi also highlights the disruptive power of Chinna Satyam's *Bhāmākalāpam* as a resistant vernacular performance (Johnson 2005). The visual aesthetics of queer diaspora, in the words of Gayatri Gopinath (2018), further threaten to expose brahmin masculinity as artifice. Drawing on the observations of Sonja Thomas (2009, 8), I would argue that it is virtually impossible to disentangle the effects of gender, caste, sexuality, and place when examining a single practice—in this case the donning of the *strī-vēṣam*—thus underscoring the dynamic flows of power and subordination across the multidimensional matrix of Kuchipudi as village *and* Kuchipudi as dance.

My vision of constructed artifice (*māyā*) is shaped by Judith Butler's ([1990] 2008, xxiv) theory that gender is a "changeable and revisable reality." It is noteworthy that the dancers of the Kuchipudi village who play the roles of *sūtradhāra*/Madhavi/Madhava in *Bhāmākalāpam* did not need Butler's insights to arrive at a similar conclusion. In place of Butler's articulations, the dancers invoked *māyā*, a word that connotes illusion and artifice, to read gender role-play onstage. Drawing on both the words of these dancers and feminist insights, I read the donning of the *strī-vēṣam* as a form of constructed artifice that creates the illusion of gender identity onstage while interrogating norms of gender, sexuality, and caste in quotidian life. As a vernacular theory of gender performance and gender performativity, constructed artifice (*māyā*) extends beyond the spaces of the Kuchipudi village and Kuchipudi dance to form the shared intellectual arc (Gautam 2016, 48) of theorizing impersonation. In other words, a hermeneutics of constructed artifice (*māyā*) is a deeply localized and transnationally salient theory on the intersectionality of gender and caste in their many guises.

Finally, the declining value ascribed to the brahmin male body in *strī-vēṣam* not only undermines the authority of brahmin masculinity, but also demands a reframing of the term "impersonation." In this study, I have restricted my scope to the guising practices of brahmin men in the Kuchipudi village and, to a lesser degree, the practice of women guising as Hindu male deities in Chinna Satyam's dance dramas. However, impersonation is far more extensive than simply the donning of a sartorial, gendered guise. Impersonation is ubiquitous across the South Asian landscape, with examples reappearing for millennia throughout literature, performance, and ritual. Whether it is the phenomenon of vocal impersonation within devotional writing or the interchangeability of deities and devotees within contemporary *rām-līlā* performances, impersonation is a quotidian occurrence in South Asia.[2] Moving away from obvious forms of guising, including the Kuchipudi brahmin male dancer in a woman's guise, engenders the capaciousness of impersonation, a practice that both reflects and undermines dominant understandings of gender, caste, and sexuality in everyday South Asia.

POSTSCRIPT

A darkened college auditorium resounds with the slow chant of three Sanskrit words: *Om Namo Nārāyaṇāya* (lit., "Salutations to Vishnu"). As light fills the auditorium, the outlines of several dancers dressed in bright hues—vibrant orange, turmeric yellow, parrot green, and royal blue—appear onstage. The dancers' faces are hidden as they prostrate on the ground, knees tucked under them, arms stretched out overhead, and palms joined in salutation (*namaskāram*). As the vocalist softly sings the invocatory phrase "*Om Namo Nārāyaṇāya,*" the dancers gradually rise up from the floor. By the third repetition, the dancers are sitting upright on their heels, arms stretched out overhead, with palms joined, pointing toward the sky. Slowly, the dancers rise to their feet and begin swaying their arms to represent the undulating waves of the cosmic ocean. They join their hands to form the hood of the snake, Ananta, and fashion their fingers to represent a conch (*śaṅkha*) and wheel (*cakra*). Finally, the dancers stand tall with palms facing outward in front of their chests, their ring fingers bent downward to form the *mudra tripatāka,* thus portraying the god Vishnu of the Hindu traditions. The rhythmic tapping of the double-barrel South Indian drum, *mṛdaṅgam,* provides an opening segue for the Kuchipudi dance item *Nārāyaṇīyam.*

The dancers who performed this piece were American college students enrolled in the theory-practice course "Dance and Embodied Knowledge in the Indian Context." In this course, students are exposed to a range of readings on the history of Indian dance, aesthetic and performance theory, and Hindu religious narratives, among other topics. As an experimental theory-practice course, students read about dance in the context of a traditional classroom setting and also learn to dance themselves. One class session per week is held in a dance studio on campus where students learn the basic movements of Kuchipudi, culminating in a final performance of the piece *Nārāyaṇīyam* at the end of the semester.

"Dance and Embodied Knowledge in the Indian Context" is a course originally conceptualized by religious studies scholar Joyce Flueckiger and Atlanta-based Kuchipudi dancer Sasikala Penumarthi. Since its conceptualization, the course has been offered at a range of private and public institutions across the eastern United States for the last two decades and has been the subject of two scholarly articles co-authored by Flueckiger and me (2013, 2019). As a dancer and scholar of Kuchipudi, I have taught the course in three academic settings: Emory University (Fall 2011), Middlebury College (Fall 2013), and UNC–Chapel Hill (Fall 2017). Aside from a few dancers trained in the dance forms of Bharatanatyam and Kathak, almost all of my students had no formal training in Indian dance and many had very little familiarity with South Asia. This meant that we began the studio sessions with very basic movements, such as how to maintain the uncomfortable half-seated position while keeping the spine curved, a stance that is now ubiquitous to both Kuchipudi and Bharatanatyam. Weeks were spent learning how to synchronize feet and arms according to a three-beat time-measure, *ta-ki-ṭa,* and four-beat time-measure, *ta-ka-dhi-mi.* This intentionality in movement builds on what Deidre Sklar (1994, 15) refers to as *kinesthetic empathy,* or the "capacity to participate *with* another's movement or another's sensory experience of movement" (emphasis added). These practices were challenging, especially for students with little or no training in dance. As one student wrote in her weekly dance journal:

> It was quite frustrating to tell my legs to do one thing and tell my arms to do another and try to combine the motion. Apparently I have rather poor control over my limbs . . . Despite my best efforts through the subsequent weeks, my movements still felt foreign and somewhat comical during practices. My thoughts centered around forcing the muscles in my fingers to curve into shapes, while I simultaneously struggled to think through the foot patterns . . . embodiment was a far-fetched dream.

Despite the rather slow and plodding pace, the final result was remarkable. By the end of the semester and with the help of several weekend practice sessions, the students donned brightly colored costumes purchased from India to perform the six-minute piece *Nārāyaṇīyam* before an audience of their friends and family. While the performance itself was short and the execution of movements often uncoordinated, these American college students experienced their own form of the Arangetram (lit., "ascent of the stage") that is now ubiquitous to many "classical" Indian dance forms (Schwartz 2004).

I mention the course "Dance and Embodied Knowledge in the Indian Context" because it is likely that the readers of this book are situated within a university setting, perhaps in the United States, Canada, or India. Having taught the course three times in three entirely different American university contexts, ranging from a small private liberal arts college to a large public state institution, I have become increasingly aware of the disruptive possibilities that a course such as this can offer. While most Kuchipudi dance classes begin by invoking the hagiography of Siddhendra and the legacy of the brahmins of the Kuchipudi village, my version of this course centered on foundational essays by Avanthi Meduri (1988) and Matthew Harp Allen (1997) that interrogate the classicization of Bharatanatyam in twentieth-century South India. Students also read the works of Anuradha Jonnalagadda (1996b), Davesh Soneji (2012), and Rumya Putcha (2015) to consider the historical development of Kuchipudi dance, particularly in relation to courtesan communities. Studio classes were framed with these critical historiographies, prompting students to be mindful of the complicated pasts their bodies inhabited through dancing a piece like *Nārāyaṇīyam*. As students prepared for their final performance, they read scholarly works on the Arangetram, inviting them to examine the symbolic capital and bodily labor undergirding their brightly colored costumes and bells imported from India (Devarajan 2011; Srinivasan 2012).

The bodies in my classroom were overwhelmingly nonbrahmin and non-male-identified. The composition of the class has included a variety of students from a range of national, cultural, and socioeconomic backgrounds, ranging from a white male student from Maine who spent his summers working on a farm to a South Asian female student with extensive training in Rukmini Arundale's style of Bharatanatyam. The absence of the brahmin male body was, at least to me, particularly striking, especially as I continued to work on this book while teaching the class. In the dance studios of Atlanta, Middlebury, and Chapel Hill, brahmin men were entirely peripheral to the embodiment of Kuchipudi.

The ability to dance while teaching and researching the history of dance reshaped my own pedagogical practices, as well as my theoretical commitments for this book. In her work on Indian dance as transnational labor, Priya Srinivasan (2012, 16–17) outlines her own methodological motivations after doing ethnographic work in dance classrooms in California:

> I increasingly questioned the social, political, and often ahistorical framework that encircles Indian dance in the United States. My love of and frustration with Indian dance drove me to find a way to write about it that made sense to me. So, the unruly spectator, a viewer who offers a nonpassive feminist perspective, was born . . . . My frustration with the current practice of Indian dance led me to study its past, which then allowed me to return to contemporary and familiar spaces with a greater understanding of their politico-historical contexts.

Prompted by Srinivasan's method of the "unruly spectator," I began to conceive of the college classroom and dance studio as the space to rewrite the script for Kuchipudi dance, bridging its contentious past and transnational present. Rather than offering a traditional guru-student model of dance learning, I invited my students to interrogate the very practice they were learning to embody. Together, we thought carefully about themes of embodiment, appropriation, and authority, all while learning to fashion our fingers in the shape of the peacock feathers adorning Krishna's crown. Beyond Sklar's (1994) conception of kinesthetic empathy, the students participated in a form of *kinesthetic interrogation* that questioned the long-standing legacy of hegemonic brahmin masculinity and the inheritance of a particular historical narrative as the foundation for Kuchipudi dance. The arc of this book, which examines both the hegemony and artifice of brahmin masculinity, reflects these feminist commitments. As a transnational form of embodiment, Kuchipudi, at least the version I teach my students, simultaneously enables the construction of hegemony and offers the site for its resistance. The convergence of embodied aesthetic practice and feminist critical insights thus enables us to rewrite the script for *Kuchipudi*, a term laden with lingering questions and performative possibilities (Arudra 1994; Allen 1997).

NOTES

INTRODUCTION

1. This description of Vedantam Satyanarayana Sarma is from a documentary film, *Kuchipudi Dance: Ancient & Modern*, Part II, produced by the India Films Division, 1973.

2. In 2014, the Telugu-speaking state of Andhra Pradesh was divided into two separate states—Telangana and Andhra Pradesh. Telugu is the primary language in both states. My fieldwork was conducted in the village of Kuchipudi, located in Andhra Pradesh, and in Hyderabad, which is now located in Telangana. I use the term "Telugu-speaking South India" (alt., "Telugu South India") to designate a linguistic region that encompasses both the states of Telangana and Andhra Pradesh. Although the states of Telangana and Andhra Pradesh create a unified conception of Telugu-speaking South India in the contemporary period, it is important to note that the Telugu language has extended across South India from the premodern period onwards. For a discussion of the polyglossia of South India, see Narayana Rao 2016, 28–30. For a broader discussion of the development of Telugu literary traditions, see Narayana Rao and Shulman 2002.

3. As Sharon Marcus (2005, 213) notes, "Straight men in queer theory are straw men, with the ironic result that male heterosexuality maintains its status as universal, normal, homogeneous, predictable, and hence immune from investigation. There could be no more powerful extension of queer theory than detailed research into straight men's desires, fantasies, attractions, and gender identifications—research unafraid to probe the differences between sexual ideology and sexual practices."

4. See also Pandey 2013, 4.

5. In a similar vein, Raka Ray (2018) makes the case for bringing colonialism in conversation with the sociology of gender.

6. For example, in her study of Syrian Christians, Thomas (2018, 9–10) critiques the interpretation of caste as solely a Hindu concept.

7. I thank Laurie L. Patton for suggesting this translation of *māyā*.

8. When joined with the roots √*kṛi* or *ā*-√*sthā, veṣa can* mean "to assume a dress" (Monier-Williams [1899] 1960, 1019).

9. Another Sanskrit term used by my interlocutors, particularly Ajay Kumar, to describe impersonation is *rūpānurūpam*. This term appears to draw on *Nāṭyaśāstra* XXXV.31–2. See Ghosh's (1961) translation of the *Nāṭyaśāstra*, vol. 2, 217.

10. Telugu belongs to the Dravidian language family, along with Tamil, Kannada, and Malayalam. Sanskrit, by contrast, is the earliest Indo-European language. Although Telugu is not part of the Indo-European language family, about 80 percent of Telugu is composed of Sanskrit loan words. Given this overlap, my interlocutors would frequently use the term *strī-vēṣam* (*strī* is the Sanskrit term for woman), as opposed to the more regional variant of *āḍa-vēṣam*. For a discussion of the relationship between Sanskrit and Telugu, see Narayana Rao and Shulman 2002. For a broader discussion of the relationship between Sanskrit and the cosmopolitan vernacular, see Pollock 2006.

11. For a full discussion of impersonation in South Asia, refer to the forthcoming edited volume *Mimetic Desires: Impersonation and Guising Across South Asia*, co-edited by Harshita Mruthinti Kamath and Pamela Lothspeich. The volume brings together the work of fifteen scholars on the subject of impersonation/guising/embodiment in South Asia, spanning the early modern and contemporary periods. The broader definition of the term "impersonation" cited here is from the introduction to the volume.

12. For uses of the term "impersonation" and/or "impersonator," see Pani 1977; Satyanarayana Sarma 1996; Kalakrishna 1996; Hansen 1998; Kapur 2004; Gopalakrishnan 2006; Nagabhushana Sarma 2012; Kaur 2013; Mukherjee and Chatterjee 2016; Multani 2017.

13. Indian feminist scholars have broadened the scope of impersonation to interpret tropes of mimicry in colonial subject formation (Roy 1998) and trace discourses on aspiration and emplacement in contemporary India (Mankekar 2015).

14. For a discussion of gender ambiguity in South Asia, see, among others, Pani 1977; Doniger 1982, 1995, 2000; Goldman 1993; Vanita and Kidwai 2001; Vanita 2002; Chatterjee 2012; Flueckiger 2013. Indian conceptions of personhood and the porousness of the body also frame the ways that practices of gender guising and impersonation appear in the South Asian context (Marriott 1976; Daniel 1984; Nabokov 2000; Smith 2006). See my recent essay in the edited volume *Refiguring the Body* (2016) for a discussion of Indian personhood in relation to Kuchipudi performance.

15. For example, in Hanne M. de Bruin's (2006) study of the South Indian theatrical style of Kattaikkuttu, *vēṣam* extends beyond outer appearance: "It represents the dramatic character's physical appearance and his or her personality, which are realized in performance through the actor's body and voice" (107).

16. I have chosen to transliterate the terms *hijṛā* and *koṭhī* according to standardized Hindi spelling.

17. Carole-Anne Tyler (2003, 2) suggests that all gender can be viewed as a socially mandated form of impersonation.

18. For Butler ([1990] 2008, xxv), "drag is an example that is meant to establish that 'reality' is not as fixed as we generally assume it to be. The purpose of the example is to expose the tenuousness of gender 'reality' in order to counter the violence performed by gender norms."

19. C. Riley Snorton (2017, 57) makes a case for reading cross-dressing as a form of *fungibility*, a practice that became a critical performance for blacks in the antebellum period.

For a discussion of cross-dressing and fetishism in the context of British imperialism, see also McClintock 1995, chap. 3.

20. As examples of scholars who use the terms "transvestism" and/or "theatrical transvestism," see Garber 1992; Senelick 2000; Hansen 1999, 2002; Suthrell 2004; Kaur 2013.

21. For a discussion of the plural term masculinities, see also De Sondy 2015, 8–9; Thangaraj 2015, 16 .

22. For a summary and critique of Connell's theorizations on hegemonic masculinity, see Inhorn 2012, 41–48. See also *Gender Reckonings: New Social Theory and Research* (2018), edited by James W. Messerschmidt et al., which substantively engages Connell's work.

23. As Marcia C. Inhorn (2012, 45) notes in her study of emergent masculinities of Arab men, masculinity should not be pigeonholed into a static binary between hegemonic and subordinated.

24. According to Halberstam (1998, 241): "[I]t is crucial to recognize that masculinity does not belong to men, has not been produced only by men, and does not properly express male heterosexuality . . . what we call 'masculinity' has also been produced by masculine women, gender deviants, and often lesbians." See also Lucinda Ramberg's (2014, 199–211) discussion of the masculinity of *jōgati*s, women who are ritually dedicated to the goddess Yellamma. Ramberg also discusses *jōgappa*s, who are people sexed as men and transformed into sacred women by the goddess Yellamma (200–201).

25. Important works on South Asian masculinities include Mrinalini Sinha's *Colonial Masculinities* (1995), Sikata Banerjee's *Make Me a Man!* (2005), Caroline Osella and Filippo Osella's *Men and Masculinities in South India* (2006), Jarrod L. Whitaker's *Strong Arms and Drinking Strength* (2011), as well as the essays in the edited volumes *Sexual Sites, Seminal Attitudes* (Srivastava 2004) and *South Asian Masculinities: Context of Change, Sites of Continuity* (Chopra, Osella, and Osella 2004). Psychoanalytic and psychological studies of South Asian men and/or masculinities include Sudhir Kakar's *The Inner World* ([1978] 2012), Ashis Nandy's *The Intimate Enemy* ([1983] 2009), and Stanley Kurtz's *All the Mothers Are One* (1992), among others. More recent scholarship that discusses South Asian masculinities includes the works of Heather Streets-Salter (2010), Craig Jeffrey (2010), Chandrima Chakraborty (2011), Joseph Alter (1992, 2011), Amanullah De Sondy (2015), Charu Gupta (2016), as well as the edited volumes *Popular Masculine Cultures in India* (Dasgupta and Baker 2013), *Masculinity and Its Challenges in India* (Dasgupta and Gokulsing 2014), *Gender and Masculinities* (Doron and Broom 2014), and *Mapping South Asian Masculinities* (Chakraborty 2015). Gayatri Gopinath's *Impossible Desires* (2005), Jasbir Puar's *Terrorist Assemblages* (2007), Junaid Rana's *Terrifying Muslims* (2011), Stanley I. Thangaraj's *Desi Hoop Dreams* (2015), and the edited volume *Asian American Sporting Culture* (2016) all provide compelling analyses of South Asian American and diasporic masculinities. Gyanendra Pandey (2013) examines black and Dalit struggles for rights in the United States and India, with a specific focus on caste, race, and masculinity (28). Lucinda Ramberg (2014, 196–200) expands discussions of masculinity to encompass kinships relations of *jōgati*s, women who are dedicated to the goddess Yellamma and sometimes serve as sons or fathers in their natal families, thus troubling normative kinship arrangements. While not focusing on masculinity directly, Sumathi Ramaswamy's *The Goddess and the Nation* (2010, 180) situates male homosociality alongside constructions of nationhood and the cartographed figure of Bharat Mata.

26. Inhorn notes a similar undertheorization of Arab masculinity in the introduction to *The New Arab Man* (2012).

27. The earliest mention of the brahmin in relation to caste hierarchy arises in *Ṛg Veda* 10.90 (*Puruṣa-sūkta*). Jarrod L. Whitaker (2011) provides an extensive discussion of the construction of masculinity in the context of the poetic hymns of the *Ṛg Veda*. In particular, he analyzes the masculinity of Vedic poet-priests in relation to the deities Indra, Soma, and Agni. For a discussion of *varṇa* and *jāti* in medieval Andhra, see also Talbot 2001, 50–55.

28. In the colonial context, Ashis Nandy ([1983] 2009, 10) posits two contrasting notions of masculinity: "The Brāhmaṇ in his cerebral, self-denying asceticism was the traditional masculine counterpoint to the more violent, 'virile', active Kṣatriya [warrior]." Also discussing colonial conceptions of masculinity, Mrinalini Sinha (1995, 2) describes the opposition between the so-called "manly Englishman" and the "effeminate *babu*," the latter being a pejorative term used to characterize elite, upper-caste Bengali men in the late colonial period. Drawing on the work of nineteenth-century Bengali writer Bankimchandra Chattopadyaya (aka Bankim), Chandrima Chakraborty (2011, 56) posits the category of ascetic nationalist martiality that brings together the Hindu masculine archetypes of the brahmin (priest) and Kshatriya (warrior). Ronojoy Sen's *Nation at Play* (2015) briefly discusses brahmins in sport. According to one calculation, since 1970 more than a third of Indian cricket players have been brahmin (Sen 2015, 229). C.J. Fuller and Haripriya Narasimhan's (2014) longitudinal study of Tamil brahmins provides further analysis of brahmin communities in South India. Although not focusing on brahmin masculinity specifically, Mary Hancock's *Womanhood in the Making* (1999), Leela Prasad's *Poetics of Conduct* (2007), and David Knipe's *Vedic Voices* (2015) are important notable studies of contemporary South Indian brahmin communities. See also Uma Chakravarti (2003) for a discussion of brahminical patriarchy and Sonja Thomas's (2018, chap. 3) extensive discussion of Namboodiri brahmins in relation to Syrian Christians in Kerala.

29. For a discussion of the thread ceremony and other life-cycle rites, see Singer 1980, 90–99. See also Olson 1977; B. Smith 1986; F. Smith 2006; Knipe 2015.

30. See also chapter 4, "Becoming a Veda," in David Knipe's *Vedic Voices* (2015).

31. Osella and Osella (2006) question whether the status of brahminhood is achieved solely by rites of initiation. For example, they note that brahmin women are treated as brahmin, despite the fact that they do not undergo initiation in a similar manner to their male counterparts. The authors conclude that "Brahmin men continue to hold to their esoteric and gender-specific knowledge and claim initiation rites as essential to man-making, while allowing that actually the rite is ineffective in the absence of many other things—biological sex, correct caste birth status, continual performance and so on" (36–37).

32. William J. Jackson's *Tyāgarāja and the Renewal of Tradition* (1994, 207–30) and Hancock's *Womanhood in the Making* (1999, 39–72) provide lengthy discussions of Smarta identity. Jackson (1994, 218) characterizes Smartas as renewers of tradition who are beyond sectarian affiliation: "They are thought of as stable tradition-bearers, yet they were innovators who popularized *brāhmaṇic* teachings and ideals among lower twice-born castes, women and *śūdras*, and they promoted Vedic ideas among Vaiṣṇava and Śaiva worshippers." Peterson and Soneji (2008, 32n1) define Smartas as "a prominent Brahmin group in south India. Traditionally linked to Sanskrit orthodoxy, temples, and monasteries, Smartas today are key players in the area of cultural production, education, and business." When defining Smarta brahmins, Prasad (2007, 12) notes that they take their name from their "adherence to smṛti ('remembered') tradition that mainly comprises the Dharmashastras and

the Dharmasutras." For discussions of Smarta brahmins in South India, see also Younger 1995, 42n30; Rudisill 2007; Fisher 2017.

33. Hancock is particularly critical of Milton Singer's ([1972] 1980) reliance on the work of Sanskritist and Smarta brahmin V. Raghavan: "Raghavan's engagement with Singer's project was consistent with already established Smārta interventions in cultural debates in India. I argue that scholarly paradigms should be seen as by-products of Smārta cultural history rather than the products of Euro-Western paradigms" (Hancock 1999, 67).

34. In 1996, Madras was renamed Chennai in line with a nationwide trend of renaming the English spellings of Indian cities in accordance with vernacular spellings in Indian languages. In this book, I use Madras to refer to the city prior to 1996 and Chennai to refer to the city after 1996. For a discussion of the renaming of Madras state to Tamil Nadu, see Ramaswamy 1997, 154–61.

35. See also Soneji 2012, 223–25.

36. According to Rudisill (2007, 62, 77), the Chennai *sabha* offers both "high-brow" culture through the performance of classical dance and Karnatak music, as well as "middle-brow" entertainment through comedy plays, also referred to as *sabha* theatre. In the case of the former, "high-brow" performances go hand in hand with the nationalist agenda to create classical performing arts, namely Bharatanatyam, the major "classical" dance form of South India. See also Rudisill (2012) for a discussion of the Chennai *sabha* and brahmin humor.

37. While some published scholarship refers to Vaidiki as Vaidika (Fuller and Narasimhan 2014, 216–17), my interlocutors colloquially referred to the group as Vaidiki. I follow the lexicon of my interlocutors, as well as the work of Jackson (1994) and Narayana Rao (2007), and refer to the group as Vaidiki. Vaidiki and Niyogi are two dominant brahmin *jāti*s in Telugu South India. Vaidiki (lit., "knowing the *Veda*") brahmins are known to perform priestly rituals, while Niyogi brahmins are traditionally considered to occupy "secular" professions, spanning from Telugu poets to village accountants (Jackson 1994, 207). For a discussion of the distinction between Vaidiki and Niyogi brahmins, particularly in comparison to Tamil brahmins, see Fuller and Narasimhan 2014, 31, 56, 216–17. For an example of the contestation between Niyogis and Vaidikis, see Velcheru Narayana Rao's afterword to his translation of Gurajada Apparao's play *Kanyāśūlkam* (2007, 159–89). For a discussion of Vaidiki pundits in the Godavari delta in Telugu South India, see Knipe 2015.

38. Fuller and Narasimhan (2014) trace the transformation of Tamil brahmins from a traditional, rural elite caste in the colonial period to a modern, urban middle-class social group in the contemporary context. Once residing in an *agrahāram*, or brahmin village in which brahmins exclusively occupy a designated street or quarter, the Tamil brahmin community has, for the most part, left rural South India and now primarily resides in urban cities in India and the United States (30–31). In this transition from rural *agrahāram* to modern cosmopolitan space, Tamil brahmins have shifted into professional and administrative employment, enabling them to occupy a new middle-class urban caste identity, colloquially referred to as "Tam Brams" (228–29).

39. The Kuchipudi *agrahāram* (brahmin quarters) is akin to the *agrahāram*s described by Knipe (2015, 23–27) in the Godavari delta of Telugu South India. For a discussion of the Sringeri *agrahāram*, see Prasad 2007, 44–47.

40. Vedantam Venkata Naga Chalapathi Rao now resides in Canada with his family and returns to the Kuchipudi village to visit his mother who still lives there.

41. The fact that Kuchipudi brahmin men dance, rather than conduct rituals, raises the possibility that this performance community is an example of a *jāti* group that sought to elevate their status by identifying with a higher *varṇa* (Kinsley 1993, 156).

42. In a chapter titled "Crossing 'Lines' of Subjectivity: Transnational Movements and Gay Identifications," Gayatri Reddy (2005) discusses transnational discourses on non-normative sexuality in relation to the *hijṛā* communities that she studies in Telugu South India.

43. See Jyoti Puri's *Women, Body, Desire in Post-Colonial India* (1999, 8) for a discussion of how sociocultural understandings of gender reinforce mandatory heterosexuality for middle- and upper-class Indian women.

44. A palpable anxiety of being read as effeminate arose in the brahmins' responses to this question, mirroring in interesting ways the discourses of masculinity and perceived effeminacy described by Sinha 1995, Krishnaswamy 2011, and Thangaraj 2015. For a discussion of effeminate gestures, see also Khubchandani 2016, 76–79 . For an alternative discussion of masculinity and effeminacy in the context of Dalits, see Gupta 2016.

45. The status given to impersonators in the Kuchipudi village counters Morcom's (2013, 172) suggestion that narratives of reform and modernization resulted in a "growing sense that female impersonators represented a 'backward' and also awkward aspect of Indian performing arts (an idea that is still very much alive today)."

46. For a detailed history of Kuchipudi, see also Nagabhushana Sarma 2016. Notably, Kuchipudi must be situated in relation to other regional performance traditions, including *yakṣagāna* (Jonnalagadda 1996b; Nagabhushana Sarma 2009), Turpu Bhagavatam (Nagabhushana Sarma 1995), and Bhagavata Mela Natakam (Jones 1963; Kothari 1977; Arudra 1986; Kothari and Pasricha 2001; Inoue 2008; Soneji 2012).

47. I have chosen to transliterate the term *devadāsī* in accordance with published scholarship (e.g., Soneji 2012) and in accordance with Sanskrit transliteration.

48. For an additional discussion of Kuchipudi and film, see Thota 2016.

49. A copy of the document is found in Jonnalagadda 1996b, appendix 1. According to poet-scholar Arudra (1994, 30), the 1763 document is "a settlement deed specifying the allocation of shares of the village between the then existing 15 dance families. The document was an agreement of mutual trust and it mentions that the grants, sanuds [land grant document], and such conferential [documents] of the land were lost, but the village had been an agraharam belonging to the original families." Putcha (2015, 5) also discusses this 1763 property document.

50. Brahmin families with the surnames Chinta, Hemadri, Pennamudi, Tadepalli, and Somayajulu also live in the village's *agrahāram*. Since these surnames were not listed on the 1763 property document, they appear to have migrated to the village at a later date. The surname Chinta is particularly prominent in the Kuchipudi village today and is also considered to be part of the list of hereditary Kuchipudi brahmin families.

51. This map is based on the observations of Pasumarti Mrutyumjaya in March 2014 and does not reflect the owners of specific households based on an assessment of property deeds or other official documentation. It also does not reflect any recent changes in households since March 2014. The purpose of the map is to give a general overview of the Kuchipudi *agrahāram*.

52. See chapter 4 in Prasad's *Poetics of Conduct* (2007), which discusses the term *sāmpradāyam* in the context of the pilgrimage town of Sringeri.

53. For a discussion of the tripartite typology of *yakṣagāna, kalāpam,* and *vēṣam,* see also Soneji 2012, 268n13; Putcha 2015, 9–10.

54. Similar responses are recorded by Philip Zarrilli (2000, 70) in his study of the all-male dance/theatrical form of Kathakali. For an alternative discussion of the reasons behind gender exclusion in Indian dance, see Subramaniam 1995.

55. Because of his skills in impersonation, Ajay is increasingly performing the role of Satyabhama in *Bhāmākalāpam* in urban centers such as Vijayawada. As an example, see the following review of Kumar's 2014 performance in *The Hindu:* www.thehindu.com/news/national/andhra-pradesh/male-dancer-floors-connoisseurs-with-bhama-kalapam/article5871830.ece (accessed August 15, 2018). Such performances are staged separately from those performed by hereditary brahmin performers such as Vedantam Venkata Naga Chalapathi Rao. Another example of a nonbrahmin impersonator is Hyderabad-based dancer Haleem Khan, who is exceptional in his skills in donning the *strī-vēṣam.*

56. See also the work of Sitara Thobani (2017) on the transnational scope of Indian classical dance, particularly in the UK.

57. The Sangeet Natak Akademi, the central government–operated arts organization in India, gives its annual prestigious SNA Award to one recipient from each of the following eight regional dance forms: Chhau, Sattriya, Odissi, Kuchipudi, Manipuri, Kathakali, Kathak, and Bharatanatyam (www.sangeetnatak.gov.in/sna/ich.php, accessed August 13, 2017). These eight dance forms are commonly referred to by the appellation "classical."

58. Notably, there is an expansive body of scholarship on Indian dance, particularly the ostensible "revival" of *devadāsī* dance into Bharatanatyam. Important scholarship on *devadāsī*s includes, among others, Frédérique Apffel-Marglin 1985; Saskia Kersenboom 1987; Anne-Marie Gaston 1992, 1996; Leslie Orr 2000; Indira Viswanathan Peterson and Davesh Soneji 2008; Hari Krishnan 2008; Davesh Soneji 2010, 2012; Amrit Srinivasan 1985, 2010; Lucinda Ramberg 2014; Anjali Arondekar 2012, 2018. Important works on the classicization of Bharatanatyam in the mid-twentieth century include, among others, those of Avanthi Meduri 1988, 1996, 2004, 2008; Matthew Harp Allen 1997, 2008; Uttara Asha Coorlawala 2004; Janet O'Shea 2007, 2008; Davesh Soneji 2010. Other important contributions to broader scholarship on Indian dance include Purnima Shah 1998, 2002; Phillip Zarrilli 2000; Ketu Katrak 2001, 2004, 2011; Pallabi Chakravorty 2008, 2017; Arthi Devarajan 2010, 2011; Priya Srinivasan 2012; Ahalya Satkunaratnam 2012, 2013; Anna Morcom 2013; Katherine Zubko 2006, 2014a, 2014b; Anusha Kedhar 2014; Margaret Walker 2016; Sitara Thobani 2017; Arya Madhavan 2017; Sreenath Nair 2017; Ruth Vanita 2018.

59. In her work on the *devadāsī* diaspora through the charitable institution Gomantak Maratha Samaj, Anjali Arondekar (2018, 111) notes: "Devadasi is a compound noun, coupling deva or god with dasi or female slave; a pan-Indian term (falsely) interchangeable with courtesan, dancing girl, prostitute and sex worker. Members of this diaspora, also referred to as kalavants (literally carriers of kala/art), shuttled between Portuguese and British colonial India for over two hundred years." For a definition of the term *devadāsī,* see also Arondekar 2012, 244.

60. For a discussion of *jōgati*s who are women who marry the goddess Yellamma and become her priests or caretakers, see Ramberg 2014. According to Ramberg, *jōgati*s are called and call themselves *devadāsī*s (3).

61. Janet O'Shea (2007, 29) defines *sadir* as "the solo, female dance form associated with the literary and musical traditions of southern India, … performed by devadasis, courtesans

and ritual officiants dedicated to temple and court service." For a discussion of the nomenclature of *sadir* and Bharatanatyam, see Arudra 1986/87.

62. A parallel revival occurred in the context of Karnatak music. As Amanda Weidman (2006, 5) notes, "This 'revival' depended on the selection, from a number of heterogeneous musical traditions, of particular sounds, performance conventions, and repertoire that would come to be identified with indigenous 'classical' music traditions of South India." In short, both music and dance were transformed to represent "classical" South Indian arts by appealing to an imagined tradition of the past. For a discussion of the classicization of Karnatak music, see Weidman 2006, 2008; Peterson and Soneji 2008; Subramanian 2006, 2008; Allen 2008.

63. See also Schwartz 2004, 19–20.

64. As an example of this tension, see Meduri's (1988) discussion of brahmin Rukmini Devi Arundale and *devadāsī* dancer T. Balasaraswati.

65. According to Vissa Appa Rao (1958, 12), a mid-twentieth-century proponent of Telugu literature and dance, "By constant observation of the different techniques of the deva-dasis, Kuchipudi artists had adapted, in turn, many forms from them but interpreted them in their own tradition." See also Soneji 2012, 267n11.

66. For a list of dance items based on Vedantam Lakshminarayana Sastry's teaching manual, see Putcha 2015, fig. 8. As Putcha notes, "With the exception of *Bhāmākalāpam,* all of these pieces belonged to female dance traditions, and most characterized a solo female character" (18).

67. See also Jonnalagadda (2016, 1062–63), who states, "the APSNA has played a decisive role in the development of dance, drama, music and cinema."

68. Putcha (2013, 101) interprets the presence of Kanchanamala as reflective of a broader trend in Kuchipudi regarding the place of the female dancer: "Kanchanamala was sent to New Delhi specifically because she represented a history of Kuchipudi and of classical dance that was yet to be written: the institutionalization of a local tradition in order to impart it to middle-to-upper-class/caste girls from Telugu families. Bharatanatyam and Kathak were among the first genres to formulate this marker of classicism, and Kuchipudi, represented by women like Kanchanamala, followed suit in short order."

69. In her article on the Kuchipudi seminar controversy, Putcha (2013, 96) reexamines the contestation in the 1958 national seminar and the subsequent "correction" in the 1959 APSNA seminar to interrogate the underlying Telugu anxieties regarding Kuchipudi's place in the minds of Tamil elite. With the hope of mirroring the female solo repertoire of Bharatanatyam, Kuchipudi proponents attempted to prove its rich tradition of female dance culture by including performances by the aforementioned female dancer Kanchanamala in the 1958 national seminar, and Vaidehi and Induvadana (both performers from hereditary *devadāsī* families) in the 1959 APSNA seminar. Putcha argues that although Kuchipudi is traditionally considered an exclusively upper-caste male dance form, its attainment of classical status paradoxically rests on the female dancing body (106). For a discussion of these two seminars, see also Bhikshu 2006, 252; Jonnalagadda 2016, 1063.

70. According to Jonnalagadda (2016, 1063), this tour was appreciated by well-known Tamil scholars and artists, including V. Raghavan, E. Krishna Iyer, Rukmini Devi Arundale, Indrani Rehman, and Ramayya Pillai.

71. The academy also organized several festivals of Andhra dance forms, including Kuchipudi and *devadāsī* dance traditions, as well as the printed publication, *Natyakala,* featuring articles on dance, drama, music, and literature (Jonnalagadda 2006, 272; 2016, 1064–65).

72. The division of Andhra Pradesh and Telangana in 2014 and the establishment of Andhra Pradesh's new state capital in Amaravati, which is regionally proximate to Kuchipudi, will undoubtedly continue to shape the importance of the Kuchipudi village.

73. There are many scholars of Indian dance and music who are also trained in performance, including Matthew Harp Allen, Hanne M. de Bruin, Pallabi Chakravorty, Arthi Devarajan, Anuradha Jonnalagadda, Anusha Kedhar, Saskia Kersenboom, Hari Krishnan, Arya Madhavan, Avanthi Meduri, Rumya Putcha, Zoe Sherinian, Davesh Soneji, Priya Srinivasan, Sitara Thobani, Amanda Weidman, and Katherine Zubko, among others.

74. See Alter 1992; Sklar 1994; Weidman 2006; Srinivasan 2012; Sherinian 2014; Zubko 2014a; Kedhar 2014; Thangaraj 2015.

75. I returned to India for follow-up research in January 2011, August 2012, March 2014, December 2015, December 2017, and July 2018.

76. As a point of comparison, see Pallabi Chakravorty's multisited ethnographic study *This Is How We Dance Now!* (2017).

77. Turpu Bhagavatam is the performance tradition of a goldsmith community from eastern Andhra Pradesh (see Nagabhushana Sarma 1995).

78. For a discussion of the contestation between Niyogis and Vaidikis, see Narayana Rao 2007; Fuller and Narasimhan 2014.

79. Even as recently as 2018, my caste became a point of discussion during a conversation with an extended family member of a deceased dancer I had previously interviewed in 2010. "Is she one of us?" the family member asked. "Yes, of course, she's Vaidiki!" responded one of my elder brahmin male interlocutors.

80. For a discussion of the insider/outsider dichotomy, particularly related to brahminical caste status, see Sarma 2001. For a discussion of coming to know one's brahmin caste affiliation in the context of ethnographic fieldwork, see Srinivas 2018, 18–24.

81. See also Dia Da Costa's (2018) essay critiquing caste innocence and caste terror by *savarṇa* academics. Thanks to Sailaja Krishnamurti for pointing me to the work of Chaudhry 2017 and Da Costa 2018.

1. TAKING CENTER STAGE: THE POET-SAINT AND THE IMPERSONATOR OF KUCHIPUDI DANCE HISTORY

1. Anuradha Jonnalagadda (1996b, 44) cites dates from Indian scholars, including Banda Kanakalingeshwara Rao and P.S.R. Appa Rao, who suggest that Siddhendra belongs to the fourteenth and fifteenth centuries; Sistla Ramakrishna Sastry and Balantrapu Rajanikanta Rao, who place him in the fifteenth century; and Vissa Appa Rao and Mohan Khokar, who place him in the seventeenth century.

2. In using the term "brahmin impersonator," I imply a hereditary Kuchipudi brahmin man who dons the *strī-vēṣam,* not a performer who impersonates brahmins.

3. For a discussion of the Tanjavur Quartet, see Weidman 2006, 62.

4. For a discussion of the term "gynemimesis," see Krishnan 2009, 386–87n1.

5. For a discussion of Iyer in *vēṣam*, see also Meduri 1996, 160; O'Shea 2007, 35; Katrak 2011, 29.

6. See also Ramberg 2014, 23–24.

7. Soneji (2012, 267n11) notes: "South Indian Brahmin men were involved in the production of courtesan dance as composers, scholar-teachers, and interpreters. Brahmin men were also involved as the scholarly collaborators of *devadāsīs* and *naṭṭuvaṉārs* in some parts of South India."

8. Later in his career, Shankar interacted with Kuchipudi guru Vedantam Lakshminarayana Sastry (Putcha 2015, 13–15).

9. According to the official website for Jacob's Pillow, Denishawn "changed the course of dance history; most of today's modern dancers trace their ancestry to Denishawn." See www.jacobspillow.org/about/pillow-history/ted-shawn/ (accessed July 29, 2018). Modern dancers who were once members of Denishawn include Martha Graham, Doris Humphrey, Charles Weidman, Pauline Lawrence, and Jane Sherman (Srinivasan 2012, 104).

10. For a discussion of the influential role of Ananda Coomaraswamy's (1918) essay "The Dance of Shiva," see Allen 1997, 83–85.

11. Additional references to Ram Gopal include his autobiography, *Rhythm in the Heavens* (1957), and a special edition of the journal *Nartanam*, including a photo-essay arranged by Modali Nagabhushana Sarma (2003).

12. In addition, Mohan Khokar's (1976) short article on male dancers covers a range of traditions, ranging from Bhagavatam Mela Natakam to Kathakali.

13. In a thought-provoking essay titled "Lingering Questions and Some Fashionable Fallacies," Arudra (1994, 29) asks, "Is Siddhendra Yogi, who supposedly originated/revived Kuchipudi, a historical personage or a legendary figure?" Arudra suggests that there is only a single *Bhāmākalāpam* text that contains a *daruvu* (metrical song) with Siddhendra's poetic signature (*mudra*). In 1990, Arudra found a *mudra* in a manuscript of the *mandulapaṭṭu*, a section of *Bhāmākalāpam* concerning love potions and charms, which apparently contains Siddhendra's *mudra*. On this basis, Arudra concludes that "with this singular piece of evidence, the historicity of Siddhendra Swami, if not that of a Yogi, is undoubtedly established; but his date and his connection with Divi-Kuchipudi are still unanswered questions" (29). Kuchipudi dance scholar Anuradha Jonnalagadda (1996b, 44) counters Arudra by noting that most *Bhāmākalāpam* manuscripts include a verse stating that the text was written by Siddhendra. Jonnalagadda concludes, "Though it is difficult in view of the paucity of authentic source materials to fix the date of Siddhendra Yogi, since the oral tradition is rather strong in this regard, it may be concluded that he must have existed in reality" (45).

14. I have surveyed the following palm-leaf manuscripts or printed texts of palm-leaf manuscripts: *Bhāmākalāpamu* R. 429, a palm-leaf manuscript from the Tirupati Oriental Research Library (ca. late nineteenth or early twentieth century); *Āṭabhāgavatam Satyabhāmā-vēṣakatha* printed by the Government Oriental Manuscripts Library Chennai (ca. late nineteenth or early twentieth century); and *Bhāmākalāpamu* R. 1924L, a text printed by the Government Oriental Manuscripts Library Chennai (ca. late nineteenth or early twentieth century). Siddhendra's name is mentioned in one palm-leaf 11b of *Bhāmākalāpamu* R. 429 and on p. 79 of the printed text of *Bhāmākalāpamu* R. 1924L. It is not mentioned in *Āṭabhāgavatam Satyabhāmā-vēṣakatha*. See Kamath 2012.

15. I am greatly indebted to Velcheru Narayana Rao, who read through the entire manuscript with me in the summer of 2011. I am also indebted to Geeta Madhuri and Anuradha Jonnalagadda for sharing the entire scanned copy of the original palm-leaf manuscript in January 2010. For a discussion of *Bhāmākalāpam* textual history, see Jonnalagadda 1996a.

16. As an example, see the first chapter of Allasani Peddana's sixteenth-century Telugu *prabandha Manucaritramu* (*The Story of Manu,* trans. Narayana Rao and Shulman, 2015) in which the poet describes the exact instances that prompted the king Krishnadevaraya to commission the text. Another example includes the first chapter of Muddupalani's *Rādhikāsāntvanamu* (*The Appeasement of Radhika: Radhika Santawanam,* trans. Mulchandani, 2011), in which the poet, who is also a courtesan performer, describes her family lineage in detail.

17. A well-known example is the performance of *Navajanārdana Pārijātam* in the town of Pithapuram, in which nine *devadāsī* troupes would perform *Bhāmākalāpam* for nine consecutive nights at the local Kuntimadhava temple. See Nataraja Ramakrishna's (1984) publication *Navajanārdanam*. See also Soneji 2012, 268n16; Putcha 2015, 11.

18. For example, when reading *Bhāmākalāpamu* R. 429 with Telugu scholar Velcheru Narayana Rao, we concluded that this palm-leaf likely belonged to Telugu courtesans (*kalāvantulu*) rather than the brahmins of the Kuchipudi village.

19. It is possible that multiple authors composed variations of *Bhāmākalāpam* for their respective performance communities. For example, Soneji (2012, 268n15) notes that "the famous poet of the Godavari delta, Gaddam Subbarayudu Sastri (d. 1940) composed individual *Bhāmākalāpam* librettos for fourteen *kalāvantulu* in the East Godavari region, including the famed Maddula Lakshminarayana and Maddula Venkataratnam."

20. In her summary of Siddhendra's hagiography, Kapila Vatsyayan ([1980] 2007, 57) states that Siddhendra was a disciple of Tirtha Narayana Yogi from Melattur. Judith Lynne Hanna (1983, 65) replicates this summary, although she notes that Siddhendra was the devotee of Tirtha Narayana Yati. See also Arudra 1994, 29.

21. According to the hagiography, Siddhendra was betrothed to a girl from a neighboring village as an infant. In his youth, the elders of the village urged Siddhendra to fulfill these vows and bring his bride back to his village (see Acharya and Sarabhai 1992, 8).

22. The summary of Siddhendra's hagiography is based on the following sources: Khokar 1957; Kanakalingeshwara Rao 1966; Kothari 1977; Rama Rao 1992; Acharya and Sarabhai 1992; Usha Gayatri 2016.

23. This practice of "vocal masquerade," as it has been called, is also present in some Sufi poetry in South Asia (Petievich 2008; Kugle 2013, 2016).

24. A.K. Ramanujan (1989b, 10) identifies vocal guising as inherent to the *bhakti* movement: "In such a *bhakti* tradition, to be male is not to be specially privileged. This may be simply a variation of the idea that in the eyes of god, the last shall be the first. Or it may spring from the idea that being male, like other kinds of privilege, is an obstacle in spiritual awareness, in attaining true inwardness."

25. Later publications on Kuchipudi dance mirror Appa Rao's language; for example, Indian dance critic and scholar Sunil Kothari (1977, 290–91) writes, "Siddhendra turned an ascetic and is considered to have established the Bhama-cult, which is later known as Madhura-Bhakti. Satyabhama, the consort of Lord Krsna, loved him passionately. Her ambition was to keep him exclusively in her embrace. The devotee worships the Lord with

such intense passion and wishes to merge with the Lord. This yearning for union with paramatma—the supersoul on part of the atma underlined this intense devotion. And it has become the governing principle of Bhakti in general." For a philosophical interpretation of *Bhāmākalāpam* through the lens of *jīvātma/paramātma*, see also Naidu 1975, 10.

26. See, among others, Kothari 1977; Vatsyayan [1980] 2007; Hanna 1983; Acharya and Sarabhai 1992; Shah 2002.

27. For a discussion of elite Smarta brahmins and the turn to *bhakti*-influenced styles, see Hancock 1999, 57.

28. Arudra (1994, 29) overtly criticizes the accounts of Banda Kankalingeshwara Rao (1966), Acharya and Sarabhai (1992), Vatsyayan ([1980] 2007), and others, characterizing them as "unauthenticated" and reliant on "unsubstantiated opinion."

29. Similarly, Vedantam Radheshyam stated: "*Bhāmākalāpam* is the struggle of the *jīvātma* becoming *paramātma*" (interview with author, Kuchipudi, March 6, 2010). Yeleswarapu Srinivas suggested: "Siddhendra Yogi saw [Kuchipudi practitioners] dance and became happy. He thought about how he can bring [*jīvātma*] into *paramātma*, and that's how he brought the true reality of Krishna, and *jīvātma* and the *paramātma*. He introduced Madhavi as a friend to join *jīvātma* to *paramātma*" (interview with author, Kuchipudi, February 17, 2010).

30. See, among others, Kanakalingeshwara Rao 1966; Naidu 1975; Kothari 1977; Rama Rao 1992; Acharya and Sarabhai 1992; Usha Gayatri 2016.

31. Related to this section, see my discussions of Kshetrayya and Siddhendra in a forthcoming *Journal of Hindu Studies* article, "Two *Bhaktas*, One District: Re-visioning Hagiographic Imagery in Telugu Performing Arts" (edited by Karen Pechilis and Amy-Ruth Holt). I also focus on the figure of Kshetrayya in a forthcoming *Indian Economic and Social History Review* article, "Kṣētrayya: The Making of a Telugu Poet" (edited by Velcheru Narayana Rao).

32. Appa Rao (1958, 8) also discusses Kshetrayya in his address on Kuchipudi in the 1958 Dance Seminar in Delhi.

33. See also Khokar 1957; Kanakalingeshwara Rao 1966; Naidu 1975; Kothari 1977.

34. Amanda Weidman (2006, 100) finds a similar trend in mid-twentieth-century English translations of Telugu compositions by the nineteenth-century poet Tyagaraja, in which the theological message was more important than the lyrics themselves: "In representing Thyagaraja as a saint, these hagiographic accounts endow him with an almost miraculous ability to rise above his circumstances." See also William J. Jackson's study of Tyagaraja (1991, 1994).

35. I thank Amy-Ruth Holt for pointing me to this image of Siddhendra at Tank Bund in Hyderabad. This image is found in my forthcoming article, "Two *Bhaktas*, One District: Re-visioning Hagiographic Imagery in Telugu Performing Arts" (edited by Karen Pechilis and Amy-Ruth Holt).

36. The Siddhendra Yogi Mahotsav in honor of Kuchipudi's founding saint is usually held annually in March. The festival was held as recently as March 2016: www.thehindu.com/news/national/andhra-pradesh/siddhendra-yogi-mahotsav-to-begin-on-march-20/article8344955.ece (accessed August 18, 2017).

37. Hawley (2015, 25) describes Raghavan as follows: "Impeccably educated, famously liberal, deeply southern, and patently Brahmin, Raghavan was perfectly suited to the task of

putting forth a narrative of Hinduism from the ground up, Hinduism in a bhakti mode—Hinduism, in fact, beyond Hinduism."

38. According to Kathryn Hansen, a move away from stylization toward realism affected the practice of impersonation in Indian theatre (pers. comm., October 22, 2016). For a discussion of Bombay versus Calcutta theatre and the decline of impersonation, see also Hansen 2002, 168, 179n16.

39. This contrasts with Calcutta theatre in which actresses replaced impersonators onstage (Hansen 2002, 168; Bhattacharya 2008, 120).

40. See Hansen's studies on impersonators published in 1998, 1999, 2002, 2004b, and 2015. In addition, her monograph, *Stages of Life: Indian Theatre Autobiographies* (2013), also includes excerpts from Jayshankar Sundari's autobiography.

41. Stage actress Nirmala Gogate, for example, lauded his beauty in a woman's guise: "[Gogate] speaks of his exquisite and soft complexion—fair with a golden tinge—which was radiant, his large eloquent eyes, his expressive hands, his delicate movements despite a slightly plump but well-proportioned body, and a dignified appearance like that of a well-born woman. All of this, she claims, brought people a new awareness and appreciation of feminine beauty" (Kosambi 2015, 269). When discussing one of Bal Gandharva's earlier performances as the character of Bhamini in the play *Manapaman*, Shanta Gokhale (2000, 36–37) writes: "Bal Gandharva had, by this time, come to embody the object of male fantasy—the woman who hid her fire under deliciously modest coquetry."

42. Barleen Kaur (2013, 196) counters Hansen's claims to suggest that although women may have attempted to emulate Bal Gandharva, "There was also a sizeable number of women in Maharashtra who were repulsed by Bal Gandharva's portrayal of 'femininity'. The women who objected to such a portrayal did so because they found his projection of femininity rather vulgar. In this sense, Bal Gandharva's impersonation also had the potential to generate a counter-structure to the model of sexuality that he was attempting to propagate."

43. Gandharva's and Sundari's Sangeet Natak Akademi awards are listed on the SNA website: www.sangeetnatak.gov.in/sna/Awardees.php?section = aa (accessed November 28, 2016).

44. See also Narayana Rao 2007, 196.

45. Sthanam also received national approbation for his impersonation; in 1956, he was awarded the national honor of Padma Shri and, in 1961, he was awarded the Sangeet Natak Akademi award. Sthanam's Sangeet Natak Akademi award is listed on the SNA website: www.sangeetnatak.gov.in/sna/Awardees.php?section=aa (accessed November 28, 2016).

46. Sumathi Ramaswamy (1997, 122) notes that the Orientalist imaginary posits a dichotomy between "the natural and inherent superiority of the rational, secular, industrious, progressive (masculine) West . . . over the irrational, spiritual, passive unchanging (feminine) East." See also Sarkar (2001, 251) and Kellen Hoxworth's (2018) fascinating discussion of Dave Carson's enactment of "The Bengalee Baboo" in the context of blackface minstrelsy in the late nineteenth century.

47. The refiguring of indigenous masculinity in the wake of the colonial encounter is not limited to the Indian context but is also documented by Afsaneh Najmabadi (2005) in her discussion of Iranian perceptions of beauty and masculinity.

48. Perhaps most famously, Gandhi overturned the colonial stereotype of the effeminate *bābu* through his own ascetic bodily practices and understandings of gender (Chakraborty

2011, 122). Related to themes of Gandhi, gender, and nationhood, see also Nandy [1983] 2009; Howard 2013; Valiana 2014. Sumathi Ramaswamy counters the perceived effeminacy of Gandhi in her *The Goddess and the Nation* (2010, 198–99).

49. For a discussion of Richard Burton's writings, see also Arondekar 2009, chap. 1.

50. Kathryn Hansen, pers. comm., October 22, 2016. Similar critiques arose in the case of Bharatanatyam dance, as previously discussed (Krishnan 2009).

51. Little is known about Vempati Venkatanarayana's practices of impersonation beyond his sobriquet *Abhinava Satyabhama* (Jonnalagadda 1993, 165; Usha Gayatri 2016, 186). According to Kuchipudi practitioners, Venkatanarayana is popularly known as one of three primary figures of Kuchipudi dance, along with Chinta Venkataramayya (1860–1949) and Vedantam Lakshminarayana Sastry (1886–1956) (Nagabhushana Sarma 2016, 49). While Venkataramayya popularized the genre of *yakṣagāna* in the Kuchipudi village and Lakshminarayana Sastry expanded the repertoire of solo items, Venkatanarayana is credited for propagating its *kalāpa* repertoire, including *Bhāmākalāpam* (Jonnalagadda 1993, 165–66; Nagabhushana Sarma 2016, 77–88). Few historical records of Venkatanarayana are available, aside for the reported accounts of scholars such as Sista Ramakrishna Sastry and Jalasutram Rukmininadha Sastry (Nagabhushana Sarma 2016, 84–87).

52. For a discussion of APSNA and their activities to promote Kuchipudi, including the 1959 APSNA seminar, see Putcha 2013; Jonnalagadda 2016.

53. Paralleling impersonation in Kuchipudi is the context of Andhra Natyam, a revival of courtesan dance promoted by Nataraja Ramakrishna and his student Kalakrishna beginning in 1970. Ramakrishna, a nonbrahmin trained by *kalāvantula* dancers, sought to promote and reinvigorate Telugu courtesan performance practices in the mid-twentieth century. Most notably, Ramakrishna learned *Navajanārdana Pārijātam* (a courtesan version of *Bhāmākalāpam*) from Pendela Satyabhama, a well-known *kalāvantula* performer in Pithapuram, a town in the east Godavari district of Andhra Pradesh. To promote and preserve Telugu courtesan performance, Ramakrishna rechristened their dance form as Andhra Natyam (lit., "Dance of Andhra") in 1970. For further discussion of Andhra Natyam, see Ramakrishna 1959, 1984; Arudra 1990; Aslesha 1994; Kalakrishna 1996; Suvarchala Devi 1997; Soneji 2012.

2. "I AM SATYABHAMA": CONSTRUCTING HEGEMONIC BRAHMIN MASCULINITY IN THE KUCHIPUDI VILLAGE

1. See Pollock (2016, 47) for the dating of Bharata's *Nāṭyaśāstra* and Zarrilli (2000, 90) for the dating of Nandikeshvara's *Abhinayadarpaṇa*.

2. For a discussion of *abhinaya* in the *Abhinayadarpaṇa*, see also *The Mirror of Gesture* [1917] 1997, 17.

3. Coorlawala (2004, 55) goes on to argue that Rukmini Arundale not only Sanskritized the dance form, but also the dancing body: "In sanskritized dance, the body is the central object and the words 'pure' and 'refinement or *samskṟīti*' serve as the ultimate arbiters applied to interpretation of emotions, selection of appropriate themes, authenticity of repertory, classicism in technique, and costumes."

4. As evidence of the Sanskritization of Kuchipudi, Banda Kanakalingeshwara Rao (1966, 30), an avid proponent of Kuchipudi, asks: "What is a classical dance? A style of

dance which has the sanctity of an authoritative ancient treatise. The earliest available treatise on dance and drama is Bharata's *Natya Sastra* . . . The Kuchipudi style of dance-drama form which is strictly based on the principles of Bharata's *Natya Sastra,* is definitely a classical style."

5. Hansen (2015, 266) notes that Sundari shifts between third- and first-person voice in his autobiography, indicating a transition from external gaze to interior exploration. For a discussion of this excerpt from Sundari's biography, see also Hansen 1999, 134–35.

6. For a discussion of the use of the term *habitus,* see Mahmood 2001, 15–16.

7. Hanne M. de Bruin (2006) outlines a comparable transformation process in the guising practices of the Tamil theatrical form of Kattaikkuttu (or Terukkuttu). Bruin notes that during the pre-performance phase, "the actor initiates the first part of the gradual transformation process from the *social* self to the dramatic *other* by applying makeup and putting on the *kaṭṭai* ornaments and a conventional costume" (109). As another example, male dancer Ram Gopal (1957, 34) describes in his autobiography that during daily practices, his teacher, Kunju Kurup, used to tell him: "You shall be the beautiful maiden Damyanti [*sic*] and I shall be your handsome prince Nala, and I want you to convince by every look, gesture and expression that you are truly, deeply in love with me." Also cited in Sinha 2017.

8. *Kuchipudi Dance: Ancient & Modern,* Part II, documentary produced by the India Films Division, 1973. In a similar vein, Nagabhushana Sarma (2012, 22) likens Satyanarayana Sarma's donning of the *strī-vēṣam* to an operation: "The three-hours of making-up, each time [Satyanarayana Sarma] did a female role was like an operation; peeling out the external demeanour and grafting a new soul into it."

9. This series of photographs of Vedantam Satyanarayana Sarma is replicated in Venkataraman and Pasricha (2005, 132–33). A similar series of photographs can be found of *kabuki* artist Nakamura Senjaku applying makeup for a young princess in Senelick's *The Changing Room* (2000, 80).

10. For a more detailed discussion of Satyabhama's braid, see Kapaleswara Rao 1996; Kamath 2012, 170–75. For a broader discussion of hair in South Asia, see Hiltebeitel 1998; Olivelle 1998.

11. The Kuchipudi female dance costume is similar to the tailored costumes of Bharatanatyam with the exception of the length of the fan between the legs. Kuchipudi fans are longer than Bharatanatyam fans; otherwise, the costumes of Kuchipudi and Bharatanatyam are virtually identical. Notably, the introduction of tailored costumes appears in the mid- to late twentieth century; pictures and videos of Vedantam Satyanarayana Sarma at the height of his career in the 1960s feature a silken sari wrapped around the body and not a tailored costume. For further discussion on the labor of the tailored costumes of Bharatanatyam, see Srinivasan 2012, chap. 7.

12. For further discussion of Andhra Natyam, see Ramakrishna 1959, 1984; Arudra 1990; Aslesha 1994; Kalakrishna 1996; Suvarchala Devi 1997; Soneji 2012.

13. Similarly, Zarrilli (2000, 70) quotes Gopi Asan, a senior Kathakali artist, as to how he was selected as a student of the Kalamandalam, the premiere Kathakali dance institute, in 1951: "Every applicant in acting was asked to put on make-up and costume in order to know whether their physical features, especially the face, was suitable for an actor. In my case, it so happened that at first sight, [senior guru] Mahakavi Vallathol commented that this boy's physical features befitted an actor and hence there was no need for me to audition!"

14. The orchestra can also include other musicians, such as those playing violin, flute, and *vīna,* who are often hired from outside the village. The composition of the orchestra for Kuchipudi dance is undoubtedly a reflection of the broader shifts in the classicization of Karnatak music (see Weidman 2006).

15. The delivery of dialogues is absent from many contemporary Kuchipudi performances enacted by nonhereditary dancers. This is due to changes implemented by Kuchipudi guru Vempati Chinna Satyam. See chapter 4 for further discussion of this change.

16. This may be because female Kuchipudi dancers are influenced by the postcolonial sanitization of *devadāsī* performance into South Indian "classical" dance (described in the introduction), and often downplay overtly erotic gestures, even when the lyrics of the songs may necessitate such suggestive movements.

17. Meera Kosambi (2015, 271) notes that after the age of forty, Marathi impersonator Bal Gandharva resorted to more exaggerated movements to compensate for his age: "Gone was the softness in his acting, now replaced by 'an excess of provocative gestures', 'little skips and jumps, neck movements, provocative smiles.'"

18. According to the *New York Times,* Satyanarayana Sarma performed in New York on March 6, 1986 (Dunning 1986). According to the *Los Angeles Times,* he performed in San Diego on March 26, 1986 (Sondak 1986). He also represented Kuchipudi at the "Congress on the Female Role as Represented on the Stage in Various Cultures" held in Denmark in September 1986, as coordinated by the International School of Theater Anthropology (ISTA) (Barba 1986, 171).

19. Satyanarayana Sarma's legacy of impersonation is also evident in scholarly accounts of his career. Hyderabad-based dancer and scholar Anuradha Jonnalagadda (1993, 132) characterizes Satyanarayana Sarma as "perhaps the greatest female impersonator of the present century." Jayant Kastuar, Kathak exponent and former secretary of the Central Sangeet Natak Akademi (the national arts organization of India), describes Satyanarayana Sarma as "one of the most outstanding dancers of our time; he has achieved rare eminence in the art of female impersonation." Jayant Kastuar's remarks are found in *Nritya Nidhi Utsav,* "Treasures of Indian Dance" (2005) in the Sangeet Natak Akademi archives.

20. While Satyanarayana Sarma does not use a Telugu equivalent for "passing," the stories he tells clearly suggest that he takes pride in his reported ability to convince his audiences as to the authenticity of his performance of gender. This resonates with Drouin's (2008, 32) claim that "the aim of passing is for the illusion [of gender] to signify as real in the public sphere. Through its investment in realness, passing is the quotidian street equivalent of theatrical cross-dressing." See also C. Riley Snorton's (2017) discussion of cross-dressing, passing, and fungibility for blacks in the antebellum period.

21. A similar account of passing is found in the Javanese tradition of impersonation *tandhak ludruk* (Sunardi 2015, 77–78). See also Hansen's (1999, 137) mention of Bal Gandharva passing as a married women undetected by the Maharani of Baroda Palace.

22. Male *nācā* actors are expected to wear a sari when enacting female roles, an expectation that Devlal did not fulfill (Flueckiger 1988, 164).

23. Kosambi (2015, 271–72) also notes the effects of age on Bal Gandharva's ability to impersonate.

24. For example, in the 2006 Siddhendra Mahotsav, an annual festival staged in the Kuchipudi village, Satyanarayana Sarma performed the lead character of Satyabhama at the age of seventy, alongside his twenty-two-year-old disciple Chinta Ravi Balakrishna playing the role of Madhavi.

25. See also Messerschmidt 2016, 10.

26. See also Inhorn 2012, 47; Messerschmidt and Messner 2018, 40.

27. For a discussion of the turbaned Sikh man and his place within heteronormative frameworks and the queer diaspora, see Puar 2007, chap. 4.

28. This contrasts with the men of Kimberley Kay Hoang's 2015 study, *Dealing in Desire,* in which men exhibit multiple masculinities that are constructed on the global frame: "These masculinities were not simply based on men's individual subjectivity; instead, men constructed and asserted their masculinities according to their desire for a world order modeled on older tropes of Western global power or the rising prominence of non-Western nations in East and Southeast Asia" (60).

29. For her foundational discussion of intersectionality, see also Crenshaw 1989.

3. CONSTRUCTING ARTIFICE, INTERROGATING IMPERSONATION: MADHAVI AS *VIDŪṢAKA* IN VILLAGE *BHĀMĀKALĀPAM* PERFORMANCE

1. The *sūtradhāra*'s opening speech quoted here is based on Banda Kanakalingeshwara Rao's *Siddhēndra-yōgī-kṛta Bhāmākalāpamu* (1967) and the handwritten script of *Bhāmākalāpam* by Vempati Chinna Satyam (ca. 1970).

2. See *Nāṭyaśāstra* XXXV.66–74 for prescribed characteristics of the *sūtradhāra.*

3. In an attempt to provide historical reasoning for this trend, Modali Nagabhushana Sarma characterizes the *sūtradhāra* as the "other," or miscellaneous, character. According to Nagabhushana Sarma, the triangulation of *sūtradhāra*/Madhavi/Madhava was introduced in the period when performances of Kuchipudi shifted from a single-person dance drama to one including more performers. As a result, the *sūtradhāra* was able to portray several roles at once and therefore functions as the "other" character (interview with author, Hyderabad, November 9, 2009).

4. *Bhāmākalāpam,* Siddhendra Mahotsav (Kuchipudi, Andhra Pradesh: March 2006, VCD). This video is courtesy of Kuchipudi resident Pasumarti Haranadh.

5. Sastry Garu is an honorific title given to any learned scholar, particularly belonging to a brahmin family. In this case, the *sūtradhāra* is referencing a supporting orchestra member when using this title.

6. Pasumarti, Bhagavatula, and Darbha are the names for hereditary brahmin families from the village of Kuchipudi. For a discussion of hereditary brahmin families of the Kuchipudi village, see the introduction.

7. Robert Cohen (2016) defines two types of direct address in Shakespearean theatre: (1) that given by the actor to the audience representing himself and/or his company of fellow actors (74–75); and (2) that given as an epilogue "by actors who retain their character identities, but who, for this concluding speech, step out of the 'play' to represent their acting company" (77). In the case of *Bhāmākalāpam,* the direct addresses of the *sūtradhāra* appear to be closer to Cohen's first designation of direct address.

8. *Bhāmākalāpam,* International Symposium on *Kalāpa* Traditions, VCD. The ellipses indicate portions of the dialogue I have edited out.

9. This character can also be referred to as Madhavudu, the Telugu form of the Sanskrit name Madhava.

10. P.V.G. Krishna Sarma also states, "Madhavi is instigating Satyabhama's character . . . Madhavi creates humor. It might not be proper etiquette, but you have to do something to create humor in audiences" (interview with author, Kuchipudi, February 9, 2010).

11. Teun Goudriaan (1978, 3) suggests that *māyā* expresses three possible meanings in the Vedic textual tradition: "In the Veda the word *māyā* can stand for various aspects of the process involved: the power which creates a new appearance, the creation of that appearance as an abstract performance, and the result of the process, i.e. the created form itself. The power, its manifestation and its result are not distinguished by name; nor does it matter if the result is real or illusory." See also Gonda 1959, 119–94; Pintchman 1994, 89.

12. The most influential Vedanta thinker is undoubtedly Shankara, the ninth-century philosopher who expounds upon the concept of Advaita Vedanta, or nondual reality, by arguing that the created world is not distinct from Brahman, or the ultimate real. For Shankara, *māyā* expresses both creative and delusive powers: "*māyā* is both creative in the sense that it brings into being the relative world and delusive, in the sense that what *māyā* creates is essentially a kind of delusion" (Pintchman 1994, 93–94). *Māyā*'s role in concealing the true nature of reality likens it to ignorance, *avidyā*, as opposed to *vidyā*, or knowledge. Tracy Pintchman (1994, 89–90) notes *māyā*'s relationship to two other important Sanskrit categories: *prakṛtī,* the principle of materiality, and *śaktī,* the cosmological principle of power. In the *Upaniṣads*, *māyā* is conflated with *prakṛtī* (see *Śvetāśvatara Upaniṣad* 4.10), while in the *Bhagavad Gītā,* the concept of *prakṛtī* is subsumed under the creative powers of *māyā* (see *Bhagavad Gītā* 7.14). While *prakṛtī* represents the result of creation, in the language of Goudriaan, *śaktī* is comparable to the power of the creative process; *māyā* ultimately encompasses both of these terms (Pintchman 1994, 90). There are many other interpretations of *māyā* beyond the Vedic and Vedantic usages of the term, particularly in relation to the concepts of *prakṛtī* in *sāṅkhya* philosophy and *śūnya* (emptiness) in Nagarjuna's articulations on Buddhist thought (Reyna 1962, 8–11, 15–22).

13. For further discussion of *rām-līlā* performances in Ramnagar/Varanasi and in the environs of Bareilly, Uttar Pradesh, see Lothspeich 2018.

14. This was confirmed to me in a follow-up discussion with Pasumarti Rattayya Sarma in January 2011. While they may not have been familiar with the specific philosophical nuances of *māyā,* it is notable that these performers selectively invoked this term, and no other, to analyze the characters of *sūtradhāra*/Madhavi/Madhava.

15. I thank Laurie L. Patton for suggesting this translation of *māyā.*

16. For a discussion of the gender of names in predominantly English-speaking societies, see Eckert and McConnell-Ginet 2003, 15–16.

17. While I have chosen not to add diacritics to proper names in this text, I have used them in this paragraph to illustrate the length of the vowels as indicative of gendered names.

18. I thank Petra Shenk for her insights on this shift in grammatical voice.

19. The importance of speech is even more apparent when examining the content of the dialogues themselves; Madhavi's playful demands for Satyabhama's jewels and nose ring, for example, delineate her gender and class status.

20. The importance of speech in the *Bhāmākalāpam* dance drama resonates with the articulations of J.L. Austin, a British philosopher of language who proposes the idea that words have performative power. In *How to Do Things with Words* (1975), a series of lectures delivered at Harvard University in 1955, Austin makes an important linguistic distinction between a constative statement and a performative utterance. In the first lecture of this series, Austin suggests that a constative statement describes the state of affairs and can be verifiable as either true or false (2–3). Rather than simply describing a state of affairs, Austin states that speech has the power to act through the performative utterance (6–7). A concrete example that Austin provides of the performative utterance is the vows of marriage: "when I say, before the registrar or altar, &c., 'I do,' I am not reporting on a marriage: I am indulging in it" (6). The very act of saying "I do" *performs* marriage, rather than simply reporting on it. The performative capacity of speech is also taken up by Butler in her discussions of gender and discourse. While Butler directly engages with Austin's theory of performative speech in *Excitable Speech* (1997), it is only in her earlier work *Bodies That Matter* ([1993] 2011) that she examines the connections between discourse, gender, and power. In *Bodies That Matter*, Butler links performativity and discourse by suggesting that "performativity must be understood not as a singular or deliberate 'act,' but, rather, as the reiterative and citational practice by which discourse produces the effects that it names" (xii). Here, Butler draws on Jacques Derrida's reading of Austin, which suggests that all performative utterances are citations in that they repeat a particular term. Butler applies Derrida's notion of citationality to her discussion of gender by suggesting that gender has the same citational structure as language: gender norms must be cited repeatedly in order to have an effect (177). For further discussion of the relationship between Austin, Derrida, and Butler, see Parker and Sedgwick 2016.

21. See also Kuiper 1979, 201.

22. See Velcheru Narayana Rao and David Shulman's translation of *Vikramorvaśīya*, titled *How Úrvashi Was Won* by Kālidāsa (2009), and Diwakar Acharya's translation of *Mṛcchakaṭikā*, titled *The Little Clay Cart* by Śūdraka (2009). Both translations are published by the Clay Sanskrit Library. Sanskrit plays that exclude the *vidūṣaka* are relatively few in number, and F.B.J. Kuiper (1979, 211–12) notes a short list of such works, including the Rama- and Krishna-focused plays of Bhasa and the dramas of Bhavabhuti. Kuiper notes that dramas categorized in the genre of *prakaraṇa* contain the character of the *vidūṣaka*, but dramas categorized as *nāṭaka* do not usually include the *vidūṣaka* (211).

23. Translated by Ghosh 1951, 224. Makeup and attire, as David Shulman (1985, 156) notes, serve to heighten this grotesque affect, and the *vidūṣaka* can appear onstage in a comic three-cornered hat and messily tied *dhoti*. For a discussion of this description of the *vidūṣaka* in the *Nāṭyaśāstra*, see Siegel 1987, 19.

24. For example, in the Sanskrit play *Priyadarśikā* (ca. seventh century CE), the brahmin *vidūṣaka* Vasantaka tells King Udayana of the many learned brahmins in the king's palace: "brahmins who know four Vedas, five Vedas, even six Vedas!" (Siegel 1987, 206). Udayana laughs at Vasantaka's ignorance as there are only four texts in the Vedic canon. The king wryly remarks that the quality of a brahmin is known by the number of Vedic texts he is versed in. In this exchange, the king outsmarts the brahmin clown in his own brahminhood (206).

25. As Shulman (1985, 160) outlines in his extensive work on the clown in Sanskrit and vernacular texts in India, the *vidūṣaka*'s primary role in Sanskrit drama serves as a comedic

foil to the *nāyaka*, and, taken together, the *vidūṣaka* and the *nāyaka* create the composite image of the royal hero.

26. The *vidūṣaka* also extends to other South Indian vernacular dramatic performance traditions, such as the previously mentioned buffoon of Tamil Special Drama (Seizer 2005), the *konaṅki* of Bhagavatamela, and the *kaṭṭiyakkāraṉ* of *kuṟavañci* (Shulman 1985, 210–11).

27. Shulman (1985, 165) describes the Brahmabandhu as a "'low' Brahmin, excluded from ritual, especially sacrificial performance." Shulman is careful to note that the *vidūṣaka* is not necessarily excluded from ritual, but just characterized in this way through the epithet (165n52). For a discussion of Brahmabandhu, see also Sarma 2001.

28. See also Novetzke (2016, chap. 4) for a discussion of brahminical authority in the thirteenth-century Marathi text, *Līḷācaritra.*

29. For example, Sunil Kothari and Avinash Pasricha's popular book *Kuchipudi: Indian Classical Dance Art* (2001), which profiles major contemporary Kuchipudi artists and includes a glossy spread of Satyanarayana Sarma in *vēṣam,* provides a brief two-sentence description on Rattayya Sarma: "Another gifted female impersonator from Pasumarti branch is Rattayya, trained by Chinta Krishnamurti. He has performed in several dance-dramas of Venkatarama Natya Mandali" (166).

30. Refer to Messerschmidt and Messner's (2018, 41–43) discussion of various forms of masculinities, including dominant, dominating, and positive masculinities.

4. *BHĀMĀKALĀPAM* BEYOND THE VILLAGE: TRANSGRESSING NORMS OF GENDER AND SEXUALITY IN URBAN AND TRANSNATIONAL KUCHIPUDI DANCE

1. As stated in the notes to the introduction, Madras was renamed Chennai in 1996 in line with a nationwide trend of renaming the English spellings of Indian cities in accordance with vernacular spellings in Indian languages. In this book, I use Madras to refer to the city prior to 1996 and Chennai to refer to the city after 1996. For a discussion of the renaming of Madras state to Tamil Nadu, see Ramaswamy 1997, 154–61.

2. In her dissertation, Anuradha Jonnalagadda (1996b, 137–40) examines Chinna Satyam's experiments with *Bhāmākalāpam,* including a paragraph discussion of his alterations to Madhavi's character. Chinna Satyam also includes a short discussion of *Bhāmākalāpam* in his article "My Experiments with Kuchipudi" (2012, 41). Notably, he focuses on his choreography of Satyabhama and does not discuss Madhavi.

3. Aware of the complexities of adapting wholesale Euro-American terminology to South Asian contexts, particularly as articulated by Gayatri Reddy (2005) and Mrinalini Sinha (2012), I use the term "gender-variant" as opposed to "transgender" or "third gender" to describe Madhavi.

4. For a discussion of Chinna Satyam's early career in film and the ways in which film movement vocabulary shapes Kuchipudi's inscription onto the female body, see Putcha 2011, chap. 4. For a discussion of the classical and cinematic elements of Chinna Satyam's "Madras Kuchipudi," see Thota 2016, chap. 4.

5. After this, in 1962, Chinna Satyam began teaching Shanta Rao, a female performer accomplished in the classical styles of Bharatanatyam and Mohiniattam. Shanta Rao financially backed Chinna Satyam to help him start the Kuchipudi Dance Academy (a precursor

to KAA). However, when she began to insist that he teach her and no one else, Chinna Satyam abandoned the efforts (Pattabhi Raman 1988/89, 47–48).

6. There is a similar heteroglossia in the context of Parsi theatre (see Hansen 2004a).

7. The narrative of Krishna's theft of the *pārijāta* tree from Indra's garden was first introduced into classical Telugu literature in Nandi Timmana's sixteenth-century *Pārijātāpaharaṇamu* (*Theft of a Tree*). For a full discussion of this narrative, see the introduction to the forthcoming translation by the Murthy Classical Library of India, which I co-translated with Velcheru Narayana Rao.

8. Another of Chinna Satyam's early dance dramas is *Ksheera Sagara Madhanam* ("Churning of the Milk Ocean"), choreographed in 1962. As Jonnalagadda (1996b, 136) states: "The first of the innovative dance dramas, [*Ksheera Sagara Madhanam*] was the first dance drama written and composed exclusively to suit the needs of Kuchipudi. It did away with the regular dialogues and was set entirely to lyrics. The earlier elaborate *Poorvaranga* [consecration of the stage] was set aside. In the stage decor, suggestive sets were introduced. Thus started the era of innovations in Kuchipudi dance with new themes, structure and performance."

9. For a discussion of the Chennai *sabha* in relation to "Brahmin taste," see Rudisill 2007, 2012.

10. In the article "My Experiments with Kuchipudi," Chinna Satyam (1996, 96) dates his experiments with *Bhāmākalāpam* as immediately following his dance drama *Padmavati Srinivasa Kalyanam,* choreographed in 1977. However, according to Chinna Satyam's son, Vempati Ravi Shankar, his father rechoreographed *Bhāmākalāpam* in the early 1970s (Vempati Ravi Shankar, pers. comm., June 13, 2011).

11. I am greatly indebted to P. Venugopala Rao for providing me a copy of Chinna Satyam's handwritten *Bhāmākalāpam* script and to G.M. Sarma for allowing me access to the 1981 recording. In the 1981 recording, a prominent nonbrahmin female performer, Sobha Naidu, played Satyabhama; a well-known male stage actor, Dharmaraj, enacted Madhavi; and a brahmin Kuchipudi dancer and cinema actress, Manju Bhargavi, enacted Krishna. In the 2011 performance in Atlanta, Sasikala Penumarthi, a longtime brahmin female student of Chinna Satyam, played Satyabhama; Vedantam Raghava, a brahmin male from the Kuchipudi village, performed Madhavi; and I enacted Krishna.

12. More recently, Vempati Ravi Shankar also passed away in 2018 due to unexpected complications from a kidney transplant, so I am indebted to have his perspectives inform my research.

13. Regarding this point, Kothari and Pasricha (2001, 205) write: "With the establishment of Kuchipudi Art Academy, Vempati Chinna Satyam ushered in a new era in Kuchipudi, training a large number of female students with a well designed repertoire for solo exposition. A bevy of thoroughly groomed young dancers appeared on the metropolitan stage of Madras and other major cities, making Kuchipudi an extremely lively dance scene."

14. When describing Sobha Naidu, Kothari and Pasricha (2001, 205) write: "A sensational discovery of the terpsichorean world Sobha Naidu sprang on the dance scene in 1969, after a thorough grounding in Kuchipudi under the watchful eye and care of Vempati Chinna Satyam for more than seven years. The prize pupil of Vempati, Sobha with her innate talent and abundant natural gifts, reed-like tall, vivacious frame and figure, with a pair of large expressive eyes, succeeded in imbibing the quintessential quality of Kuchipudi in a remarkable

manner. She became synonymous with Vempati's style." While Kothari and Pasricha seem to suggest that Naidu began training with Chinna Satyam seven years prior to 1969, an article in *Sruti* magazine suggests that she began her training at the age of fourteen, in 1969 (see Iyenger 1989). See also Naidu 2012.

15. Sobha Naidu, email correspondence, November 7, 2009. See also Naidu 2012, 68.

16. Sobha Naidu, email correspondence, November 7, 2009.

17. For a discussion of the *jaḍa vṛtāntam*, see also Kamath 2012.

18. The Vaishnava style of wrapping the sari is found in the 1981 recording of *Bhāmākalāpam*.

19. Sudha Gopalakrishnan (2006, 141) notes a similar shift in costuming in the case of Kutiyattam, specifically in the drama *Toranayuddhanka* in which the character Ravana describes a quarrel between Shiva and Parvati: "In this scene, the actor in the guise of Ravana has to have great dexterity while changing roles in quick succession as Siva and Parvati. The change into a woman is indicated merely by taking the end of the lower garment and fastening it on the waist, but the transformation of the facial expression and demeanor from the masculine to the feminine is subtle yet powerful."

20. After distinguishing between these three contingent dimensions, Butler ([1990] 2008, 187) goes on to lay the groundwork for her theory of gender performativity: "If the anatomy of the performer is already distinct from the gender of the performer, and both of those are distinct from the gender of the performance, then the performance suggests a dissonance not only between sex and performance, but sex and gender, and gender and performance. As much as drag creates a unified picture of 'woman'...it also reveals the distinctness of those aspects of gendered experience which are falsely naturalized as a unity through the regulatory fiction of heterosexual coherence. *In imitating gender, drag implicitly reveals the imitative structure of gender itself—as well as its contingency*" [emphasis in original].

21. Anuradha Jonnalagadda, in discussion with author, Hyderabad, fall 2009. For a discussion of various types of gender-variant characters, see *Nāṭyaśāstra* XXXIV.70–81. Also see *Vikramorvaśīya* 3.1, in *How Úrvashi Was Won* by Kālidāsa (2009, 89), for an example of the *kañcukī* as the guardian of women's domestic space in Sanskrit drama. For a survey of gender-variant roles in early South Asian texts, see also Reddy 2005, 18–22.

22. For a discussion of the term *hijṛā* and the *koṭhī-hijṛā* spectrum, see Reddy 2005; Morcom 2013; Dutta and Roy 2014.

23. See Reddy's discussion of the *hijṛā* sex/gender system, particularly the penetrative/penetrated model of sexual practice in the third chapter of *With Respect to Sex* (2005, 44–77).

24. Drawing on the discourse of his grandmother, Johnson (2001, 2) uses the term "quare" as the black vernacular for queer.

25. Regarding these practices, Johnson (2001, 13) notes: "Performance practices such as vogueing, snapping, 'throwing shade,' and 'reading' attest to the ways in which black gays, lesbians, bisexuals, and transgender people devise technologies of self-assertion and summon the agency to resist."

26. For a critique of Livingston's film *Paris Is Burning*, see hooks 1992, chap. 9.

27. See introduction for a full discussion of South Indian Smarta brahmins.

28. Notably, my interlocutors did not frequently use the Telugu vernacular *maga-vēṣam* or the more Sanskritized *puruṣa-vēṣam*. Rather, they usually referred to the character (i.e., donning Krishna's role, Shiva's role, etc.). This contrasts with *strī-vēṣam*, which was employed more frequently.

29. One important exception to this claim is Vempati Ravi Shankar's performance of the dual-gendered role of Ardhanarishvara in the KAA production *Ardhanareeswaram*, first staged in 1998. In the end of the dance drama, Ravi Shankar, who enacts the lead character of Shiva up to this point, appears as Ardhanarishvara in a costume that distinguishes his body as half female (Parvati) and half male (Shiva), divided by a long dark veil. For a discussion of this dance drama, see Jonnalagadda 2012, 52–53. Another notable exception is Venku, who under Chinna Satyam's guidance first donned the *strī-vēṣam* for the documentary *The Temple and the Swan* (1995).

30. Packert (2010, 25–26) goes on to state that, for many, artistic representations of Krishna is "kitsch par excellence . . . the highly feminized (at least to Euro-American eyes) rendition of Krishna also generates, for some, potential concerns about the seeming imbalance among taste, gender, art, and religion. The same issues are also encountered in debates about Christian art, as Colleen McDannell explains: 'Art was given characteristics that Western culture defines as masculine: strength, power, nobility. Kitsch became associated with stereotypical feminine qualities: sentimentality, superficiality, and intimacy.'"

31. See also Amy-Ruth Holt's "Sacred Androgyny and Jayalalitha's Ritual Embodiment in Tamil Politics" (2018, 16) for a discussion of Krishna in artistic representation.

32. See Halberstam's new preface to the twentieth anniversary edition of *Female Masculinity* (2018) for a discussion of the utility of the term "female masculinity."

33. Similarly, Halberstam (2012, 258–59) states that while drag queen performances veer toward the flamboyant, drag king performances reflect constraint and a quiet machismo.

34. For discussions of Chinna Satyam's choreography, see also Kamath 2011; Penumarthi 2012.

5. LONGING TO DANCE: STORIES OF KUCHIPUDI BRAHMIN WOMEN

1. Although I interacted with Rajyalakshmi during my fieldwork in the village in 2010, all quotes by Rajyalakshmi are from the transcript of the 2014 interview.

2. For a discussion of marriage patterns and examples of women's songs upon departure from their natal homes, see Raheja and Gold, *Listen to the Heron's Words* (1994, chap. 3).

3. Margaret Trawick includes an extensive discussion of marriage patterns in South India in chapter 4 of her 1992 book *Notes on Love in a Tamil Family.* Thanks to Leela Prasad for pointing me to this work.

4. For example, Rajayalakshmi's sons Venku and Raghava both married women from outside the village.

5. Lakshminarasamma also passed away a few years after my interview with her.

6. Rajyalakshmi seemed entirely unconcerned with Mutyam's presence and was open to answering our questions, a point that was evident to me when I returned to her house for a follow-up visit in July 2018 without Mutyam. During the return visit, Rajyalakshmi again spoke about her experiences of learning dance.

7. See Anne Mackenzie Pearson's *"Because It Gives Me Peace of Mind": Ritual Fasts in the Religious Lives of Hindu Women* (1996) for a discussion of the meaning that women attribute to Hindu votive rituals, *vrats*.

8. For a discussion of *habitus* and embodied practice, see also Mahmood 2001, 15–16; 2005, chap. 5.

9. Although I extensively interacted with Baliakka during my fieldwork in Hyderabad in 2009–10 and in all of my follow-up visits, all quotes by Baliakka are from the transcript of the 2014 interview.

10. The story of Ekalavya appears in *Mahābhārata* 1(7)123. This translation of the narrative is from Buitenen 1973, 270–73.

11. See my 2011 interview with Vempati Ravi Shankar in the arts journal *Kalaparva*, "Vempati Ravi Shankar: Following His Father's Footsteps," http://commentary.kalaparva.com/2011/06/vempati-ravi-shankar-following-his.html (accessed March 22, 2017).

12. During the interview, Baliakka often alternated between referring to her experiences in the first-person singular ("I") and the first-person plural ("we"), presumably referencing herself and her sisters. It is common for Indian language speakers to employ the first-person plural ("we") when referring to oneself, perhaps as a signal of both individual and collective experience. Joyce Flueckiger notes that Hindi speakers often colloquially refer to themselves using the first-person plural *hum* (pers. comm., September 26, 2018). In this case, Baliakka's deferral to collective voice includes her experiences as well as those of her sisters, thereby providing further legitimacy to her narrative.

13. Baliakka's school, Abhinayavani Nritya Niketan, was established following her marriage, with the support of her brahmin husband and father-in-law who are, incidentally, not from the Kuchipudi village.

14. Soneji (2012, 187) goes on to state that both *noṭṭusvaram* and *mōṭi* "stood outside the canon of the hereditary courtly repertoire (*catirkkaccēri*) of the prereform period and were not 'classical' or religious enough to be integrated into postreform-period reinvented Bharatanāṭyam of the urban middle class."

15. Baliakka's sister, Kameshwari, also continues to teach, but, due to health-related reasons in her family, she has minimized her teaching commitments.

16. For a recording of Satyanarayana Sarma as Satyabhama, see the documentary *Kuchipudi Dance: Ancient & Modern*, Part II, produced by the India Films Division, 1973.

CONCLUSION

1. Anna Morcom (2013, 172) also notes this decline in impersonation practices but dates the decline to the late nineteenth or early twentieth century, as opposed to the contemporary period.

2. Impersonation is attested in a range of literary sources including premodern Sanskrit epic texts (Goldman 1993; Doniger 2000, 2004; Vanita and Kidwai 2001), *bhakti* devotional literature (Ramanujan 1989; Hawley 2000; Pechilis 2012), and Sufi and Urdu poetry (Petievich 2008; Kugle 2013). For a full discussion of impersonation in South Asia, see the forthcoming edited volume *Mimetic Desires: Impersonation and Guising Across South Asia*, co-edited by Harshita Mruthinti Kamath and Pamela Lothspeich.

BIBLIOGRAPHY

PRIMARY TEXTS AND TRANSLATIONS

The Appeasement of Radhika: Radhika Santawanam by Muddupalani. 2011. Translated by Sandhya Mulchandani. New Delhi: Penguin Books.

Āṭabhāgavatam Satyabhāmā-vēṣakatha. 1999. In *Bhāmākalāpamu,* edited by P. Jayamma. Chennai: Government Oriental Manuscripts Library, 1–69.

The Bhagavad Gita. 2008. Translated by Laurie Patton. New York: Penguin Books.

Bhāmākalāpam. 1970. Handwritten script by Vempati Chinna Satyam. Chennai: Kuchipudi Art Academy.

Bhāmākalāpamu R. 1924L. 1999. In *Bhāmākalāpamu,* edited by P. Jayamma. Chennai: Government Oriental Manuscripts Library, 70–103.

Bhāmākalāpamu R. 429. n.d. Tirupati: Tirupati Oriental Research Institute.

Bhāmākalāpamu (Pārijātamu). 1913. Edited by Mangu Jagannatha Rao. Kakinada.

The Demon's Daughter: A Love Story from South India. 2006. Translated by Velcheru Narayana Rao and David Shulman. Albany: State University of New York Press.

Girls for Sale: Kanyasulkam, A Play from Colonial India. 2007. Written by Gurajada Apparao. Translated by Velcheru Narayana Rao. Bloomington: Indiana University Press.

How Úrvashi Was Won by Kālidāsa. 2009. Translated by Velcheru Narayana Rao and David Shulman. Clay Sanskrit Library. New York: New York University Press and JJC Foundation.

Kamasutra by Vatsyayana Mallanga. 2009. Translated by Wendy Doniger and Sudhir Kakar. New York: Oxford University Press.

Kṣētrayya padamulu. 1963. 2nd edition. Edited by Vissa Appa Rao. Rajahmundry: Saraswati Power Press.

Kūcipūḍī-bhāmākalāpamu. [1967] 1982. Edited by Vedantam Parvatisam. Kuchipudi: Sri Balaji.

The Story of Manu by Allasani Peddana. 2015. Translated by Velcheru Narayana Rao and David Shulman. Murthy Classical Library of India. Cambridge, MA: Harvard University Press.

The Little Clay Cart by Śūdraka. 2009. Translated by Diwakar Acharya. Clay Sanskrit Library. New York: New York University Press and JJC Foundation.

The Mahābhārata. Vol. 1: The Book of the Beginnings. 1973. Translated and edited by J.A.B. van Buitenen. Chicago: University of Chicago Press.

The Mahābhārata. Vol. 3: Book 4: The Book of Virata; Book 5: The Book of Effort. 1978. Translated and edited by J.A.B. van Buitenen. Chicago: University of Chicago Press.

The Mirror of Gesture: Being the Abhinaya Darpaṇa of Nandikeśvara. [1917] 1997. Translated by Ananda Coomaraswamy and Gopala Kristnayya Duggirala. New Delhi: Munisharam Manoharlal.

The Nāṭyaśāstra Ascribed to Bharata Muni, Volume I. 1951. Translated by Manmohan Ghosh. Calcutta: Asiatic Society of Bengal.

The Nāṭyaśāstra Ascribed to Bharata Muni, Volume II. 1961. Translated by Manmohan Ghosh. Calcutta: Asiatic Society of Bengal.

Nāṭyaśāstra: Text with Introduction, English Translation, and Indices in Four Volumes. 1998. Translated by N.P. Unni. Vol. 14. Delhi: Nag.

Sarva Śabda Saṃbōdhinyākhyōyam. [1875] 2004. Translated by Sri Paravastu Srinivasacarya. New Delhi: Asian Educational Services.

Siddhēndra-yōgī-kṛta Bhāmākalāpamu. 1967. Edited by Banda Kanakalingeshwara Rao. Hyderabad: Andhra Pradesh Sangeet Natak Akademi.

The Sound of the Kiss or The Story That Must Never Be Told. 2002. Translated by Velcheru Narayana Rao and David Shulman. New York: Columbia University Press.

Upaniṣads. 1998. Translated by Patrick Olivelle. Oxford: Oxford World Classics.

AUDIO-VISUAL MATERIAL

Bhāmākalāpam. 1959. Parts 1–3. Produced by Chinta Krishna Murthy. Vijayawada: All India Radio, July 7. Mp3.

Bhāmākalāpam. 1981. Produced by Vempati Chinna Satyam. Madras. VCD.

Bhāmākalāpam. 2006. Siddhendra Mahotsav. Kuchipudi, Andhra Pradesh: March. VCD.

Bhāmākalāpam. 2011. Atlanta: Emory University, September 23–24. DVD.

Bhāmākalāpam. 2011. International Symposium on *Kalāpa* Traditions. Hyderabad: University of Hyderabad, January 20. VCD.

The Evolution of Kuchipudi. 2004. Mumbai: Kuchipudi Kalakendra, March 6. VCD.

Heritage Dances of India. 1973. Directed by T.A. Abraham. Mumbai: Ministry of Information and Broadcasting, Films Division. VCD.

I am Satyabhama. 2013. Directed by Dulam Satyanarayana. DSN Films.

Kuchipudi Dance: Ancient & Modern, Parts I–II. 1973. Directed by T.A. Abraham. Mumbai: Ministry of Information and Broadcasting, Films Division. VCD.

Kuchipudi Nrityotsava. 1995. New Delhi: Sangeet Natak Akademi Archives, V3138, January 31. VHS.

Kuchipudi Nrityotsava. 1997. New Delhi: Sangeet Natak Akademi Archives, V4281. VHS.

Lakshminarayana Sastry, Vedantam conversing with Balasaraswati. 1960. New Delhi: Sangeet Natak Akademi Archives, V1240. VHS.

Nritya Nidhi Utsav. 2005. "Treasures of Indian Dance." New Delhi: Sangeet Natak Akademi Archives, V7448, April 27. VHS.
Paris Is Burning. 1991. Directed by Jennie Livingston. Burbank, CA: Miramax Films. DVD.
Sangeet Natak Akademi Nrityotsava. 1995. New Delhi: Sangeet Natak Akademi Archives, Photo 42456, January 31. Photograph.
Sangeet Natak Akademi Nrityotsava. 1995. New Delhi: Sangeet Natak Akademi Archives, V3138, January 31. VHS.
The Temple and the Swan. 1995. Produced by Vempati Chinna Satyam and Sujatha Vinjamuri, and directed by Vinay Dumale. Madras.

RECORDED INTERVIEWS

Balatripurasundari, Chavali (Vempati). March 28, 2014. Hyderabad.
Bhargavi, Manju. March 8, March 18, and April 6, 2010. Chennai.
Bhikshu, Aruna. October 9, 2009. Hyderabad.
Chari, Vasanthalakshmi, and Narasimha Chari. November 28, 2009. Chennai.
Gnana Prasunamba, Pasumarti. March 25, 2014. Kuchipudi. Interview conducted with Pasumarti Mrutyumjaya.
Jonnalagadda, Anuradha. April 28, 2010. Hyderabad.
Kalakrishna. August 18, 2009. Hyderabad.
Katyayani, Hari (Vempati). March 27, 2014. Vijayawada.
Keshav Prasad, Pasumarti. October 10, 2009. Kuchipudi.
Khan, Haleem. December 21, 2015. Hyderabad.
Krishna Murthy, Josyula. March 10 and April 30, 2010. Kuchipudi.
Krishna Sarma, Pasumarti Venugopala. February 5 and 9, and March 10, 2010. Kuchipudi.
Kumar, Ajay. January 31, 2010. Vijayawada.
Lakshminarasamma, Bhagavatula. March 25, 2014. Kuchipudi. Interview conducted with Pasumarti Mrutyumjaya.
Lakshminarasamma, Pasumarti. March 26, 2014. Chennai. Interview conducted with Pasumarti Mrutyumjaya.
Lakshminarasamma, Vedantam, March 24, 2014. Kuchipudi. Interview conducted with Pasumarti Mrutyumjaya.
Mosalikanti, Kishore. March 20, 2010. Chennai.
Nagabhushana Sarma, Modali. October 7, October 29, November 6, and December 18, 2009. Hyderabad.
Nageswara Sarma, Yeleswarapu. February 17, 2010. Kuchipudi.
Naidu, Sobha. November 12, 2009. Hyderabad.
Narasimham, B.L. March 1 and March 3, 2010. Kuchipudi.
Penumarthi, Sasikala. December 6, 2011. Atlanta.
Radheshyam, Vedantam. March 6, 2010. Kuchipudi.
Rajyalakshmi, Vedantam. March 24, 2014. Kuchipudi. Interview conducted with Pasumarti Mrutyumjaya.
Rama Murthy, Bhagavatula. March 12, 2010. Kuchipudi.
Rama Rao, Uma. October 4, 2009. Hyderabad.
Rama Seshamma, Vempati. March 24, 2014. Kuchipudi. Interview conducted with Pasumarti Mrutyumjaya.

Ramakrishna, Nataraja. November 20, 2009 and January 23, 2010. Hyderabad.
Ramalingasastry, Vedantam. March 11, 2010. Kuchipudi.
Ramu, Vedantam. April 3, 2010. Chennai.
Rattayya Sarma, Pasumarti. January 26, February 11, and February 14, 2010. Kuchipudi.
Ravi Balakrishna, Chinta. March 8, 2010. Kuchipudi.
Ravi Shankar, Vempati. March 30 and April 8, 2010. Chennai.
Satyanarayana Sarma, Vedantam. January 18, 2011. Kuchipudi.
Sethuram, Bhagavatula. March 3, 2010. Kuchipudi.
Sitarama Anjaneyulu, Chinta. March 11, 2010. Kuchipudi.
Srinivas, Yeleswarapu. February 17, 2010. Kuchipudi.
Suvarchala Devi, K.L.V.N. November 9 and 18, 2009. Hyderabad.
Swarajyalakshmi, Vempati. March 26, 2014. Chennai. Interview conducted with Pasumarti Mrutyumjaya.
Udaya Bhaskaramma, Chinta. March 25, 2014. Kuchipudi. Interview conducted with Pasumarti Mrutyumjaya.
Venkata Naga Chalapathi Rao, Vedantam. April 30, 2010. Vijayawada.
Venkateswarlu, Pasumarti. March 11, 2010. Vijayawada.
Yagnarayana Sarma, Bhagavatula. March 26, 2014. Chennai.

SECONDARY SOURCES

Abu-Lughod, Lila. 1990. "Can There be a Feminist Ethnography?" *Women and Performance: A Journal in Feminist Theory* 5(1): 7–27.

Acharya, C.R., and Mallika Sarabhai. 1992. *Understanding Kuchipudi.* New Delhi: Indira Gandhi National Centre for the Arts in association with Darpana Academy of Performing Arts, Ahmedabad.

Adams, Tony E., and Stacy Holman Jones. 2008. "Autoethnography Is Queer." In *Handbook of Critical and Indigenous Methodologies,* edited by Norman K. Denzin, Yvonna S. Lincoln, and Linda Tuhiwai Smith, 373–90. Thousand Oaks, CA: Sage Publications.

Allen, Matthew Harp. 1997. "Rewriting the Script for South Indian Dance." *TDR* 41(3): 63–100.

———. 2008. "Standardize, Classicize, and Nationalize: The Scientific Work of the Music Academy of Madras, 1930–52." In *Performing Pasts: Reinventing the Arts in Modern South India,* edited by Indira Viswanathan Peterson and Davesh Soneji, 90–129. New Delhi: Oxford University Press.

Alter, Joseph S. 1992. *The Wrestler's Body: Identity and Ideology in North India.* Berkeley: University of California Press.

———. 2011. *Moral Materialism: Sex and Masculinity in Modern India.* New Delhi: Penguin Books.

Andavilli, Satyanarayana, and Pemmaraju Surya Rao. 1994. *Dr. Vempati: Maestro with a Mission.* Vijayawada: S.S.V. Associates.

Andhra Pradesh Sangeet Natak Akademi. 1959. *Souvenir on Kuchipudi Natya Seminar.* Hyderabad: Andhra Pradesh Sangeet Natak Akademi.

Apffel-Marglin, Frederique. 1985. *Wives of the God-King: The Rituals of the Devadasis of Puri.* New York: Oxford University Press.

Appa Rao, Vissa. 1958. "Kuchipudi School of Dance." In *Papers and Programme Presented at the Dance Seminar of the Sangeet Natak Akademi*, March–April. New Delhi: Sangeet Natak Akademi.

———.1959. "Kuchipudi School of Dancing." In *Souvenir on Kuchipudi Natya Seminar*, 10–22. Hyderabad: Andhra Pradesh Sangeet Natak Akademi.

Apte, Vaman Shivaraman. 1995. *The Practical Sanskrit-English Dictionary.* Delhi: Motilal Banarsidass.

Arondekar, Anjali. 2009. *For the Record: On Sexuality and the Colonial Archive in India.* Durham, NC: Duke University Press.

———. 2012. "Subject to Sex: A Small History of the Gomantak Maratha Samaj." In *South Asian Feminisms,* edited by Ania Loomba and Ritty A. Lukose, 244–63. Durham: Duke University Press.

———. 2018. "Caste, Sexuality, and the *Kala* of the Archive." In *Gender, Caste and the Imagination of Equality,* edited by Anupama Rao, 109–35. New Delhi: Women Unlimited.

Arudra. 1986. "Bhagavata Mela: The Telugu Heritage of Tamil Nadu." *Sruti* 22 (April): 18–28.

———. 1986/87. "The Renaming of an Old Dance: A Whodunit Tale of Mystery." *Sruti* 27/28 (December/January): 30–31.

———. 1989. "Background & Evolution of Kuchipudi Dance." *Sruti* 54 (March): 17–19.

———. 1990. "Kalavantulu of Andhra Natyam." *Sangeet Natak* 97 (July–September): 46–55.

———. 1991. *Samagra Āndhra Sāhityam.* Vijayawada: Prajasakti Bookhouse.

———. 1994. "Lingering Questions & Some Fashionable Fallacies." *Sruti* 115 (April): 29–31.

———. 2011. *Dance Traditions of Andhra.* Hyderabad: Sthree Sakthi.

Ashton, Martha Bush. 1969. "Yakshagana: A South Indian Folk Theatre." *TDR* 13(3): 148–55.

Aslesha, Ram. 1994. "The Andhra Devadasi Dance Tradition: Three Seminars Held in Quick Succession." *Sruti* 122 (November): 17–20.

Austin, J.L. 1975. *How to Do Things with Words.* Oxford: Oxford University Press.

Baker, Roger. 1994. *Drag: A History of Female Impersonation in the Performing Arts.* With contributions by Peter Burton and Richard Smith. New York: New York University Press.

Bakhtin, Mikhail M. 1981. *The Dialogic Imagination: Four Essays.* Edited by Michael Holquist and translated by Caryl Emerson and Michael Holquist. Austin: University of Texas Press.

Banerjee, Sikata. 2005. *Make Me a Man! Masculinity, Hinduism, and Nationalism in India.* Albany: State University of New York Press.

Barba, Eugenio. 1986. "International School of Theater Anthropology (ISTA): Congress on the Female Role as Represented on the Stage in Various Cultures." *TDR* 30(2): 171–72.

Beauvoir, Simone de. [1949] 1989. *The Second Sex.* Translated by H.M. Parshley. New York: Vintage Books.

Bhabha, Homi. 1984. "Of Mimicry and Man: The Ambivalence of Colonial Discourse." *Discipleship: A Special Issue on Psychoanalysis* 28 (Spring): 125–33.

Bhaskaran, Suparna. 2004. *Made in India: Decolonializations, Queer Sexualities, Trans/national Projects.* New York: Palgrave Macmillan.

Bhattacharya, Rimli. 2008. "Dutta, Golap/Sukumari." In *The Oxford Encyclopedia of Women in World History,* Vol. 1, edited by Bonnie G. Smith, 120. Oxford: Oxford University Press.

Bhikshu, Aruna. 2006. "Tradition and Change: Transpositions in *Kuchipudi.*" In *Performers and Their Arts: Folk Popular, and Classical Genres in a Changing India,* edited by Simon Charsley and Laxmi Narayana Kadekar, 248–65. New Delhi: Routledge.

Bourdieu, Pierre. 1977. *Outline of a Theory of Practice.* Cambridge Studies in Social and Cultural Anthropology (Book 16). Cambridge: Cambridge University Press.

———. 1989. "Social Space and Symbolic Power." *Sociological Theory* 7(1): 14–25.

Boyarin, Daniel. 1998. "Gender." In *Critical Terms for Religious Studies,* edited by Mark C. Taylor, 117–36. Chicago: University of Chicago Press.

Bronner, Yigal. 2010. *Extreme Poetry: The South Asian Movement of Simultaneous Narration.* New York: Columbia University Press.

——— and Gary A. Tubb. 2008. "Blaming the Messenger: A Controversy in Late Sanskrit Poetics and Its Implications." *Bulletin of SOAS* 71(1): 75–91.

Bruin, Hanne M. de. 2006. "Donning the *Vēṣam* in Kaṭṭaikkūttu." In *Masked Ritual and Performance in South India: Dance, Healing, and Possession,* edited by David Shulman and Deborah Thiagarajan, 107–34. Center for South and Southeast Asian Studies. Ann Arbor: University of Michigan Press.

———. 2007. "Devadāsīs and Village Goddesses of North Tamil Nadu." In *The Power of Performance: Actors, Audiences, and Observers of Cultural Performances in India,* edited by Heidrun Brückner, Elisabeth Schömbucher, and Phillip B. Zarrilli, 53–83. New Delhi: Manohar.

Burton, Richard F. 1851. *Scinde; or, The Unhappy Valley, Volume II.* London: Richard Bentley, New Burlington Street.

Butler, Judith. [1990] 2008. *Gender Trouble: Feminism and the Subversion of Identity.* New York: Routledge.

———. 1993. "Gender Imitation and Insubordination." In *The Lesbian and Gay Studies Reader,* edited by Henry Abelove, Michele Aina Barale, and David Halperin, 307–20. New York: Routledge.

———. [1993] 2011. *Bodies That Matter: On the Discursive Limits of "Sex."* New York: Routledge.

———. 1997. *Excitable Speech: A Politics of the Performative.* New York: Routledge.

———. 2004. *Undoing Gender.* Routledge: New York.

Caldwell, Sarah. 1999. *Oh Terrifying Mother: Sexuality, Violence and the Worship of the Goddess Kāḷi.* Delhi: Oxford University Press.

———. 2006. "Kali and Kuli: Female Masquerade in Kerala Ritual Dance." In *Masked Ritual and Performance in South India: Dance, Healing, and Possession,* edited by David Shulman and Deborah Thiagarajan, 184–207. Center for South and Southeast Asian Studies. Ann Arbor: University of Michigan Press.

Carman, John, and Vasudha Narayanan. 1989. *The Tamil Veda: Piḷḷaṉ's Interpretation of the Tiruvāymoḻi.* Chicago: University of Chicago Press.

Case, Sue-Ellen. 1998. *Feminism and Theatre.* New York: Routledge.

Chakraborty, Chandrima. 2011. *Masculinity, Asceticism, Hinduism: Past and Present Imaginings in India.* New Delhi: Permanent Black.

———, ed. 2015. *Mapping South Asian Masculinities: Men and Political Crisis.* London: Routledge.

Chakravarti, Uma. 2003. *Gendering Caste through a Feminist Lens.* Calcutta: Stree.

Chakravorty, Pallabi. 2008. *Bells of Change: Kathak Dance, Women and Modernity in India.* Oxford: Seagull Books.

———. 2010. "From Interculturalism to Historicism: Reflections on Classical Indian Dance." In *The Routledge Dance Studies Reader,* edited by Alexandra Carter and Janet O'Shea, 273–84. London: Routledge.

———. 2017. *This Is How We Dance Now! Performance in the Age of Bollywood and Reality Shows*. New Delhi: Oxford University Press.

Charsley, Simon, and Laxmi Narayana Kadekar, eds. 2006. *Performers and Their Arts: Folk, Popular, and Classical Genres in a Changing India*. New Delhi: Routledge.

Chatterjee, Indrani. 2012. "When 'Sexuality' Floated Free of Histories in South Asia." *Journal of Asian Studies* 71(4): 945–62.

Chatterjee, Sudipto. 2007. *The Colonial Staged: Theatre in Colonial Calcutta*. London: Seagull Books.

Chaudhry, Ayesha. 2017. "Islamic Legal Studies: A Critical Historiography." In *The Oxford Handbook of Islamic Law*, edited by Anver M. Emon and Rumee Ahmed, 1–40. Oxford: Oxford University Press.

Chinna Satyam, Vempati. "My Guru, My Mentor." *Nartanam: A Quarterly Journal of Indian Dance* 2(2): 28–32.

———. 2012. "My Experiments with Kuchipudi." *Nartanam: A Quarterly Journal of Indian Dance* 12(3): 36–43.

Chopra, Radhika, Caroline Osella, and Filippo Osella, eds. 2004. *South Asian Masculinities: Context of Change, Sites of Continuity*. New Delhi: Women Unlimited: An Associate of Kali for Women.

Chowdhry, Neelam Man Singh. 2011. "The Naqqals of Chandigarh: Transforming Gender on the Musical Stage." *Journal of Punjab Studies* 18(1/2): 203–16.

Cleto, Fabio. 1999. "Introduction: Queering the Camp." In *Camp: Queer Aesthetics and the Performing Subject: A Reader*, edited by Fabio Cleto, 1–42. Ann Arbor: University of Michigan Press.

Clooney, Francis X. 2014. *His Hiding Place Is Darkness: A Hindu-Catholic Theopoetics of Divine Absence*. Stanford, CA: Stanford University Press.

Cohen, Lawrence. 1995. "The Pleasures of Castration: The Postoperative Status of Hijras, Jankhas, and Academics." In *Sexual Nature, Sexual Culture*, edited by Paul R. Abramson and Steven D. Pinkerton, 276–304. Chicago: University of Chicago Press.

Cohen, Robert. 2016. *Shakespeare on Theatre: A Critical Look at His Theories and Practices*. London: Routledge.

Connell, R.W. 1987. *Gender and Power*. Stanford, CA: Stanford University Press.

———. 1995. *Masculinities*. Cambridge: Polity Press.

———. 2000. *The Men and the Boys*. Cambridge: Polity Press.

——— and James W. Messerschmidt. 2005. "Hegemonic Masculinity: Rethinking the Concept." *Gender and Society* 19(6): 829–59.

Coomaraswamy, Ananda K. [1918] 1957. *The Dance of Shiva: On Indian Art and Culture*. New York: Noonday Press.

———. 1930. "Two Leaves from a Seventeenth-Century Manuscript of the Rasikapriyā." *Metropolitan Museum Studies* 3(1): 14–21.

———. 1933. "On Translation: Māyā, Deva, Tapas." *Isis* 19(1): 74–91.

Coorlawala, Uttara Asha. 1992. "Ruth St. Denis and India's Dance Renaissance." *Dance Chronicle* 15(2): 123–52.

———. 2004. "The Sanskritized Body." *Dance Research Journal* 36(2): 50–63.

Crenshaw, Kimberlé. 1989. "Demarginalizing the Intersection of Race and Sex: A Black Feminist Critique of Antidiscrimination Doctrine, Feminist Theory and Antiracist Politics." *University of Chicago Legal Forum* 1989(1): 139–67.

Da Costa, Dia. 2018. "Caste-Ignorant Worlds of Progressive Academics." *RAIOT*. Accessed January 13, 2019. http://raiot.in/academically-transmitted-caste-innocence/
Daniel, E. Valentine. 1984. *Fluid Signs: Being a Person in the Tamil Way*. Berkeley: University of California Press.
Dasgupta, Rohit K., and K. Moti Gokulsing, eds. 2014. *Masculinity and Its Challenges in India: Essays on Changing Perceptions*. Jefferson, NC: McFarland & Company.
Dasgupta, Rohit K., and Steven Baker, eds. 2013. *Popular Masculine Cultures in India: Critical Essays*. Kolkata: Setu Prakashani.
Daugherty, Diane, and Marlene Pitkow. 1991. "Who Wears the Skirts in Kathakali?" *TDR* 35(2): 138–56.
De Sondy, Amanullah. 2015. *The Crisis of Islamic Masculinities*. London: Bloomsbury.
Dehejia, Vidya, ed. 1997. *Representing the Body: Gender Issues in Indian Art*. New Delhi: Kali for Women and Book Review Literary Trust.
———. 2009. *The Body Adorned: Dissolving Boundaries between Sacred and Profane in India's Art*. New York: Columbia University Press.
Desmond, Jane. 1991. "Dancing Out the Difference: Cultural Imperialism and Ruth St. Denis's 'Radha' of 1906." *Signs* 17(1): 28–49.
Devarajan, Arthi. 2010. "'Natya From Within': A Practical Theology-Based Analysis of Classical Indian Dance Pedagogy in the United States." PhD diss., Emory University.
———. 2011. "Ascending Capital: The Economy of Performance at the *Arangetram* (Indian Classical Dance Debut)." Unpublished paper.
———. 2012. "Reviewed Work: *Unfinished Gestures: Devadasis, Memory, and Modernity in South India* by Davesh Soneji." *Journal of Asian Studies* 71(4): 1181–83.
Dixit, M. 2013. "*Begum Barve*: Embodiment of Subversive Fantasy." *Studies in South Asian Film and Media* 5(1): 25–36.
Doniger, Wendy. 1982. *Women, Androgynes, and Other Mythical Beasts*. Chicago: University of Chicago Press.
———. 1984. *Dreams, Illusions, and Other Realities*. Chicago: University of Chicago Press.
———. 1995. "The Criteria of Identity in a Telugu Myth of Sexual Masquerade." In *Syllables of Sky: Studies in South Indian Civilization in Honour of Velcheru Narayana Rao*, edited by David Shulman, 103–32. Delhi: Oxford University Press.
———. 2000. *The Bedtrick: Tales of Sex and Masquerade*. Chicago: University of Chicago Press.
———. 2004. "Self-Impersonation in World Literature." *Kenyon Review* 26(2): 101–25.
———. 2016. *Redeeming the* Kamasutra. New York: Oxford University Press.
Doron, Assa, and Alex Broom, eds. 2014. *Gender and Masculinities: Histories, Texts and Practices in India and Sri Lanka*. London: Routledge.
Drouin, Jennifer. 2008. "Cross-Dressing, Drag, and Passing: Slippages in Shakespearean Comedy." In *Shakespeare Redressed: Cross-Gender Casting in Contemporary Performance*, edited by James C. Bulman, 23–56. Madison: Fairleigh Dickinson University Press.
Dumont, Louis. [1970] 1980. *Homo Hierarchicus: The Caste System and Its Implications*. Chicago: University of Chicago Press.
Dunning, Jennifer. 1986. "Freedom of Gender in Dances from India." *New York Times*, March 6.
Dutta, Aniruddha, and Raina Roy. 2014. "Decolonizing Transgender in India: Some Reflections." *TSQ: Transgender Studies Quarterly* 1(3): 320–37.

Eck, Diana. 1998. *Darśan: Seeing the Divine Image in India.* Third Edition. New York: Columbia University Press.
Eckert, Penelope, and Sally McConnell-Ginet. 2003. *Language and Gender.* Cambridge: Cambridge University Press.
Emigh, John, with Ulrike Emigh. 1986. "Hajari Bhand of Rajasthan: A Joker in the Deck." *TDR* 30(1): 101–30.
Erdman, Joan L. 1987. "Performance as Translation: Uday Shankar in the West." *TDR* 31(1): 64–88.
Farrier, Stephen. 2016. "That Lip-Synching Feeling: Drag Performance as Digging the Past." In *Queer Dramaturgies: International Perspectives on Where Performance Leads Queer,* edited by Alyson Campbell and Stephen Farrier, 192–209. New York: Palgrave Macmillan.
Feit, Candace. 2016. "Mortal to Divine and Back: India's Transgender Goddesses." *New York Times,* July 24. Accessed July 30, 2016. www.nytimes.com/2016/07/25/world/asia/india-transgender.html
Ferris, Leslie, ed. 1993. *Crossing the Stage: Controversies on Cross-Dressing.* New York: Routledge.
Fisher, Elaine M. 2017. *Hindu Pluralism: Religion and the Public Sphere in Early Modern South India.* Oakland: University of California Press.
Flueckiger, Joyce Burkhalter. 1988. "'He Should Have Worn a Sari': A 'Failed' Performance of a Central Indian Oral Epic." *TDR* 32(1): 159–69.
———. 1996. *Gender and Genre in the Folklore of Middle India.* Ithaca, NY: Cornell University Press.
———. 2005. "Guises, Turmeric, and Recognition in the Gangamma Tradition of Tirupati." In *Incompatible Visions: South Asian Religions in History and Culture, Essays in Honor of David M. Knipe,* edited by James Blumenthal, 35–49. Madison: Center for South Asia, University of Wisconsin.
———. 2006. *In Amma's Healing Room: Gender and Vernacular Islam in South India.* Bloomington: Indiana University Press.
———. 2013. *When the World Becomes Female: The Guises of a South Indian Goddess.* Bloomington: Indiana University Press.
———. 2015. *Everyday Hinduism.* West Sussex, UK: Wiley Blackwell.
Flueckiger, Joyce Burkhalter, and Harshita Mruthinti Kamath. 2013. "Dance and Embodied Knowledge in the Indian Context." *Practical Matters* 6. Accessed September 26, 2018. http://practicalmattersjournal.org/2013/03/01/dance-embodied-knowledge/
Foucault, Michel. [1961] 2009. *History of Madness.* London: Routledge.
———. [1976] 1990. *The History of Sexuality, Volume 1: An Introduction.* Translated by Robert Hurley. New York: Vintage Books.
Fujito, Minoru, and Michael Shapiro, eds. 2006. *Transvestism and the Onnagata Traditions in Shakespeare and Kabuki.* Kent, UK: Global Oriental.
Fuller, C.J., and Haripriya Narasimhan. 2014. *Tamil Brahmins: The Making of a Middle-Class Caste.* Chicago: University of Chicago Press.
Gannon, Shane. 2011. "Exclusion as Language and the Language of Exclusion: Tracing Regimes of Gender through Linguistic Representations of the 'Eunuch.'" *Journal of the History of Sexuality* 20(1): 1–27.

Garber, Marjorie. 1992. *Vested Interests: Cross-Dressing and Cultural Anxiety.* New York: Routledge.

Gaston, Anne-Marie. 1992. *Śiva in Dance, Myth and Iconography.* Delhi: Oxford University Press.

———. 1996. *Bharata Natyam: From Temple to Theatre.* New Delhi: Manohar.

Gautam, Sanjay K. 2016. *Foucault and the Kamasutra: The Courtesan, the Dandy, and the Birth of* Ars Erotica *as Theater in India.* Chicago: University of Chicago Press.

Gnoli, Raniero. 1985. *The Aesthetic Experience According to Abhinavagupta.* Vol. 62. Varanasi: Chowkambha Sanskrit Series Office.

Gokhale, Shanta. 2000. *Playwright at the Centre: Marathi Drama from 1843 to the Present.* Calcutta: Seagull Books.

Gold, Ann Grodzins. 2000. *Fruitful Journeys: The Ways of Rajasthani Pilgrims.* Prospect Heights, IL: Waveland Press.

Goldman, Robert. 1993. "Transsexualism, Gender, and Anxiety in Traditional India." *Journal of the American Oriental Society* 113(3): 374–401.

Gonda, Jan. 1959. "The 'Original' Sense and Etymology of Skt. *māyā.*" In *Four Studies in the Language of the Veda,* Disputationes Rheno-Trajectinae, vol. 3, 119–94. The Hague: Mouton.

Gopal, Ram. 1957. *Rhythm in the Heavens: An Autobiography.* London: Secker and Warburg.

Gopalakrishnan, Sudha. 2006. "The Face and the Mask: Expression and Impersonation in Kutiyattam, Krishnattam, and Noh." In *Masked Ritual and Performance in South India: Dance, Healing, and Possession,* edited by David Shulman and Deborah Thiagarajan, 135–46. Center for South and Southeast Asian Studies. Ann Arbor: University of Michigan Press.

Gopinath, Gayatri. 2005. *Impossible Desires: Queer Diasporas and South Asian Public Cultures.* Durham: Duke University Press.

———. 2018. *Unruly Visions: The Aesthetic Practices of Queer Diaspora.* Durham: Duke University Press.

Goudriaan, Teun. 1978. *Māyā: Divine and Human.* Delhi: Motilal Banarsidass.

Gramsci, Antonio. 1971. *Selections from the Prison Notebooks.* London: Lawrence & Wishart.

Gupta, Charu, ed. 2012. *Gendering Colonial India: Reforms, Print, Caste, and Communalism.* Hyderabad: Orient Blackswan.

———. 2016. *The Gender of Caste: Representing Dalits in Print.* Seattle: University of Washington Press.

Gupt, Somnath. 2005. *The Parsi Theatre: Its Origins and Development.* Translated and edited by Kathryn Hansen. Calcutta: Seagull Books.

Gyatso, Janet. 2003. "One Plus One Makes Three: Buddhist Gender, Monasticism, and the Law of the Non-Excluded Middle." *History of Religions* 43(2): 89–115.

Haberman, David. 1988. *Acting as a Way of Salvation: A Study of Rāgānuga Bhakti Sādhana.* Delhi: Motilal Banarsidass.

Halberstam, Jack. 1998. *Female Masculinity.* Durham, NC: Duke University Press.

Hall, Kira. 1997. "'Go Suck Your Husband's Sugarcane!': Hijras and the Use of Sexual Insult." In *Queerly Phrased: Language, Gender, and Sexuality,* edited by Anna Livia and Kira Hall, 430–60. New York: Oxford University Press.

——— and Mary Bucholtz, eds. 1995. *Gender Articulated: Language and the Socially Constructed Self.* New York: Routledge.

Hancock, Mary Elizabeth. 1999. *Womanhood in the Making: Domestic Ritual and Public Culture in Urban South India*. Boulder, CO: Westview Press.

Handelman, Don. 1995. "The Guises of the Goddess and the Transformation of the Male: Gangamma's Visit to Tirupati and the Continuum of Gender." In *Syllables of Sky: Studies in South Indian Civilization in Honour of Velcheru Narayana Rao*, edited by David Shulman, 281–335. Delhi: Oxford University Press.

Hanna, Judith Lynne. 1983. *The Performer-Audience Connection: Emotion to Metaphor in Dance and Society*. Austin: University of Texas Press.

———. 1988. *Dance, Sex, and Gender: Signs of Identity, Dominance, Defiance, and Desire*. Chicago: University of Chicago Press.

Hansen, Kathryn. 1992. *Grounds for Play: The Nauṭaṅkī Theatre of North India*. Berkeley: University of California Press.

———. 1998. "Stri Bhumika: Female Impersonators and Actresses on the Parsi Stage." *Economic and Political Weekly* 33(35): 2291–300.

———. 1999. "Making Women Visible: Gender and Race Cross-Dressing in the Parsi Theatre." *Theatre Journal* 51(2): 127–47.

———. 2002. "A Difference Desire, a Different Femininity: Theatrical Transvestism in the Parsi, Gujarati, and Marathi Theatres (1850–1940)." In *Queering India: Same-Sex Love and Eroticism in Indian Culture and Society*, edited by Ruth Vanita, 163–80. New York: Routledge.

———. 2004a. "Language, Community and the Theatrical Public: Linguistic Pluralism and Change in the Nineteenth-Century Parsi Theatre." In *India's Literary History: Essays on the Nineteenth Century*, edited by Stuart Blackburn and Vasudha Dalmia, 60–86. New Delhi: Permanent Black.

———. 2004b. "Theatrical Transvestism in the Parsi, Gujurati, and Marathi Theatres (1850–1940)." In *Sexual Sites, Seminal Attitudes: Sexualities, Masculinities and Culture in South Asia*, edited by Sanjay Srivastava, 99–122. New Delhi: Sage Publications.

———. 2013. *Stages of Life: Indian Theatre Autobiographies*. London: Anthem Press.

———. 2015. "Performing Gender and Faith in Indian Theater Autobiographies." In *Speaking of the Self: Gender, Performance, and Autobiography in South Asia*, edited by Anshu Malhotra and Siobhan Lambert-Hurley, 255–80. Durham: Duke University Press.

Hardy, Friedhelm. 1983. *Viraha-Bhakti: The Early History of Kṛṣṇa Devotion in South India*. Delhi: Oxford University Press.

Hawley, John Stratton. 1981. *At Play with Krishna: Pilgrimage Dramas from Brindavan*. Princeton, NJ: Princeton University Press.

———. 1984. *Sur Das: Poet, Singer, Saint*. Seattle: University of Washington Press.

———. 1986. "Images of Gender in the Poetry of Krishna." In *Gender and Religion: On the Complexity of Symbols*, edited by Caroline Walker Bynum, Stevan Harrell, and Paula Richman, 231–56. Boston: Beacon Press.

———. 2000. "Krishna and the Gender of Longing." In *Love, Sex, and Gender in the World Religions*, edited by Joseph Runzo and Nancy M. Martin, 239–56. Oxford: Oneworld.

———. 2009. *The Memory of Love: Sūrdās Sings to Krishna*. New York: Oxford University Press.

———. 2012. *Three Bhakti Voices: Mirabai, Surdas, and Kabir in Their Times and Ours*. New York: Oxford University Press.

———. 2015. *A Storm of Songs: India and the Idea of a Bhakti Movement.* Cambridge, MA: Harvard University Press.

———. 2017. *Into Sūr's Ocean: Poetry, Context, and Commentary.* Harvard Oriental Series 83. Cambridge, MA: Harvard University Press.

Hess, Linda. 2006. "An Open-Air Ramayana: Ramlila, the Audience Experience." In *The Life of Hinduism,* edited by John Stratton Hawley and Vasudha Narayanan, 115–39. Berkeley: University of California Press.

———. 2015. *Bodies of Songs: Kabir Oral Traditions and Performative Worlds in North India.* Oxford: Oxford University Press.

Hiltebeitel, Alf. 1980. "Śiva, the Goddess, and the Disguises of the Pāṇḍavas and Draupadī." *History of Religions* 20(1/2): 147–74.

———. 1998. "Hair Like Snakes and Mustached Brides: Crossed Gender in an Indian Folk Cult." In *Hair: Its Power and Meaning in Asian Cultures,* edited by Alf Hiltebeitel and Barbara D. Miller, 143–76. Albany: State University of New York Press.

Hoang, Kimberly Kay. 2015. *Dealing in Desire: Asian Ascendancy, Western Decline, and the Hidden Currencies of Global Sex Work.* Berkeley: University of California Press.

Holdrege, Barbara. 2015. *Bhakti and Embodiment: Fashioning Divine Bodies and Devotional Bodies in Kṛṣṇa Bhakti.* New York: Routledge.

——— and Karen Pechilis, eds. 2016. *Refiguring the Body: Embodiment in South Asian Religions.* Albany: State University of New York Press.

Holt, Amy-Ruth. 2018. "Sacred Androgyny and Jayalalitha's Ritual Embodiment in Tamil Politics." Paper presented at the Impersonation in South Asia Symposium, Annual Conference on South Asia, Madison, Wisconsin, October 11–14.

hooks, bell. 1992. *Black Looks: Race and Representation.* Boston: South End Press.

Howard, Veena R. 2013. *Gandhi's Ascetic Activism: Renunciation and Social Action.* Albany: State University of New York Press.

Hoxworth, Kellen. 2018. "Racial Impressions, Capital Characters: Dave Carson Brownfaces the Empire." Paper presented at the Impersonation in South Asia Symposium, Annual Conference on South Asia, Madison, Wisconsin, October 11–14.

Humes, Cynthia Ann. 1996. "Becoming Male: Salvation through Gender Modification in Hinduism and Buddhism." In *Gender Reversals and Gender Culture: Anthropological and Historical Perspectives,* edited by Sabrina Petra Ramet, 123–37. London: Routledge.

Hymes, Dell. 2015. *Breakthrough into Performance.* Rimini: Guaraldi.

Ingalls, Daniel H. H. 1962. "Words for Beauty in Classical Sanskrit Poetry." *Indological Studies in Honor of W. Norman Brown,* edited by Ernest Bender, 87–107. New Haven, CT: American Oriental Society.

Inhorn, Marcia C. 2012. *The New Arab Man: Emergent Masculinities, Technologies, and Islam in the Middle East.* Princeton, NJ: Princeton University Press.

Inoue, Takako. 2008. "Between Art and Religion: *Bhāgavata Mēḷa* in Thanjavur." *Senri Ethnological Studies* 71: 103–34.

Iyengar, B.R.C. 1989. "Interview: Happy Days as Satyam's Student." *Sruti* 54 (March): 32–33.

Jackson, William J. 1991. *Tyāgarāja: Life and Lyrics.* Delhi: Oxford University Press.

———. 1994. *Tyāgarāja and the Renewal of Tradition: Translations and Reflections.* Delhi: Motilal Banarsidass.

Jeffrey, Craig. 2010. *Timepass: Youth, Class, and the Politics of Waiting in India.* Stanford, CA: Stanford University Press.

Johnson, E. Patrick. 2001. "'Quare' Studies, or (Almost) Everything I Know about Queer Studies I Learned from My Grandmother." *Text and Performance Quarterly* 21(1): 1–25.

———. 2003. *Appropriating Blackness: Performance and the Politics of Authenticity.* Durham: Duke University Press.

———. ed., 2016. *No Tea, No Shade: New Writings in Black Queer Studies.* Durham: Duke University Press.

———. and Mae G. Henderson, eds. 2005. *Black Queer Studies: A Critical Anthology.* Durham: Duke University Press.

Jones, Clifford Jones. 1963. "The Bhāgavata Mēḷa Nāṭakam, A Traditional Dance-Drama Form." *Journal of Asian Studies* 22(2): 193–200.

Jonnalagadda, Anuradha. 1993. *Kuchipudi Dance Who Is Who.* Bombay: Kuchipudi Mahotsav.

———. 1995. "Crossed Swords over Andhra Natyam: New Developments." *Sruti* 134 (November): 13–14.

———. 1996a. "Bhamakalapam Texts: An Analysis." *Kuchipudi Mahotsav '96 Souvenir,* 78–81. Mumbai: Kuchipudi Kalakendra.

———. 1996b. "Tradition and Innovations in Kuchipudi Dance." PhD diss., University of Hyderabad, Sarojini Naidu School of Performing Arts, Fine Arts and Communication.

———. 2004. "Guru Vempati Chinna Satyam: An Epoch Maker." *Nartanam: A Quarterly Journal of Indian Dance* 4(3): 23–30.

———. 2006. "*Kuchipudi*: Changing Patterns of Patronage." In *Performers and Their Arts: Folk Popular, and Classical Genres in a Changing India,* edited by Simon Charsley and Laxmi Narayana Kadekar, 266–76. New Delhi: Routledge, 2006.

———. 2008. "60 Years of Kuchipudi." *Nartanam: A Quarterly Journal of Indian Dance* 8(1): 7–20.

———. 2012. "The Dance Dramas of Vempati Chinna Satyam." *Nartanam: A Quarterly Journal of Indian Dance* 12(3): 44–54.

———. 2016. "Development of Dance: Kuchipudi." In *Contemporary History of Andhra Pradesh and Telangana AD 1956–1990s,* edited by V. Ramakrishna Reddy, 1062–72. Hyderabad: EMESCO Books.

Jordan, Kay. 2003. *From Sacred to Profane Prostitute: A History of the Changing Legal Status of the Devadasis in India 1857–1947.* Delhi: Manohar.

Kakar, Sudhir. [1978] 2012. *The Inner World: A Psychoanalytic Study of Childhood and Society in India,* 4th edition. New York: Oxford University Press.

———. 1990. *Intimate Relations: Exploring Indian Sexuality.* Chicago: University of Chicago Press.

Kalakrishna. 1996. "The Art of Female Impersonation." *Kuchipudi Mahotsav '96 Souvenir,* 66–67. Mumbai: Kuchipudi Kalakendra.

Kamath, Harshita Mruthinti. 2011. "Vempati Ravi Shankar: Following His Father's Footsteps." *The Kalaparva.* Accessed March 22, 2017. http://commentary.kalaparva.com/2011/06/vempati-ravi-shankar-following-his.html

———. 2012. "Aesthetics, Performativity and Performative *Māyā:* Imagining Gender in the Textual and Performance Traditions of Telugu South India." PhD diss., Emory University.

———. 2016. "Bodied, Embodied, and Reflective Selves: Theorizing Performative Selfhood in South Indian Performance." In *Refiguring the Body: Embodiment in South Asian*

Religions, edited by Barbara A. Holdrege and Karen Pechilis, 109–29. Albany: State University of New York Press.

——— and Joyce Burkhalter Flueckiger. 2019. "From Bells to *Bottus:* Analyzing the Body and Materiality of Indian Dance in an American University Context." In *The Wiley-Blackwell Companion to Material Religion,* edited by Vasudha Narayanan, 241–68. Hoboken, NJ: Wiley-Blackwell.

Kanakalingeshwara Rao, Banda. 1966. "The Kuchipudi Dance-Drama." *Marg* 19(2): 30–36.

Kapaleswara Rao, Chaganti. 1996. "Jada Bharatam." *Kuchipudi Mahotsav '96 Souvenir,* 82–85. Mumbai: Kuchipudi Kalakendra.

Kapur, Anuradha. 1990. *Actors, Pilgrims, Kings and Gods: The Ramlila at Ramnagar.* Calcutta: Seagull Books.

———. 2004. "Impersonation, Narration, Desire, and Parsi Theatre." In *India's Literary History: Essays on the Nineteenth Century,* edited by Stuart Blackburn and Vasudha Dalmia, 87–118. New Delhi: Permanent Black.

Kapur, Ratna. 2001. "Imperial Parody." *Feminist Theory* 2(1): 79–88.

Katrak, Ketu H. 2001. "Body Boundarylands: Locating South Asian Ethnicity in Performance and in Daily Life." *Amerasia Journal* 27(1): 2–33.

———. 2004. "'Cultural Translation' of Bharata Natyam into 'Contemporary Indian Dance': Second-Generation South Asian Americans and Cultural Politics in Diasporic Locations." *South Asian Popular Culture* 2(2): 79–102.

———. 2011. *Contemporary Indian Dance: New Creative Choreography in India and the Diaspora.* London: Palgrave Macmillan.

Katyal, Anjum. 2001. "Performing the Goddess: Sacred Ritual into Professional Performance." Photo-essay with Naveen Kishore. *TDR* 45(1): 96–117.

Kaur, Barleen. 2013. "Problematizing Androgyny: Female Impersonation in Indian Theatre." In *Interdisciplinary Alter-Natives in Comparative Literature,* edited by E.V. Ramakrishna, Harish Trivedi, and Chandra Mohan, 190–98. New Delhi: Sage Publications.

Kedhar, Anusha. 2014. "Flexibility and Its Bodily Limits: Transnational South Asian Dancers in an Age of Neoliberalism." *Dance Research Journal* 46(1): 23–40.

Kersenboom, Saskia. 1987. *Nityasumaṅgalī: Devadasi Tradition in South India.* Delhi: Motilal Banarsidass.

Khokar, Mohan. 1957. "Bhagavata Mela and Kuchipudi." *Marg* 10(4): 27–36.

———. 1976. "Male Dancers." *Illustrated Weekly of India.* March: 24–29.

Khubchandani, Kareem. 2016. "Snakes on the Dance Floor: Bollywood, Gesture, and Gender." *Velvet Light Trap* 77 (Spring): 69–85.

———. 2018. "Cruising the Ephemeral Archives of Bangalore's Gay Nightlife." In *Queering Digital India: Activisms, Identities, Subjectivities,* edited by Rohit K. Dasgupta and Debanuj DasGupta, 72–93. Edinburgh: Edinburgh University Press.

Kinsley, David R. 1979. *The Divine Player: A Study of Kṛṣṇa Līlā.* Delhi: Motilal Banarsidass.

———. 1993. *Hinduism: A Cultural Perspective.* Edgewood Cliffs, NJ: Prentice Hall.

Knipe, David M. 2015. *Vedic Voices: Intimate Narratives of Living Andhra Tradition.* New York: Oxford University Press.

Kosambi, Meera. 2015. *Gender, Culture, and Performance: Marathi Theatre and Cinema before Independence.* New Delhi: Routledge.

Kothari, Sunil. 1977. "The Dance-Drama Tradition of Kuchipudi, Bhagavata Mela Nataka and Kuravanji with Special Reference to Rasa Theory as Expounded in Bharata's Natyasastra." PhD diss., Department of Dance, M.S. University of Baroda.

——— and Avinash Pasricha. 2001. *Kuchipudi: Indian Classical Dance Art.* New Delhi: Abhinav Publications.

Kripal, Jeffrey J. 1998. *Kālī's Child: The Mystical and the Erotic in the Life and Teachings of Ramakrishna.* 2nd edition. Chicago: University of Chicago Press.

Krishnamurthy, Yamini. 1973. "Satya Bhama: The Aesthetic Ideal of Womanhood." *Times of India*: 19–25.

Krishnan, Hari. 2008. "Inscribing Practice: Reconfigurations and Textualizations of Devadasi Repertoire in Nineteenth and Early Twentieth Century South India." In *Performing Pasts: Reinventing the Arts in Modern South India,* edited by Indira Viswanathan Peterson and Davesh Soneji, 71–89. New Delhi: Oxford University Press.

———. 2009. "From Gynemimesis to Hypermasculinity: The Shifting Orientations of Male Performers of South Indian Court Dance." In *When Men Dance: Choreographing Masculinities across Borders,* edited by Jennifer Fisher and Anthony Shay, 378–91. Oxford: Oxford University Press.

Krishnaswamy, Revathi. 2011. *Effeminism: The Economy of Colonial Desire.* Ann Arbor: University of Michigan Press.

Kugle, Scott. 2010. *Homosexuality in Islam: Critical Reflection on Gay, Lesbian, and Transgender Muslims.* Oxford: Oneworld.

———. 2013. "Dancing with Khusro: Gender Ambiguities and Poetic Performance in a Delhi *Dargah.*" In *Rethinking Islamic Studies: From Orientalism to Cosmopolitanism,* edited by Carl W. Ernst and Richard C. Martin, 245–65. Columbia: University of South Carolina Press.

———. 2016. *When Sun Meets Moon: Gender, Eros, and Ecstasy in Urdu Poetry.* Chapel Hill: University of North Carolina Press.

Kuiper, F.B.J. 1979. *Varuṇa and Vidūṣaka: On the Origin of the Sanskrit Drama.* Amsterdam: North-Holland.

Kurtz, Stanley. 1992. *All the Mothers Are One: Hindu India and the Cultural Reshaping of Psychoanalysis.* New York: Columbia University Press.

Lal, Ruby. 2005. *Domesticity and Power in the Early Mughal World.* Cambridge: Cambridge University Press.

Livia, Anna, and Kira Hall, eds. 1997. *Queerly Phrased: Language, Gender, and Sexuality.* New York: Oxford University Press.

Lloyd, Moya. 2007. *Judith Butler: From Norms to Politics.* Cambridge: Polity Press.

Lothspeich, Pamela. 2018. "Embodied Divinities on the *Ramlila* Stage." Paper presented at the Impersonation in South Asia Symposium, Annual Conference on South Asia, Madison, Wisconsin, October 11–14.

Madhavan, Arya, ed. 2017. *Women in Asian Performance: Aesthetics and Politics.* London: Routledge.

Mahmood, Saba. 2001. "Feminist Theory, Embodiment, and the Docile Agent: Some Reflections on the Egyptian Islamic Revival." *Cultural Anthropology* 16(2): 202–36.

———. 2005. *Politics of Piety: The Islamic Revival and the Feminist Subject.* Princeton, NJ: University of Princeton Press.

Mangai, A. 2015. *Acting Up: Gender and Theatre in India, 1979 Onwards.* New Delhi: Left-Word Books.

Mani, Lata. 1998. *Contentious Traditions: The Debate on Sati in Colonial India.* Berkeley: University of California Press.

Mankekar, Purnima. 2015. *Unsettling India: Affect, Temporality, Transnationality.* Durham: Duke University Press.

Marcus, Sharon. 2005. "Queer Theory for Everyone: A Review Essay." *Signs* 31(1): 191–218.

Marriott, McKim. 1976. "Hindu Transactions: Diversity without Dualism." In *Transaction and Meaning: Directions in the Anthropology of Human Issues,* edited by Bruce Kapferer, 109–42. Philadelphia: Institute for the Study of Human Issues.

Martin, Nancy M. 2010. "Mirabai Comes to America: The Translation and Transformation of a Saint." *Journal of Hindu Studies* 3(1): 12–35.

McClintock, Anne. 1995. *Imperial Leather: Race, Gender, and Sexuality in the Colonial Contest.* New York: Routledge.

McGlotten, Shaka. 2016. "Black Data." In *No Tea, No Shade: New Writings in Black Queer Studies,* edited by E. Patrick Johnson, 262–86. Durham: Duke University Press.

McLain, Karline. 2009. *India's Immortal Comic Books: Gods, Kings, and Other Heroes.* Bloomington: Indiana University Press.

Meduri, Avanthi. 1988. "Bharatha Natyam—What Are You?" *Asian Theatre Journal* 5(1): 1–22.

———. 1996. "Nation, Woman, Representation: The Sutured History of the Devadasi and Her Dance." PhD diss., New York University.

———. 2004. "Bharatanatyam as a Global Dance: Some Issues in Research, Teaching, and Practice." *Dance Research Journal* 36(2): 11–29.

———. 2008. "Temple Stage as Historical Allegory in Bharatanatyam: Rukmini Devi as Dancer-Historian." In *Performing Pasts: Reinventing the Arts in Modern South India,* edited by Indira Viswanathan Peterson and Davesh Soneji, 133–64. New Delhi: Oxford University Press.

Menon, Jisha. 2013. "Queer Selfhoods in the Shadow of Neoliberal Urbanism." *Journal of Historical Sociology* 26(1): 100–19.

Mernissi, Fatima. 1987. *Beyond the Veil: Male-Female Dynamics in Modern Muslim Society.* Bloomington: Indiana University Press.

Messerschmidt, James W. 2016. *Masculinities in the Making: From the Local to the Global.* London: Rowman and Littlefield.

——— and Michael A. Messner. 2018. "Hegemonic, Nonhegemonic, and 'New' Masculinities." In *Gender Reckonings: New Social Theory and Research,* edited by James W. Messerschmidt, Patricia Yancey Martin, Michael A. Messner, and Raewyn Connell, 35–56. New York: New York University Press.

———, Patricia Yancey Martin, Michael A. Messner, and Raewyn Connell, eds. 2018. *Gender Reckonings: New Social Theory and Research.* New York: New York University Press.

Mezur, Katherine. 2005. *Beautiful Boys/Outlaw Bodies: Devising Kabuki Female-Likeness.* New York: Palgrave Macmillan.

Mitchell, Lisa. 2009. *Language, Emotion, and Politics in South India: The Making of a Mother Tongue.* Bloomington: Indiana University Press.

Mohanty, Chandra Talpade. 1991. "Introduction: Cartographies of Struggle: Third World Women and the Politics of Feminism." In *Third World Women and the Politics of Feminism,* edited by Chandra Talpade Mohanty, Ann Russo, and Lourdes Torres, 1–47. Bloomington: Indiana University Press.

———. 2013. "Transnational Feminist Crossings: On Neoliberalism and Radical Critique." *Signs* 38(4): 967–91.

Monier-Williams, Sir Monier. [1899] 1960. *A Sanskrit-English Dictionary.* London: Oxford University Press.

Morcom, Anna. 2013. *Illicit Worlds of Indian Dance: Cultures of Exclusion.* New York: Oxford University Press.

Mruthinti, Harshita. 2006. "Dancing the Divine Female: Diasporic Women's Encounters with the Hindu Goddess through Indian Classical Dance." *Journal of Asian American Studies* 9(6): 271–99.

Mukherjee, Tutun, and Niladri R. Chatterjee. 2016. *Androgyny and Female Impersonation in India: Nari Bhav.* New Delhi: Niyogi Books.

Multani, Angeli. 2017. "'Just like a Woman': Female Impersonation, Gender Construction and Role Play in *Begum Barve.*" In *Women in Asian Performance: Aesthetics and Politics,* edited by Arya Madhavan, 39–51. London: Routledge.

Muñoz, José Esteban. 1999. *Disidentifications: Queers of Color and the Performance of Politics.* Minneapolis: University of Minnesota Press.

Murali Sankar, K.N. 2016. "Kala Krishna: It's Tough to Depend on Dance." *The Hindu.* February 4. Accessed January 27, 2019. www.thehindu.com/features/friday-review/kala-krishna-its-tough-to-depend-on-dance/article8188567.ece

Nabokov, Isabelle. 2000. *Religion against the Self: An Ethnography of Tamil Rituals.* New York: Oxford University Press.

Nagabhushana Sarma, Modali. 1995. *Folk Performing Arts of Andhra Pradesh.* Hyderabad: Telugu University.

———. 2002. "Vedantam Laxminarayana Sastry: His Life, Times and Achievement." *Nartanam: A Quarterly Journal of Indian Dance* 2(2): 7–24.

———. 2003. "Ram Gopal and His World of Dance: An Essay in Visuals." *Nartanam: A Quarterly Journal of Indian Dance* 3(4): 35–50.

———. 2004. "The Artist as Visionary: Guru Vempati Chinna Satyam's Contribution to Kuchipudi." *Nartanam: A Quarterly Journal of Indian Dance* 4(3): 5–22.

———. 2009. "Chinta Venkataramaiah and the Kuchipudi Yakshagana Tradition." *Nartanam: A Quarterly Journal of Indian Dance* 9(2): 5–37.

———. 2012. "The Man Who Beguiles Women: Vedantam Satyanarayana Sarma and the Art of Female Impersonation." *Nartanam: A Quarterly Journal of Indian Dance* 7(4): 7–24.

———. 2013. *"Naṭakāvatamsa" Sthānaṃ Narasiṃhārāvu: naṭa jīvana prasthānaṃ.* Chennai: Kalatapasvi Creations.

———. 2016. *Kuchipudi:* Gurus, *Performers and Performance Traditions.* Hyderabad: Ranga Sampada.

——— and Mudigonda Veerabhadra Sastry, eds. 1995. *History and Culture of the Andhras.* Hyderabad: Telugu University.

Naidu, M.A. 1975. *Kuchipudi Classical Dance.* Hyderabad: Andhra Pradesh Sangeet Natak Akademi.

Naidu, Sobha. 2012. "A Tribute to the Master." *Nartanam: A Quarterly Journal of Indian Dance* 12(3): 67–68.

Nair, Sreenath. 2017. "Rasatrialogue: The Politics of the Female Body in Asian Performance." In *Women in Asian Performance: Aesthetics and Politics,* edited by Arya Madhavan, 159–72. London: Routledge.

Najmabadi, Afsaneh. 2005. *Women with Mustaches and Men without Beards: Gender and Sexual Anxieties of Iranian Modernity.* Berkeley: University of California Press.

Narayan, Uma. 1997. *Dislocating Cultures: Identities, Traditions, and Third World Feminism.* New York: Routledge.

Nandy, Ashis. [1983] 2009. *The Intimate Enemy: Loss and Recovery of Self under Colonialism.* New Delhi: Oxford India Paperbacks.

Narayana Rao, Velcheru. 1991. "A *Rāmāyaṇa* of Their Own: Women's Oral Tradition in Telugu." In *Many Rāmāyaṇas: The Diversity of a Narrative Tradition in South Asia,* edited by Paula Richman, 114–36. Berkeley: University of California Press.

———. 1995. "Coconut and Honey: Sanskrit and Telugu in Medieval Andhra." *Social Scientist* 23(10–12): 24–40.

———. 2003. "Multiple Literary Cultures in Telugu: Court, Temple, and Public." In *Literary Cultures in History: Reconstructions from South Asia,* edited by Sheldon Pollock, 383–436. Berkeley: University of California Press.

———. [2004] 2007. "Purana." In *The Hindu World,* edited by Sushil Mittal and Gene Thursby, 97–115. New York: Routledge.

———. 2016. *Text and Tradition in South India.* New Delhi: Permanent Black.

——— and David Shulman. 2002. *Classical Telugu Poetry: An Anthology.* Berkeley: University of California Press.

Narayanan, Vasudha. 1987. *The Way and the Goal: Expressions of Devotion in the Early Śrī Vaiṣṇava Tradition.* Washington, DC: Institute for Vaishnava Studies and Center for the Study of World Religions, Harvard University.

———. 1994. *The Vernacular Veda: Revelation, Recitation, and Ritual.* Columbia: University of South Carolina Press.

———. 2000. "Diglossic Hinduism: Liberation and Lentils." *Journal of American Academy of Religion* 68(4): 761–79.

———. 2003. "Gender in a Devotional Universe." In *The Blackwell Companion to Hinduism,* edited by Gavin Flood, 569–87. Oxford: Blackwell Publishing.

Newton, Esther. 1979. *Mother Camp: Female Impersonators in North America.* Chicago: University of Chicago Press.

Novetzke, Christian Lee. 2011. "The Brahmin Double: The Brahminical Construction of Anti-Brahminism and Anti-caste Sentiment in the Religious Cultures of Precolonial Maharastra." *South Asian History and Culture* 2(2): 232–52.

———. 2016. *The Quotidian Revolution: Vernacularization, Religion, and the Premodern Public Sphere in India.* New York: Columbia University Press.

Olivelle, Patrick. 1998. "Hair and Society: Social Significance of Hair in South Asian Traditions." In *Hair: Its Power and Meaning in Asian Cultures,* edited by Alf Hiltebeitel and Barbara D. Miller, 11–50. Albany: State University of New York Press.

Olson, Carl. 1977. "The Existential, Social, and Cosmic Significance of the Upanayana Rite." *Numen* 24(2): 152–60.

Orgel, Stephen. 1996. *Impersonations: The Performance of Gender in Shakespeare's England.* Cambridge: Cambridge University Press.

Orr, Leslie. 2000. *Donors, Devotees, and Daughters of God: Temple Women in Medieval Tamilnadu.* New York: Oxford University Press.

O'Shea, Janet. 2003. "At Home in the World? The Bharatanatyam Dancer as Transnational Interpreter." *TDR* 47(1): 176–86.

———. 2007. *At Home in the World: Bharata Natyam on the Global Stage.* Middletown, CT: Wesleyan University Press.

———. 2008. "Serving Two Masters? Bharatanatyam and Tamil Cultural Production." In *Performing Pasts: Reinventing the Arts in Modern South India,* edited by Indira Viswanathan Peterson and Davesh Soneji, 165–93. New Delhi: Oxford University Press.

Osella, Caroline and Filippo. 2006. *Men and Masculinities in South India.* London: Anthem Press.

Packert, Cynthia. 2010. *The Art of Loving Krishna: Ornamentation and Devotion.* Bloomington: Indiana University Press.

Pandey, Gyanendra. 2013. *A History of Prejudice: Race, Caste, and Difference in India and the United States.* Cambridge: Cambridge University Press.

Pandian, M.S.S. 2016. *Brahmin & Non-Brahmin: Genealogies of the Tamil Political Present.* New Delhi: Permanent Black.

Pani, Jivan. 1977. "The Female Impersonator in Traditional Indian Theatre." *Sangeet Natak* 45 (July–September): 37–42.

Parker, Andrew, and Eve Kosofsky Sedgwick. 2016. "Introduction to *Performativity and Performance.*" In *The Performance Studies Reader,* edited by Henry Bial and Sara Brady, 226–32. London: Routledge.

Parvati Devi, P.N. 1999. *Āndhra Sāhityamulo Satyabhāma Pātra Citraṇamu.* Vijayawada: Navodaya.

Patel, Deven M. 2014. *Text to Tradition: The* Naiṣadhīyacarita *and Literary Community in South Asia.* New York: Columbia University Press.

Pattabhi Raman, N. 1988/89. "Dr. Vempati Chinna Satyam: Modernizer of a Tacky Dance Tradition." *Sruti* 51–52 (December): 47–54.

Patton, Laurie L., ed. 1994. *Authority, Anxiety, and Canon: Essays in Vedic Interpretation.* Albany: State University of New York Press.

———. 2004. "*Samvada* as a Literary and Philosophical Genre: An Overlooked Resource for Public Debate and Conflict Resolution." *Evam: Forums on Indian Representation,* 177–90. Delhi: Samvad: India.

Pearson, Anne Mackenzie. 1996. *"Because It Gives Me Peace of Mind": Ritual Fasts in the Religious Lives of Hindu Women.* Albany: State University of New York Press.

Pechilis, Karen. 2012. "Gender." In *Brill's Encyclopedia of Hinduism,* edited by Knut Jacobsen, Vol. 4, 788–805. Leiden: Brill.

———. 2012. *Interpreting Devotion: The Poetry and Legacy of a Female* Bhakti *Saint.* London: Routledge.

Penumarthi, Sasikala. 2012. "The Expressions of a Master." *Nartanam: A Quarterly Journal of Indian Dance* 12(3): 89–91.

Peterson, Indira Viswanathan. 2011. "Multilingual Dramas at the Tanjavur Maratha Court and Literary Cultures in Early Modern South India." *Medieval History Journal* 14(2): 285–321.

———. 2011/12. "The Evolution of Kuṟavañci Dance Drama in Tamil Nadu: Negotiating the 'Folk' and the 'Classical' in the Bhārata Nāṭyam Canon." *Nartanam: A Quarterly Journal of Indian Dance* 11(4): 5–54.

——— and Davesh Soneji, eds. 2008. *Performing Pasts: Reinventing the Arts in Modern South India.* New Delhi: Oxford University Press.

Petievich, Carla. 2002. "Doganas and Zanakhis: The Invention and Subsequent Erasure of Urdu Poetry's 'Lesbian' Voice." In *Queering India: Same-Sex Love and Eroticism in Indian Culture and Society,* edited by Ruth Vanita, 47–60. New York: Routledge.

———. 2004. "Rekhti: Impersonating the Feminine in Urdu Poetry." In *Sexual Sites, Seminal Attitudes: Sexualities, Masculinities, and Culture in South Asia,* edited by Sanjay Srivastava, 123–46. New Delhi: Sage Publications.

———. 2008. *When Men Speak as Women: Vocal Masquerade in Indo-Muslim Poetry.* New Delhi: Oxford University Press.

Pintchman, Tracy. 1994. *The Rise of the Goddess in the Hindu Tradition.* New York: State University of New York Press.

———. 2007. *Women's Lives, Women's Rituals in the Hindu Tradition.* Oxford: Oxford University Press.

Pitkow, Marlene B. 2001. "Putana's Salvation in *Kathakali*: Embodying the Sacred Journey." *Asian Theatre Journal* 18(2): 238–48.

———. 2011. "The Good, The Bad, and The Ugly: Kathakali Female's and the Men Who Play Them." In *Between Fame and Shame: Performing Women—Women Performers in India,* edited by Heidren Brückner, Hanne M. de Bruin, and Heike Moser, 223–43. Wiesbaden, Germany: Harrassowitz Verlag.

Pollock, Sheldon. 2006. *The Language of the Gods in the World of Men: Sanskrit, Culture, and Power in Premodern India.* Berkeley: University of California Press.

———, trans. and ed. 2016. *A Rasa Reader: Classical Indian Aesthetics.* New York: Columbia University Press.

Prakash, Brahma. 2016. "Performing Bidesiyā in Bihar: Strategy for Survival, Strategies for Performance." *Asian Theatre Journal* 33(1): 57–81.

Prasad, Leela. 2007. *Poetics of Conduct: Oral Narrative and Moral Being in a South Indian Town.* New York: Columbia University Press.

Puar, Jasbir. 2007. *Terrorist Assemblages: Homonationalism in Queer Times.* Durham: Duke University Press.

Puranam, Madhavi. 2011a. "The Allure of Satyabhama." *The Hindu,* February 11. Accessed January 20, 2019. www.thehindu.com/features/friday-review/dance/The-allure-of-Satyabhama/article15293242.ece

———. 2011b. "The International Symposium on Kalapa Traditions." *Nartanam: A Quarterly Journal of Indian Dance* 11(1): 83.

Puri, Jyoti. 1999. *Woman, Body, Desire in Post-Colonial India: Narratives of Gender and Sexuality.* New York: Routledge.

Putcha, Rumya. 2011. "Revisiting the Classical: A Critical History of Kuchipudi Dance." PhD diss., University of Chicago.

———. 2013. "Between History and Historiography: The Origins of Classical Kuchipudi Dance." *Dance Research Journal* 45(3): 91–110.

———. 2015. "Dancing in Place: Mythopoetics and the Production of History in Kuchipudi." *Yearbook for Traditional Music* 47: 1–26.

Radhakrishnan, Sarvepalli. [1927] 2008. *Indian Philosophy, Volume 2.* 2nd edition. Oxford: Oxford University Press.

Raghavan, V. 1993. "Sanskrit Drama in Performance." In *Sanskrit Drama in Performance,* edited by Rachel Van M. Baumer and James R. Brandon, 9–44. New Delhi: Motilal Banarsidass.

Raheja, Gloria Goodwin and Ann Grodzins Gold. 1994. *Listen to the Heron's Words: Reimagining Gender and Kinship in North India.* Berkeley: University of California Press.

Rama Rao, Uma. 1992. *Kuchipudi Bharatam or Kuchipudi Dance: A South Indian Classical Dance Tradition*. New Delhi: South Asia Books.
Ramakrishna, Nataraja. 1959. "Āndhra dēśamlo dēvadāsīla ārādhana, kēḷikā nṛtyamulu." In *Souvenir on Kuchipudi Natya Seminar*, 70–73. Hyderabad: Andhra Pradesh Sangeet Natak Akademi.
———. 1984. *Navajanārdanam*. Hyderabad: Perini International.
Ramalingasastry, Vedantam. 2000. *Telugulo Kūcipūḍi Nāṭaka Vikāsamu*. Sri Venkateswara D.T.P. Center: Pamarru.
Ramanujan, A.K., trans. and ed. 1973. *Speaking of Siva*. London: Penguin Books.
———. 1989a. "Is There an Indian Way of Thinking? An Informal Essay." *Contributions to Indian Sociology* 23(41): 41–58.
———. 1989b. "Talking to God in the Mother Tongue." *Manushi* 50/51/52: 9–14.
———. 2005. *Hymns for the Drowning: Poems for Viṣṇu by Nammāḻvār*. New Delhi: Penguin Books.
———, Velcheru Narayana Rao, and David Shulman, trans. 1994. *When God Is a Customer: Telugu Courtesan Songs by Kṣetrayya and Others*. Berkeley: University of California Press.
Ramaswamy, Sumathi. 1997. *Passions of the Tongue: Language Devotion in Tamil India, 1891–1970*. Berkeley: University of California Press.
———.2010. *The Goddess and the Nation: Mapping Mother India*. Durham: Duke University Press.
Ramberg, Lucinda. 2014. *Given to the Goddess: South Indian Devadasis and the Sexuality of Religion*. Durham: Duke University Press.
Rana, Junaid. 2011. *Terrifying Muslims: Race and Labor in the South Asian Diaspora*. Durham: Duke University Press.
Ray, Raka. 2018. "Postcoloniality and the Sociology of Gender." In *Gender Reckonings: New Social Theory and Research*, edited by James W. Messerschmidt, Patricia Yancey Martin, Michael A. Messner, and Raewyn Connell, 73–89. New York: New York University Press.
Reddy, Gayatri. 2005. *With Respect to Sex: Negotiating Hijra Identity in South India*. Chicago: University of Chicago Press.
Reyna, Ruth. 1962. *The Concept of Maya: From the Vedas to the 20th Century*. Bombay: Asia Publishing House.
Richmond, Farley P. 1993. "Sanskrit Drama in Performance." In *Sanskrit Drama in Performance*, edited by Rachel Van M. Baumer and James R. Brandon, 74–109. New Delhi: Motilal Banarsidass.
———, Darius L. Swann, and Phillip B. Zarrilli. 1990. *Indian Theatre: Traditions of Performance*. Honolulu: University of Hawaii Press.
Roy, Kumkum. 2011. *The Power of Gender and the Gender of Power: Explorations in Early Indian History*. New Delhi: Oxford University Press.
Roy, Parama. 1998. *Indian Traffic: Identities in Question in Colonial and Postcolonial India*. Berkeley: University of California Press.
Rubin, Gayle. 1975. "The Traffic of Women: Notes on the 'Political Economy' of Sex." In *Toward an Anthropology of Women*, edited by Rayna R. Reiter, 157–210. New York: Monthly Review Press.

Rudisill, Kristen. 2007. "Brahmin Humor: Chennai's Sabha Theater and the Creation of Middle-Class Indian Taste from the 1950s to the Present." PhD diss., University of Texas at Austin.

———. 2012. "Everyday Flamboyancy in Chennai's *Sabha* Theatre." *Asian Theatre Journal* 29(1): 276–90.

Sangari, Kumkum, and Sudesh Vaid, eds. 1999. *Recasting Women Essays in Indian Colonial History.* Rutgers: Rutgers University Press.

Sarkar, Tanika. 2001. *Hindu Wife, Hindu Nation: Community, Religion, and Cultural Nationalism.* Bloomington: Indiana University Press.

Sarma, Deepak. 2001. "When Is a Brahmin a *Brahmabandhu,* an Unworthy or Wicked Brahmin? Or When Is the *Adhikārin,* Eligible One, *Anadhikārin,* Ineligible?" *Methods & Theory in the Study of Religion* 13: 82–90.

Satkunaratnam, Ahalya. 2012. "Dance: Classical Tradition." In *Brill's Encyclopedia of Hinduism,* edited by Knut A. Jacobsen, Helene Basu, Angelika Malinar, and Vasudha Narayanan. Accessed January 14, 2019. http://dx.doi.org.proxy.library.emory.edu/10.1163/2212-5019_beh_COM_000384

———. 2013. "Staging War: Performing Bharata Natyam in Colombo, Sri Lanka." *Dance Research Journal* 45(1): 81–108.

Satyanarayana Sarma, Vedantam. 1996. "Bhrukunsuvus of Kuchipudi," *Kuchipudi Mahotsav '96 Souvenir,* 86–87. Mumbai: Kuchipudi Kalakendra.

Schechner, Richard. 1993. *The Future of Ritual: Writings on Culture and Performance.* London: Routledge.

———. 2015. *Performed Imaginaries.* London: Routledge.

——— and Linda Hess. 1977. "The Ramlila of Ramnagar [India]." *Drama Review* 21(3): 51–82.

Schwartz, Susan. 2004. *Rasa: Performing the Divine in India.* New York: Columbia University Press.

Schweig, Graham M. 2007. "The Divine Feminine in the Theology of Krishna." In *Krishna: A Sourcebook,* edited by Edwin F. Bryant, 441–74. Oxford: Oxford University Press.

Scott, Joan W. 1986. "Gender: A Useful Category of Historical Analysis." *American Historical Review* 91(5): 1053–75.

Sedgwick, Eve Kosofsky. [1990] 2008. *Epistemology of the Closet.* Berkeley: University of California.

———. 2003. *Touching Feeling: Affect, Pedagogy, Performativity.* Durham: Duke University Press.

Seizer, Susan. 2005. *Stigmas of the Tamil Stage: An Ethnography of Special Drama Artists in South India.* Durham: Duke University Press.

Sen, Ronojoy. 2015. *Nation at Play: A History of Sport in India.* New York: Columbia University Press.

Senelick, Laurence. 2000. *The Changing Room: Sex, Drag and Theatre.* London: Routledge.

Shah, Purnima. 1998. "Transcending Gender in the Performance of Kathak." *Dance Research Journal* 30(2): 2–17.

———. 2002. "State Patronage in India: Appropriation of the 'Regional' and 'National.'" *Dance Chronicle* 25(1): 125–41.

Shahani, Nishant. 2003. "'Resisting Mundane Violence': Feminism and Queer Identity in Post-colonial India." *Michigan Feminist Studies* 17: 27–46.

———. 2011. "What Can Queer Theory Learn from Feminism in India?: Reversing Epistemological Frameworks." *Thamyris/Intersecting* 22: 225–42.

Shekhar, Indu. 1960. *Sanskrit Drama: Its Origin and Decline*. Leiden, Neth.: E.J. Brill.

Sherinian, Zoe C. 2014. *Tamil Folk Music as Dalit Liberation Theology*. Bloomington: Indiana University Press.

Shulman, David Dean. 1980. *Tamil Temple Myths: Sacrifice and Divine Marriage in the South Indian Saiva Tradition*. Princeton, NJ: Princeton University Press.

———. 1985. *The King and the Clown in South Indian Myth and Poetry*. Princeton, NJ: Princeton University Press.

———. 1995. "First Man, Forest Mother: Telugu Humanism in the Age of Kṛṣṇadevarāya." In *Syllables of Sky: Studies in South Indian Civilization in Honour of Velcheru Narayana Rao*, edited by David Shulman, 133–64. Delhi: Oxford University Press.

———. 1997. "Embracing the Subject: Harṣa's Play within a Play." *Journal of Indian Philosophy* 25(1): 69–89.

———. 2012. *More than Real: A History of the Imagination in South India*. Cambridge, MA: Harvard University Press.

———. 2016. *Tamil: A Biography*. Cambridge, MA: Harvard University Press.

——— and Deborah Thiagarajan, eds. 2006. *Masked Ritual and Performance in South India: Dance, Healing, and Possession*. Center for South and Southeast Asian Studies. Ann Arbor: University of Michigan Press.

Siegel, Lee. 1987. *Laughing Matters: Comic Tradition in India*. Chicago: University of Chicago Press.

Singer, Milton. [1972] 1980. *When a Great Tradition Modernizes: An Anthropological Approach to Indian Civilization*. Chicago: University of Chicago Press.

Singh, Lata. 2009. "Fore-grounding the Actresses' Question: Bengal and Maharastra." In *Theatre in Colonial India: Play-House of Power*, edited by Lata Singh, 270–94. New Delhi: Oxford University Press.

Sinha, Ajay. 2017. "Iconology of a Photograph." *Art and Vernacular Photographies in Asia* 8(1). Accessed July 29, 2018. http://hdl.handle.net/2027/spo.7977573.0008.106

Sinha, Mrinalini. 1995. *Colonial Masculinity: The 'Manly Englishman' and the 'Effeminate Bengali' in the Late Nineteenth Century*. Manchester, UK: Manchester University Press.

———. 2012. "A Global Perspective on Gender: What's South Asia Got to Do with It?" In *South Asian Feminisms*, edited by Ania Loomba and Ritty A. Lukose, 356–74. Durham: Duke University Press.

Sklar, Deidre. 1994. "Can Bodylore Be Brought to Its Senses?" *Journal of American Folklore* 107(423): 9–22.

Smith, Brian K. 1986. "Ritual, Knowledge, and Being: Initiation and Vedic Study in Ancient India." *Numen* 33(1): 65–89.

Smith, David. 2010. "Beauty and Words Relating to Beauty in the *Rāmāyaṇa*, the *Kāvyas* of Aśvaghoṣa, and Kālidāsa's Kumārasambhava." *Journal of Hindu Studies* 3(1): 36–52.

Smith, Frederick. 2006. *The Self Possessed: Deity and Spirit Possession in South Asian Literature and Civilization*. New York: Columbia University Press.

Snorton, C. Riley. 2017. *Black on Both Sides: A Racial History of Trans Identity*. Minneapolis: University of Minnesota Press.

Sondak, Eileen. 1986. "Classical Indian Dance Comes to Casa Del Prado." *Los Angeles Times,* March 26. Accessed Janaury 20, 2019. http://articles.latimes.com/1986-03-26/entertainment/ca-607_1_indian-dance

Soneji, Davesh. 2004. "Performing Satyabhāmā: Text, Context, Memory and Mimesis in Telugu-Speaking South India." PhD diss., McGill University.

———. 2008. "Memory and the Recovery of Identity: Living Histories and the Kalavantulu of Coastal Andhra Pradesh." In *Performing Pasts: Reinventing the Arts in Modern South India,* edited by Indira Viswanathan Peterson and Davesh Soneji, 283–312. New Delhi: Oxford University Press.

———. 2010, ed. *Bharatanatyam: A Reader.* Delhi: Oxford University Press.

———. 2012. *Unfinished Gestures: Devadāsīs, Memory, and Modernity in South India.* Chicago: University of Chicago Press.

Sontag, Susan. 1999. "Notes on 'Camp.'" In *Camp: Queer Aesthetics and the Performing Subject: A Reader,* edited by Fabio Cleto. 53–65. Ann Arbor: University of Michigan Press.

Spivak, Gayatri Chakravorty. 1988. "Can the Subaltern Speak?" In *Marxism and the Interpretation of Culture,* edited by Cary Nelson and Lawrence Grossberg, 271–313. Chicago: University of Illinois Press.

Srinivas, Tulasi. 2018. *The Cow in the Elevator: An Anthropology of Wonder.* Durham: Duke University Press.

Srinivasan, Amrit. 1985. "Reform and Revival: The Devadasi and Her Dance." *Economic and Political Weekly* 20(44): 1869–76.

———. 2010. "Reform or Conformity? Temple 'Prostitution' and the Community in the Madras Presidency." In *Bharatanatyam: A Reader,* edited by Davesh Soneji, 139–59. New Delhi: Oxford University Press.

Srinivasan, Priya. 2012. *Sweating Saris: Indian Dance as Transnational Labor.* Philadelphia: Temple University Press.

Srivastava, Sanjay, ed. 2004. *Sexual Sites, Seminal Attitudes: Sexualities, Masculinities and Culture in South Asia.* New Delhi: Sage Publications.

Story, Kaila Adia. 2016. "On the Cusp of Deviance: Respectability Politics and the Cultural Marketplace of Sameness." In *No Tea, No Shade: New Writings in Black Queer Studies,* edited by E. Patrick Johnson, 362–79. Durham: Duke University Press.

Streets-Salter, Heather. 2010. *Martial Races: The Military, Race, and Masculinity in British Imperial Culture, 1857–1914.* New York: Manchester University Press.

Stryker, Susan and Stephen Whittle, eds. 2006. *The Transgender Studies Reader.* New York: Routledge.

Subrahmanyam, Padma. 1997. *Natya Sastra and National Unity.* Kerala: Sri Ramavarma Government Sanskrit College Tripunithura.

Subramanian, Lakshmi. 2006. *From the Tanjore Court to the Madras Music Academy: A Social History of Music in South India.* New Delhi: Oxford University Press.

———. 2008. "Embracing the Canonical: Identity, Tradition, and Modernity in Karnatak Music." In *Performing Pasts: Reinventing the Arts in Modern South India,* edited by Indira Viswanathan Peterson and Davesh Soneji, 43–70. New Delhi: Oxford University Press.

Subramaniam, V. 1995. "Gender Monopolies in Indian Classical Dance: A Sociological Analysis of Cause and Context." *Sangeet Natak* 117/118: 3–13.

Sunardi, Christina. 2015. *Stunning Males and Powerful Females: Gender and Tradition in East Javanese Dance.* Urbana: University of Illinois Press.

Suthrell, Charlotte. 2004. *Unzipping Gender: Sex, Cross-Dressing and Culture.* New York: Berg Publishers.

Suvarchala Devi, K.V.L.N. 1997. *Andhranatyam: The Lasya Dance Tradition of Andhra.* Hyderabad: Abhinaya.

Swapnasundari. 2010. *Vilasini Natyam: Bharatam of Telugu Temple and Court Dancers.* Hyderabad: Swapnasundari.

Talbot, Cynthia. 2001. *Precolonial India in Practice: Society, Region, and Identity in Medieval Andhra.* Oxford: Oxford University Press.

Thangaraj, Stanley I. 2015. *Desi Hoop Dreams: Pickup Basketball and the Making of Asian American Masculinity.* New York: New York University Press.

———, Constancio R. Arnaldo Jr., and Christina B. Chin, eds. 2016. *Asian American Sporting Cultures.* New York: New York University Press.

Thiagarajan, Premalatha. 2017. "Gender and Ethnicity in Indian Classical Dance in Malaysia." *Asian Theatre Journal* 34(1): 97–121.

Thobani, Sitara. 2017. *Indian Classical Dance and the Making of Postcolonial National Identities: Dancing on Empire's Stage.* London: Routledge.

Thomas, Sonja. 2018. *Privileged Minorities: Syrian Christianity, Gender, and Minority Rights in Postcolonial India.* Seattle: University of Washington Press.

Thompson, George. 1997. "Ahaṃkāra and Ātmastuti: Self-Assertion and Impersonation in the Ṛgveda." *History of Religions* 37(2): 141–71.

Thota, Katyayani. 2009. "Vendantam Raghavaiah." *Nartanam: A Quarterly Journal of Indian Dance* 9(2): 38–40.

———.2016. "Stage to Screen, and Back: A Study of the Dialogue Between Kuchipudi and Telugu Cinema." PhD diss., University of Hyderabad.

Trawick, Margaret. 1992. *Notes on Love in a Tamil Family.* Berkeley: University of California Press.

Trivedi, Poonam. 2010. "Shakespeare and the Indian Image(nary): Embod(y)ment in Versions of *A Midsummer Night's Dream.*" In *Re-playing Shakespeare in Asia,* edited by Poonam Trivedi and Minami Ryuta, 54–75. New York: Routledge.

Troka, Donna Jean, Kathleen LeBesco, and Jean Bobby Noble, eds. 2002. *The Drag King Anthology.* New York: Harrington Park Press.

Tyler, Carole-Anne. 2003. *Female Impersonation.* New York: Routledge.

Ullman, Sharon. 1995. "'The Twentieth Century Way': Female Impersonation and Sexual Practice in Turn-of-the-Century America." *Journal of the History of Sexuality* 5(4): 573–600.

Usha Gayatri, M. 2016. *Kuchipudi Art and Satyabhama.* New Delhi: B.R. Rhythms.

Valiana, Arafaat A. 2014. "Recuperating Indian Masculinity: Mohandas Gandhi, war and the Indian diaspora in South Africa (1899–1914)." *South Asian History and Culture* 5(4): 505–20.

van der Veer, Peter. 1987. "Taming the Ascetic: Devotionalism in a Hindu Monastic Order." *Man New Series* 22(4): 680–95.

———. 1988. *Gods on Earth: The Management of Religious Experience and Identity in a North Indian Pilgrimage Centre.* London: Berg Publishers.

Vanita, Ruth, ed. 2002. *Queering India: Same-Sex Love and Eroticism in Indian Culture and Society.* New York: Routledge.

———. 2018. *Dancing with the Nation: Courtesans in Bombay Cinema.* New York: Bloomsbury Academic.

——— and Saleem Kidwai, eds. 2001. *Same-Sex Love in India: Readings from Literature and History.* New York: Palgrave Macmillan.

Varadpande, M.L. 1992. *History of Indian Theatre: Loka Ranga Panorama of Indian Folk Theatre.* New Delhi: Abhinav Publications.

Vatsyayan, Kapila. [1974] 2007. *Indian Classical Dance.* New Delhi: Publications Division, Ministry of Information and Broadcasting, Government of India.

Viresalingam, Kandukuri. 1970. *Autobiography of Kandukuri Veersalingam Pantulu,* Part I. Translated by V. Ramakrishna Rao and T. Rama Rao. Rajahmundry: Addepally.

Venkataraman, Leela. 2012. "Manju Barggavee Speaks of Her Great Guru." *Nartanam: A Quarterly Journal of Indian Dance* 12(3): 74–80.

——— and Avinash Pasricha. 2005. *Indian Classical Dance: Tradition in Transition.* New Delhi: Roli Books.

Wadley, Susan. 1980. "Hindu Women's Family and Household Rites in a North Indian Village." In *Unspoken Worlds: Women's Religious Lives,* edited by Nancy Falk and Rita Gross. San Francisco: Harper and Row.

Walker, Margaret E. 2016. *India's* Kathak *Dance in Historical Perspective.* London: Routledge.

Weidman, Amanda. 2006. *Singing the Classical, Voicing the Modern: The Postcolonial Politics of Music in South India.* Durham: Duke University Press.

———. 2008. "In Search of the Guru: Technology and Authenticity in Karnatak Music." In *Performing Pasts: Reinventing the Arts in Modern South India,* edited by Indira Viswanathan Peterson and Davesh Soneji, 225–51. New Delhi: Oxford University Press.

Whitaker, Jarrod L. 2011. *Strong Arms and Drinking Strength: Masculinity, Violence, and the Body in Ancient India.* Oxford: Oxford University Press.

Younger, Paul. 1995. *The Home of the Dancing Śivaṉ: The Traditions of the Hindu Temple in Citamparam.* New York: Oxford University Press.

Zarrilli, Phillip B. 2000. *Kathakali Dance-Drama: Where Gods and Demons Come to Play.* London: Routledge.

———. 2007. "Embodying the Lion's 'Fury': Ambivalent Animals, Activation, and Representation." In *The Power of Performance: Actors, Audiences, and Observers of Cultural Performances in India,* edited by Heidrun Brückner, Elisabeth Schömbucher, and Phillip B. Zarrilli, 235–60. New Delhi: Manohar.

Zubko, Katherine. 2006. "Embodying *Bhakti Rasa* in Bharata Natyam: An Indian Christian Interpretation of *Gayatri Mantra* through Dance." *Journal of Hindu-Christian Studies* 19: 37–44.

———. 2008. "Embodying Bhakti Rasa: Dancing across Religious Boundaries in Bharata Natyam." PhD diss., Emory University.

———. 2014a. *Dancing Bodies of Devotion: Fluid Gestures in Bharata Natyam.* Lexington, KY: Lexington Books.

———. 2014b. "Dancing the *Bhagavadgītā:* Embodiment as Commentary." *Journal of Hindu Studies* 7(3): 392–417.

INDEX

Page numbers in *italics* refer to illustrations.

Abhinavagupta, 23
abhinaya, 57–58. See also *āhārya abhinaya* (costume and makeup); *āṅgika abhinaya* (gait and bodily movement); *vācika abhinaya* (speech)
Abhinayadarpaṇa, 58
Abhinayavani Nritya Niketan, 149, 192n13
Abul Hassan Qutb Shah, Nawab of Golconda (Tana Shah). *See* Tana Shah
āhārya abhinaya (costume and makeup), 57–64, 66–67, 112, 114, 116, 128, 183n11; Baliakka, 157; quick changes, 190n19; Vedantam Ragava, 112; Venku, 55, *60–61*, 62. *See also* makeup
Andhra Natyam, 62, 182n53
Andhra Pradesh Sangeet Natak Akademi (APSNA), 24, 25, 26, 52, 69–70, 176n67
āṅgika abhinaya (gait and bodily movement), 57, 58, 66–68, 114, 116, 117, 128; Satyanarayana Sarma, 74; Venku, 55
Allen, Matthew Harp, 22, 166, 177n73
All India Radio, 25
Amar Chitra Katha (*ACK*) comic books, 130
Andal, 39
anti-nautch movement, 21–22, 34, 35, 41, 46–47, 53
Appa Rao, Vissa, 24–25, 40, 43, 44, 46, 176n65
APSNA. *See* Andhra Pradesh Sangeet Natak Akademi (APSNA)
Arangetram, 144–45, 165, 166
Ardhanareeswaram, 191n29
Arondekar, Anjali, 175n59, 182n49
Arudra, 14–15, 41, 42, 174n49, 178n13, 180n28
Arundale, Rukmini, 11, 22–23, 25, 35, 40, 67, 70
Asan, Gopi, 183n13
Austin, J.L., 187n20

Bakhtin, Mikhail, 107
Balakrishna, Chinta Ravi. *See* Ravi Balakrishna, Chinta
Balatripurasundari, Chavali (Baliakka), 108, 132, 134–37, 145–152, *151*, 153–58
Balatripurasundari temple. *See* Ramalingeshvara and Balatripurasundari temple
Bhagavad Gita, 186n12
bhakti, 23, 39–44, 46, 53, 72, 91–92, 179–80n25; *madhura-bhakti*, 40
Bhāmākalāpam, 1, 2, 18, 33, 37–42, 51, 80–103, 178n13, 178n19; Chinna Satyam, 104–5, 108, 109, 111–23, 125–28, 132–33; female students, 28, 65, 67; Krishna Murthy, 138; Radheshyam and, 180n29; recording of, 25; Satyanarayana Sarma, 52, 68–73, 70, 138; texts and manuscripts, 38, 41, 178n14; Venku, 55–56,

60–61, 62, 73–74. *See also* Madhava; Madhavi; *Navajanārdana Pārijātam;* Satyabhama
Bharata: *Nāṭyaśāstra,* 22, 23, 37, 39, 58, 82, 96, 118, 183n4
Bharatanatyam (dance), 22–26, 37, 107, 144, 153, 165, 175n57, 183n11; renaming from *sadir*, 22, 175–176n61; "revival," 22–24, 26, 34–35, 53, 58, 104, 123, 175n58
Bhargavi, Manju, 109, 119, 127, 128–30, 189n11
Bhujangaraya Sarma, S.V., 108
black queer studies, 122, 123–24, 190n25
Bodies That Matter (Butler), 101, 124, 187n20
Bourdieu, Pierre, 10, 135, 144–45
brahmin (term), xv, 12
brahminical patriarchy. *See* patriarchy
Bruin, Hanne M. de, 170n15, 177n73, 183n7
Burton, Richard F., 49–50, 182n49
Butler, Judith, 8, 163, 187n20; *Bodies That Matter,* 101, 124, 187n20; gender identity and gender performance (distinction), 118; *Gender Trouble,* 6, 8, 9, 75, 93, 103, 118, 123, 170n18, 190n20; views of drag, 8, 101, 124, 170n18, 190n20

Caldwell, Sarah, 98
camp aesthetics, 125
Candaini, 74
caste, 29–30, 38, 57, 78, 155, 162–63; in *Bhāmākalāpam,* 84, 99–100; Chinna Satyam and, 104, 127; *devadāsīs* (*kalāvantulu*) and, 35, 153
Chakraborty, Chandrima, 172n28, 181–182n48
Chakravarti, Uma, 155
Chakravorty, Pallabi, 23, 177n73
Chalapathi Rao, Vedantam Venkata Naga. *See* Venkata Naga Chalapathi Rao, Vedantam (Venku)
Chandalika (Tagore), 108
Chattopadyaya, Bankimchandra, 172n28
Chaudhry, Ayesha, 30
Chinna Satyam, Vempati, 19, 104–9, 131, 143, 160189n13; *Bhāmākalāpam,* 104–5, 108, 109, 111–23, 125–28, 132–33, 163, 188n2, 189nn10–11; *Ardhanareeswaram,* 191n29; daughter (Baliakka) and, 134, 145–50; death, 152, 156; *Ksheera Sagara Madhanam,* 189n8; Sasikala Penumarthi and, 29; wife (Swarajyalakshmi) and, 142–46, 150
Cleto, Fabio, 125
Cohen, Robert, 185n7
Connell, Raewyn, 8–9, 75, 78
Coomaraswamy, Ananda K., 36
Coorlawala, Uttara Asha, 58, 182n3
Corey, Dorian, 124
Cosmic Dance of Siva, 36
costume. See *āhārya abhinaya* (costume and makeup)
Crenshaw, Kimberlé, 5
cymbals. See *naṭṭuvāṅgam* (cymbals)

Dalits, 152,
Denishawn, 36, 178n9
Derrida, Jacques, 187n20
devadāsī (term), 21, 174n47, 175n59
devadāsīs (*kalāvantulu*), 21–24, 34, 35, 38, 40–41, 53, 135, 152–55, 178n7; Appa Rao on, 176n65; *Bhāmākalāpam* and, 179n17, 179n19; Kshetrayya and, 43; *sadir* and, 175–76n61
Devarajan, Arthi, 21, 144–45
Devlal, 74, 184n22
Dharmaraj, 125, 132, 189n11
dialogue lip-synching. *See* lip-synching
diaspora, queer. *See* queer diaspora
drag, 7–8, 101, 124, 125, 131, 170n18, 190n20
drag kings, 131, 191n33
Dravidianism, 46
Drouin, Jennifer, 8, 184n20
drums and drumming. See *mṛdaṅgam* (South Indian drum)
Durga, Kanaka, 147

effeminacy, 13, 49, 50, 76, 181–82n48
Erdman, Joan, 36
erotic aesthetics (*śṛṅgāra*), 22, 67, 96, 184n16

feminism, 4–9, 54, 78,163, 166–67, 170n13
femininity, 75, 131, 181n42
film, 15, 106, 109, 143
Flueckiger, Joyce, 7, 51, 74, 136, 165, 192n12
Foucault, Michel, 12
Fuller, C. J.: *Tamil Brahmins*: 173n38

gait and bodily movement. See *āṅgika abhinaya* (gait and bodily movement)
Gandharva, Bal, 47–48, 52, 65–66, 181nn41–43, 184n17, 184n21, 184n23
Gandhi, Mohandas, 181–82n48
Gangamma *jātara* (festival), 7, 51, 77, 136
Gender Trouble (Butler), 6, 8, 9, 75, 93, 118, 123, 170n18, 190n20
Gogate, Nirmala, 181n41
Gokhale, Shanta, 181n41
Gold, Ann Grodzins, 27, 136, 142, 158
Gopal, Ram, 36, 37, 178n11, 183n7

Gopalakrishnan, Sudha, 82, 190n19
Gopinath, Gayatri, 106, 122–23, 163
Goudriaan, Teun, 186n11
guising, vocal. *See* vocal guising
Gujarati theatre, 47, 48, 59, 63. *See also* Sundari, Jayshankar
Gupta, Charu, 4

habitus, 59, 144–45
Halberstam, Jack, 9, 131, 132, 133, 171n24, 191nn32–33
Hancock, Mary: *Womanhood in the Making*, 11, 44, 50, 77, 173n33
Hansen, Kathryn, 34, 47–48, 65–66, 181n38, 183n5
Haranadh, Pasumarti (Hari), 12, 18, 26, 27, 159
Haravilasam, 128, 130
Hawley, John Stratton, 39, 40, 180–81n37
heteronormativity, 13, 106, 122–23, 125, 133, 161, 163
hijṛā, 122, 163
Hymes, Dell, 2

Ibrahim, Ramli, 37
Inhorn, Marcia C., 76, 171n23
International Symposium on *Kalāpa* Traditions, 83, 83, 95
intersectionality, 4–5, 32, 78, 155
Iyer, E. Krishna, 11, 34, 70

Jackson, William J., 172n32, 173n37
jīvātma (individual soul), 40, 42, 46, 92, 180n29
jōgatis, 152–53, 175n60
Johnson, E. Patrick, 106, 122, 123–24, 190nn24–25
Jonnalagadda, Anuradha, 14–17, 29, 51, 70, 106, 118–19, 166, 176n67; on Chinna Satyam's Madhavi, 118, 120; on *Ksheera Sagara Madhanam*, 189n8; on Satyanarayana Sarma, 184n19; view of Siddhendra, 177n1, 178n13

KAA. *See* Kuchipudi Art Academy (KAA)
Kalakrishna, 62–63
Kalakshetra (Rukmini Arundale institution), 23, 35, 107
Kalamandalam, 183n13
kalāpas, 18–19, 20, 102, 107, 108, 121, 182n51
kalāvantulu (courtesans). See *devadāsīs (kalāvantulu)*
Kalidasa: *Vikramorvaśīya*, 96
Kanakalingeshwara Rao, Banda, 25, 26, 40–41, 43, 44, 46, 70, 138, 182–83n4
Kanchanamala, Maranganti, 25, 176n68–69
Kapur, Anuradha, 63
Karnataka Devadasis Bill, 153
Karnatak music, 64, 107, 108, 184n14
Kastuar, Jayant, 184n19
Kathak (dance), 21, 37, 49–50, 175n57, 176n68
Kathakali (dance), 21, 35, 37, 63, 175n57, 183n13
Kathakali Dance-Drama (Zarrilli), 37, 63,
Katrak, Ketu, 107
Kattaikuttu, 170n15, 183n7
Kaur, Barleen, 181n42
Keshav Prasad, Pasumarti, 18, 42, 63–64
Khan, Haleem, 51, 175n55
Khokar, Mohan, 51
Khubchandani, Kareem, 122, 125
kinesthetic empathy, 27–28, 165, 167
kojja, 121–22, 161, 163
Kondala Rao, Bala, 127
Kondala Rao, Pasumarti, 141
Kosambi, Meera, 181n41, 184n17, 184n23
Kothari, Sunil, 179–80n25; *Kuchipudi*, 188n29, 189–90nn13–14Krishna, 167, 191n30; in *Bhāmākalāpam*, 33, 82, 84, 87–91, *90*, 95, 97, 98, 100, 117; in Chinna Satyam's *Bhāmākalāpam*, 105, 108, 114, 117, 118, 119, 180n29; in comic books, 130; Siddhendra and, 33, 39, 42, 51; *Sri Krishna Parijatam*, 107–8; women in role of, 107, 109, 127–33, *129*, 189n11
Krishna Murthy, Chinta, 25, 52, 69, 70, 91, 102, 138, 141
Krishnan, Hari, 34–35, 177n73
Krishna Sarma, Pasumarti Venugopala (P.V.G.), 18, 89, 90–91, 93, 156, 186n10
Ksheera Sagara Madhanam (Chinna Satyam), 189n8
Kshetrayya, 43, 44, 157
Kuchipudi Art Academy (KAA), 104–9, 111, 121, 127–28, 131, 132, 145, 160, 161; *Ardhanareeswaram*, 191n29; Chavali Balatripurasundari and, 134, 145–48, 150; Kothari and Pasricha on, 189n13; post-Chinna Satyam, 150, 156, 157; Vempati Swarajyalakshmi and, 143
Kuchipudi Classical Dance (Naidu), 41–42
Kuchupudi: Indian Classical Dance Art (Kothari and Pasricha), 188n29, 189–90nn13–14
Kumar, Ajay, 20, 111, 175n55
Kutiyattam, 82, 96–97, 190n19

Lakshminarasamma, Vedantam, 137, 140–142, 144, 156
Lakshminarayana Sastry, Vedantam, 15, 24–26, 53, 69, 106, 109, 182n51

lip-synching, 64, 115–16
Livingston, Jennie: *Paris Is Burning*, 124

Madhava, 5, 81–83, 87–92, 94–98, 103, 162, 163; in Chinna Satyam's *Bhāmākalāpam*, 111, 112, 114, 117, 118, 119
Madhavi, 5, 64, 80–105, *84*, *90*, 108, 162, 163; in Chinna Satyam's *Bhāmākalāpam*, 104–5, 108, 111–27, *113*, *115*, *126*, 127, 132–23; P.V.G. Krishna Sarma on, 186n10
"Madras Kuchipudi" (term), 105
Māhabhārata, 134, 147, 192n10
Maharaj, Birju, 37
Mahmood, Saba, 59
makeup, 55, 59, *60–61*, 62–64, 128, 183nn7–9, 187n23; *Nāṭyaśāstra*, 58
Malayalam, 96–97, 170n10
Malaysia, 37
Malini, Hema, 109
Manikkavacakar, 39
Mankekar, Purnima, 152
Marathi theatre, 47, 48, 184n17. *See also* Gandharva, Bal
Marcus, Sharon, 169n3
masculinity, 8–13, 50, 172n28; emergent (used by Inhorn), 57, 76, 171n23; Halberstam views, 131, 171n24; hegemonic, 9, 57, 75–79, 161, 162, normative, 2, 9, 57, 76–77, 78–79, 102–3
māyā (constructed artifice), 5–6, 32, 81, 89–93, 101, 102, 119, 162, 163; as Indian philosophical concept, 92, 186nn11–12
McDannell, Colleen, 191n30
McGlotten, Shaka, 122, 124
McLain, Karline, 130
Meduri, Avanthi, 23, 166, 177n73
Menon, Jisha, 123
Messerschmidt, James W., 9, 75
Mirabai, 39, 40
Mitchell, Lisa, 43
Morcom, Anna, 174n45
mōṭi, 152, 192n14
movement. See *āṅgika abhinaya* (gait and bodily movement); kinesthetic empathy
mṛdaṅgam (South Indian drum), 12, 64, 164
Mrutyumjaya, Pasumarti (Mutyam), 141–45, 157, 191n6
Muñoz, José Esteban, 124, 127
music, 55, 64, 82, 83, 116, 147, 184n14. *See also* Karnatak music; *mṛdaṅgam* (South Indian drum); *naṭṭuvāṅgam* (cymbals)
Muthulakshmi Reddi, S., 21
Muttukkannammal, R., 152
Mutyam. *See* Mrutyumjaya, Pasumarti (Mutyam)
muṭiyēṯṯu, 98
Muvva (village), 43

Nagabhushana Sarma, Modali, 29, 66, 69, 70–71, 183n8, 185n3
Naidu, M.A., 41–42
Naidu, Sobha, 109, 111, 127, 132, 189n11, 189–90n14
Nammalvar, 39
Nandikeshvara, 58
Nandi Timmana, 189n7
Nandy, Ashis, 172n28
Narasimha Rao, Sthanam, 48–49, 52, 181n45
Narasimhan, Haripriya: *Tamil Brahmins*, 173n38
Narayana Rao, Velcheru, 18, 145, 155,
Nārāyanīyam, 164, 165, 166
Nataraja, 36
naṭṭuvāṅgam (cymbals), 55, 64, 82, 83, 89, 112, 117, 154
Nāṭyaśāstra (Bharata), 22, 37, 58, 96, 183n4; "classical" dance and, 23; eunuch figure in, 118; Siddhendra and, 39; *sūtradhāra*, 82
nautch, movement against. *See* anti-nautch movement
Navajanārdana Pārijātam, 38, 179n17, 182n53
Newton, Esther, 7–8, 124–125
Niyogi, 30, 173n37
noṭṭusvaram, 152, 192n14
Novetzke, Christian, 12, 100

orchestra, 55, 64, 82, 83, 84–85, 89, 116, 184n14; in dialogue, 84–85, 94–95, 97–98
Orientalism, 36–37, 49–50, 76, 181n46
Osella, Caroline, 10, 172n31
Osella, Filippo, 10, 172n31
O'Shea, Janet, 175–76n61

Packert, Cynthia, 130, 191n30
padams, 43, 157
Padmavati Srinivasa Kalyanam, 128, 189n10
Pai, Anant, 130
Pani, Jivan, 74
paramātma (divine soul), 40, 42, 46, 91, 92, 180n25, 180n29
Pārijātāparahaṇamu, 189n7
Paris Is Burning (Livingston), 124
Parsi theatre, 19, 47, 48. *See also* Gujarati theatre; Marathi theatre
Parvati, 69, 190n19, 191n29
Parvatisam, Vedantam, 119–20, 138

Pasricha, Avinash: *Kuchipudi*, 188n29, 189–90nn13–14
patriarchy, 30, 135, 153–54, 155, 163
Pattabhi Raman, N., 107
Pavlova, Anna, 36
Pechilis, Karen, 39
Pedda Satyam, Vempati, 106
Penumarthi, Sasikala, 26, *110*, *113*, 119, 125, 126, *126*, 127, 150; "Dance and Embodied Knowledge in the Indian Context," 165; Emory performance (2011), 29, 108, 189n11; view of Dharmaraj, 132
Perayya Sastry, Tadepalli, 106
performative speech, 187n20
Peterson, Indira Viswanathan, 11, 172n32
Pillai, Muthukumar, 34
Pintchman, Tracy, 186n12
Potti Sreeramulu Telugu University, 25
Prahlada Sarma, Vedantam, 69, 141
prakṛtī, 186n12
Prasad, Leela, 172–73n32,
Puar, Jasbir, 75–76
Puranam, Madhavi, 73
Putcha, Rumya, 15, 24, 46, 106, 166, 176n66, 176nn68–69

queer diaspora, 106, 122–23, 126, 133, 16
"queer optic" (Gopinath), 123
queer theory, 122–26, 169n3, 190n24–25

Radhakrishnan, Sarvepalli, 48–49
Radheshyam, Vedantam, 18, 67, 180n29
Raghava, Vedantam, 20, 29, *112*, 120, 125, 189n11, 191n4; mother (Rajyalakshmi) of, 121, 137–40
Raghavan, V., 40, 44, 70, 173n33, 180–81n37
Raghavayya, Vedantam, 106
Raheja, Gloria Goodwin, 27, 136, 142, 158
Rajyalakshmi, Vedantam, 121, 137–40, *139*, 141, 142, 145, 153–54, 191n6
Ramakrishna, Nataraja, 182n53
Ramalingasastry, Vedantam, 18, 159
Ramalingeshvara and Balatripurasundari temple, 14, *15*, 19, 68; on map, 17
Ramanujan, A.K., 179n24
Ramaswamy, Sumathi, 45–46, 171n25, 181n46, 182n48
Rāmāyaṇa, 82, 145, 155
Ramberg, Lucinda, 152–53, 171nn24–25, 175n60
Rāmcaritmānas (Tulsidas), 92
Rao, Banda Kanakalingeshwara. *See* Kanakalingeshwara Rao, Banda
Rao, Shanta, 188–89n5
Rao, Sthanam Narasimha. *See* Narasimha Rao, Sthanam
Rao, Vedantam Venkata Naga Chalapathi. *See* Venkata Naga Chalapathi Rao, Vedantam (Venku)
Rao, Velcheru Narayana. *See* Narayana Rao, Velcheru
Rattayya Sarma, Pasumarti, 5, 18, 55, 63–66, 73–74, 92–93, 102–3, 162, 188n29; as *sūtradhāra*/Madhavi/Madhava, 89–90, 91, 103
Rattaya Sarma, Vedantam, 73, 109, 119–20, 140
Ravi Balakrishna, Chinta, 18, 42, 59, 65, 68, 159; as *sūtradhāra*/Madhavi/Madhava, 82–83, *83*, 89, 91, 185n24
Ravi Shankar, Vempati, 105, 108, 147, 149, 150, 156, 189n10, 189n12, 191n29
Ravi Varma, Raja, 130
Reddi, S. Muthulakshmi. *See* Muthulakshmi Reddi, S.
Reddy, Gayatri, 174n42, 188n3
Reddy, Kamala, 127
Rehman, Indrani, 70
Rudisill, Kristen, 173n36; "Brahmin taste," 11, 127, 162–63,

Sabhapatayya, Muvvanallur, 34
sadir, 22, 175–76n61
St. Denis, Ruth, 36
sāmpradāyam, 11, 18, 31, 50–51, 131; Chinna Satyam and, 149, 160; as "culture brokers," 77; queer Other to, 123; Siddhendra and, 122; Venku, 56; women and girls and, 134, 154, 155, 158
Sangeetha Rao, Patrayani, 108
Sangeet Natak Akademi (New Delhi), 24–25, 66, 70, 71, 184n19; awards, 48, 70, 73, 175n57, 181n45; *Nrityotsava* festival, 72
Sanskritization, 5, 23, 58, 91, 92, 182–83nn3–4
Sarma, Modali Nagabhushana. *See* Nagabhushana Sarma, Modali
Sarma, Pasumarti Rattayya. *See* Rattayya Sarma, Pasumarti
Sarma, Pasumarti Venugopala (P.V.G.) Krishna. *See* Krishna Sarma, Pasumarti Venugopala (P.V.G.)
Sarma, S.V. Bhujangaraya. *See* Bhujangaraya Sarma, S.V.
Sarma, Vedantam Prahlada. See Prahlada Sarma, Vedantam
Sarma, Vedantam Satyanarayana. *See* Satyanarayana Sarma, Vedantam
Sastry, D.S.V., 55

Satyabhama, 2, 7, 13, 19, 26, 27, 63–71, 160; in Chinna Satyam's *Bhāmākalāpam*, 109, *110*, 111, *113*, 128; erotic expression, 67; Madhavi and, 5–6, 80–91, *84*, *90*, 93–103; Satyanarayana Sarma as, 1, 2, 52, 57, 68–73, 78; Siddhendra and, 40, 42; Siddhendra prescription (for all Kuchipudi men), 2, 33, 39, 51, 63, 78, 121, 122, 132; Sthanam as, 48; Venku as 55–56, *60–61*, 62, 73–74; women as, 108, 109, *110*, 111, 128, 132, 133; women proscribed from role, 138
Satyabhama, Pendela, 182n53
Satya Hariscandra, 48
Satyanarayana Sarma, Vedantam, 1–2, *3*, 52, 66, 90, 91, 102–3, 184n20; *āṅgika*, 67; Baliakka evocation, 157; costume and makeup, 59; death, 32, 72, 156, 161; hegemonic masculinity, 9, 57, 76, 78; Jonnalagadda and Kastuar on, 184n19; Krishna Murthy and, 52, 138, 141; Nagabhushana Sarma on, 183n8; photography of, 62; as Satyabhama, 1, 2, 52, 57, 68–73, 78; Siddhendra Mahotsav (2006), 83, 185n24; US tours, 107; wife (Lakshminarasamma) and, 15, 24–26, 53, 69, 106, 109, 140–42
Schechner, Richard, 81, 92, 93
Schweig, Graham, 130
Scinde, or The Unhappy Valley (Burton), 49–50
Seizer, Susan, 19, 89, 94
Sen, Ronojoy: *Nation at Play*, 172n28
Shah, Tana. *See* Tana Shah
Shakespearean theatre, 7, 85, 185n7
Shankar, Uday, 24, 36, 37, 178n8
Shankara, 186n12
Shawn, Ted, 36–37
Shiva, 128, 130, 131, 132, 190n19, 191n29
Shudraka: *Mṛcchakaṭikā*, 96
Shulman, David Dean, 96, 97, 101,–88n25, 188n27
Siddhendra, 14–15, 33, 37–46, 51–54, 57, 179nn20–21; Arudra view, 42, 178n13; hagiography, 38–39; historical dating, 33, 177n1; Kothari on, 179; *mūrti* (image), *45*; Ravi Balakrishna view, 91; Satyabhama prescription (all Kuchipudi men must perform), 2, 33, 39, 51, 63, 78, 121, 122, 132; Yeleswarapu Srinivas on, 180n29. See also *Bhāmākalāpam*
Siddhendra Kalakshetra, 14, 18, 20, 28, 30, 68, 140, 159, 160; founding, 25; on map, 17; Rattayya Sarma, 102; Vedantam Lakshminarasamma, 141; Vedantam Radheshyam, 67; Yeleswarapu Srinivas, 65
Siddhendra Mahotsav, 82–83, 180n36, 185n24
Sikh men, 76
Singer, Milton, 44, 173n33
Singh, Lata, 50
Sinha, Mrinalini, 4, 5, 49, 78, 162, 172n28
Sklar, Deidre, 27–28, 165, 167
Smartas, 11, 15, 18, 24, 44, 46, 126–27, 172–73n32–33
Soneji, Davesh, 11, 15, 172n32; *Unfinished Gestures*, 21, 23–24, 35, 152–53, 166, 178n7, 179n19, 192n14
Snorton, C. Riley, 170n19, 184n20
speech. *See* performative speech; *vācika abhinaya* (speech)
Spivak, Gayatri, 21, 153
Sri Krishna Parijatam, 107–8, 109, 128, 132
Srinivas, Tulasi, 136–37
Srinivas, Yeleswarapu, 18, 65, 66, *90*, 159, 180n29
Srinivasan, Priya: as performer, 177n73; *Sweating Saris*, 20, 23, 27, 28, 105, 134, 149, 166
śṛṅgāra. *See* erotic aesthetics (*śṛṅgāra*)
Sriramamurti, Gurajada, 43
Sthanam. *See* Narasimha Rao, Sthanam
strī-vēṣam (term), 1, 6
Sundari, Jayshankar, 47, 49, 52, 59, 63
sūtradhāra, 81–85, 87–92, 94–98, 103, 160; in Chinna Satyam's *Bhāmākalāpam*, 111–12, *112*, 114, 118, 119; Chinta Ravi Balakrishna as, *83*; Nagabhushana Sarma view, 185n3
Swarajyalakshmi, Vempati, 142–45, 150, 156
Sweating Saris (Srinivasan), 20, 23, 27, 28, 105, 134, 149, 166,

Tagore, Rabindranath: *Chandalika*, 108
Tamil Brahmins (Fuller and Narasimhan), 173n38
Tamil language, 44–46
Tamil Special Drama, 19, 85, 89, 94, 95, 188n26
Tana Shah, 15–16
Telugu arts, 44, 48, 69, 82, 155
Telugu language, 6, 43–44, 46, 107, 152, 169n2, 170n10; and gender identity, 94, 95
Thangaraj, Stanley I., 75
Thiagarajan, Premalatha, 37
Thobani, Sitara, 37, 106
Thomas, Sonja, 5, 163, 169n6
Thota, Katyayani, 106
Timmana, Nandi, 189n7
Toranayuddhanka, 190n19
transnational Kuchipudi dance, 29, 104–33, 160–61, 165–67
Trawick, Margaret, 191n3
Tulsidas: *Rāmcaritmānas*, 92

Turpu Bhagavatam, 29, 177n77
Tyagaraja, 180n34
Tyāgarāja and the Renewal of Tradition (Jackson), 172n32

The Unhappy Valley (Burton). See *Scinde, or The Unhappy Valley* (Burton)
"unruly spectator," 27, 166
upanayanam, 10–11, 12
Uṣā-pariṇayam, 19, 52, 65, 66, 69, 70, 71

vācika abhinaya (speech), 57, 58, 64–66, 116. *See also* vocal guising; vocal register
Vaidiki, 11, 12, 18, 30, 135, 173n37, 177n79
Vaishnava, 39, 40, 41, 114, 172n32
Vallathol, Mahakavi, 183n13
Van Vechten, Carl, 37
Vatsyayan, Kapila, 179n20, 180n28
Vedanta, 92, 93, 186n12
Vedas, 92, 172n32, 186n11, 187n24
Venkata Naga Chalapathi Rao, Vedantam (Venku), 12, 20, 55–56, *60–61*, 62, 67, 73–74, 90; on *āṅgika abhinaya*, 66; Canada residence, 173n40; on Madhavi portrayal of father (Vedantam Rattayya Sarma), 119–20; mother (Rajyalakshmi) of, 121; normative masculinity, 77; on Satyabhama by a female dancer, 111; Seattle performance, 162; *Temple and the Swan*, 191n29
Venkataraman, Leela, 128
Venkatarama Natya Mandali, 52, 69, 188n29
Venkataramayya, Chinta, 182n51
Venkatanarayana, Vempati, 52, 68, 182n51
veṣa (Sanskrit term), 6
vēṣam (Telugu term), 6
Victoria Theatrical Company, 47
vidūṣaka (clown), 81, 82, 96–103, 125–26, 187–88nn22–27
Vikramorvaśīya, 96
Viresalingam, Kandukuri, 21, 43
Vishnu, 39, 128, 161, 164
Vivekananda, 49
vocal guising, 31, 34, 39, 40, 42, 46, 179n24
vocal register, 65–66, 116

Walker, Margaret, 37, 50
Weidman, Amanda, 176n62, 177n3, 180n34
Whitaker, Jarrod L., 172n27
womanhood, 47–48, 49, 59, 76, 77, 99, 130–31; nationalist ideals, 50; parody and, 99, 101, 125. *See also* femininity
Womanhood in the Making (Hancock), 11, 44, 173n33
women performers, 65–66, 67, 152, 156, 157, 176n69; Baliakka, 147–50; Chinna Satyam and, 109, 111, 121, 128, 131–33, 145–46, 148; in Chinna Satyam's *Bhāmākalāpam*, 105, 108, 112, 127; exclusion and social prescription against, 47, 77, 135, 138, 145–49, 152; ostensibly outperformed by Satyanarayana Sarma, 74, 77; Sasikala Penumarthi, *110, 113, 126*; Sobha Naidu, 109, 111. *See also* anti-nautch movement; *devadāsīs* (*kalāvantulu*)
women's mosque movement (Egypt), 59

yakṣagānas, 18–19, 20, 102, 107, 121, 161, 182n51. See also *Uṣā-pariṇayam*
Yellamma, 152–53, 171n24–25

Zarrilli, Phillip: *Kathakali Dance-Drama*, 37, 63, 175n54
Zubko, Katherine, 23, 177n73

CPSIA information can be obtained
at www.ICGtesting.com
Printed in the USA
LVHW052255160519
618152LV00002B/2/P

9 780520 301665